Arnulfo L. Oliveira Memorial Library

The Medieval Life of King Alfred the Great

ENGLAND: South of the Humber AD 850–1000

# The Medieval Life of King Alfred the Great

A Translation and Commentary on the Text
Attributed to Asser

Alfred P. Smyth

First published 2002 by
PALGRAVE
Houndmills, Basingstoke, Hampshire RG21 6XS and
175 Fifth Avenue, New York, N. Y. 10010
Companies and representatives throughout the world

PALGRAVE is the new global academic imprint of
St. Martin's Press LLC Scholarly and Reference Division and
Palgrave Publishers Ltd (formerly Macmillan Press Ltd).

ISBN 0–333–69917–3

This book is printed on paper suitable for recycling and made from fully managed and sustained forest sources.

A catalogue record for this book is available from the British Library.

Library of Congress Cataloging-in-Publication Data
Asser, John, d. 909.
    [De Rebus gestis Aelfredi. English]
    The medieval life of King Alfred the Great : a translation and commentary on the text attributed to Asser / translated with a commentary by Alfred P. Smyth.
        p. cm.
    Includes bibliographical references (p. ) and index.
    ISBN 0–333–69917–3
        1. Alfred, King of England, 849–899. 2. Great Britain—Kings and rulers—Biography. 3. Anglo–Saxons—Kings and rulers—Biography. 4. Great Britain—History—Alfred, 871–899. I. Smyth, Alfred P. II. Title.

DA153 .A8213 2001
942.01′64′092—dc21
[B]
                                                        2001048206

10   9   8   7   6   5   4   3   2   1
11   10   09   08   07   06   05   04   03   02

Printed and bound in Great Britain by
Antony Rowe Ltd, Chippenham, Wiltshire

*In Memory
of
My Mother,
Mary Josephine O'Brien*

# Contents

# Abbreviations

| | |
|---|---|
| *Annals of St. Neots* | Also known as The East Anglian Chronicle |
| *Æthelweard*, ed. Campbell | A. Campbell, ed., *Chronicon Æthelweardi: The Chronicle of Æthelweard* (Nelson Medieval Texts: London, 1962) |
| A.S.C. | Anglo-Saxon Chronicle |
| A.S.C., MS.A., ed. Bately | J.M. Bately, ed., *The Anglo-Saxon Chronicle: A Collaborative Edition, iii. Manuscript A* (gen. eds., D. Dumville and S. Keynes; Cambridge, 1986) |
| A.S.E. | *Anglo-Saxon England*, ed. P. Clemoes *et al.* (Cambridge, 1972–) |
| Birch no. 561 | Charter no. 561 in W de G. Birch, ed., *Cartularium Saxonicum: A Collection of Charters Relating to Anglo-Saxon History* (4 vols. London, 1964; reprint of 1885–99 edn) |
| East Anglian Chronicle | Also known as *The Annals of St. Neots* |
| E.H.D. | *English Historical Documents*, D.C. Douglas, gen. ed., Vol. 1 edited by D. Whitelock (London, 1968, reprint of 1955 edn) |
| Eng. Hist. Rev. | *English Historical Review* |
| Historia Regum | in T. Arnold, ed., *Symeonis monachi opera omnia* (Rolls Series, vol. 1: 1882) |
| *HR 1* and *HR 2* | Two different recensions of extracts and summaries from the *Life* of King Alfred incorporated into the *Historia Regum* attributed to Symeon of Durham |

Keynes and Lapidge,          S. Keynes and M. Lapidge, transl. *Alfred the Great:*
*Alfred the Great*           *Asser's Life of King Alfred and Other Contemporary*
                             *Sources* (Harmondsworth, 1983)

*Life of Alfred,*            W.H. Stevenson, ed., *Asser's Life of King Alfred,*
ed. Stevenson                introd. by D. Whitelock (Oxford reprint 1959 of
                             1904 edn.)

Sawyer no. 346               Charter no. 346 in P.H. Sawyer, *Anglo-Saxon*
                             *Charters: an Annotated List and Bibliography* (Roy.
                             Hist. Soc., London, 1968)

Smyth, *Alfred the Great*    A.P. Smyth, *King Alfred the Great* (Oxford, 1995)

Worcester Latin Chronicle    Also known as *The Chronicle of Florence of Worcester*
                             and *The Chronicle of John of Worcester*

# Acknowledgement

I am grateful to Oxford University Press for kind permission to reproduce passages in revised form from Chapters 6, 11 and 13 of my book on *King Alfred the Great* (1995).

# Preface

I have been greatly assisted by the scholarly advice of my colleague Christopher Chaffin, Department of Classics, University of Kent, who has collated my translation of the *Life* of King Alfred with the Latin of Stevenson's Parker-Cotton text, and whose own immense understanding of Late Antique Latin authors has brought invaluable insights to bear on the *Life*. Mr Eric Christiansen, New College, Oxford, has also kindly read the translation and saved me from a number of infelicities. He has also provided numerous helpful comments on early English placenames and on historical issues raised in the text. I remain indebted to all those colleagues who encouraged me to publish the biography of King Alfred in 1995, and who are acknowledged in that volume. This book owes much to the inspiration of Dr Roy Hart, whose independent researches have transformed our understanding not only of the Anglo-Saxon Chronicle and *The Chronicle of John of Worcester*, but of learning in the late Anglo-Saxon period generally. This work was begun during a busy time in my life at St. George's House, Windsor Castle. I remain indebted to my friends and colleagues at Windsor who did so much to ensure that I had time for my own research. I must especially thank Very Rev. Patrick Mitchell, The then Dean of Windsor; Group Captain Ian Madelin; Mr Michael Orger and my Assistant, Mrs Sue Pendry. Sadly, Sir Patrick Palmer, the Governor and Constable of the Castle, who showed me so many kindnesses during my time at Windsor, died before I could thank him in this volume. The translation was completed at Canterbury Christ Church University College, where I am grateful to the Principal and Vice-Principal for their making precious space available in my day to include my personal research. Ms Leonie James provided me with invaluable assistance in my work as Director of Research during the final months of writing, as we struggled with other pressing administrative matters. Professor Sean Greenwood and his colleagues in the Department of History at Christ Church have offered me friendship as well as support. My wife, Margaret, has helped as always with bibliographical matters. Mrs Alison Guy and Dr Katia Pizzi have gone to great lengths to help with reading proofs. Audrey Green has provided invaluable help with the index. A particular word of thanks should be recorded for Luciana O'Flaherty of Palgrave and Ruth Willats for the special interest which they have taken in the production of this publication.

This book is dedicated to the memory of my mother who first taught me to stand up for what I believed to be right.

Canterbury, 2001

# Introduction

We should expect that the medieval biography of Anglo-Saxon England's greatest king would attract its fair share of scholarly interest and scrutiny. Alfred the Great occupies a two-fold pivotal role in English historiography – first as the historical ninth-century scholar-king who saved Wessex and southern England from conquest at the hands of Danish invaders, and second, as an iconic hero in the saga of England's imperial destiny, the darling of Victorian nationalism. The study of how Alfred was perceived by later generations of the English establishment is almost as complex as the study of the historical king. What fuels the uncertainty surrounding our assessment of King Alfred is the fact that the only surviving medieval manuscript of the king's *Life* was destroyed in 1731, and that other surviving fragments of the work, as well as an early printed edition, suggest even the lost manuscript may itself have been seriously flawed. It is important for all students of the subject to understand that the translation and commentary presented in this edition represent a minority view that has been vigorously challenged since I first offered my ideas on this subject in my biography of King Alfred the Great in 1995. In summary, I believe that the medieval *Life* of King Alfred the Great is not what its author claims it to be. The author introduces himself in this work as Asser, a Welsh monk and scholar, who was the personal tutor of King Alfred. It is my contention that the *Life* of King Alfred is not a contemporary biography but a medieval forgery written at Ramsey Abbey in Huntingdonshire in *c.* AD 1000 by the monk Byrhtferth, who was also the author of a wide range of other historical and scientific works.

Those few scholars who have in the past doubted, and continue today to question the authenticity of the *Life* of King Alfred are neither guilty of unpatriotic acts nor of trying to sabotage 'the subject', nor – as one more hysterical critic has put it – of 'dishonouring the dead'. It has certainly never been my intention to be guilty of any one of those things, but there are times when the pursuit of free enquiry may have to cause upset in the order of paradise. Serious doubts would be raised about the health of any discipline where no significantly new questions had been asked, much less answers given, over 150 years of successive scholarly commentaries on one of the most central works of medieval English history. When historical investigation fails to concern itself with posing new and sometimes difficult questions about the past, it is unlikely to come up with answers which offer new insights into our understanding of it. No one takes it amiss in scholarly circles that we should question some minor – and occasionally major – assumptions regarding traditional interpretations of, say, the Viking Wars or the Norman Conquest.

When W.H. Stevenson published his scholarly edition of the Latin text of the *Life* of King Alfred the Great in 1904, he protested in his Preface that he had 'attempted to approach it without any bias for or against it'. Even if Stevenson failed to honour fully his commitment in his vast commentary on the *Life*, he did at least thoroughly review the welter of arguments put forward by those who had questioned its authenticity throughout the nineteenth century. In reality, however, while he faced each formidable objection to the authenticity of Asser's authorship in its turn, Stevenson likewise dismissed all of them in spite of his own admission that nothing was certain; that the objections were formidable; and that proof of authenticity of Asser's authorship was impossible to come by. Unfortunately for Alfredian studies, Stevenson's limited caution and all of his caveats have not always been taken into account by later scholars. For even as he presented what was immediately accepted as a definitive case in favour of the authenticity of this work, Stevenson was extraordinarily defensive about the outcome of the debate. He admitted that in spite of his 250-page commentary and notes, he 'had to qualify almost every statement or conclusion with a "possibly", a "perhaps", or a "probably"'.[1] And although he may not himself have been conscious of it, he was forever looking over his shoulder at how the nineteenth-century historical establishment might view this highly sensitive subject. Already by 1900, belief in the authenticity of Asser as the biographer of King Alfred had become nothing less than an article of scholarly faith for some. As he reached the conclusion to his Preface, Stevenson declared: 'The profession of belief in its authenticity by such eminent historians as Kemble, Pauli, Stubbs, and Freeman agrees with my own conclusion.'[2] It is not always a healthy sign to find one scholar appealing to the authority of another, when struggling to win acceptance for a contested opinion. Besides, neither Stubbs nor Pauli could be described as fervent in their belief in Asser. Were they airing their own reasonable scholarly doubts on points of detail today, both men might find themselves described as 'controversial' in the tense atmosphere of current scholarly debate.

It is clear from reading Stevenson's labyrinthine commentaries that he himself regarded the question of who wrote this extraordinary *Life* of King Alfred the Great as an ongoing question for further study. When Dorothy Whitelock came to write an updated introduction to Stevenson's edition in 1959, not only did she feel it was unnecessary to alter a line of the 1904 edition, but she declared: 'Stevenson did his work so well that the fifty-five years which have elapsed since he published his edition of Asser have brought to light little new material.' While acknowledging a few helpful notes on the subject by Sisam, Wheeler and Schütt, she believed that Stevenson remained sound, for instance, on matters relating to placenames, and that 'little needs correction in what Stevenson says of the Anglo-Saxon Chronicle'. But Chronicle studies *had* moved on, and continue to move on, and the role of the translated Chronicle remains pivotal in our understanding of the *Life* of Alfred. As for arguments against the authenticity of Asser's authorship of King Alfred's *Life*, Whitelock believed that during the first half of the twentieth century 'no arguments of any weight against it have been published since Stevenson wrote' – this in the face of V.H. Galbraith's crucial paper presented as a Creighton Lecture in London in 1949. Galbraith's more developed criticisms of the *Life* of Alfred which appeared in 1964 were dismissed by Whitelock three years later in her *Stenton Lecture* on *The Genuine Asser*. Whitelock included a partial translation of the *Life* of Alfred in her monumental *English Historical Documents* volume of 1955. Her translation exhibited all the meticulous attention to detail which characterised so much of her scholarly work, but it included less than one third of the chapters in the whole text and significantly omitted several of the more problematic and contradictory passages. Her omission of Chapter 74 with its key passages on King Alfred's illnesses – all of which are unique to the medieval *Life* – can be explained only by Whitelock's unwillingness to confront such problematical evidence.

Some, at least, of the scholarly tension in the debate which centres on the text of the *Life* of Alfred arises from a misunderstanding of the translation process, as it does also from a misunderstanding of the nature of historical debate. All language – however precise – affords us only an approximation of the complete thought process which inspired a speaker or writer in the first instance. Translation takes us, in turn, one step further away again from the original intentions of the author. Even simultaneous translation of speeches of latter-day politicians may lead to serious misunderstandings. Translation serves only to deflect meaning through yet another surface of the prism, and translation of an early medieval text – the transmission of which may have been contaminated by extraneous material – is inevitably open to a variety of interpretations. No one questions the scholarly integrity of Whitelock and the Stenton school. Her views on the authorship of the *Life* of Alfred were sincerely held, but they were held with such passion and authority that – given the complex relationship between scholarship and patronage – little room was left for an alternative view.

Keynes and Lapidge, in their translation of the *Life* of Alfred in 1983, kept in step with Stevenson's commentary and notes of 1904 in regard to all the significant arguments, pausing here and there to qualify his ideas by way of minor adjustments. In essence, the 1983 English translation carried a commentary which mirrored Stevenson's thesis and supported Whitelock's pronouncements on the debate regarding authenticity. The translation of

1983 was heavily influenced by a scholarly position taken up by Stenton and sustained by Whitelock. That is not to say that the 1983 translation was 'bad' or lacking in scholarly integrity. Like all translators of a problematical text, its editors had to follow a consistent approach, and once having committed themselves to a 'genuine Asser' thesis, they were left with no choice but to render the text in a consistent way – opting for legitimate interpretations which remained in line with Stevenson's and Whitelock's approach. But while interpretations may be legitimate, it is also necessary to allow for alternative meanings in a text. The 1983 English translation of key Latin passages in the *Life* of King Alfred which contain glaring contradictions (in the original) or which might be suggestive of an authorship after King Alfred had died, was rendered, on occasion, to yield a sense that was supportive of a 'genuine Asser' thesis. Other telling errors and inconsistencies within the Latin text as it has come down to us were amended to conform with current scholarly orthodoxies. Some aspects of the text, however, were more needlessly altered. King Alfred's enemies, consistently described by his medieval biographer as *Pagans*, were turned into *Vikings*, giving a false sense of ninth-century immediacy to a narrative of uncertain date.

The present translation lays no claim to represent the definitive and original Latin text in English, for that is impossible due to the loss of the only complete medieval manuscript. Furthermore, this translation has been produced under the influence of an alternative interpretation regarding the origins, the authorship and the date of the medieval *Life* of King Alfred the Great. There is no sense in which I present this work as the 'true' version of Alfred's *Life* with all the pejorative implications that might have for earlier printed editions of the text. Historians know that because of the uncertainties surrounding this medieval *Life*, there is no 'true' version. Much controversy could be avoided if this fact were grasped by all contributors to the debate. But neither is it right to hold that one viewpoint is as good as another. This translation does strive to provide the reader with an English version of King Alfred's *Life* which is as close as possible to the Latin text as it survives in Archbishop Parker's 1574 printed edition – as edited by Stevenson, and supplemented with key passages from the other surviving medieval fragments of the *Life*. Nothing has been silently omitted or amended. I have also identified (by use of italics) those passages which the medieval author borrowed into his Latin narrative from the Old English text of the Anglo-Saxon Chronicle. This will allow readers for the first time to assess the magnitude of the author's indebtedness to the Anglo-Saxon Chronicle when compiling his *Life* of Alfred. It will be made clear in the Commentary that Byrhtferth of Ramsey involved himself more than any other Anglo-Saxon historian in producing versions of the Chronicle text – both in the copying and continuation of vernacular editions and in the compiling of Latin versions of the

Chronicle to serve regional needs in southern, eastern and northern England. My aim is to provide students of Anglo-Saxon history with a translation which allows them to form their own opinion as to the value of the *Life* of King Alfred. While no translator can be free of personal bias, I have consciously striven to provide a translation which stays as close as possible to the original Latin.

The Stenton–Whitelock thesis to the effect that the historical bishop, Asser, is the genuine author of the *Life* of King Alfred still enjoys widespread acceptance in leading scholarly circles today, and it must be said that my views on this subject are still those of a dissenting minority. On 8 December 1995, Professor Keynes came to the defence of Asser's authorship in *The Times Higher Education Supplement*[3] arguing that the *Life* of Alfred contained no errors or anachronisms that would be fatal to its authenticity and that it did not serve any identifiable purpose of a later forger. Keynes followed this initial salvo with a much lengthier and more constructive review of my work in 1996.[4] Professor Lapidge took up his pen for *The Times Higher Education Supplement*, in a more personal vein than Professor Keynes.[5] I had argued – and continue to argue – that the *Life* of King Alfred owes a marked dependence for its hagiographical motifs, on the *Life* of Gerald of Aurillac which was written in *c*. 940 by Odo of Cluny. Lapidge insisted that for this argument to hold good, it was necessary for verbal links to be demonstrated between the Latin in Odo's *Life* of Gerald and that in the *Life* of King Alfred.[6] Historians are aware that medieval writers were quite capable of borrowing literary motifs from other authors without imitating their Latin style. Lapidge went on to challenge any argument which suggested similarities between the style of Byrhtferth of Ramsey and the author of the *Life* of Alfred, in a vein not always consistent with what this scholar had written previously on Byrhtferth's style elsewhere. I replied to this contribution more in sorrow than in anger on 29 March 1996.[7] Professor Lapidge's notion that if he could prove it was not Byrhtferth of Ramsey who wrote the *Life* of King Alfred, then 'the principal pillar [in my biography of King Alfred] is removed and the book collapses under the weight of its own pomposity' is as misplaced as it is intellectually flawed. The major brunt of my argument regarding the *Life* of King Alfred remains essentially the same as that of Galbraith. This is a source which from its own internal organisation and the content of its narrative proclaims itself to have been written long after its subject, King Alfred, had died. Critics of my thesis must address the multitude of problems inherent in the narrative as well as the issue of why there is such an overwhelming Ramsey connection with this text – regardless of what Byrhtferth's personal contribution to it may have been. And like Galbraith and others before him, I remain unconvinced that the glaring contradictions within the text can be put down to a naive biographer offering pious theological and Gregorian insights on the duties of an early medieval ruler. For while it may have been just possible for a ruler suffering from intermittent serious illness to lead, on occasion, in war, it was never possible for a man to have been highly literate and completely illiterate at one and the same time. And that is precisely what this *Life* tells us about its king. As for the Ramsey dimension, this cannot be discussed in crude topographical terms as a place too far removed from Alfredian Wessex to offer a plausible location for King Alfred's biographer. Ramsey was the intellectual power-house of tenth- and eleventh-century Monastic Reform, and since I first wrote on this subject in 1995, the argument for a Ramsey dimension has grown ever more compelling rather than less.

It is interesting to find that while Professor Lapidge hoped for the speedy 'collapse' of my case, and Professor Keynes predicted that 'the establishment will strike back ... [with] arguments of sufficient weight to flatten a book as fat as this', the central concern of both scholars was with my views on the *Life* of King Alfred. Yet my biography of the king concerned itself at length with Alfred's military career, with the all-important Anglo-Saxon Chronicle and with the king's own writings. And while I agree with Professor Nelson that I allowed the spectre of Asser to loom too large in my biography of Alfred, I did nevertheless devote great space to the study of so many other aspects of King Alfred's life.[8] It was inevitable, given the deeply unsatisfactory state of the 'Genuine Asser' debate during the 1980s, that my biography of King Alfred should become preoccupied with the biography written by 'Asser'. A major argument in my study on King Alfred centred on the case that too much emphasis had been placed in the past on studying the medieval *Life* of the king and too little time had been devoted to the study of Alfred's own writings for the evidence they shed on his personality, his intellectual concerns, and on his thought world generally. While Professor Keynes lamented the destructive approach which I had taken in my investigation of Anglo-Saxon sources, Eric Christiansen took a more balanced view involving a wider vision beyond the obsessive preoccupation with the 'genuine Asser', pointing to 'a far more credible Alfred than we have yet seen'.[9] Professor Campbell, while holding fast to 'genuine Asser' orthodoxies, was generous enough to point out that even if I were completely wrong about the authorship of the *Life* of King Alfred, my 1995 biography had important things to say about the Alfredian annals.[10] The Alfredian annals, forming the core of the Anglo-Saxon Chronicle, have a major bearing on the *Life* of Alfred where they appear by way of a Latin translation embedded in that work. It is difficult not to conclude that the hysterical reception with which my views on the *Life* of King Alfred were greeted by a few scholars in 1995, proves the point that 'Asser's *life* of Alfred' had been allowed to develop into a scholarly black hole over the past century. And that black hole has drawn far too much scholarly energy into its destructive vortex, precluding progress in other aspects of

Anglo-Saxon studies and stifling constructive debate and a free exchange of ideas.

The caravan has rolled on – for many scholars at least – since 1995, and much new work is coming forward to enrich our understanding of ninth- and tenth-century England. Richard Abels' book on King Alfred contains an appendix on 'The Authenticity of Asser's Life of King Alfred',[11] which, as its title suggests, adheres to traditional thinking on this subject. But Abels provides a fair and reasoned survey in a brief space which brings many complex strands in the argument up to date, and wisely refrains from offering too many solutions. Pauline Stafford has produced her *Queen Emma and Queen Edith*,[12] which although it has little bearing on Alfredian England, sheds much light on the eleventh century – a time which many scholars are now coming to realise had a crucial bearing on the rewriting of the Anglo-Saxon past. Stafford's treatment of the *Encomium Emmae*, a celebratory piece on Queen Emma which contains definite echoes of passages from the *Life* of Alfred adds to our understanding of the social and political background to this work.[13] An ongoing series of detailed studies on the Anglo-Saxon Chronicle, including its Alfredian sections, have been undertaken by Janet Bately, Roy Hart, David Dumville and other scholars, with the result that simplistic views on the manuscript transmission of the Chronicle which were in vogue as late as the 1970s and 1980s have now given way to a much more complex and sophisticated picture. It is fair to say that notions of an Abingdon Chronicle, and of the relationship between the A-Text and later recensions, have been revolutionised by Hart's researches – based as they are, on independent scholarly insights into late tenth- and early eleventh-century English historiography. It is also the case that in spite of the highly charged nature of the debate over the authorship of the *Life* of Alfred – at times verging on scholarly meltdown – some scholars who hold the orthodox view on authenticity, are nevertheless moving towards the centre ground. Since the first publication of my views on a Ramsey origin for the *Life* of Alfred in 1995, Professor Lapidge has endorsed Hart's researches on the Ramsey Annals as a source which began life at Ramsey in *c.* AD 1000 – precisely the time when Byrhtferth was active there. Lapidge has also come to accept the possibility that Byrhtferth was responsible for the compilation of the tenth-century section of the Worcester Latin Chronicle, later ascribed to John of Worcester.[14] So we now have a situation where Byrhtferth of Ramsey is acknowledged to have been responsible for, or closely associated with, no less than three compilations which contain summaries or – as some might argue – alternative manuscript readings of the *Life* of King Alfred dating to *c.* AD 1000. These Byrhtferthian renderings of material from Alfred's *Life* are found in the Northumbrian Chronicle, the Worcester Latin Chronicle and in much more fragmentary (but none the less definite) form in the Ramsey Annals.

And the date of all three recensions of material from Alfred's *Life* coincides precisely with the age of the oldest, only surviving and more complete manuscript of the *Life* (British Library Cotton MS Otho A.Xii). So the Ramsey connection and a date of *c.* 1000 have been reinforced by scholars from both sides of the debate, and the figure of Byrhtferth remains at centre stage.

Other English translations of the *Life* of King Alfred the Great include those of J.A. Giles in his *Six Old English Chronicles* of 1848; followed in 1854 by the Revd. J. Stevenson's translation in his *Church Historians of England.* A more recent translation by L. Cecil Jane appeared in New York in 1960, where its editor presented a sensible and cautious appraisal of the difficulties presented by this text.

# Translation of the *Life* of King Alfred

# Important Notice

CHAPTER HEADINGS: All chapter headings have been inserted by the present translator of the *Life*, and are not original to the medieval text.

CHAPTER NUMBERING: The numbering of chapters follows that of Stevenson's 1904 edition. This allows easy reference to Stevenson's Latin text which forms the basis of this translation. A small number of Stevenson's chapters have been split up, and are distinguished by letters *a, b, c,* attached to the original chapter number.

*Typescript in italics*: Indicates those passages (now in English translation) which the medieval author borrowed from the Anglo-Saxon Chronicle.

**Typescript in bold:** Indicates passages which may not have originally belonged to the text of the *Life* of King Alfred.

[Square Brackets]: Words in square brackets have been added by the present translator.

<u>Words underlined</u>: Words underlined include unidentified placenames and other proper names in the medieval author's text, as well as titles of works (now in translation) which he quotes by name.

## The Author's Dedication

To my venerable and most pious lord, to Alfred king of the Anglo-Saxons, ruler of all the Christians of the island of Britain,[1] Asser least of all the servants of God, wishes thousandfold prosperity in this life and in the next, according to the prayers of his fervent desires.

# 1
# Alfred's Birth and Royal Descent

## AD 849

In the year of the Incarnation of the Lord, 849,[2] Alfred, king of the Anglo-Saxons was born at the royal estate which is called Wantage in the region which is called Berkshire. That region is so called from <u>Berroc</u> Wood where the box-tree grows most abundantly. His genealogy is constructed in the following way:

> King Alfred was the son of[3] King *Æthelwulf, who was the son of Ecgberht, who was the son of Ealhmund, who was the son of Eafa, who was the son of Eoppa, who was the son of Ingild. Ingild and Ine – that famous king of the West Saxons – were two full brothers. Of these, Ine made the journey to Rome and there ending this present life* honourably, he went to the heavenly country to reign with Christ. *They were the sons of Cenred, who was the son of Ceolwald, who was the son of Cuda, who was the son of Cuthwine, who was the son of Ceawlin, who was the son of Cynric, who was the son of Creoda, who was the son of Cerdic, who was the son of Elesa* [who was the son of Esla], *who was the son of Gewis,* from whom the Britons call all that people the Gegwis. *Gewis was the son* [of Wig, who was the son of Freawine, who was the son of Freothegar,][4] *who was the son of Brond, who was the son of Beldeag, who was the son of Woden, who was the son of Frithowald, who was the son of Frealeaf, who was the son of Frithuwulf, who was the son of Finn, [who was the son of] Godwulf, who was the son of Geata.*

This Geata the pagans for a long time worshipped as a god. Of him the poet Sedulius makes mention in his <u>Paschal Hymn</u>,[5] saying thus:[6]

> 'Seeing that Pagan poets strive to parade their fictitious tales in bombastic measures and with tragedy's wailing, or with [comedy's] ridiculous Geta, or by means of whatever kind of poetic art you like, they renew the raging contagion of abominable deeds and sing of monumental wickedness, and in scholarly manner they relate many lies in Egyptian[7] books. Why then should I, accustomed to chanting praises in songs of David upon an instrument of ten strings, and who take my place with awe in the holy choir, chanting heavenly words in gentle diction – why should I be silent on the illustrious miracles of Christ who bore us Salvation?'

*This Geata was the son of Tœtwa, who was the son of Beaw, who was the son of Sceldwea, who was the son of Heremod, who was the son of Itermod, who was the*

*son of Hathra, who was the son of Hwala who was the son of Bedwig, who was the
son of Seth, who was the son of Noah, who was the son of Lamech, who was the
son of Methuselah, who was the son of Enoch, [who was the son of Jared], who was
the son of M[ah]alaleel, who was the son of Cainan, who was the son of Enos, who
was the son of Seth, who was the son of Adam.*

### 2
### Alfred's Maternal Kindred

Concerning the genealogy of his mother. Alfred's mother was called Osburh,
a deeply religious woman who was noble in character as well as by birth. She
was the daughter of Oslac, the famous cup-bearer of King Æthelwulf.[8] This
Oslac was a Goth by race, for he was descended from the Goths and Jutes,
namely from the line of *Stuf and Wihtgar, two brothers* and also ealdormen,[9]
*who received rule over the Isle of Wight from their uncle, King Cerdic, and from his
son, Cynric, their cousin. They slew a few* nearby British inhabitants of the
island, as many as they were able to find on it, *at a place called
Guuihtgaraburhg*.[10] The other inhabitants of the island had either already been
slain or had fled as exiles.

[AD 850]

### 3
### The Men of Devon Fight the Pagans,
### and Pagans Winter on Sheppey

## AD 851

*In the year of the Incarnation of the Lord 851*: the third year from the birth of
King Alfred. *Ealdorman Ceorl of Devon, with the men of Devon, fought against
the pagans at a place called Uuicganbeorg, and the Christians had the victory.*
   In the very same year, *the pagans wintered for the first time on the island called*
Sheppey, which means 'Sheep Isle'.[11] It lies in the River Thames between the
East Saxons and the men of Kent, but it is nearer to Kent than to the East
Saxons. In it (i.e. on Sheppey) an excellent monastery has been built.[12]

### 4
### Pagans Attack Canterbury and London

*In the same year,* a great army of pagans with *350 ships came into the Thames
estuary. They laid waste Canterbury*, the city of the men of Kent, [and
London][13] which is situated on the northern bank of the River Thames on the

border of the East Saxons and the Middle Saxons, but that city, nevertheless, belongs in truth to the East Saxons.[14] *They put Beorhtulf, king of the Mercians to flight along with all his army* who had come to do battle against them.

## 5
## The West Saxons are Victorious over the Pagans at <u>Aclea</u>

*After these things had happened there, the* aforesaid *army* of the pagans *went into Surrey, a region situated on the southern bank of the River Thames*, to the west of Kent. *And Æthelwulf, king* of the Saxons *and his son, Æthelbald, fought with the whole army* for a very long time *in the place which is called <u>Aclea</u>,* which means 'Oak Field'. And there, when both sides had fought most vigorously and courageously for a long time, *the greater part of the pagan host was completely destroyed and slain, so that never in any region in one day, before or since, have we heard of such slaughter of them. The Christians* honourably *gained a victory* and were masters of the place of slaughter.[15]

## 6
## A Pagan Fleet is Defeated at Sandwich[16]

*In the same year, Athelstan*[17] *and Ealdorman Ealhhere slew a great army* of pagans *in Kent, in a place called Sandwich. They captured nine of their ships. The others escaped by flight.*

[852]

## 7
## The Mercians and West Saxons Attack the Welsh

### AD 853

*In the year of the Incarnation of the Lord, 853*: the eleventh[18] year from the birth of King Alfred. *Burgred, king of the Mercians, besought Æthelwulf, king* of the West Saxons, by means of messengers, that *he might help him bring under his rule the* midland *Britons* who live between Mercia and the Western Sea and who struggled excessively against him. As soon as King Æthelwulf had received his embassy, mobilising an army, *he went with King Burgred to the land of the Britons*[19] *and* immediately on entering it, devastating that race, *he brought it under the rule of Burgred.* When he had done this, he returned home.

## 8
## The Infant Alfred is Sent to Rome

*In the same year King Æthelwulf sent his son* – the previously mentioned *Alfred* – honourably *to Rome*, in the company of a great number of nobles and non-nobles. *At that time the lord, Pope Leo, was then ruling the Apostolic See. He anointed* the same child, Alfred, fully ordaining *him as king,*[20] *and he confirmed him*, receiving him as an adopted son.

## 9
## Pagan Victories in Kent. Alfred's Sister Weds

*In this year also* Ealdorman *Ealhhere, along with the men of Kent, and Huda with the men of Surrey, fought* bravely and courageously *against an army of Pagans in* the island which is called in English, *Thanet*, and which in the British language [is called] <u>Ruim</u>.[21] *At first, the Christians were victorious, but* when the battle was continued for a long time *a great many fell on both sides or* were engulfed by water so that *they drowned. And both those ealdormen were laid low* there.

*In this year also, after Easter, Æthelwulf king* of the West Saxons, gave *his daughter* as queen *to Burgred, king of the Mercians*, at the royal estate[22] called Chippenham. And the marriage was celebrated with royal ceremony.

[854]

## 10
## Pagans Winter on Sheppey

## AD 855

*In the year of the Incarnation of the Lord 855*: the seventh year from the birth of the aforementioned king. A great army of *Pagans spent the* entire *winter in the* aforementioned *Isle of Sheppey*.[23]

## 11
## Alfred Goes to Rome a Second Time
## His Father, Æthelwulf, Bestows Gifts and Marries a New Queen

*In the same year*, the said revered *King Æthelwulf freed a tenth part of his entire kingdom*[24] from all royal service and taxation *and by a* perpetual *written grant he sacrificed it to* the One and Threefold *God* on the Cross of Christ[25] *for the redemption of his soul* and [the souls] of his ancestors.

*And in the same year he [i.e. King Æthelwulf] journeyed to Rome with great honour,* taking his aforementioned son, Alfred, on that same journey with him for a second time.[26] *For he loved him more than his other sons.*[27] *And he remained there for one full year. And when it was completed he returned to his own country, bringing with him* Judith, *the daughter of Charles* [the Bald], *king of the Franks.*

## 12
## King Æthelbald Rebels against his Father[28]

But meanwhile, while King Æthelwulf was lingering beyond the sea for so short a time, a certain infamous thing[29] which was contrary to the practice of all Christians, arose to the west of Selwood. For King Æthelbald [son of King Æthelwulf], and Ealhstan bishop of the church of Sherborne, together with Eanwulf ealdorman of the shire of Somerset,[30] are said to have plotted that King Æthelwulf should not be received again into the kingship when he returned from Rome. Very many people ascribe this misfortune, unheard of in all previous ages, to the bishop and to the ealdorman alone, and it was on their advice that the deed was proposed. There are also many who attribute the deed solely to royal insolence because that king [Æthelbald] was obstinate in this affair and in many other perversities, as we have heard from the report of certain men, and as was proved by the outcome of the following event.

For as King Æthelwulf was returning from Rome, that same son, with all his counsellors – or rather traitors – tried to perpetrate so great a villainy as to banish the king from his own kingdom. But neither did God permit this to happen nor did the nobles of all Saxony[31] consent. For lest the irremediable danger to Saxony from civil war might grow more fierce and cruel day by day, with father and son at war – or rather with the whole people in rebellion against both of them – by the indescribable clemency of the father and with the assent of all the nobles, the hitherto united kingdom was divided between father and son. The eastern districts were assigned to the father and the western, on the other hand, to the son. For where the father ought by right to have reigned, there the wicked and obstinate son was reigning. For the western portion of the Saxon land has always been more important than the eastern.[32]

## 13
## King Æthelwulf Returns with his Carolingian Queen

*When therefore King Æthelwulf returned* from Rome, all *that people* as was right, so *rejoiced at the coming* of their lord[33] that had he permitted it, they would have wished to expel his obstinate son, Æthelbald, along with all his counsellors from his part of the whole kingdom. But as we have said, he, exercising excessive clemency and prudent counsel, would not wish it to be so, lest danger should befall the kingdom.[34]

Without any dispute or ill feeling on the part of his nobles, he ordered that Judith, daughter of King Charles [the Bald] whom he had received from her father, was to sit beside him on the royal throne until the end of his life, although this was contrary to the perverse custom of that people. For the people of the West Saxons do not allow their queen to sit beside the king, nor do they permit her to be called 'queen' but 'king's wife'.[35]

The older people of that land say that this questionable and infamous thing arose on account of a certain stubborn and malevolent queen of that same people. For she so acted against her lord and all the people in every way, that not only did she merit so much hatred against herself that she was driven from her queenly throne, but she also handed down the same deadly deprivation to all those queens who came after her.

For on account of the very great malice of that queen, all the inhabitants of that land swore *en masse* that they would never allow any king to reign over them who chose to command his queen to sit beside him in his lifetime, on the royal throne. And because many, in my opinion, are not aware how this perverse and detestable custom which is contrary to the custom of all Teutonic[36] peoples, first came into being in Saxony, it seems to me that I should explain it a little more fully. I have heard this story from my lord, Alfred the truth-teller,[37] king of the Anglo-Saxons, who still often relates it to me. And again, he had heard it from many reliable witnesses, indeed for the most part [from people] who remembered the event.

## 14
### The Tale of the Wicked Queen, Eadburh

There was in Mercia in recent times a certain restless king called Offa who incited fear in all neighbouring kings and regions round about him, and who commanded a great dyke to be built between Britain[38] and Mercia from sea to sea. Beorhtric, king of the West Saxons, received in marriage the daughter of that same [King Offa] who was called Eadburh.[39] And immediately on gaining the king's friendship and taking power over almost all of the kingdom, she began to live the life of a tyrant after the manner of her father. She detested every man whom Beorhtric esteemed and she did all things hateful to God and men. All those whom she was able to accuse, she accused before the king, and so she deprived them by treachery of either life or power. And if she was not able to gain her wish from the king, she killed them with poison. This was undoubtedly the case with a certain youth who was most dear to the king, whom when she was not able to accuse him before the king, she slew him with poison. That same king, Beorhtric, is said to have partaken of some of the poison unknowingly. She had intended not to give the poison to the king but to the boy, but the king took it first and so they both perished.

## 15
## Queen Eadburh's Exile and Death

When, therefore, King Beorhtric was dead, because she [Eadburh] could no longer live among the Saxons, sailing overseas with innumerable treasures, she made her way to Charles,[40] the most famous king of the Franks. When she stood before the throne bringing many gifts to the king, Charles said:

'Eadburh, choose whom you wish between me and my son, who stands with me on this throne.'

She foolishly replying without thinking, said:

'If the choice is given to me, I choose your son, since he is younger than you.'

Charles answering her and ridiculing her, said:

'Had you chosen me, you would have had my son: but because you have chosen my son, you shall have neither me nor him.'

He did nevertheless grant her a great convent of nuns, in which having set aside the secular habit, and having assumed the clothing of the nuns, she performed the office of abbess for a very few years. For just as she is said to have lived in an unreasonable way in her own country, so she was perceived to live even more irresponsibly among an alien people. When at last she was caught openly being defiled by a man of her own nation, she was driven out of the monastery by the command of King Charles[41] and in a reprehensible way, led a life of poverty and misery up until her death. So, in the end, in the company of a single slave boy, begging daily – as we have heard from many who saw her – she died miserably in Pavia.[42]

## 16
## King Æthelwulf's Will

*King Æthelwulf*, then, *lived for two years after he arrived from Rome.* In this time he – among many other good activities in this present life – reflecting that he was to go the way of all flesh, commanded that a will or rather a document of recommendation be drawn up, so that his sons should not dispute unduly among themselves after their father's death. In this he took care to command in writing, in an orderly form, a division of the kingdom between his sons, namely the two eldest;[43] of his personal inheritance between his sons, daughter, and his relatives; and of the money which should be over and above after his death, between [the good of] his soul and his sons and nobles. We have decided to record a few things out of many in connection with this wise and well-considered policy for posterity to imitate, namely, those which are considered to pertain most of all to the need of the soul. As for the rest, it is not necessary to insert into this little work[44] what pertains to human affairs, lest by its length it should engender disgust in its readers as well as in those who would wish to listen to it.[45] For the benefit of his soul, then, which from the first flowering of his youth he had been zealous to care for in all things, he prescribed that his successors after him until the final Day of Judgement were always to support with food, drink and clothing, one poor person, whether native or stranger, from every ten hides throughout all his hereditary land,[46] provided such land was inhabited by men and flocks and was not waste. He prescribed also that a great sum of money should be taken to Rome every year[47] for the benefit of his soul,[48] namely 300 mancuses which were divided there in this way: 100 mancuses in honour of St. Peter – more particularly for the buying of oil to fill all the lamps in that apostolic church on the eve of Easter and also at cockcrow (on Easter Sunday); and 100 mancuses in honour of St. Paul on the same condition, for the provision of oil in the church of St. Paul the apostle, for the filling of lamps on Easter Eve and at cockcrow; 100 mancuses also for the universal and apostolic pope.

## 17
## The Reign of King Æthelbald

*When King Æthelwulf was dead* [and was buried in Winchester][49] *his son Æthelbald,* contrary to the prohibition of God and to the dignity of Christians, and also contrary to the custom of all pagans,[50] ascending the bed of his father, married Judith, the daughter of Charles, king of the Franks,[51] incurring much ill repute from all who heard of it. He *ruled over* the government of *the kingdom of the West Saxons for two and a half*[52] unbridled *years* after (the death of) his father.[53]

## [17B][54]
## [The Royal Anointing of King Edmund of East Anglia]

## AD 856

The year of the Incarnation of the Lord, 856, and the eighth year from the birth of Alfred,[55] the second year of the emperor Charles III, but in the eighteenth year of Æthelwulf, king of the West Saxons. Hunberht, bishop of the East Angles, with much joy and with the greatest honour at the royal estate which is called Burua, where the royal seat then was, anointed with oil and consecrated to be king, the most glorious Edmund who was then in the fifteenth year of his age, on the sixth day of the week, and on the twenty-fourth of the month, the day of the nativity of Our Lord.

[859]

## 18
## Pagans Sack Winchester

### AD 860

*In the year of the Incarnation of the Lord, 860*: the twelfth year from the birth of King Alfred. *Æthelbald* [king of the West Saxons, died] *and was buried in Sherborne, and his brother, Æthelberht, added Kent, Surrey and also Sussex to his dominion* as was fitting.[56] *During his days, a great army* of pagans, *coming by sea,* aggressively *attacked* the city of *Winchester and sacked it.*[57] When they were returning to their ships with great booty, *Osric, ealdorman of Hampshire with his men, and Ealdorman Æthelwulf with the men of Berkshire* valiantly *intercepted them.* Battle was truly joined. *The pagans were* everywhere *cut to pieces* and when they were no longer able to resist, they fled like women, *and the Christians were masters of the place of slaughter.*

## 19
## Death of King Æthelberht

*Æthelberht, then, reigned for five years* peacefully, lovingly, and with honour, and went the way of all flesh to the great sorrow of his people. *He lies in Sherborne*, buried honourably beside his brother.

[861]
[862]
[863]
[864]

## 20
## Pagans Ravage East Kent

### AD 864 [recte 865][58]

*In the year of the Incarnation of the Lord, 864.*[59] *The Pagans* spent the winter *on the Isle of Thanet and concluded a* firm *treaty with the men of Kent. The men of Kent promised to give money to them for the keeping of the treaty. Meanwhile, however, the Pagans*, like foxes, secretly bursting out of their camp *by night, broke the treaty, and scorning the promise of money* – for they knew they would obtain more money from stolen booty than from peace – *ravaged the entire eastern region of Kent.*

## 21
## Æthelred Becomes King.
## The Arrival of the Great Army of Pagans

### AD 866

*In the year of the Incarnation of the Lord, 866*: the eighteenth year from the birth of King Alfred. *Æthelred, the brother of King Æthelberht, began to reign over the kingdom of the West Saxons. And in the same year, a great* fleet *of Pagans came to* Britain[60] *from the Danube.*[61] *They spent the winter in the kingdom of the* East Saxons, which in English is called East Anglia.[62] *There the* greater part of the *army was supplied with horses.*

But, to speak in the manner of those who sail, lest we be carried far away amidst such great slaughters of wars and calculations of years – weakening our ship for too long, by means of waves and sails, and sailing too far from land – I think we ought to return to that subject which specially incited me to this work. That is to say, I think what little that has come to my knowledge concerning the character of the infancy and boyhood of my venerable lord, Alfred, king of the Anglo-Saxons, should be inserted briefly in this place.

## 22
## Alfred's Childhood

Now he was cherished by his father and mother, and indeed by everybody with a universal and immense love more than all his brothers.[63] He was always brought up at the royal court and was inseparable from it.[64] Growing up through his infancy and boyhood, he was seen to be more handsome in form than all his brothers and more lovable in his facial expression, in his speech and in his manners. From when he was in swaddling clothes, before all things and among all the commitments of this present life, a yearning for wisdom along with nobility of birth filled up the nature of his noble mind. But alas! through the unworthy neglect of his parents[65] and of those who brought him up, he remained an illiterate[66] until his twelfth year or even longer. But he was an intelligent listener to Saxon poems[67] by day and by night, most often hearing them recited by others, and, apt to be taught, he learnt them by heart. A keen huntsman, not in vain does he toil incessantly in every art of hunting. For no one else could compare with him in skill and success in that art, just as in all other gifts of God, as we ourselves have so often seen.[68]

## 23
## A Book Prize from Alfred's Mother[69]

When therefore on a certain day his mother showed a certain book of Saxon poetry which she had in her hand, to him and to his brothers[70] she said: 'I will give this book to whichever of you is able to learn it the sooner.' Alfred, prompted by this utterance, or rather by Divine inspiration, and enticed by the beauty of the initial letter of the book, replying thus to his mother, he said – anticipating his brothers, who were senior in age though not in grace[71] –

'Will you truly give this book to that one of us who can understand it the soonest and read it aloud[72] before you?'

At this, smiling and rejoicing, and reassuring him she said: 'Yes, I will give it to him.' Then, immediately, taking the book from her hand, he went to his tutor and read[73] it. And when it was read, he took it back to his mother and read it aloud.

## 24
## Alfred Learns the Divine Office and Keeps a Book of Hours

After this he learnt the order of the Divine Office,[74] that is the services of the hours and then certain psalms and many prayers. He collected these into one book which he took around with him everywhere in his clothing, and was inseparable from it[75] for the sake of prayer throughout the course of this present life, by day and night – as we ourselves have seen. But alas! he was not able to satisfy his longing for what he desired most, namely the liberal arts, for as he used to say, there were at that time no good readers[76] in the entire kingdom of the West Saxons.

## 25
## Alfred Lamented his Lack of Opportunity for Learning

He used to assert with repeated laments and sighs from his innermost heart that among all the difficulties and losses[77] of this present life, this was the greatest, namely, that during that time when he had the (right) age and leisure, and was equal to learning, he did not have the tutors.[78] But when he was more advanced in age he did have teachers and writers to some little extent, but he was not able to read.[79] For he was more incessantly preoccupied, nay rather, disturbed, by day and by night, both with sicknesses unknown to all the physicians of this island and with the cares of royal office at home and abroad, and also with the assaults of Pagans by land and sea. But nevertheless, among the difficulties of this present life – from infancy to the present day – and as I believe up until his death[80] – just as he did not previously forsake that insatiable longing [for knowledge],[81] so he does not cease even now to long for it.

## 26
## The Progress of the Great Pagan Army

### AD 867

*In the year of the Incarnation of the Lord, 867*: the nineteenth year from the birth of King Charles [recte Alfred].[82] *The* aforementioned *army* of the Pagans *removed from the East Angles to the city of York,* which is situated on the northern bank of the river Humber.[83]

## 27
## The Pagans Capture York and Slay the Kings of the Northumbrians

*At that time a very great strife,* prompted by the devil, *had arisen among the Northumbrians,* as always happens to a people which has incurred the hatred of God. *For the Northumbrians, at that time,* as we have said,[84] *had expelled their* legitimate *king, called Osberht,* from the kingdom, *and had placed* a certain tyrant, called *Ælla, who was not of royal descent* at the head of their realm. But on the arrival of the Pagans, by Divine counsel and with the help of the magnates, that strife had abated to some little extent for the common good. *Osberht and Ælla, uniting their men and gathering an army went to the town of York.* On their arrival, the Pagans immediately took to flight, and took care to defend themselves within the defences of the city. Perceiving their flight and terror, *the Christians resolved to* pursue them even inside the defences of the city and to *break down the wall, and this they did.* For in those days, up until then,[85] the city did not have strong and stable walls.[86] *When the Christians had breached the wall as they had proposed,* and when many of them had entered the city at the same time as the Pagans, *the Pagans* driven by pain and necessity fell fiercely upon them, *slew them,* put them to flight and overthrew them *within and without [the city].* Almost all the crowd of the Northumbrians was annihilated there and *the two kings were slain. The remainder, however, who escaped, made peace with the Pagans.*

## 28
## Bishop Ealhstan of Sherborne Dies

*In this same year Ealhstan, bishop of the church of Sherborne, going the way of all flesh, was buried* in peace *in Sherborne after he had ruled the bishopric* honourably[87] *for fifty years.*

## 29
## Alfred's In-Laws

# AD 868

*In the year of the Incarnation of the Lord, 868*: the twentieth year from the birth of King Alfred. The same aforementioned and venerable King Alfred, who was at that time recognised by the rank of joint-ruler,[88] espoused and took a wife from Mercia of noble family, namely the daughter[89] of Æthelred, who was called Mucill, a count of the Gaini.[90] The mother of this woman was called Eadburh, from the royal lineage of the king of the Mercians. We ourselves with our very own eyes frequently saw her for many years before her death.[91] She was a venerable woman who for many years after the death of her husband remained a most chaste widow until her [own] death.

## 30
## The Siege of Nottingham

*In the same year the aforementioned army* of the Pagans leaving the Northumbrians *came into Mercia and reached Nottingham* which means Tigguocobauc in Brittonic and 'House of Caves'[92] in Latin, *and* in that year *they spent the winter in that place.* On their arrival there, *Burgred king of the Mercians and all the magnates of that people* immediately *sent messengers to Æthelred, king of the West Saxons, and to his brother Alfred,* humbly imploring[93] them *that they would give them help, so that they would be able to fight against the* aforementioned [Pagan] *army.* They easily obtained [their wish]. For *the brothers* promptly [fulfilling their] promise, *collecting an* immense *army from every part of the kingdom went to Mercia and arrived at Nottingham,* of one mind in seeking battle. *And when the Pagans* – defended by the protection of the fortress – *refused to give battle* and the Christians were not equal to breaching the wall, *a peace was made between the Mercians and the Pagans* and the two brothers, Æthelred and Alfred, returned home with their forces.

## 31
## The Pagans Return to York

**AD 869**

*In the year of the Incarnation of the Lord, 869*: the twenty-first year from the birth of King Alfred. *The* aforementioned *army* of Pagans, riding back to the Northumbrians, *went up to the city of York and remained there for a whole year.*

## 32
## The Pagans Move to Thetford

**AD 870**

*In the year of the Incarnation of the Lord, 870*: the twenty-first[94] year from the birth of King Alfred. *The army* of Pagans mentioned above *passed through Mercia to the East Angles, and they spent the winter there in a place which is called Thetford.*

## 33
## The Slaying of King Edmund

*In the same year, Edmund, king of the East Angles, fought* fiercely[95] *against that army*, but alas! he was slain there with a large number of his men. *The* Pagans rejoicing exceedingly, [those] *enemies dominated the place of slaughter and subjected that entire region to their rule.*

## 34
## Ceolnoth, Archbishop of Canterbury Dies

*In the same year, Ceolnoth archbishop of Canterbury, going the way of all flesh*, was buried in peace in that same city.[96]

## 35
## The Pagans Attack Wessex and Take Reading

**AD 871**

*In the year of the Incarnation of the Lord, 871*: the twenty-third year from the birth of King Alfred. *The army* of the Pagans of hateful memory, leaving the East Angles, *entered the kingdom of the West Saxons and came to* the royal estate which is called *Reading*, situated on the southern bank of the river Thames in that district[97] which is called Berkshire. *On the third day after their arrival there, [two] of their counts*[98] with a great part of the (army) *rode out to plunder*, while the others constructed a defensive earthwork between the two rivers, Thames and Kennet, on the right hand [southern] side of the same royal estate. *Æthelwulf, ealdorman* of the district of Berkshire, along with his comrades, *opposed them in a place called Englefield* and the battle was fought there courageously on both sides. When both sides had resisted there for a long time, *and one count of the Pagans had been slain* and the greater part of their army was destroyed, [the Pagans] escaped by flight *and the Christians*, gaining the victory, *were masters of the place of slaughter.*

## 36
## A Christian Assault on Reading is Repulsed with Slaughter

*Four days after these things had happened there, King Æthelred and his brother Alfred*, having united their men and *having gathered together an army, went to Reading.* When they had reached the gate of the fortress by slaying and overthrowing all the Pagans whom they found outside the fortress, the Pagans were none the slower to fight, and like wolves bursting out of all the gates entered the fray in full force. *Both sides fought* it out fiercely *there* for a long time, *but* alas! in the end the Christians turned their backs and *the Pagans, gaining the victory, were masters of the battlefield. And Ealdorman Æthelwulf*, already mentioned, *fell* there along with others.

## 37
## The Christians Prepare for Battle at Ashdown

*The Christians* were moved by the pain and the shame of this, and *four days later* with all their men and fully committed, they *went forth to battle against the* aforementioned *army in a place which is called Ashdown*, which in Latin means 'Hill of the Ash'. *But the Pagans, dividing into two bands*, prepared shield walls of equal size – for they then had two kings and many earls – *giving* the middle *part of the army to the two kings and the other to all the earls.*[99]

The Christians seeing this, they also divided their army into two bands in precisely [the same way] and formed their shield walls no less swiftly. But Alfred and his men, reached the place of battle sooner and in a better state of readiness, as we have heard from the truth-telling reporting of those who saw it.[100] For undoubtedly his brother, King Æthelred, was still in his tent at prayer, hearing Mass, declaring excessively that he would not leave from that place alive before the priest had finished Mass, and that he would not abandon the service of God for that of man.[101] And so he did. The faith of the

Christian king signified much with the Lord as will be shown more clearly by that which follows.

## 38
## Alfred Takes on Two Pagan Divisions at Ashdown before the Arrival of his Brother, the King

*The Christians, then, had determined that King Æthelred with his forces should begin the battle against the two* Pagan *kings, while his brother Alfred* with his divisions should know that he *was to* try the fortune of *battle against all the earls* of the Pagans.[102]

Things had thus been firmly arranged on both sides, when the king delayed a very long time in prayer, and the Pagans, prepared, arrived sooner at the place of conflict. Alfred, who was then joint-ruler,[103] was not able to drive away the enemy lines any longer. He either had to withdraw from the battlefield or burst out against the enemy forces before the arrival of his brother in the battle. Then, at last, boldly and like a wild boar, he drew up his Christian forces against the enemy army as he had earlier proposed, although the king had not yet come. So, relying on God's counsel and supported by His help, he drew the shield-wall together in an orderly way, and immediately advanced his war-banners against the enemy. **Finally King Æthelred, having completed the prayers with which he was occupied, arrived, and having invoked the great Ruler of the world, at once entered the battle.**[104]

## 39
## The Pagan Army is Slaughtered

But it must be made known at this point to those who are ignorant of the fact, that the place of battle was not equally advantageous to the belligerents. For the Pagans had already occupied the higher ground and the Christians were drawing up their line of battle from a lower position. There was moreover, in that place, a solitary quite stunted thorn tree, which we ourselves have seen with our own eyes,[105] around which the hostile lines of battle clashed violently, with an immense clamour on all sides – the one espousing the side of wrongdoing, the other fighting for life, loved ones and fatherland. When both sides had been fighting[106] to and fro courageously and with excessive cruelty for some long time, the Pagans, by Divine judgement, took to scandalous flight, being no longer able to bear the onslaught of the Christians, and because the greater part of their forces had been slain. One of the two kings of the Pagans and five of their counts were slain and *many thousands on the Pagan side fell*, slaughtered in that place – dispersed over the entire breadth of the flat countryside of Ashdown.[107]

*So, King Bægscecg, the old Count Sidroc, the young Count Sidroc, Count Osbern, Count Fræna, and Count Harold, were killed there, and the entire army of the Pagans was driven in flight* until nightfall and into the following day until they reached the fortress from which they had [earlier] gone forth. *The Christians pursued them until nightfall, laying them low* everywhere.

## 40
## The Crisis Deepens for the West Saxons

**[To whom, when losses of such a kind of the present life, wrongly, were not sufficient for the [wealth]-seeking Foreigners][108]**

When these things had happened there, *King Æthelred with his brother Alfred*, having again united their forces *to fight against the Pagans, after fourteen days came to Basing.* Although they [the Saxons] clashed violently on all fronts and resisted for a long time, *the Pagans won the victory* and were masters of the place of slaughter.[109] *When the battle was over, another army* of Pagans came from lands overseas and *joined itself to the [enemy] company.*[110]

## 41
## King Æthelred Dies

*And in the same year after Easter,*[111] the above-mentioned *King Æthelred, went the way of all flesh, having ruled the kingdom for five years* through many tribulations – vigorously, with honour and in good repute. *He was buried in Wimborne monastery* [where] he awaits the coming of the Lord and the first resurrection with the just.

## 42
## Alfred is Made King and is Defeated at Wilton

In that year the above-mentioned *Alfred*, who up to that time when his brothers were alive had been recognised as joint-ruler,[112] *received the rule of the whole kingdom* immediately after the death of his brother with the assent of the Divine will and with the full accord of all the inhabitants of the kingdom.[113]

And even while his previously named brother [Æthelred] was alive, Alfred could most easily have taken over the government with the consent of all, had he deigned to do so. For without a doubt he was superior to all of his brothers together,[114] both in wisdom and in all good habits, and furthermore because he was warlike beyond measure and victorious in almost all battles.[115]

*When he had begun to reign for a whole month*, almost against his will – for truly he did not think that he alone, unless he were supported by Divine assistance, could ever endure such great severity of the Pagans, since he had already sustained great losses of many men while his brothers were still alive – *he fought* most fiercely *with a few men* who were very much outnumbered, *against the whole army* of Pagans *on* a hill which is called *Wilton*, lying on the southern bank of the river *Guilou* [Wylye], from which river the whole district takes its name. *When both sides had been fighting*[116] fiercely and courageously from different directions *for no small part of the day, the Pagans* perceiving with their own eyes the full extent of their danger, and no longer enduring the attack of their enemies, turned their backs and fled. But alas! by ensnaring the great daring of the pursuers,[117] they entered into the battle again and seizing the victory, they *held the place of slaughter*. Nor should it seem strange to anyone that the Christians had a small number of men in this battle: for *the Saxons* for the most part *in that one year, in eight*[118] *battles against the Pagans*, were destroyed in great numbers.[119] *In those eight battles one king of the Pagans and nine earls*[120] *along with innumerable men were slain. This does not include the* innumerable *attacks* by day and by night *which* the oft-mentioned *Alfred and individual ealdormen*[121] of that race with their followers *and* also very many *king's thegns*[122] *had fought* without wearying and zealously *against the Pagans.* How many thousands of the pagan army were slain in these frequent attacks – apart from those who were slain in the eight battles mentioned above – is unknown except to God alone.

## 43
## The Saxons Make Peace

*In this year also the Saxons concluded a peace with the Pagans* on this condition that they should depart from them, which they [the Pagans] complied with.

## 44
## The Pagan Army in London

## AD 872

*In the year of the Incarnation of the Lord, 872*: the twenty-third from the birth of King Alfred. *The army* of the Pagans already mentioned *went to London and wintered there and the Mercians concluded a peace with them.*

## 45
## The Pagans Leave London for Northumbria

### AD 873

*In the year of the Incarnation of the Lord, 873*: the twenty-fourth year from the birth of King Alfred. *The* frequently mentioned *army*, leaving London *went into the region of the Northumbrians and it wintered there in the district called Lindsey*,[123] *and the Mercians* again *concluded a peace with them.*

## 46
## The Pagans Conquer All Mercia
## King Burgred is Driven out and Ceolwulf is
## Established in His Place

### AD 874

*In the year of the Incarnation of the Lord, 874*: the twenty-fifth year from the birth of Alfred. *The* frequently mentioned *army leaving Lindsey entered Mercia and it wintered in the place which is called Repton.*

*They compelled Burgred also, king* of the Mercians, *to abandon his kingdom* against his will *and to depart overseas and to go to Rome in the twenty-second year of his reign.* He did not live long after *he reached Rome, where he died and he was buried* honourably *in the church of St. Mary in the <u>Schola</u> of the Saxons*,[124] where he awaits the coming of the Lord and the first resurrection with the just.

After he had been expelled, *the Pagans subjected the whole kingdom of the Mercians to their rule. But they entrusted*[125] *it to* the agreed custody of *a certain foolish thegn, whose name was Ceolwulf, on the* deplorable *condition that if they wished to have it again at any time, he should give it* peaceably *to them. He gave hostages to them under this provision and he swore that in no way would he go against their will* but that he would be obedient to them in all things.

## 47
## The Great Army of Pagans Divides into Two

### AD 875

*In the year of the Incarnation of the Lord, 875*: the twenty-sixth year since the birth of King Alfred. *The* frequently mentioned *army, leaving Repton*, divided into two companies. *One part under Halfdan went straight to the region of the Northumbrians and it wintered there beside the river which is called Tyne and* subjected the whole region of the Northumbrians to its rule, and they plundered some of the Picts and Strathclyde [Britons].

The other part, under *three kings* of the Pagans – *Guthrum,*[126] *Osscytil* and *Anvind* – went to the place which is called *Cambridge*[127] and wintered there.

## 48
## Alfred Fights the Pagans at Sea

*In the same year, King Alfred fought a naval battle at sea against six*[128] *ships of the Pagans. He captured one of them, the rest escaped by flight.*

## 49
## Beginning of King Alfred's Second War
## The Pagan Army Invades Wessex and Occupies Wareham and Exeter

### AD 876

*In the year of the Incarnation of the Lord, 876*: the twenty-sixth[129] year since the birth of Alfred. *The* frequently mentioned *army* of the Pagans, leaving Cambridge[130] by night *entered* the fortress[131] which is called *Wareham*. This is a convent of nuns [situated] between two rivers – the Frome and Tarrant – in the district[132] which is called in Brittonic <u>Durngueir</u>,[133] and which in Saxon is called Dorset. It is sited in the most secure position on earth, except on the western side where it is joined to the land.

*With this army King Alfred concluded a* firm *peace on this condition that they should depart from him. The army gave him,* without any controversy, *as many selected hostages as he alone chose. And they also swore an oath on* all the relics in which the king placed most confidence after God – *and on which they had never before been willing to swear for any race – that they would most quickly depart from his kingdom.*[134] *But* following their custom and using their usual trickery; and disregarding the hostages, their oath, and promise of [good] faith, *one night they broke the treaty,* slew all the horsemen[135] which they held, *and* turning from there, *they headed* unexpectedly *for* another place – called *Exeter* in Saxon, <u>*Cairuuisc*</u> in Brittonic, and *civitas Exae* in Latin – situated on the eastern bank of the river Exe [*Uuisc*] near to the southern sea which flows between Gaul and Britain. [The Pagan army] spent the winter there.

## 50
## Halfdan Settles His Men in Northumbria

*In the same year, Halfdan* king *of* that [other] part [of the Pagan army] of *the Northumbrians*[136] *divided up the* whole *region* between himself and his followers, *and he and his army tilled that land.*

## 50B[137]

In that year, Rollo invaded Normandy with his forces. This same Rollo, Duke[138] of the Normans, confident with his army, while wintering in 'Old' Britain or England,[139] experienced a vision one night of what was soon surely to come to pass. Much more may be read of this Rollo in the [Norman] annals.

## 50C

## [AD 877]

[This chapter, as printed by Stevenson, represents an interpolation from Roger of Wendover, which was based in turn on a fanciful version of the East Anglian Chronicle (*Annals of St. Neots*).]

## 50D[140]

## AD 877

In this year the army of the Pagans left Wareham, some on horseback and some in ships. And when they came to the place which is called Swanage, one hundred and twenty of the ships were lost. But then King Alfred pursued the army that was on horseback, until it came to Exeter. There he took hostages and an oath from them that they would depart forthwith.

## 51[141]
## Mercia is Divided between the Invaders and Ceolwulf
## a Foolish King's Thegn

## AD 877

*In the month of August*[142] *in that same year, the army went into Mercia and gave part of that* region of the Mercians *to Ceolwulf,* a certain foolish thegn[143] of the king, *and part of it they divided among themselves.*[144]

## 52
## The Danes Attack Chippenham

### AD 878

*In the year of the Incarnation of the Lord, 878*: the twenty-seventh[145] since the birth of King Alfred. *The* frequently mentioned *army* leaving Exeter *came to Chippenham,*[146] a royal estate which is situated in the left-hand part [i.e. north] of Wiltshire on the eastern bank of the river which is called <u>Abon</u> [Avon] in Brittonic, and it wintered there.[147] And through their hostilities, *they compelled many of that race* through both poverty and trepidation *to sail overseas*[148] *and they reduced almost all the inhabitants of that region*[149] *to their rule.*

## 53
## Alfred Retreats to Somerset and Turns to Guerrilla Warfare

*At that time, Alfred,* the frequently mentioned king, *with a few* of his nobles and also with certain knights and vassals[150] *spent his life in great tribulation* and disturbance *in the wooded and marshy*[151] *places* of the district[152] of Somerset. For he had nothing on which to live, apart from that which he might take by frequent raids either secretly or openly, from the Pagans and even from Christians who had submitted to the rule of the Pagans.

## 53A[153]
## King Alfred Burns the Cakes[154]

And, as it is read in the Life of the holy father, Neot, he lay hidden for a long time in the house of one of his cowherds.[155] It happened one day that a countrywoman – the wife of that cowherd – was preparing to bake loaves, and that king [i.e. Alfred], sitting by the hearth was preparing his bow and arrows and other instruments of war. But when that unhappy woman observed that the loaves placed near the fire were burning, she quickly ran and removed them, scolding the unconquerable king, saying:

'Look here, man! You hold back from turning the loaves which you see burning, but you're glad to eat them when freshly cooked.'

That unfortunate woman did not reckon in the slightest that he was King Alfred, who waged so many wars against the Pagans and who gained so many victories from them.[156]

# 54

## The Brother of Ivar and Halfdan is Slain while Invading Devon
## The Fortress of <u>Cynuit</u> is Described

*In the same year*[157] *the brother of Ivar and Halfdan*[158] *sailed to*[159] Devon with *twenty-three ships* from the region[160] of Dyfed where he had wintered after slaughtering many of the Christians there. *He was slain there* [in Devon] by the thegns of the king [Alfred], meeting an unhappy end in front of the fortress[161] of <u>Cynuit</u>, *along with 1,200*[162] *of his men* while doing harm.

For many of the thegns of the king [Alfred] had shut themselves up along with their men in that fortress as a place of refuge. But when the Pagans perceived that the fortress was unprepared and altogether unfortified and that it only had defences[163] erected after our custom,[164] yet they did not try to break into it, because that place, by the lie of the land, is the safest on every side except on the east as we ourselves have seen. They began to lay siege to it thinking that those men, would be compelled to surrender by hunger and thirst, and siege, since there is no water near that fortress. But it did not happen as they reckoned. For the Christians, long before they would be exposed to suffer want in any way, were Divinely prompted, and judged it were far better to merit either death or victory. They burst out unexpectedly and in such hostile manner against the Pagans at dawn, and they destroyed most of the enemy along with their king in the first attack, a few escaping by fleeing to the ships.[165]

# 55

## Alfred Builds a Fort on Athelney and Rallies His Men.
## They Rejoice to See Him

*In the same year after Easter,*[166] *Alfred, with a few followers, made a fortress in a place which is called Athelney and from that fortress he waged war* tirelessly *along with his Somerset vassals against the Pagans. And again, in the seventh week after Easter*[167] *he rode to Egbert's Stone which is in the eastern part of the forest called Selwood* – in Latin *sylva magna* and in Brittonic <u>Coit Maur</u> – *and there all the inhabitants of the district of Somerset and of Wiltshire, and all the inhabitants of the district of Hampshire* – who had not sailed overseas for fear of the Pagans[168] – *met up with him. On seeing the king*, they received him as was right, as one restored [from the dead] after such great tribulations, and *they were filled with* immense *joy. And there they made a camp for one night.* As the following dawn broke, *the king moved camp from there and went to the place which is called Iley*[169] *and made a camp there for one night.*

# 56
## Alfred's Crucial Victory in the Second War
## The Battle of Edington,
## Guthrum's Baptism at Aller and the Peace of Wedmore

*When the following morning dawned, he [King Alfred] moved* his war-banners and came *to the place called Edington. And fighting* ferociously, forming a dense shield-wall *against the whole army* of the Pagans, and striving long and bravely, through God's will at last he gained the victory. *He overthrew the Pagans* with great slaughter, *and* smiting the fugitives, *he pursued them as far as the fortress.* He took away everything which he found outside the fortress – men, horses and cattle, and the men he slew immediately. He boldly pitched his camp with all his army before the gates of the pagan fortress. *When he had remained there for fourteen days, the Pagans* were terrified by hunger, cold and fear, and in the end by despair. They *sought peace on this condition that the king [Alfred] should take* as many named[170] hostages from them as he wished and that he should give none to them. Indeed never before had they made peace with anyone on such terms.[171] When the king had heard their delegation, he was moved to pity, as is his wont,[172] and he took named hostages from them – as many as he wished for. After they [the hostages] had been received, *the Pagans swore in addition that they would leave his kingdom* immediately.[173] *Furthermore, their king, Guthrum, promised to accept Christianity and to undergo Baptism at the hand of King Alfred. And he and his men fulfilled all these things as they had promised. And after [three]*[174] *weeks, Guthrum, king* of the Pagans, *along with thirty*[175] *of the choicest men of his army came to King Alfred at a place called Aller, near Athelney. King Alfred raised him from the sacred font of Baptism,* receiving him as his adopted son. *His chrism-loosing was* on the eighth day *at* the royal estate which is called *Wedmore. He [Guthrum] remained with the king for twelve nights after his Baptism and the king bountifully bestowed many and excellent buildings*[176] *on him and on* all *his men.*

# 57
## The Pagans Withdraw from Wessex to Cirencester

## AD 879

*In the year of the Incarnation of the Lord, 879*: the twenty-eighth[177] since the birth of King Alfred. *The same Pagan army, rising up out of Chippenham* as it had promised, *went to Cirencester* which is called <u>Cairceri</u> in Brittonic and which is in the southern part of the [territory of the] Hwicce,[178] *and it remained there for one year.*

## 58
## Another Pagan Army Arrives at Fulham

*In the same year, a* great *army* of Pagans[179] sailing from overseas parts *came into* the River Thames and united with the former army,[180] but nevertheless wintered in a place which is called *Fulham beside the River Thames.*

## 59
## An Eclipse of the Sun

*In the same year there was an eclipse of the sun* between Nones and Vespers, but nearer to Nones.[181]

## 60
## The Pagan Army at Cirencester Moves to East Anglia

### AD 880

*In the year of the Incarnation of the Lord, 880*: the twenty-ninth[182] year since the birth of King Alfred. *The* frequently mentioned *army* of the Pagans, *leaving Cirencester went to the East Angles and dividing out that region*[183] *they began to dwell there.*

## 61
## The Fulham Army Departs for the Continent

*In the same year the army of the Pagans which had wintered at Fulham*, leaving the island of Britain and *sailing* once more *overseas, went to* Eastern *Francia and remained for one year in that place which is called Ghent.*[184]

## 62
## The Progress of the Pagan Army in Francia

### AD 881

*In the year of the Incarnation of the Lord, 881*: the thirtieth[185] year since the birth of King Alfred. *The* previously mentioned *army went further into Francia. The Franks fought against them*[186] *and when the battle was over, the Pagans finding horses, became mounted warriors.*

## 63
## The Pagan Army Sails up the Meuse

## AD 882

*In the year of the Incarnation of the Lord, 882*: the thirty-first[187] year since the birth of King Alfred. *The* previously mentioned *army drew its ships up the river which is called the Meuse, [and went] much*[188] *further into Francia, and wintered there for one year.*

## 64
## Alfred Wins a Naval Victory against the Pagans

*And in the same year, Alfred, king* of the Anglo-Saxons *fought a battle at sea against the* Pagan *ships.*[189] *He took two of their ships, having slain all who were in them. The two* commanders *of the other* two *ships with all their comrades, being very much wearied by the battle and by their wounds*, laying down their arms and on bended knee, and with humble entreaties, *gave themselves up to the king.*

## 65
## The Pagan Army in Francia Reaches Condé

## AD 883

*In the year of the Incarnation of the Lord, 883*: the thirty-second[190] year since the birth of King Alfred. *The* previously mentioned *army*[191] *drew its ships along the river which is called the Scheldt*, and sailing against the stream *to* the convent of nuns which is called *Condé, it remained there one year.*[192]

[884]

## 66
## A Detachment of Pagans from Francia Attack Rochester
## Alfred Comes to the Relief of the Town

## AD 884 [*recte* 885][193]

*In the year of the Incarnation of the Lord, 884*: the thirty-third[194] year since the birth of King Alfred. *The previously mentioned army divided into two bands. One band went* to *East* Francia *and the other* coming to Britain, reached Kent and *laid siege to the city which is called Rochester* in Saxon, situated on the eastern bank of the River Medway. *The Pagans* at once *constructed a* strong *fortification*[195] in front of the gate of this place. *Nevertheless,* they were not able to storm the city because *those citizens defended themselves* courageously *until King Alfred bearing help to them arrived with a* great *army.*[196] *Then the Pagans, leaving their stronghold and abandoning* all *the horses* in it which they had taken with them from Francia as well as the greater part of their captives, *fled* immediately *to their ships* on the sudden arrival of the king. The Saxons at once seized the spoil of captives and horses which had been abandoned by the Pagans. *And thus the Pagans,* compelled by great necessity, *returned again to Francia in that same summer.*

## 67
### Alfred's Fleet Invades East Anglia

*In the same year, Alfred, king* of the Anglo-Saxons *sent his fleet from Kent* filled with warriors, directing it *against the East Angles* in order to take booty. *When they came to the mouth of the River Stour, thirteen*[197] *ships of the Pagans,* prepared for battle, immediately *encountered them. A naval battle was begun,* and with fierce fighting on either side, *all the Pagans were slain, and all the ships were captured* along with all of their riches. *When the* victorious royal *fleet was sleeping,*[198] the Pagans who inhabited the region of the East Angles, gathering ships from every quarter, confronted the royal fleet at sea in the mouth of the same river. *When a naval battle was joined the Pagans had the victory.*

## 68
### Carolingian Family History

*In the same year, a wild boar*[199] *attacked Carloman,*[200] *king of the Western Franks,* as he was hunting boars, *and* tore him apart with its horrendous tusk, *and [so] smote him with* a miserable *death. His brother* Louis[201] *had died in the previous year, who was himself also king of the Franks. For they were both sons of Louis,*[202] king of the Franks. *That Louis died in the* above-mentioned *year in which there was an eclipse of the sun.*[203] *And that Louis* [the Stammerer] *was the son of Charles*[204] king of the Franks, *whose daughter* Judith, *Æthelwulf, king of the West Saxons, received as his queen* with the consent of her father.

## 69
### The Pagan Army is Defeated in Germany

*In the same year a great army* of Pagans[205] *came* from Germany *into the region of the Old Saxons* which in Saxon is called <u>Eald Seaxum</u>.[206] *Against which [Pagans] the same Saxons and Frisians having united their forces fought* courageously *twice in that one year. In those two*[207] *battles, the Christians had the victory* by the assistance of the Divine mercy.

## 70
## Charles the Fat Becomes King of the Western Franks
## More Carolingian Family History

*And in the same year, Charles* [the Fat],[208] king of the Alemmani, with the voluntary consent of all,[209] *received the kingdom of the Western Franks and all the kingdoms which lie between the Tyrrhenian Sea and that bay of sea* which lies between the Old Saxons and the Gauls[210] *with the exception of the kingdom of Brittany. This Charles was the son of* King Louis [the German][211] *and that same Louis was the brother of Charles* [the Bald][212] king of the Franks *who was the father of* Queen *Judith* mentioned above. *The two brothers were the sons of Louis* [the Pious].[213] *Louis* in truth *was the son of Pepin or Charles* [Charlemagne].[214]

## 71
## Alfred's Friendship with Pope Marinus

*In this same year Pope Marinus, of blessed memory, went the way of all flesh. He, on account of the* love and *entreaties of Alfred, king* of the Anglo-Saxons,[215] kindly *freed the Saxon* Schole *abiding in Rome, from all* tribute and tax. He also *sent back* many *gifts to that same king, among which he gave* no small *piece of the* most holy and most venerable *cross on which* Our Lord Jesus *Christ hung* for the salvation of all mankind.[216]

## 72
## The Pagans in East Anglia Break their Truce

*In that year also, the army of the Pagans*[217] *which had settled among the East Angles* dishonourably *broke the peace* which it had concluded *with King Alfred.*

## 73
## The Author Returns to His Life of King Alfred
## He Promises to be Brief

That I may return, therefore, to that point from where I have digressed, lest by a long-lasting voyage, I be compelled to pass by the harbour of longed-for rest. I shall as I promised, undertake to set forth what little – as much as has come to my knowledge – concerning the life, manners, and favourable conversation and also not a little of the deeds of my lord, Alfred, king of the Anglo-Saxons, after he married that aforementioned[218] and venerable wife of the race of the noble Mercians. And, God granting, I promise [to write] succinctly and briefly lest by a long-winded explanation of every fresh detail, I offend the minds of the highly critical.[219]

## 74[220]

## Alfred is Struck down with an Illness at His Wedding Feast[221]

When therefore he had celebrated the wedding which was held in Mercia with honour and solemnity in the presence of innumerable people of both sexes,[222] and after lengthy feasting by day and by night, he was suddenly seized – in the presence of all the people – with a sudden and immense pain which was unknown to all physicians. For it was unknown to all those who were then present, and even to those who perceived [it] right up to the present day, from what source such an illness could arise. But alas! the worst thing is that for such a long time from his twentieth year up to his fortieth and even longer, it [i.e. his illness] could be prolonged incessantly through so many cycles of years. There are many who supposed that this happened through the applause[223] and witchcraft of the people around him; others that it came from the jealousy of the devil who is always envious of good men; others that it was caused by some uncommon kind of fever; others thought it was due to piles, which kind of most troublesome affliction he had, even from early childhood.[224]

Some time before, he had gone to Cornwall with a view to hunting, and by Divine inspiration, he turned aside, acting on his own initiative[225] in order to pray at a certain church[226] in which St. Gueriir rests and where St. Neot now also reposes.[227] For he was a diligent visitor of holy places also from early childhood for the sake of praying and alms-giving. There he remained prostrated for a long time in silent prayer; and thus he besought the mercy of the Lord, to the extent that Almighty God in His immense clemency, might change the torments of this present and troublesome infirmity for some other lighter illness, on this condition nevertheless, that the [new] illness should not appear on the outside of his body lest he might become useless and despised. For he feared leprosy and blindness or some other such disease, which soon make men, upon whom they fall, both useless and despised.[228]

When he had finished his prayer, he set off on the journey he had begun, and not long after that time, as he had besought in his prayer, he felt himself to be divinely healed of that bodily pain, so that it was to be entirely rooted out, even though as a pious humble petitioner through devout prayer and frequent supplication to God, he had contracted this bodily pain in the first flowering of his youth.

For if I may speak of his benevolence of mind and of his devotion to God – succinctly and briefly, even if presented back-to-front – when in the first flowering of his youth before he married his wife, he wished to strengthen his own mind in the commandments of God, and he realised he was not able to abstain from carnal desire, and [fearing][229] that he would incur the anger of God if he did anything contrary to His will, he very often – rising secretly at cock-crow and in the morning hours – visited churches and relics of the saints in order to pray.[230] And there he used to pray, prostrating himself for a long while and turning himself totally [to God], whereby Almighty God, on account of His mercy, would the more robustly strengthen his mind in the love of His service by means of some infirmity which he might be able to bear but which nevertheless would not render him unworthy or useless in earthly affairs.[231] When he had often done this with great devotion of mind, after a short interval of time he contracted the previously mentioned bodily affliction of the piles through the gift of God.[232] In which illness, labouring long and painfully for many years, he despaired even of life, until after he had made his prayer, [God] took it away entirely from him.

But alas! when it was taken away another more troublesome [disorder] seized him, as we have said, at his wedding feast, and this wore him out incessantly by night and day from the twentieth year of his age up to his forty-fifth year.[233] But if at any time through the mercy of God that illness were banished for one day or a night, or even for the interval of only one hour, nevertheless the fear and dread of that terrible bodily pain never left him, but rendered him almost useless, as it seemed to him, in Divine as well as in human affairs.

## 75
## King Alfred's Children
## The Prep School at the Royal Household

Now there were born to him by the abovementioned wife[234] sons and daughters, namely, Æthelflæd the first-born, and after her Edward and then Æthelgifu, and after her, Ælfthryth, and then Æthelweard, besides those who were surprised by an early death in infancy, among whose number was. . . . [235] Æthelflæd, when the time of her marriage came, was joined in matrimony to Eadred,[236] ealdorman of the Mercians. Æthelgifu, devoting her virginity to God, and subjected to and consecrated under the monastic rule of life, entered the service of God.[237] Æthelweard, the youngest of all, by Divine counsel and through the admirable forethought of the king, was given over to the pleasures of reading and writing[238] along with all the noble infants of almost the entire region, and indeed along with many non-noble ones as well, under the diligent care of tutors.

In that school, books in both languages – Latin as well as Saxon – were diligently read. They also had the leisure for writing, so that before they had the strengths suitable for manly skills – hunting as well as other arts appropriate to nobles – they appeared devoted and intelligent in the liberal arts.

Edward and Ælfthryth were always brought up in the royal court[239] with the great diligence of their tutors and nurses and indeed with a great love from all; and indeed they remain there to this day,[240] and displaying humility, kindness and tenderness towards all – both natives and foreigners – and showing great obedience to their father. Nor are they allowed to live without being occupied, or by being negligent without a liberal education, among the other concerns of the present life which are suitable for nobles; for they have zealously learnt the Psalms, and books [written in] Saxon, and especially Saxon poems and they very frequently make use of books.[241]

## 76
## Alfred: Saint, Scholar, Headmaster, Emperor and Super-king

Meanwhile, therefore, the king between wars and frequent hindrances of the present life, as well as the attacks of the Pagans and the daily illnesses of his body, did not leave off from presiding over the government of the kingdom; engaging in every art of hunting; instructing all his goldsmiths and craftsmen, falconers, hawk-handlers[242] and dog-handlers;[243] making buildings according to his own new design – more venerable and more precious, surpassing the tradition of his ancestors; reading Saxon books aloud and especially learning Saxon poems by heart[244] and in commanding others [to do likewise]. And he, on his own, [did all of these things] assiduously and most zealously with all his might.

He was also accustomed to hearing daily the Divine Services[245] and the Mass, and certain psalms and prayers, as well as celebrating the Day and Night Hours and frequenting churches at night-time – as we have said – in order to pray in secret from his followers.[246]

He applied himself with diligence in alms-giving and in generosity both to natives and to newcomers from all nations, displaying the greatest and incomparable affability and pleasantness towards all men, and ingeniously investigating into unknown things.[247]

And many Franks, Frisians, Gauls, Pagans, Welsh, Scots and Bretons, freely submitted themselves to his lordship – nobles as well as non-nobles and he had royal power over them all just as over his very own people as befitted his [royal] status, and he cherished, honoured and enriched them all[248] with wealth and power.[249]

He was also in the habit of listening earnestly and attentively to Divine Scripture read aloud by native [clergy], but also if by chance someone had come from elsewhere, he would likewise listen to prayers with foreigners.[250] He also cherished his bishops and all order of clerics, his ealdormen[251] and nobles, his *ministeriales* together with all his *familiares*,[252] with a wonderful affection. He never ceased in the midst of other duties, to undertake on his own, day and night,[253] to supervise their sons who were brought up in the royal court in all good behaviour and to instruct them in literacy – cherishing them no less than his own children.

## 76A[254]
## Alfred's Constant Lament for His Lack of Education and his Thirst for Knowledge

Yet, as if he took no comfort from all these things and as if he suffered no other distress, inwardly or outwardly, he used to groan in anxious sorrow and lament with daily and nightly sighing to the Lord, and to all those who were adopted by him in close affection, that Almighty God had made him lacking in Divine wisdom and in the liberal arts. In this he was on a par with the pious, most illustrious and richest Solomon, king of the Hebrews, who despising all present glories and riches, first demanded wisdom from God and he even found both – wisdom and present glory – as it is written:

'Seek ye first the Kingdom of God and his righteousness, and all these things shall be given unto you.'[255]

But God who is always the observer of our inward minds and who is the prompter of our thoughts and all good desires, and who is also a most generous enabler, so that good desires may be accomplished, and who never prompts anyone to desire [something] good, without also generously providing what each one well and justly desires to have – prompted the mind of the king from within, not without, as it is written: 'I will hear what the Lord God speaks in me.'[256] Whenever he was able, he would acquire helpers in his good intention, who would help him towards the desired wisdom that he might obtain what he so greatly desired. So, like the most prudent bee,[257] which at dawn of day in summertime, arising from its beloved cells, and setting off in a straight line, swiftly flying on its uncertain journey through the air, descends onto many and varied blossoms of herbs, of plants and of fruits, and finds and carries back home what pleases it most – so King Alfred directed the eyes of his mind afar-off, seeking abroad what he did not have within, that is, within his own kingdom.[258]

## 77

# Wærfærth, Bishop of Worcester, together with a Team of Mercian Scholars, join the Seminar of the Illiterate King

And then God, being unable to tolerate such a well-intentioned and most just complaint any longer, sent some reliefs for the goodwill of the king – certain luminaries, namely, Wærfærth bishop of the church of Worcester, who was well instructed in Divine Scripture, and who at the king's command, first translated the books of the *Dialogues* of Pope Gregory[259] and his disciple, Peter, painstakingly and most elegantly, from Latin into the Saxon language, sometimes rendering sense for sense.[260] And after that [came] Plegmund from the race of the Mercians, archbishop of the church of Canterbury,[261] a venerable man and one possessed of wisdom; also Æthelstan and Wærwulf, priests and chaplains,[262] learned men of Mercian race. These four men, King Alfred called to himself from Mercia, and he exalted them with many honours and with powers in the kingdom of the West Saxons, in addition to those which Archbishop Plegmund and Bishop Wærfærth had in Mercia.

By the teaching and wisdom of all these men, the desire of the king [for learning] was ever increased and satisfied. For by day and by night, whenever he had any freedom, he ordered books to be read aloud before him by such men, for he would not ever allow himself to be without one or other of them. He obtained a notion, therefore, of almost all books, although he was not as yet able by himself to understand anything from books. For he had still not begun to read anything.[263]

## 78

# Alfred Sends to Gaul for Grimbald and John

However since the royal greed – which was nevertheless laudable – was still not satisfied, he sent emissaries overseas to Gaul to find tutors, and from there he summoned Grimbald, a priest and monk, that venerable man, the best of singers, and most learned in every way in ecclesiastical customs and in Divine Scriptures, and adorned in all good habits.[264] And he also [summoned] John, likewise a priest and monk, a man of the keenest intelligence and most learned in all the arts of literary discipline and accomplished in many other arts.[265] By their teaching, the king's way of thinking was much enlarged and he enriched and honoured them with great authority.

# 79
## The Author is Summoned to King Alfred from Wales
## Their First Meeting at Dean, the Author's Convalescence at
## Winchester, and his Terms of Entering the King's Service, are
## Described

In those times,[266] I also was summoned by the king and I came to the Saxon land from the western and furthest parts of Britain. When I had resolved to come to him through great expanses of territory, I reached the region of the Right-Hand [southern][267] Saxons which is called Sussex in the Saxon language, accompanied by guides of that race. And there I first saw the king on the royal estate which is called Dean.[268] When I had been kindly received by him, and during the various exchanges[269] of our opinions, he asked me most firmly to devote myself to his service and to become his <u>familiaris</u>, and to relinquish for his sake, all that I had in the left-hand [northern] part and to the west of the Severn, and he promised also to give me back a greater recompense. And this he did. I replied:

'I cannot promise such things incautiously and rashly.'

For it seemed unjust to me to abandon those very holy places in which I had been brought up, educated, tonsured, and – finally – ordained, for the sake of some earthly honour and power, unless I were forced and compelled.
  To this he said:[270]

'If you cannot agree to accede to this, then at least give half of your service to me, so that for six months you may be with me and for the same length of time you may be in Britain.'

To which I replied:

'I cannot agreeably and rashly promise this without the counsel of my people.'

But when I realised that he truly desired my service, although I did not know why, I promised that I would return to him after six months – my life being spared – with a reply such as would be useful to me and to my people and agreeable to him. And when this response seemed acceptable to him, and a pledge having been given to return at the appointed time, riding away from him on the fourth day, we returned to our native country. But when we had departed from him,[271] a violent fever seized me in the city of Winchester[272] in which I laboured without remission for twelve months and one week, day and night, without any hope of life. And when, at the appointed time, I had not returned to him as I had promised, he sent letters[273] to me earnestly asking the cause of my delay and urging me to make haste in riding to him. But when I could not ride to him, I sent another letter to him which disclosed the cause of my delay and which sent back word that I would fulfil what I had promised if I were able to recover from that illness. Therefore when the sickness had departed, by the advice and permission of all my people, and for the benefit of that holy place and of all its inhabitants, I devoted myself to the service of the king as I had promised on this condition, that for six months of every year I should remain constantly with him. Either if I were able to prolong [my stay] for six months in alternate succession with him, or otherwise I should remain three months in Britain and three months in the Saxon land, and that [Saxon land] would be helped by the rudiments of learning[274] of St. David, yet in every case according to our strength. For our people hoped that if I should come to the notice and friendship of that king [Alfred] by some kind of agreement, they might suffer less tribulations and injuries on the part of King Hyfaidd who often plundered that monastery and the *parochia*[275] of St. David, sometimes by the expulsion of those overseers who were in charge of it, just as, on one of those occasions, he expelled my relative Archbishop Nobis as well as myself.[276]

## 80
## The Welsh Kings Submit to Alfred's *Imperium*

At that time and for long before, all the regions[277] of the right-hand [southern] part of Britain belonged to King Alfred and they belong to him still,[278] since Hyfaidd along with all the inhabitants of the region of Dyfed, compelled by the power of the six sons of Rhodri [Mawr][279] had submitted himself to the royal *imperium*. Likewise Hywel son of Rhys, king of Glywysing and Brochfael and Ffyrnfael, the sons of Meurig, kings of Gwent, compelled by the power and tyranny of Ealdorman Eadred,[280] and of the Mercians, besought the same king of their own accord that they might have lordship and protection[281] from him against their enemies. Similarly Elise son of Tewdwr, king of Brycheiniog, driven by the power of the same sons of Rhodri, sought of his own accord the lordship of the aforementioned king. And Anarawd, son of Rhodri, along with his brothers, finally deserting the friendship of the Northumbrians, from which they had no good but only harm, came into the presence of the king, earnestly seeking friendship. When he had been honourably received by the king, and accepted as a son at the hand of a bishop in Confirmation,[282] and enriched with the greatest gifts, he submitted himself along with all his people to the lordship of the king on the same condition as Æthelred[283] with his Mercians, namely that in all things he would be obedient to the royal will.

## 81
## The Author Begins his Tutorials with the Illiterate King and is Given Great Gifts

Nor was it in vain that all of these [Welsh rulers] acquired the king's friendship. For those who desired to increase their earthly power, got that; those who desired money, got money; those who desired friendship, got friendship; and those who desired both, got both. All, however, had love, protection and defence[284] on every side in so far as the king himself along with all his people was able to defend himself. When therefore I came to him at the royal estate which is called *Leonaford*,[285] I was received honourably by him and remained with him in his court[286] on that stint for eight months, during which I read aloud from those books which he wished and which we had to hand. For it is his own most frequent habit by day and by night – amid all his other hindrances of mind and body – either himself to read books aloud or to listen to others reading them. And when I often sought permission from him to return, I was in no way able to obtain my wish. When I had at length decided absolutely to implore him for this permission, I was summoned to him at dawn on the vigil of Christmas [i.e. Christmas Eve] and he gave two letters to me in which there was a manifold list of all the items which were in the two monasteries which in the Saxon language are called Congresbury and Banwell.[287] And he gave to me, on that same day, those two monasteries, with everything which was in them, as well as an exceedingly precious silken mantle,[288] and a strong man's load of incense. And he added these words:

'I do not give these small things, because at a later time I am unwilling to give you greater.'

For at a later and unexpected time he did give me Exeter along with all the diocese[289] which pertained to it in Saxon territory and in Cornwall, as well as innumerable daily gifts of earthly riches of every kind which it would be tedious to enumerate in this place lest they should cause aversion to [my] readers.[290] But do not let anyone think that I have mentioned such gifts in this place out of any kind of empty glory, or in flattery, or for the desire of seeking greater honour, because I testify in the presence of God that I have not done so, but [rather I mention the gifts] so that I may make public to those who do not know, how profuse his generosity [really] is.

He then immediately gave me permission to ride to those two monasteries which were crammed full of all good things, and from there to return to my native land.

## 82
### [*The Author Reverts to Translating the Anglo-Saxon Chronicle*]
### The Pagan Army in Francia Lays Siege to Paris

### AD 886

*In the year of the Incarnation of the Lord, 886*: the thirty-fifth[291] year since the birth of Alfred. *The* frequently mentioned *army*[292] *fleeing once again from the region* [of the East Franks], *came* to the region of the *West* Franks. *Entering with their ships the river which is called the Seine* and navigating a long way against the stream, *they reached the city of Paris*[293] *and wintered there.* They laid out a camp on both sides of the river near the bridge so that they might prevent the citizens from crossing the bridge – because that city is situated on a little island in the middle of the river – and they laid siege to that city for that entire year. But by the merciful favour of God and by the citizens' courageous defence of themselves, they were not able to storm the fortifications.

## 83
### Alfred Restores the City of London

*In the same year, Alfred, king* of the Anglo-Saxons,[294] *restored* with honour the city of *London* and he made it habitable – after the burning of cities and the slaughter of people.[295] *He entrusted it to Æthelred, ealdorman*[296] *of the* Mercians. *To this king [i.e. Alfred], all the Angles and Saxons – those* who had formerly been dispersed everywhere or *who were not*[297] *in captivity with the Pagans*[298] – turned voluntarily and *submitted themselves to his rule.*

## 84
### The Pagan Army Abandons the Siege of Paris

### AD 887

*In the year of the Incarnation of the Lord, 887*: the thirty-sixth[299] since the birth of Alfred. *The army* of the Pagans mentioned above, *abandoned* the city of *Paris* without damaging it, and since they were not able to profit themselves in any other way, *rowing under the bridge, they directed their fleet* a long way *upstream against the Seine until* at last *they reached the* mouth of the river which is called the *Marne. Then* leaving the Seine, they diverted into the mouth of the Marne, and *sailing* far *up it* for a long time until at last, and not without toil, *they reached* a place which is called *Chézy* which is a royal residence. *They wintered there for a whole year. In the following year, they entered* the mouth of the river which is called *the Yonne* – not without great loss to the region – *and they remained there for one year.*

## 85
## Arnulf and Other Kings Inherit a Fragmented Carolingian Empire

*In that year, Charles [the Fat], king of the Franks went the way of all flesh. But Arnulf, his brother's son, had expelled him from the kingdom in the sixth week before his death. As soon as he [Charles the Fat] was dead, five kings were ordained and the kingdom*[300] *was torn up*[301] *into five parts.* But nevertheless, the principal seat of the kingdom went to Arnulf – justly and meritoriously – if it had not been for the way in which he had dishonourably wronged his uncle. *The other four kings also promised* fealty and *obedience to Arnulf* as was fitting, *for none of those four kings had a hereditary right to the kingdom on the paternal side, except Arnulf alone.* Five kings, therefore, were immediately ordained on the death of Charles [the Fat], but the imperial authority (<u>imperium</u>) remained in the possession of Arnulf. The division of the kingdom, therefore, was as follows: *Arnulf received the regions east of the River Rhine; Rudolf took the interior part of the kingdom; Odo the western kingdom; Berengar and Guy received Lombardy as well as those regions which are on that side of the mountains.* Nevertheless, *they did not preserve* so great and *such* remarkable *kingdoms peacefully between themselves. They fought two full-scale battles against each other and very often devastated those kingdoms by turns as one expelled the other from his kingdom.*[302]

## 86
## The Alms of King Alfred and His People are Taken to Rome

*In the same year in which the army on leaving Paris* went to Chézy, Æthelhelm, *ealdorman* of Wiltshire,[303] *took the alms of King Alfred and of the Saxons to Rome.*

## 87[304]
## *The Author Finally Returns to his Life of King Alfred*

In the same year also [AD 887], the frequently mentioned Alfred, king of the Anglo-Saxons, by Divine inspiration began for the first time to read and to interpret at the same time on one and the same day. But in order that this may be made more openly accessible to those who do not know, I shall take care to explain the reason for this late beginning.

## 88

## Alfred is Miraculously Taught to Read by His Tutor
## The King's Notebooks Old and New

For when, one day, we were both sitting in the royal chamber,[305] having a discussion on this and that, as was usual, it happened that I read a passage aloud to him from a certain book. When he had listened intently to it with both ears, and had thoroughly examined it in the depth of his mind, he suddenly showed me a little book,[306] which he purposely carried in the fold of his cloak, in which were written the Daily Offices and certain psalms and prayers, which he had read[307] in his youth. He ordered me to commit that passage to writing in the same little book. I, hearing this, and[308] recognising in part his benevolent intellect and also his devout wish in relation to the study of Divine wisdom, rendered immense thanks to Almighty God – although silently, stretching out my palms to Heaven – who had in-grafted such great devotion for the study of wisdom in the royal heart. But when I could find no vacant place in that same little book, in which to write such a quotation, since it was crammed full of many matters, I delayed for a little while especially as I was eager to provoke the fine intellect of the king to a greater knowledge of Divine Scriptures. When he urged me to write it down as quickly as possible, I said:

> 'Would it please you if I should write this passage separately on another little sheet of parchment? For it is not known whether we might find at some time one or more such passages which might please you, and if this should happen unexpectedly, we shall rejoice to have kept it apart.'

And hearing this he said:

> 'That is good counsel.'

On hearing this, I rejoiced and I quickly prepared a booklet of four folds to be at hand, at the beginning of which I wrote down the quotation, – not unbidden. And on that same day I wrote into that same booklet at his command, no fewer than three passages which were pleasing to him, as I had foretold. And after that, during our daily discussions while investigating this topic, finding other equally pleasing quotations, the booklet became filled up and not undeservedly, as it is written:

> 'The just man builds upon a small foundation and little by little proceeds to greater things.'[309]

Like the most productive bee, hastening far and wide over the marshes in its searchings, he open-mouthedly[310] and unceasingly collected many and various flowers of Divine Scripture[311] with which he closely filled the cells of his heart.

## 89
### King Alfred Progresses in His Study of Biblical Exegesis Miraculously Begun on 11 November 887. More about the King's Handbook

As soon as that first passage had been written, he was immediately eager to read and to translate in the Saxon language and after that to train many others. And just as we are warned by the fortunate thief, who recognising the Lord Jesus Christ, his Lord and indeed Lord of all things, as He hung beside him on the venerable gibbet of the Holy Cross, who with trusting prayers and turning only his bodily eyes on Him, because he was unable to do anything else, for he was totally transfixed with nails, he cried aloud with humble voice:

'Christ remember me, when you shall come into your kingdom.'[312]

He first began to learn the rudiments of the Christian faith on the gibbet, and this [king] likewise,[313] although in a different manner because of his royal power, presumed by the Divine inspiration, to begin on the rudiments of Holy Scripture on the feast of the venerable Martin.[314] And he began to learn those flowers collected here and there from various masters and to bring them together into the body of one little book, although all mixed up, and as the occasion arose. And he expanded it so much until it almost reached the size of a psalter. He wished it to be called his Enchiridion, that is his 'handbook', because most resourcefully, he had it to hand by day and by night. As he then used to say, he found no small comfort in it.[315]

## 90
### A Digression on the Gallows Metaphor[316]

But just as it was written by a certain wise man, a long time ago:

'The minds of those are watchful who have the conscientious concern for ruling'[317]

I think I should be exceedingly watchful since I have just before made some comparison – although in a different way – between the fortunate thief and the king. For the gallows are exceedingly hateful to everyone and are held in evil [repute] everywhere. But what can one do if he cannot escape from there or run away, nor by any means improve his condition as he remains there? He must therefore, whether he is willing or unwilling, endure what he suffers in mourning and in sadness.

## 91
## Alfred, Invalid and Super-king now in his Forty-fifth Year

The king was pierced by many nails of tribulations although firmly estab-lished in royal power. For from his twentieth year until his forty-fifth year, in which he now is,[318] he has been unceasingly worn out by the most serious attack of an unknown bodily pain, so that he does not have relief for a single hour, in which he does not either suffer from that infirmity, or else mourn-fully under the dread of it, he is almost driven to despair.

Furthermore, he was disturbed – and not without cause – by the constant attacks of foreign peoples which he continually sustained by land and sea without any quiet interval of peace. What shall I say of his frequent expedi-tions and battles against the Pagans and of the never-ending responsibility of governing his kingdom?

What shall I say of his daily [concern][319] with nations which dwell from the Mediterranean to the furthest limit of Ireland? For we have read letters and seen gifts which have been sent to him from Jerusalem[320] by [Abel][321] the patriarch. What shall I say of the cities and towns which he restored and of others which were built where there had never been any before? Or of the buildings of gold and silver incomparably made at his instructions?[322] Or of the royal halls and chambers[323] marvellously constructed of stone and timber at his command? Or of the royal residences of stone removed at the royal command from their ancient position and erected most seemingly in more fitting locations?[324]

And what shall I say[325] of the great disturbance and dispute with his own people – not to mention his own bodily pain – who were willing voluntarily to undertake little or no labour for the common needs of the kingdom?[326]

Just as an excellent pilot strives to guide his ship,[327] crammed full of many riches, to the longed-for secure harbour of his native country, although almost all his sailors are exhausted, similarly he alone – once he had taken upon himself the government of the kingdom – supported by Divine help would not allow [that government] to totter or waver although set among the various driving waves and whirlpools of this present life. He continuously and most wisely asserted his right over, and bound to his own will and for the common good of the whole kingdom, his bishops and ealdormen[328] and the most noble men and the thegns[329] who were most dear to him, as well as his heads of religious houses[330] to whom after the Lord and the king, the power of the entire kingdom seems, as is right, to be placed under.[331] [He asserted his right] by gently teaching, flattering, exhorting, commanding, and eventually – after long patience – by punishing sharply the disobedient and by showing in every way hatred of vulgar stupidity and obstinacy. But if amid these royal exhortations, his orders are not carried out[332] because of the laziness of the people, or things which were begun late in time of emergency were unfinished and did not turn out profitably for those who were engaged on them – *I speak of fortifications*[333] *ordered by him and which* have not yet been begun, or *having begun very late were not brought to perfect completion, – and when enemy forces broke in by land and sea*, or as often happened *from both those directions*, then those who opposed the imperial decrees[334] felt ashamed with a vain repentance when almost ruined. I call it 'vain repentance' on the authority of Scripture where innumerable men grieve, having been frequently laid low by the very great damage from the many treacherous deeds they have perpetrated. But although – alas the pity of it! – the well-spoken[335] are miserably saddened through this and are moved to tears through the loss of their fathers, wives, children, servants, slaves, female slaves, their labours and all their equipment, what help is detestable repentance when it cannot hasten to help their slain relatives, nor buy back captives from hateful captivity, nor even occasionally be in a position to help those who have escaped, since they do not have anything by which to sustain their own life? Therefore, those who are very much destroyed repent with a late repentance and they then grieve that they carelessly looked down upon the royal commands and they praise very much the royal wisdom with all their voices and they promise to perform with all their strength what they previously refused to do – that is concerning the construction of fortresses and of other things for the common good of the whole kingdom.[336]

## 92
## Alfred Founds a Monastery at Athelney

I do not think it beneficial to omit in this place his vow and the most excellently thought-out plan which he was in no way able to pass over in prosperity or adversity. For when in his usual way he was pondering on the need of his soul among other good things which he zealously and very constantly pursued by day and by night, he commanded that two monasteries should be built. One [was] for monks in a place which is called Athelney, which is surrounded on all sides by a very great boggy and impassable fen as well as by water, which no one can in any way approach except by dug-out canoes[337] or by one bridge which has been constructed between the two citadels by protracted labour. At the western end of which bridge a most secure citadel of most beautiful workmanship was set up at the command of the aforementioned king. In this monastery he assembled monks of diverse peoples and from every quarter and set them up in that place.[338]

## 93

### The Decline of English Monasticism
### Alfred Cannot Find West Saxon Postulants

At first he had no one – noble or free man – of his own nation, who would of his own accord submit to the monastic life, apart from infants who, because of the tenderness of their ineffectual age, were unable either to choose good or reject evil. For without doubt, for many past cycles of years the desire for the monastic life had been utterly lacking in all of that people as well as among many other peoples. Although many monasteries had been built in that region and endure to this day, yets none holds to that rule of life in an orderly way.[339] I am not sure why: whether on account of the attacks by foreign peoples who very often and savagely burst in from land and sea, or else because of the very great abundance of riches of every sort, of that people [i.e. the West Saxons], because of which I think this kind of monastic life came all the more into contempt. For this reason he strove to assemble monks of different race in that monastery.[340]

## 94

### Gauls, Gaulish Infants and Pagan Youths are Pressed into
### Monastic Life at Athelney

First he established John, namely a priest and monk, who was an Old Saxon by race,[341] as abbot, and then he established some priests and deacons from across the sea. But when with them he had not as yet as great a number as he wished, he also brought together many of that same Gaulish nation, among whom there were some infants[342] whom he ordered to be educated in that same monastery, and at a later time to be raised into the monastic habit. In that monastery also we saw one of the Pagan nation – a mere youth[343] – who was educated there and enduring in the monastic habit,[344] and truly he was not the last of them to do so.

## 95

### A Foul Deed at Athelney that Needs Exposing

A crime was perpetrated at a certain time in that monastery which I would not quietly consign to the oblivion of a dumb silence, even though the villainy is unworthy. For throughout all Scripture, the foul deeds of the unrighteous are inter-sown with the venerable deeds of the righteous, just as tares and cockles[345] among fields of wheat. Naturally, good deeds [are related] so that they may be praised, followed, and equalled, and that their adherents should be deemed worthy of every revered honour. But evil deeds [are recorded] so that they may be censured, execrated and avoided in every way, and that their imitators be accused with all hatred, contempt and vengeance.[346]

## 96
## Gaulish Monks Plan to Slay Abbot John

At a certain time, through diabolical prompting, a certain priest and deacon of the Gaulish nation from among the aforementioned monks, were provoked by some [hidden] envy against their abbot, the aforementioned John. They were secretly so very much embittered that in the manner of the Jews they plotted against and betrayed their lord through deception. For they deceitfully instructed two young slaves of the same Gaulish nation who were hired with a bribe, so that in the night-time when all were sleeping heavily in delightful peace of body, they would enter, armed, the wide-open church and they were to shut it again after themselves in the normal way, and hidden in that church they were to await the coming of the abbot on his own. When he was to enter the church secretly and alone in his usual manner in order to pray, and as he would bow himself in front of the holy altar, bending his knees to the ground, [then] seizing upon him fiercely, they were to slay him then and there. And dragging his lifeless body from there, they were to fling it down in front of the door of a certain prostitute, as if he had been slain while dealing with whores. Thus they plotted, adding crime to crime, as it is said:

'The last error shall be worse than the first.'[347]

But the Divine mercy, which always comes to the assistance of the innocent, to a great extent frustrated an evil plan of evil men, so that it did not turn out completely as they had intended.[348]

## 97
## Abbot John Escapes.
## His Assailants, together with All who were Involved in the Plot, are Tortured to Death

When, therefore, all the evil instruction had been explained with great care and talked over by the evil instructors to their evil listeners, with the onset and assistance of night and with freedom from punishment having been promised, the two armed brigands shut themselves in the church, awaiting the coming of the abbot. When John, at midnight, secretly – as was his custom and unknown to anyone – entered the church in order to pray and on bended knees bowed down before the altar, those two brigands suddenly burst upon him with naked swords and harmed him with cruel wounds. But he was both sharp with accustomed intelligence and – as we have heard about him from certain sources – was a man not wanting in the arts of war, if he had not striven after a better [form of] learning. Immediately he heard the sound of the brigands, he rose up fiercely against them[349] before he even saw them, or before he was wounded by them, and crying out he struggled against them as he was able, shouting that they were devils and not men. He did not know otherwise, for he did not believe that men would dare so. Nevertheless, he was wounded before his own people reached him.

His own people, therefore, woken up by this din, but also having heard the word 'devils' were exceedingly terrified as well as being unaccustomed [to this], and also those [others] – like the Jews, the betrayers of their lord – ran together, hither and thither to the doors of the church. But before they [Abbot John's followers] reached them, the brigands had fled by a precipitous passage to their lairs in a nearby fen,[350] leaving the abbot half-alive. Then the monks collected their half-alive master[351] and carried him back home with sighing and grief, but the cunning plotters did not weep any less than the innocent. However, the mercy of God did not allow so great a crime to go unpunished. The brigands who perpetrated this deed and all who persuaded them of so great a wickedness, were captured and bound, and underwent a most foul death through various tortures.[352] Having related these events, let us return to the main theme.[353]

## 98
## Alfred Founds a Convent for Nuns at Shaftesbury

The same aforementioned king ordered the other monastery to be built near the east gate of Shaftesbury[354] as a residence proper for nuns. In it he appointed as abbess, his own daughter, Æthelgifu, a virgin dedicated to God.[355] With her also many other noble nuns[356] live in the same monastery, serving God in the monastic life. These two monasteries he abundantly enriched[357] with landed possessions and with every wealth.[358]

## 99
## The Saintly Alfred Hands over one Half of His Service and of All His Riches to God, Night and Day[359]

When these matters had been so decreed, as was his usual habit, he thought within himself what he might be able to add which would be more pleasing for his pious intention, and what was not vainly embarked upon, was usefully hit upon and even more usefully observed. For he had once heard that which was written in the Law, that the Lord has promised to return His tithe many times and that He had faithfully observed [this promise] to return His tithe many times.[360] Spurred on by this example and wishing to transcend the custom of his predecessors,[361] this pious planner pledged himself devoutly and faithfully with all his heart that he would give to God the half part of his service by day and by night, as well as one half part of all the riches which with justice and moderation came to him annually. He strove to fulfil this promise, exactly and wisely, in as far as human discretion is able to judge and observe. But as was his habit, in order that he might cautiously avoid what is warned against in another place in Divine Scripture: 'If you offer correctly, but do not divide justly, you sin,'[362] he considered how he might justly divide what he had willingly devoted to God. And, as Solomon says: 'the heart of the king – (that is his counsel) – is in the hand of the Lord.'[363] Having learnt this counsel from on high, he ordered his ministers[364] first to divide all the tax revenue[365] from any one year into two equal parts.

## 100
### The First Half of the King's Revenues are Subdivided into Three. One Third of This First Half is Given to Alfred's Warriors and Household Thegns

When these things had been so divided, he awarded the first part [of his revenues] to be allocated to secular business. He instructed that this should be further separated into three parts.[366] The first part of this division, he bestowed, annually, on his fighting men;[367] and likewise on his noble thegns who stayed in turns at the royal court serving in many offices. The royal household was regularly managed at all times in three relays, for the followers[368] of the aforementioned king were prudently divided into three companies so that the first company stayed at the royal court for one month serving night and day. When the month was finished and another company had arrived, the first returned home and stayed there for two months, everyone caring for his own needs. And so, the second company, when its month was accomplished, and the third [company] had arrived, returned home and stayed there for two months. And also this [third company] having finished one month of service went home when the first company had arrived, and remained there for two months. And by an arrangement of this kind,[369] the administration in the royal court is taken in relay at all times of this present life.

## 101
## The Second and Third Portions of the First Half of the King's Revenues are Given to Craftsmen and Foreigners

To such men, then, he bestowed the first part of the above-mentioned three portions, but to each one according to his own particular rank and also according to his own particular office.[370] He gave the second portion to his workmen[371] who were skilled in every earthly building technique[372] and whom he had assembled and made ready from many nations in almost countless numbers. The third portion of the same [first half of the king's revenues] he cheerfully spent on foreigners from every nation, who came to him from places far and near asking money from him – and also to those who did not ask – [he gave] according to each one's own rank – [and he spent] with marvellous stewardship and in a praiseworthy way as it is written: 'God loves a cheerful giver.'[373]

## 102
## The Second Half of the King's Revenues are Subdivided into Four Parts and Devoted to God.
## One Quarter is Given to the Poor of Every Nation;
## One Divided between the Monasteries of Athelney and Shaftesbury;
## One Given to Alfred's School; and
## One to Other Monasteries in Wessex, Mercia and even Beyond[374]

The second part of all his riches, which came to him annually from all his wealth and which were assigned to the treasury[375] he devoted to God with all his will, as we said a little while back, and he ordered his ministers to divide it carefully into four equal parts on this understanding, that the first part of this sub-division would be paid most discerningly to the poor of every nation who came to him. He used to call to mind in this connection that as far as human discernment is able to ensure, the opinion of the holy Pope Gregory ought to be observed, where he makes the wise suggestion concerning how alms ought to be divided, saying thus:

> 'Do not give little to whom you should give much, nor much to whom you should give little, nor nothing to whom you should give something, nor something to whom you should give nothing.'[376]

The second part [of these four portions] he gave to the two monasteries which he himself had ordered to be built and to those serving God in them – concerning which we discussed at length a short while ago.[377] The third part he gave to the school which he had most carefully assembled from many nobles of his own nation and also from boys who were not of noble birth.[378] He gave the fourth part to neighbouring monasteries, around all Saxony and Mercia, and also in some years he either distributed [gifts] by turns and according to his ability, to churches and to the servants of God dwelling in them, in Wales and Cornwall; Gaul, Brittany, Northumbria; and sometimes even in Ireland; or he intended to dispense alms to them at a later time if his life and prosperity continued.[379]

## 103
## Alfred Resolves
## to Devote Half of His Own Personal Time, Day and Night, to God

When these things had been systematically settled by the same king, being mindful of that passage of Divine Scripture where it is said that 'he who wishes to give alms, must begin with himself',[380] he planned wisely what he might offer to God by way of his own service of his body and mind. For he proposed to make an offering to God in this [spiritual] matter no less than in that of material riches.[381] He proposed to offer to God a half portion of his mental and bodily service in so far as infirmity, ability and means would permit, and he vowed that he would give [this] back to God of his own accord both in daytime and night-time, and with all his strength. But because he was not at all able to distinguish the difference between the hours of night on account of the darkness, nor of the daytime hours because of the most frequent density of rain and cloud, he began to plan how by a fixed method of calculation and without any hesitation, he might be able to keep this promise of his vow unchangingly up until his death, while relying on the mercy of God.

## 104
## Alfred Invents the Lantern Clock[382]

When he had pondered these things for some time, having found at last useful and discerning counsel, he ordered his chaplains to bring a sufficient amount of wax, and when they had brought it, he ordered it to be weighed against pennies in a pair of balances. When as much wax had been measured out as the equivalent of seventy-two pennies in weight, he ordered the chaplains to make six candles, each of equal size, so that each candle would be twelve inches long and have the inches marked along it.[383] Thus, when this plan had been devised, those six candles shone brightly, night and day for twenty-four hours, without failing in the presence of the holy relics of many of the elect of God, which accompanied him always and everywhere.[384]

But sometimes the candles were not able to burn and shine for a whole day and night up to that same hour as that at which they were lit on the previous evening – doubtless because of the violence of the blustering winds which sometimes blew day and night without ceasing, through the entrance of churches and of windows, through walls and wooden panelling, or through the tiny cracks in partitions, and also through the fineness of tents. So, the candles were forced to burn out more quickly than they ought, so that they had finished their course before the [proper] hour. He planned, therefore, how he might be able to prevent such great blowing of winds.

Having skilfully and wisely devised a plan, he ordered a lantern to be made most beautifully out of wood and ox horn. For white ox-horns when scraped down thinly by a tool are no less translucent than a small glass vessel. When this lantern was thus so marvellously made from wood and horns, as we have said above, at night the candle placed in it, being in no way hindered by blasts of winds, burned as brightly on the outside as within, because he had ordered the door at the opening of this lantern also to be made out of horns. When the instrument had been so made in this way, six candles – one after another – burned for twenty-four hours without ceasing, neither too rapidly nor too slowly. And when they went out, others were lit.

## 105
## Champion of the Poor

When all these things had been arranged in an orderly way, he was eager to guard the half-portion of his service which he had consecrated to God, and even to increase it in so far as ability and means and also, of course, his illness, would allow. He was a painstaking judge in the investigation of the truth in judgements, and in this especially on account of his concern for the poor,[385] for whom he exerted himself wonderfully by day and night among his other obligations of this present life. For the poor had no helpers – or very few – in all of that kingdom, except for him alone, because truly, almost all the magnates and nobles of that region had turned their minds more to secular preoccupations rather than to Divine. For each one regarded more his individual advantage in worldly affairs rather than the common good.[386]

## 106A
## Diligent Judge

In judgements he also earnestly strove after[387] the advantage of his people – nobles and non-nobles. For they very frequently disagreed most obstinately among themselves in the assemblies of the counts and officials,[388] so that almost none of them would concede that any judgement by the counts and officials was right.[389] Compelled by this persistent and most obstinate disagreement, they would pledge themselves to submit to the king's separate judgement, and both parties quickly hastened to do so. Yet he who knew that there was some injustice on his part in that lawsuit would not willingly assent to the judgement of such a judge, although compelled to come against his will in accordance with the force of law[390] and pledge. For he knew that not one of his evil deeds could lie hidden there for a moment. And not surprisingly, since this king was a most discerning investigator in judicial business as in all other matters. For he carefully investigated all the judgements of almost the whole of his country[391] which were made in his absence, to see whether they were just or unjust, and truly if he were able to discover anything inequitable in those judgements, he would on his own initiative mildly ask those judges either in person or through some of his other followers[392] as to why they had judged so wickedly, whether from ignorance or on account of ill-will or whatever, that is for love or fear of one party or hatred of the others[393] or even out of greed for someone's money.

Finally, if those judges openly confessed that they had given such judgements therefore, because they could know no better in those cases, then he, discerningly and moderately refuting their ignorance and folly, would speak to them saying:

'I am greatly astonished at your insolence that by God's gift and mine, you have appropriated the office and status of Wise Men, but you have neglected the study and practice of wisdom.[394] Therefore I command you either to relinquish on the spot the offices of worldly power which you hold, or else to apply yourselves with much greater zeal to the study of wisdom.'

## 106B
## Alfred's Magnates are Sent back to School

On hearing these words, the counts and officials strove with all their might to turn themselves to the task of learning justice, for they were terrified and stood corrected as though by the greatest punishment. Almost all the counts, officials and ministers[395] who were illiterate from childhood, applied themselves in a marvellous way in the art of letters, preferring to learn an unaccustomed discipline, however laboriously, rather than relinquish their offices of power.

But if anyone were not capable of making progress in the study of reading and writing,[396] either because of age or from too great a slowness of an unpractised intellect, he ordered his son, if he had one, or some other of his relatives or even if he had no other, then his own man – either freeman or slave – whom he had long before advanced to reading, to read aloud Saxon books to him, day and night, whenever he had any leisure. And sighing greatly from the depths of their hearts, they bewailed that they had not applied themselves to such studies in their youth, perceiving the youth of this age to be happy who were fortunately able to be trained in the liberal arts, and deeming themselves to be unhappy indeed, who had neither learnt in their youth nor in old age, although they had longed for [learning] with avidity.[397] But we have set forth the alacrity of old and young for learning to read in order to add to [your] knowledge of the aforementioned king.[398]

# Commentary

# 1
# A Tour around the Manuscripts

## The importance of the *Life* of King Alfred

The *Life* of King Alfred attributed to Asser occupies a central place in English historical writing, not only because of its acceptance by scholars as the earliest extant biography of an English king – and indeed of any English lay person – but because its subject is Alfred the Great of Wessex whom Asser, the self-proclaimed author of the *Life*, claims to have known as a tutor and a friend. The immediacy of this extraordinary source is heightened by the author's claim to be writing his biography while the king was still living – in Alfred's forty-fifth year – in AD 893.[1] The author follows the progress of Alfred's life from his birth which he dates to AD 849 down to his succession to the kingship of Wessex in 871; through his First and Second Wars and to the eve of the invasion of England by Hæsten's Danish army – or Alfred's Last War – in 892.

This *Life* attributed to Asser presents us with an enduring image of Alfred, youngest and most favoured son of Æthelwulf of Wessex, destined to outlive and to succeed all his brothers in the kingship of the West Saxons. It shows us a hero-king, torn between his duties as leader of the West Saxon war band and the promptings of his immense piety which drove him to emulate the asceticisms of the Desert Fathers. All the while as he struggles between the duties imposed by his public office and the burden of his conscience, he is racked by painful illness which is endured with saintly fortitude as part of his spiritual struggle against the desires of the flesh. Alfred in this *Life* never achieves the status of an established scholar. He is portrayed, rather, as an obsessive – a king obsessed with illness and with his own personal need to overcome illiteracy. He is equally obsessed with the need to enforce literacy on the great men of his realm. He is obsessive, too, in matters of justice, holding postmortems on 'nearly all the judgements which were passed in his absence anywhere in his realm'. In addition to his extraordinary military, scholarly and judicial programmes, Alfred, we are told, offered no less than half of his time, day and night, to the service of God. This work attributed to Asser rounds off the hagiographical portrait of its hero with an overall image of Alfred as a great inventor and a generous patron of the arts. In short, the *Life* shows us Alfred as the idealised Christian king. It is the portrait of Alfred Super-King.

However idealised and sycophantic this *Life* may be, that in itself ought not necessarily to invalidate its claim to have been written during Alfred's lifetime and by a confidant of the king. I find myself in agreement with Professor Nelson in that there is nothing essentially inauthentic in the portrayal of Alfred as a conscientious, pious and suffering servant of God.[2] I would also accept that even the exaggerated portrayal of the characteristics of such a king would not necessarily mark the *Life* off as a later forgery *per se*. For whether or not the *Life* was written by the historical Asser or by Byrhtferth of Ramsey, similar monastic and hagiographical angles of vision might have been brought to bear on Alfred's life-story. Yet the all-pervading ecclesiastical spiritual agenda in this allegedly contemporary *Life* of a secular lord, and the multitude of contradictory statements embedded in that agenda, ought to have made supporters for the validity of Asser's authorship more cautious and more critical in their wholesale acceptance of some of its more extravagant hagiographical detail. As long ago as 1842, Thomas Wright communicated a paper to the Society of Antiquaries in which he cast serious doubts on the authenticity of the *Life* of Alfred as a work composed by Asser, bishop of Sherborne, during the lifetime of the king.[3] Wright was troubled by the unfinished nature of the *Life*, by what he considered to be legendary elements in its make-up – such as Alfred's invention of horn lanterns – and by its heavy reliance on the Anglo-Saxon Chronicle for providing detail on Alfred's career. Wright also noted the author's anachronism in referring to the *parochia* or diocese of Exeter which was not formally constituted until AD 1050, and he observed, too, lapses in the author's Latinity from the imperfect into the present tense when speaking of Alfred.[4] This last point cast doubts on whether the subject of the narrative was still alive at the time of writing. Finally, Wright noted the confused and contradictory accounts offered on Alfred's early education and on the mysterious illness which is alleged in the *Life* to have plagued the king's career. Wright's arguments were hampered by his reliance on poor textual editions of the *Life* and by the limitations of textual criticism in his own day. He believed, for instance, the text of the Anglo-Saxon Chronicle (on which the *Life* of Alfred had so heavily relied) to be considerably later than Asser's time, and he was understandably confused by Archbishop Matthew Parker's additions to the original text of the *Life* of Alfred, such as material taken from the East Anglian Chronicle (*Annals of St. Neots*) in the first printed edition of the *Life* in 1574.[5] Wright's study led him to believe that the *Life* of King Alfred was a late tenth- or eleventh-century forgery compiled at St. Neots in Huntingdonshire. In this Wright was extraordinarily near the mark. In 1995 I concluded that the *Life* of Alfred had been written in *c.* AD 1000 within the scholarly circle of Byrhtferth, a monk and master of the monastic school at Ramsey which lies only 15 miles north of St. Neots, and also in Huntingdonshire. The problems identified by Wright have continued to exercise the minds of a small but significant number of scholars for well over a century. Since Asser clearly outlived his royal master by some ten years, dying as bishop of Sherborne in Dorset in 909,[6] why did he not continue the biography of Alfred up to the latter's death in 899? By breaking off his account in midstream, Asser lost what would have been for him a golden opportunity to dwell in detail on the king's Last War as a grand finale to his military career, and he also forfeited the opportunity to discuss in detail the programme of scholarly writing and translations for which Alfred is justly famous. And although the author claims to be writing in 893, the biography follows Alfred's life in strict chronological terms only up to 887.[7] So, questions immediately present themselves. Did the original *Life* of which no complete medieval manuscript survives, follow the career of the king down to the time of his death, or did the author break off his narrative at 887 or 893 because he had grown tired of the project, or because he had no further reason to proceed with it, or because his sources of information failed him at that point? To these questions we must return, but they are by no means the most serious or most urgent in requiring answers.

W.H. Stevenson published what was to become the definitive edition of Asser's *Life* in 1904 in which he sought to purify the text of Archbishop Parker's interpolations and sixteenth-century printing errors; and provided scholars with a clear indication of what he considered to belong to the Cottonian manuscript (the most extensive single manuscript of the *Life* to have survived into modern times); what parts of the original text had been used by John (*alias* Florence) of Worcester; and what were later interpolations.[8] But Stevenson, although he agonised at length over the undoubted problems inherent in the *Life*'s account of Alfred's illnesses and education (to name but two difficulties), was committed to the notion of the authenticity of Asser's authorship.[9] His scholarly commentary, excessive and sometimes confused, has provided the quarry from which all subsequent commentators and translators of the *Life* of Alfred have drawn liberally. Stevenson, in his zeal to defend Asser, brushed Wright's arguments aside by the familiar, but unworthy tactic of undermining faith in his opponent's scholarly integrity, through denigrating Wright's strenuous defence of the authenticity of another 'absurd forgery *De situ Britanniae*'.[10] If Wright could be proved wrong in his estimation of one historical text, then who would accept his opinion on another? Considering that Wright's paper appeared more than half a century before Stevenson's edition of the *Life* of Alfred, and bearing in mind that Wright touched on most of the major issues which have caused concern to more recent and able historians, Stevenson's attempts to show up Wright as an unscholarly amateur reaching 'a most lame and impotent conclusion' which derived in part 'from later monkish fabrications' was unwarranted and unjust.[11] Wright's concern that this work attributed to Asser was a collection of eulogy and anecdote grafted on to a translation of the Anglo-Saxon Chronicle (and so posing problems regarding its status as a contemporary and independent source on King Alfred) was scorned by Stevenson as 'merely matter of opinion'. Stevenson's attack demonstrated his fundamental lack of appreciation as a textual scholar, of the historian's approach to his subject.[12] The debate over the authenticity or otherwise of Asser's *Life* of King Alfred developed into a battle between linguists constrained, in this particular case, by the limited value of their textual evidence, and historians whose lines of inquiry arose – in Galbraith's words – 'from subjective impression'.[13]

If as Maitland observed 'Asser was supremely fortunate in the hands of Mr. Stevenson',[14] he did not fare so happily under the scrutiny of V.H. Galbraith, who first expressed his doubts on Asser in his Creighton Lecture at the University of London in 1949 and who later developed his views into open rejection of the source as a contemporary document from Alfred's reign, in a chapter entitled 'Who Wrote Asser's Life of Alfred?' in his *Introduction to the Study of History* in 1964. Galbraith, who read Stevenson's 328 pages of Introduction and Notes with great care, concluded:

> The whole book is a sustained rearguard action in which every difficulty is looked firmly in the face, and then not so much explained, as explained away.[15]

Galbraith's 'difficulties' and his arguments used to disprove Asser's authorship of the *Life* of Alfred were in many ways similar to those of Wright. He refused to accept Stevenson's explanation for the apparent anachronism in relation to the *parochia* of Exeter; he made much of the contradictions in the account of Alfred's illnesses; of the changes from imperfect to present tense, and of motifs which he viewed as drawn from folklore and legend.[16] Galbraith gave new emphasis to problems presented by other aspects of Asser's text – its debt to Einhard's *Life* of Charlemagne, its dedication to Alfred as 'ruler of all Christians of the island of Britain' (a nonsense in Galbraith's view), and its referring to Alfred as 'king of the Anglo-Saxons', when in his time Alfred ruled only Wessex and parts of Mercia.[17] 'In general,' Galbraith concluded, 'it reads like the life of a man no longer alive' presented in the form of a 'hagiographical picture of Alfred as a neurotic invalid'.[18] He saw the *Life* of Alfred as a forgery which he ascribed to Leofric, bishop of Devon and Cornwall from 1046, and bishop of Exeter from 1050.[19] Galbraith believed the purpose of the forgery was to facilitate or justify the amalgamation of the two bishoprics of Devon and Cornwall, and the moving of Leofric's episcopal seat from Crediton in Cornwall to a safer location in Exeter – hence the prominence given in the *Life* to Alfred's gift of Exeter to Asser.[20] In Galbraith's opinion, Leofric began his work with the notion of writing about a dead king, but stopped at 893 and revised his text by inserting references to Alfred and others in the present tense in order to lend a false aura of contemporaneity to his narrative.[21] This ploy saved Leofric the embarrassment of not knowing much of Alfred's later translations and concealed his ignorance of the precise time when Asser was advanced by King Alfred to the bishopric of Sherborne.

Galbraith's study, in spite of its dependence on the work of earlier scholars, ranks as one of the most important pieces of historical writing in Great Britain in the twentieth century. This is not just because he challenged the authenticity of Asser's authorship of Alfred's *Life*, and it is in spite of his error in ascribing that authorship to an eleventh-century bishop of Exeter. Galbraith was essentially asserting the historian's role as presenter of the past – not as individual scholars or as a whole national consciousness might *wish* to be shown it, but to present it in so far as it can be objectively reconstructed, through the scholarly integrity of one observer's angle of vision. Challenges to the authenticity of the *Life* of Alfred struck deep at the establishment's view of what sort of king Alfred ought to have been. The *Life* of Alfred had served as propaganda not only for medieval English kings and for bishops of the Reformation: it also had its uses in the romantic and imperial age of nineteenth-century Britain. Those who believed in a divine destiny for the British Empire, could conveniently see its origins in Asser's Super-King of Wessex – a man of simple life and virtue, but also a warrior with superhuman resolve and genius. 'The Victorians,' Nelson reminded us, 'fashioned Alfred's kingdom in their own image' and that image had a huge bearing on late nineteenth-century scholarship.[22] Wright's voice of dissent in 1842 or that of Howorth in 1876–7[23] failed to win the backing of leading historians such as Edward Freeman (1823–92) or Bishop Stubbs (1825–1901). The ideas of the doubters of Asser were consigned to the wilderness in an imperial Britain that looked upon forgery as a peculiarly villainous craft and which saw any tampering with a major source of English history as tantamount to an unpatriotic act. Queen Victoria and Prince Albert had named their second son after Alfred the Great in 1844, while in death at Frogmore, they themselves were portrayed on monuments with all the trappings of an Alfredian 'Saxon' fantasy. As the nineteenth century neared its end, Britain braced itself to celebrate with millenary fervour the anniversary of her most celebrated and beloved of medieval kings. Winchester acquired its massive statue of Alfred the Great in 1901,[24] and although two major wars with Germany in the early twentieth century killed off the romantic Germanic and Albertian dimension of the Alfred saga, the West Saxon king-myth survived in the national consciousness to present a trimmed-down interpretation of early English greatness.

No one can deprive Alfred of the credit for commissioning a modest fleet of longships to withstand Danish seaborne attacks on his coasts. It was understandable for Lord Rosebury, then former Prime Minister – and carried along by the euphoria of Alfred mania in 1901 – to see 'the British fleet [as] the offspring of his [Alfred's] own poor ships'.[25] It was quite another thing for Stenton to state in his *Anglo-Saxon England* of 1947: 'the recorded beginnings of the English navy lie in the small fleet of large vessels built by Alfred.'[26] The rhetoric generated by Alfredian historiography had, under Stenton, taken on new meaning in a Britain which had endured the menace of invasion in two world wars. And while the outsized and impracticable longships employed by Alfred in 896 prefigured conquering *Dreadnoughts* for the late Victorians,[27] for Stenton they had become a symbol of an embattled island's defences against the Reich. Nationalist images, and the myths that sustain them, die hard, and it took real intellectual courage to go against the tide. Galbraith's papers on Asser in 1949 and 1964 still encountered an academic establishment in hostile mood to any changes in the received teaching on Alfred as enshrined in Stevenson's inordinately long commentary on Asser's text. Stenton had already accepted Stevenson as 'the definitive authority' on the *Life* of Alfred[28] prior to Galbraith's bombshell, and he accepted the *Life* attributed to Asser as 'a very naive, but sincerely intimate biography'.[29]

Dorothy Whitelock rose to the defence of Asser, Stevenson and especially of Stenton, with *The Genuine Asser* – her riposte to Galbraith – delivered appropriately as *The Stenton Lecture* at the University of Reading in 1967. An additional stated aim of Whitelock was 'to clear Bishop Leofric from the accusation of being a forger'.[30] Many of the points which she raised can still be argued for or against the authenticity of the *Life*, and in her unguarded moments Whitelock indulged in the kind of speculation which she derided in the works of other scholars. Her musings that Asser may have left off from writing the *Life* of Alfred in 893 in order to help the king with the translation of Boethius' *Consolation of Philosophy*[31] shows how she could heap one piece of speculation upon another, for the notion that Asser was connected with the translation of Boethius's *De Consolatione Philosophiae* rests on two unsupported statements of William of Malmesbury.[32] A number of her arguments – such as those regarding Alfred's supposed alliance with Welsh rulers – are inaccurate,[33] while others were patently false. Her idea, for instance, that the author of Alfred's *Life* confined himself 'to datable contemporary records ... rejecting legendary matter' was a nonsense, as was the notion that a passing reference to St. Gueriir was 'the nearest approach to a miraculous element in the *Life*'.[34] Whitelock did succeed in showing that Leofric could not have written the *Life* of Alfred, and her arguments here were based on sound chronological and contextual grounds. She argued that the Cottonian manuscript (Otho A.xii) of the *Life* of Alfred pre-dated Leofric of Exeter by about 50 years[35] and she rightly pointed out that the Exeter episode in the *Life* constitutes far too minor a feature in that work to justify reasons for constructing an elaborate forgery around an issue which a would-be fabricator allowed to become lost in the body of an otherwise lengthy and irrelevant text.[36] But the effect of her paper on the Asser debate was extraordinary. The contest appeared to have ended in outright victory for the orthodox school, as exemplified by Whitelock and Stenton. In subsequent years a handful of scholars dared to call into question some points of detail in Alfredian sources and to acknowledge the contemporary propaganda value inherent in those sources. Such contributions were sporadic and lacked an overview of the Alfredian debate. More importantly, they rarely questioned the received dogma on Asser, confining themselves instead to less sensitive Alfredian materials. They were received by the academic establishment as mere fine-tuning – not all of it welcome – to a thesis which was considered unassailable and which remained unchallenged in its essentials. The effect of Whitelock's personal defence of Stenton, and of her *ex cathedra* teaching on Asser's authorship of the *Life* of Alfred, was to elevate all sections of that problematical text to the status of a sacred canon in Anglo-Saxon Studies. In 1983, the editors of the Penguin translation of *Asser's Life of King Alfred* felt confident in excluding all reference from their bibliography to either Wright's or Howorth's papers in the nineteenth century, or to Galbraith's Creighton Lecture. They declared Galbraith's argument to have been 'promptly and comprehensively demolished by Dorothy Whitelock'.[37] But they felt impelled to exorcise the ghost of Galbraith from the subject of Asser's text once and for all by reviewing some 'main points at issue'.[38] In an uncharacteristically brief sortie into the graveyard of Galbraith's arguments, the authors concluded:

> In short, the case against the authenticity of Asser's *Life* of King Alfred does not stand up to scrutiny, and any lingering doubts should be laid peacefully to rest.[39]

Few now remained who shared Galbraith's unease in relation to Asser and his supposed *Life* of the king of Wessex.

## Manuscripts of the *Life*

The *Life* of King Alfred survives in one major recension, together with four other fragmentary or abridged versions of the work which are incorporated in a series of Latin chronicles, all of which were compiled at *c*. AD 1000. Those chronicles were compiled as part of a larger enterprise to copy out and continue the record of the ninth-century vernacular Anglo-Saxon Chronicle which was begun in King Alfred's reign. While the original Chronicle had begun life in Alfredian Wessex, its continuation and proliferation in both Old English and Latin versions were carried out at Ramsey Abbey (in Huntingdonshire) at the turn of the millennium. Ramsey Abbey had been founded by Oswald, Bishop of Worcester in 968. Oswald, along with Archbishop Dunstan of Canterbury and Bishop Æthelwold of Winchester spearheaded the reconstruction and reform of English monasticism in the aftermath of the Viking onslaught which had virtually wiped out the monasteries of the Danelaw. Oswald had founded Ramsey as the first of the new Fenland houses and it was intended at the outset to be a centre not only of spirituality but also of great scholarship, where the *Lives* of England's saints and martyrs could be written up, distributed and preserved.[40] One such *Life*, the account of the *Passio* or martyrdom of King Edmund of East Anglia, who had been tortured to death by Vikings in 869, was written as a blueprint for the Ramsey school of hagiographers by Abbo of Fleury in *c*. 987. Abbo, who visited and taught at Ramsey from 986 to 988, was one of the leading European scholars of his day, and his presence at Ramsey (which enjoyed numerous other Fleury connections) testifies to the pre-eminence of the role of that monastery in the revival of English learning at the turn of the millennium.[41] Ramsey already had an able young scholar, Byrhtferth, almost certainly working there before Abbo arrived, and Byrhtferth was to absorb the teaching and Latin style of Abbo as well as acquire his master's interests not only in hagiography but in mathematical and scientific knowledge. Byrhtferth's earliest and most enduring interest was in the compilation of annals and chronicles and it is important to recognise from the outset that he was responsible for the compilation of at least three and very probably all four of the Latin chronicles which incorporate abridged versions of the *Life* of King Alfred.

### The Cottonian Manuscript

King Alfred's *Life* survived in its fullest form into modern times in one solitary (and by then composite) manuscript (Cotton MS Otho A.xii). It was part of the library of Sir Robert Cotton (1571–1631). That unique source was destroyed in the blaze which consumed 114 priceless volumes when Cotton's library was severely damaged in the fire at Ashburnham House in the Little

Dean's Yard, Westminster, on 23 October 1731. Cotton had acquired the manuscript of Alfred's *Life* by 1621, but one of its previous owners, Matthew Parker (1504–75), Archbishop of Canterbury and erstwhile master of Corpus Christi College, Cambridge, published the first printed edition of the text in 1574. Parker had a transcript of the manuscript made for his own use while preparing his edition, which survives as Cambridge Corpus Christi College MS 100.[42] This transcript was assumed by Stevenson[43] to be largely free of annotations and interpolations of Parker and his secretaries, which they are believed to have added to the Cottonian manuscript, and which appear in his printed edition. Similar Parkerian additions and alterations are also present to a lesser extent in yet another and slightly later transcript, BL Cotton Otho A.xii*.[44] Parker's edition was reprinted in Frankfurt in 1602 by Camden who, in addition to reproducing Parker's additions and incorporating his marginal glosses into the original text, also inserted the outrageous anecdote to prove that Oxford already possessed a university in King Alfred's reign.[45] A second new edition of the work was published by Francis Wise at Oxford University Press in 1722.[46] Although this was only nine years before the fire which destroyed the only surviving medieval manuscript, Wise did not personally consult either that manuscript or the Corpus transcript for his edition, and his work incorporated interpolations and errors of Parker and Camden, and of their printers. Wise employed the antiquary, James Hill, who collated the Cotton manuscript with Camden's printed edition, a task which was poorly undertaken, but Hill also supplied a lithographic facsimile of the first fourteen lines of the Cotton manuscript of the *Life* for Wise's edition.[47] This precious piece of evidence relating to the lost manuscript of the *Life* shows us the text of Asser's supposed dedication to his 'esteemed and most holy lord, Alfred' written in rustic capitals followed by the opening lines of the text proper. The text began with a large initial, opening a line of smaller capitals, followed by a second line of rustic capitals, followed in turn by five lines of text in Caroline minuscule. This Caroline script was used for Latin texts in England from *c.* 950 onwards.[48] Stevenson dated the script from the drawing supplied by Hill in Wise's edition, to 'the early part of the eleventh century'[49] and the general appearance of the drawing clearly suggests that we are dealing with a pre-Conquest date for the Cotton manuscript text of the *Life* of Alfred. Some words of caution need to be registered at this stage. Parker claimed his manuscript of the *Life* was written in Latin letters – presumably Caroline minuscule as represented in Hill's drawing. But Parker also claimed a resemblance between the script in his Cotton manuscript and that of other manuscripts of King Alfred's translation of the *Pastoral Care*, which were written not in Caroline minuscule, but in Anglo-Saxon characters.[50] Humphrey Wanley was later (in 1721) to challenge Parker's opinion, by stating that only proper names in the Cotton manuscript of Alfred's *Life* were written in Saxon letters, the main text of the *Life* being in 'the English hand of that time' – i.e. the Caroline minuscule which he dated to *c.* 1000.[51] Wanley, who was by the standards of his day a skilled palaeographer, believed the Cotton manuscript had been written by several hands, and he dated the first and earliest of these to *c.* 1000–1 and the remaining hands to much the same time.[52] This precise judgement was based, as Sisam showed, on Wanley's comparison of the manuscript text of Alfred's *Life* with a charter of King Æthelred the Unready (Cotton Augustus ii. 22) dealing with land at Long Itchington, Warwickshire, and dating to 1001.[53] So Hill's facsimile and Wanley's observations both suggest a date of *c.* AD 1000 for the lost Cottonian manuscript of the *Life* of Alfred. Hart has made a strong case on textual as well as palaeographical grounds for identifying the hand of the Long Itchington diploma and of the facsimile of the opening lines of the Cottonian text of Alfred's *Life* as the work of a Worcester-trained scribe of *c.* AD 1000.[54] Ramsey was a daughter house of Worcester and its scriptorium at the turn of the millennium was a much more active centre with more able scholars at work there than at the parent foundation at Worcester. It was Byrhtferth at Ramsey, after all, who had been commissioned to write the *Life* of Oswald of Worcester, soon after that bishop (who had founded Ramsey) died in 992. We shall see that the four abridged versions of the *Life* of King Alfred that survive in Latin Chronicles, all have a strong Ramsey and Byrhtferthian connection.[55]

It is scarcely surprising to find that there is frequent disagreement between the accounts of scholars who examined the Cottonian manuscript prior to its destruction. Wanley identified several hands in the manuscript in 1721, but already, back in 1600, Thomas James, the first Bodley's librarian, who saw the work in the library of Lord Lumley, claimed 'it was written by two diverse scribes at the least, whereof the later parte of the book ... is by much in my opinion the latest.'[56] Yet even the later hand had some 'Saxon letters', by which James presumably meant that even the later of the two scripts may have been pre-Conquest in date.[57] Sir John Spelman (died 1643) returned to the issue of an earlier and later hand in the manuscript, but it is not clear from his report whether what he perceived as the later hand was that of an interpolator or of a main scribe.[58] Spelman did distinguish between this later hand and annotations of Archbishop Parker, written in Parker's characteristically red pen. Wise also discussed an earlier and later hand in the manuscript in 1722 and was informed by Wanley, who consulted the manuscript, that the later hand was at work from part of Chapter 88 to the end of Chapter 98.[59] In other words, Wanley believed that the bulk of the manuscript from its beginning, down to beyond the last of the annals which it incorporates – that is, to a little after AD 887 – was all in the same hand. And that hand was similar to that of the Long Itchington diploma of 1001. We shall never know whether the script for Chapters 99 to 106 at the end of the *Life* reverted to that of the first or earlier hand, or whether it was written by one of those several hands observed by Wanley, who was one of Wise's advisers.[60] The picture is further confused by James's pronouncement[61] that the text in the neighbourhood of Chapter 83 was in the later hand – a hand incidentally which he considered to be much later than the first or earlier hand. Several of these commentators, including Wise,[62] show some confusion in distinguishing Archbishop Parker's annotations from other hands in the text. In short, the Cotton manuscript Otho A.xii of the *Life* of Alfred seems to have been written in two main hands, the first of which almost certainly dated to *c*. 1000, and had a Worcester and perhaps (by implication) a Ramsey and Byrhtferthian provenance, but we have little indication of the date of the later hand or hands in this manuscript except to say that the manuscript as a whole was considered to be pre-Conquest in date. Our knowledge of the lost manuscript, then, depends on a surviving lithographic drawing of its opening lines, the printed editions of Parker, Camden and Wise; the transcripts made for Parker's use, and the opinions expressed by a range of scholars and antiquaries who inspected the manuscript prior to its destruction in 1731.

### Byrhtferth's Northumbrian Chronicle

Hart and Lapidge convincingly and independently showed in 1981–82 that the first five sections of the *Historia Regum* formerly attributed to Symeon of Durham (and including abstracts from the *Life* of Alfred) were compiled by Byrhtferth, a monk and teacher at Ramsey Abbey in Huntingdonshire at the turn of the tenth century.[63] The agreement of these two scholars, who although working independently of each other, concurred on every significant detail, brought about a major breakthrough in our understanding of Anglo-Saxon source material. Byrhtferth of Ramsey, who hitherto had ranked as an obscure yet significant figure in the world of late Anglo-Saxon scholarship, rapidly emerged as the major historical writer in England at the turn of the millennium. Byrhtferth's school at Ramsey came to be seen as a more important centre than Winchester or Canterbury, and immensely more important than Worcester or York, the diocesan seats of Ramsey's founding bishop, Oswald. By 1929, S.J. Crawford had identified Byrhtferth as the author of the *Life* of St. Oswald, a saint's *Life* which was regarded as one of the more important sources of tenth-century English history.[64] Lapidge added to Byrhtferth's portfolio by confirming that the *Life* of Saint Oswald and also that of Saint Ecgwine were produced by Byrhtferth[65] as were, of course, his *Manual* or *Enchiridion*[66] and several other known Byrhtferthian works, including the account of the martyrdom of Saints Æthelberht and Æthelred of Kent, together with his computistical treatise. Hunter Blair had already demonstrated in 1964 that the early section in the *Historia Regum* (*HR 1*) was clearly not the work of Symeon of Durham but of an earlier compiler. He recognised, too, that the run of annals from 849 to 887 was yet another recension of annalistic entries which originally formed the framework of the *Life* of King Alfred, and he suggested (contradicting Stevenson)[67] that the compiler of that early section of the *Historia Regum* (now known to be Byrhtferth) may have worked from a manuscript different from that of Cotton Otho A.xii which was available to Parker and Wise.[68] It should be stressed that the recension of the *Life* of King Alfred, which Byrhtferth incorporated into his Northumbrian Chronicle, included not only the annalistic framework on which the *Life* is built, but it also included abridged sections of the hagiographical text which fills out the framework of the *Life*, and in several cases there are significant differences between the Cottonian and Northumbrian recensions. Whitelock believed that the manuscript source behind the extract from the *Life* of Alfred in the first five sections of the *Historia Regum* (*HR 1*) was not only different from Cotton Otho A.xii but had a reading that was superior to it.[69] Lapidge was more cautious in his assessment of the textual evidence, suggesting that at least in one case (the designation of placenames with the *æt* formula), Byrhtferth, the compiler of the first five parts of the *Historia*, may have altered the original text of the *Life* of Alfred, which could in this one respect at least, have had identical readings with the Cotton manuscript.[70] It is also possible, however, that the *æt* formula for placenames was original to the text of the *Life* of Alfred and that Parker or one of his 'apprentices' expunged it from the Cottonian text in an effort to normalise its Latin. In Lapidge's opinion, 'there is some possibility that it was the Cotton manuscript which Byrhtferth used' in his Northumbrian Chronicle.[71] Stevenson was of the view that the extracts from Alfred's *Life* in the early section of the *Historia Regum* (*HR 1*) followed the Cottonian manuscript.[72] He pointed out *inter alia* that *HR 1* 'had most of the errors [as shared by the Cotton manuscript] in the reckoning of the king's age'.[73] Lapidge was also tending towards that view. We must therefore conclude that a manuscript of the *Life* of King Alfred was available for Byrhtferth of Ramsey to include in his historical compilation sometime between 987 and *c.* 1015 – at about the very time when the Cotton manuscript of the *Life* was written. It is the known existence of the *Life* of Alfred by this early date which invalidated Galbraith's thesis for Leofric's forging of the *Life* in the mid-eleventh century.

Hart entitled the first five sections of the chronicle formerly ascribed to Symeon of Durham as Byrhtferth's Northumbrian Chronicle[74] and identified two distinct recensions – the earliest or York recension (BNC Y) surviving in a late manuscript (BL Royal 13, A 6) of a mid twelfth-century compilation known as the *Historia post Bedam*, and a later recension originating at Durham (BNC D) surviving as part of *HR 1* in the compilation attributed to Symeon of Durham. The first part of the text of the *Historia post Bedam* was transcribed by Roger of Howden down to the year 802 and incorporated into Roger's Chronicle.[75] The earlier York abridgement of Alfred's *Life* follows the Cottonian and Worcester Latin Chronicle[76] versions closely, but it also has its own variants and additions. This York recension was prepared for a Northumbrian readership, having fewer glosses on southern placenames than the Cottonian version or that preserved in the Worcester Latin Chronicle.[77] Hart tentatively dated the York recension of the abridged *Life* of King Alfred to *c*. AD 990.

When Byrhtferth compiled his Durham recension of the abridgement of King Alfred's *Life* – in Byrhtferth's Northumbrian Chronicle (BNC D) – he had access to Abbo of Fleury's *Passio* of Saint Edmund of East Anglia, as is evident from the treatment of the annal for 870.[78] This, together with an insertion regarding Viking attacks on Fleury (under AD 881), suggests that Byrhtferth worked after the period 986–8 when Abbo visited and taught at Ramsey Abbey.[79] Hart first argued for the Cottonian Otho A.xii manuscript of the *Life* of Alfred to have been the source of Byrhtferth's summary from that *Life* which he included in his Northumbrian Chronicle – *HR 1* of the *Historia Regum*.[80] He later altered his opinion and concluded that Byrhtferth worked from his York recension of the *Life* (BNC Y) when compiling the later Durham version (BNC D).[81] This Durham recension preserved in the *Historia Regum* exhibits a more developed hostility towards the Danish invaders than the earlier York or Cottonian version, a point which prompted Hart to suggest that BNC D was compiled after the Danish attacks of 1013 which resulted in the exile of Æthelred the Unready. He suggested that the Durham recension *HR 1* was completed by Byrhtferth at Ramsey at the behest of Archbishop Wulstan II who was appointed to rule the York and Worcester dioceses in 1002.[82]

### The Worcester Latin Chronicle attributed to John (*alias* Florence) of Worcester

Extensive extracts from the *Life* of Alfred were also incorporated into the *Chronicon ex chronicis* which was attributed to John (and formerly to Florence) of Worcester.[83] This Chronicle compilation did undergo continuation and revision at the hands of the monks, Florence (who died in 1118) and John (who continued the work down to 1140) – both of Worcester. Hence it was known from the sixteenth century, but more particularly from Thorpe's English Historical Society edition of 1848, as *The Chronicle of Florence of Worcester*.[84] In recent times it has acquired the more politically correct but equally inexact title of *The Chronicle of John of Worcester*.[85] Hart argued a case in 1983 that the English material in this Chronicle, stretching from AD 450 down to AD 1016, was compiled and continued by one man and he identified its compiler (and for the later parts its author) as Byrhtferth of Ramsey.[86] Hart entitled Byrhtferth's Latin chronicle which lay behind the text of the compilation of Florence and John of Worcester as the Worcester Latin Chronicle, and it will be the practice here to refer to this work in Hart's terms. McGurk in his edition of the Chronicle in 1995, rejected Hart's thesis out of hand and clung to the established view of an eleventh-century compilation undertaken at Worcester sometime between 1095 and 1143.[87] One year later, in 1996, Lapidge published a remarkable vindication, in part at least, of Hart's scholarly conclusions. Lapidge's study began with Byrhtferth's Life of Saint Oswald, which was written between 997 and 1002. He recognised 'unmistakable verbal links' and 'many parallels' between John's *Chronicon* and Byrhtferth's *Life* of Oswald.[88] Lapidge emphatically and rightly rejected the idea that John of Worcester had borrowed from Byrhtferth's *Life* of Saint Oswald and argued instead for John having used a lost Latin chronicle, which was in turn based on a version of the Anglo-Saxon Chronicle for at least that period from 958 to 992 – that time when there is a demonstrable overlap between the Chronicle of John of Worcester and Byrhtferth's *Life* of Oswald. Lapidge went yet further and conceded that 'it is not impossible that the hypothetical chronicle was also composed at Ramsey in the late tenth century, perhaps by Byrhtferth himself, but such suppositions await proof.'[89] Few matters pertaining to the attribution of authorship of annals from the tenth and eleventh centuries are amenable to 'proof' in any accepted sense of that term. Lapidge in his own analysis of the five diverse and disjointed sections of the Northumbrian Chronicle finally attributed that work to Byrhtferth of Ramsey on no better evidence than Hart attributed the authorship of the Worcester Latin Chronicle also to Byrhtferth. But Lapidge did concede that the Ramsey and Byrhtferth case for the origins of the Worcester Latin Chronicle as a whole was strong, pointing to Ramsey's high standing in historical research; Byrhtferth's acknowledged compilation of the Northumbrian Chronicle; together with the existence of the Ramsey Annals and 'the possibility that the B-text of the Anglo-Saxon Chronicle was at Ramsey by *c.* 1000' – when, it may be added, Byrhtferth was the only Ramsey scholar who could have been responsible for the compilation of the B-text.[90]

In his earlier study of the Northumbrian Chronicle, Lapidge set out his criteria for attributing the work to Byrhtferth as based on 'stylistic features' of the Latin, together with 'habits of mind and use of sources'[91] – not the stuff of which 'proof' is made, but nevertheless valid indicators as to the identity of an early medieval author. In identifying the author of the Northumbrian Chronicle, Lapidge did not have the advantage of having a whole section of annals already attributable to Byrhtferth as in the case of parallels between the Worcester Chronicle (958–992) and passages from the *Life* of Oswald. For clearly the case for Byrhtferth's direct involvement in part at least of the Worcester Latin Chronicle is overwhelming. Lapidge's concession that John of Worcester relied on a Chronicle most probably compiled by Byrhtferth at Ramsey, and spanning, at the very least, that period from 958 to 992 was dictated by the overwhelming weight of evidence already marshalled by Hart. The fact that Lapidge was not prepared to apply the same criteria to any earlier part of the Worcester Chronicle – in the face of compelling stylistic, organisational and numerous other criteria – was driven by altogether different considerations. To concede that Byrhtferth might have had a hand in any earlier parts of the Worcester Latin Chronicle would have immediately involved Lapidge in the admission that Byrhtferth unaccountably and for a *third* time, had incorporated a large-scale abridgement of the *Life* of King Alfred in yet another of his chronicles. More embarrassingly, McGurk who edited the Worcester Chronicle and who rejected any Byrhtferthian involvement out of hand, did concede that the personal outburst under the Alfredian annal for 897, 'is unexplained and unexpected, and is reminiscent, if more restrained, of some of Byrhtferth's outbursts'.[92]

The Worcester Latin Chronicle incorporates an abridgement of the *Life* of King Alfred as found in the Cotton manuscript. This abridgement includes not only the Alfredian annals down to 887, but also large portions of the hagiographical text. These extracts were copied from a manuscript of King Alfred's *Life* which embodied several of the errors of the lost Cottonian manuscript. This led Stevenson to the firm belief that the extracts from King Alfred's *Life* in Florence of Worcester's Chronicle (i.e. the Worcester Latin Chronicle) were copied from the Cotton manuscript.[93] A compiler may have worked from the actual Cottonian source,[94] correcting and editing as he thought fit, but he also used another recension. That other recension of the *Life* which was used for inclusion in the Worcester Latin Chronicle is more closely related to the abridged text now found in the East Anglian Chronicle (or *Annals of St. Neots*, see below). The Worcester Latin Chronicle shares a number of words and variant spellings with the East Anglian Chronicle's abridgement of Alfred's *Life*, and the two versions omit, for instance, the second half of Chapter 21, all of Chapter 25, and from Chapters 79 to 81. Both recensions amend the date of Chapter 66 from 884 to 885.[95] A possible explanation of the relationship between the fuller Cottonian recension of the *Life* of Alfred and the abridged versions in the East Anglian Chronicle and the Worcester Latin Chronicle may be summarised as follows. The *Life* of King Alfred was first abridged by the compiler of the East Anglian Chronicle and that same abstract was later used by the compiler of the Worcester Latin Chronicle. But the compiler of the Worcester Latin Chronicle also added in to his chronicle more extensive sections of the hagiographical text from the *Life* which shows that he used, in addition, a text of the fuller version which may have been identical with the Cottonian recension. We shall see that since Byrhtferth of Ramsey was responsible for this entire historical output, we are not dealing with manuscript recensions in the conventional sense. Byrhtferth may have had several different versions of the *Life* of King Alfred on the drawing board at any one time. Most of those versions were designed to fill gaps in his ambitious programme to supply regional chronicles for the whole of Anglo-Saxon England. No less than four such Byrhtferthian abridgements from chronicles for Northumbria, East Anglia and southern England survive. We must be careful, therefore, as to what significance we attach to variant readings or to particular arrangements of his material. Such differences between recensions may not relate to a conventional manuscript transmission from one copyist to another over, say, a century or more of time, but rather to different versions of a text in the mind of one prolific author and compiler who wrote tirelessly over perhaps thirty years or more of his life.

## The East Anglian Chronicle (or *Annals of St. Neots*)

*The Annals of St. Neots* was the name given to a unique manuscript surviving within a composite volume.[96] The chronicle – for such it is – was copied out by two scribes, most probably at Bury St. Edmunds at some time between *c.* 1120 and 1140,[97] and contains annals and extracts from saints' *Lives* which are mainly concerned with the history of East Anglia. The title *Annals of St. Neots* was given to this collection by the antiquary John Leland, who discovered the work when he visited St. Neots Priory in Huntingdonshire between 1540 and 1544[98] and who at first, may have wrongly ascribed the authorship of the work to Asser.[99] Leland's unique manuscript eventually came into the possession of Archbishop Parker, who collated material from the St. Neots annals with the Cottonian text of his *Life* of Alfred. This amounted to a double conflation of two medieval texts, because the so-called *Annals of St. Neots* had from their medieval beginnings – like Byrhtferth's Northumbrian Chronicle and the Worcester Latin Chronicle – incorporated abridged sections of the *Life* of King Alfred. Parker caused immense confusion for all subsequent students of these texts by marrying portions of the abridged *Life* of Alfred from the St. Neots annals to the fuller Cottonian manuscript text of the *Life* in his 1574 edition. Hart suggested renaming the *Annals of St. Neots*, The East Anglian Chronicle, on the grounds that they were largely a chronicle of East Anglian affairs from the time of Julius Caesar's invasion of Britain up to the year 914.[100] The re-naming of this source has now much to recommend it. While the chronicle contains a version of the *Life* of St. Neot, its contents on the whole relate to East Anglian affairs rather than to one particular and obscure house. The compilation also includes abstracts from Abbo of Fleury's *Passio* of St. Edmund of East Anglia; an abridgement of the *Life* of King Alfred; extracts from Frankish and Norman annals; as well as a version of the Anglo-Saxon Chronicle – most probably the A-Text Precursor – from 455 as far as 914 when the chronicle ends. Hart tentatively dated the time of actual composition of this work to the late tenth century, ascribing its authorship, first to a monk of Ramsey Abbey who was a contemporary and perhaps a pupil of Byrhtferth, and later identifying the author as Byrhtferth himself.[101] Hart set the outside limits for the date of authorship as any time from 985 to 1140 – the latter date being the time of the latest scribe who worked on the surviving manuscript text.[102]

The compiler of the East Anglian Chronicle made extensive use of the *Life* of Alfred, but he omitted thirty-two of its chapters, and some of the remainder he only partially transcribed.[103] This abridgement omits Alfred's genealogy, and accounts of his birth and childhood, as well as of his learning and character. Hart was of the opinion that the compiler of the East Anglian Chronicle worked from the same Cottonian manuscript of the *Life* of Alfred as that used by Archbishop Parker, and he explained the extensive variant readings of the East Anglian Chronicle text as due to collations by its compiler with a very early text of the Anglo-Saxon Chronicle (the A-Text Precursor), and by the introduction of explanatory material to elucidate the text of Alfred's *Life*.[104] Whitelock's argument that the *Annals of St. Neots* (in the case of the 885 annal) share with the later part of the *Historia Regum* (*HR* 2) a superior reading of the *Life* of Alfred to that found in Cotton Otho A.xii, stands in opposition to Hart's views.[105] The significance of that observation has been very much reduced, however, with the realisation in more recent studies that all these versions of King Alfred's *Life* – as well as the early eleventh-century chronicles in which they are now embedded – were the work of one compiler.[106] Hart's views on the manuscript of Alfred's *Life* which lay behind the *Annals of St. Neots* were summed up as follows:

> Such variants as exist [between the text of the *Annals of St. Neots* and the Cottonian manuscript of the *Life* of Alfred] appear to be due entirely to minor errors in transcription, or to the East Anglian chronicler [i.e. compiler of the *Annals of St. Neots*] seeking to elucidate the text of Asser by introducing or substituting words or phrases from other sources, known to be before him as he wrote.[107]

Because the East Anglian Chronicle has been associated for so long with the text of the *Life* of King Alfred, an accurate estimation of its date of composition is very important for Alfredian studies. The association between the East Anglian Chronicle and the *Life* of Alfred goes back much further than the time of Parker, who conflated the two sources in an effort to publish as much material as he could find on the subject of King Alfred. We have seen how from their inception, the so-called St. Neots annals had themselves incorporated extensive material from the *Life* of Alfred, and it was this which may have prompted Leland – when he discovered the manuscript in the 1540s – to attribute their authorship to Asser.[108] While Hart argued cogently for a late tenth- or early eleventh-century date for the compilation of the East Anglian

Chronicle,[109] Dumville and Lapidge opted for a date of compilation between 1120 and 1140.[110] The fact that Hart's detailed, and on the whole convincing, arguments were contemptuously dismissed in a two-line footnote[111] rather than answered point by point, lends little credibility to the pronouncements of his critics. Among Hart's strongest arguments for a date *c.* 1000 were his comparisons between the East Anglian Chronicle and Byrhtferth's Northumbrian Chronicle. Both sources, he argued, made use of the same early version of the Anglo-Saxon Chronicle (the A-Text Precursor) – as indeed did the compiler of the Worcester Latin Chronicle. The East Anglian Chronicle and the Northumbrian Chronicle also used the Royal Frankish Annals, Bede's *Historia Ecclesiastica*, the *Life* of King Alfred, and Abbo's *Passio* of St. Edmund. The Latin style and phrasing, together with highly specific and intrusive Byrhtferthian comments, are common to both chronicles. The structural arrangement of this similar material was handled in the same way by the compiler of Byrhtferth's Northumbrian Chronicle and by the compiler of the East Anglian Chronicle, using sets of annals for continuity, and the textual treatment was also very similar in both cases. It scarcely needs stressing that both compilations included an abridged version of the *Life* of King Alfred to cover the period 845 to 887. Hart observed how while in the fuller Cottonian recension, the Scandinavian invaders are invariably described as *pagani* or 'pagans', that term is altered in both the Northumbrian Chronicle and the East Anglian Chronicle to read as either *Dani* or *Nordmanni* – adding: 'it would be an extraordinary coincidence if chroniclers from two different centres were to make this same alteration consistently and independently, particularly if they were writing at different periods.' Hart also pointed to the fact that Byrhtferth's Northumbrian Chronicle and the East Anglian Chronicle both end well before the dates at which they were composed, and both are orientated towards the affairs of a particular Anglo-Saxon kingdom – Northumbria and East Anglia, respectively.

Dumville and Lapidge failed to provide a convincing explanation as to why a twelfth-century compiler would cut short an historical compilation (beginning at 60 BC), at 914. Their suggestion that by bringing the work to a conclusion in the early tenth century, with the foundation of the Norman duchy, the compilers had fulfilled their remit, is in no way convincing.[112] The editors' notion that the ending of the work in 914 paved the way for a subsequent volume (which no longer exists) was – on their own admission – speculative.[113] Dumville and Lapidge concluded that the presence of extracts from Norman annals in the East Anglian Chronicle betrays a post-Conquest date for that compilation.[114] Hart argued for the transmission of this material via pre-Conquest links between Normandy and the English Danelaw.[115] Norman Annals – in the usually understood sense of that term – originated in the mid-eleventh century and are considered contemporary from the late eleventh century.[116] It is, of course, possible that a work such as the East Anglian Chronicle – ending in 914 – could have borrowed from a compilation which did not come into existence until *c.* 1066, but it is no less probable that the same scattered information which was borrowed by the East Anglian compiler was made available from precursor texts of the Norman annals, which have since been lost. No surviving set of Norman annals can be shown to be the exact source of the East Anglian Chronicle's entries.[117] Dumville's statement on this extremely complex issue constitutes no more than one writer's unsubstantiated personal opinion, and sidesteps the glaring lack of detailed study of the Norman texts involved:

> Whatever annalistic or chronicling activity may have occurred in Normandy before this period [*c.* 1066], there seems no reason to place the composition of the parent text of these Norman Annals before the second half of the eleventh century.[118]

Almost all the so-called Norman material in the East Anglian Chronicle pre-dates the foundation of the Norman duchy in 911, and belongs, therefore, ultimately to Frankish sources rather than to things Norman. The modern editors of the *Annals of St. Neots* did not provide an adequate explanation for the existence of so many entries from the Norman annals either squeezed in and abbreviated at the ends of lines, or in the margins of the only surviving medieval manuscript of the text.[119] Apart from the 633 entry which is of mixed English and 'Norman' content, all of these marginal or end-of-line annals deal exclusively with 'Norman' annalistic matters and their peripheral position in the manuscript of the *Annals of St. Neots* (although all appear to be written in the main or text hand) could suggest that the twelfth-century scribe of this work was incorporating 'Norman' material into an older compilation. While we may agree with Hart that the surviving text of the East Anglian Chronicle 'has the appearance of a copy from an exemplar, rather than something being compiled at the time of writing [in the twelfth century] from a variety of sources,'[120] it is possible that the two twelfth-century scribes copied an earlier version of the East Anglian Chronicle dating from *c.* 1000 and incorporated into that copy an early series of entries from a later eleventh-century set of Norman annals. The twelfth-century scribes of the surviving manuscript would not, in that case, have been acting as general compilers, but were rather adding in a prepared and coherent set of Norman abstracts into an earlier compilation, of which they were making a new and conflated copy. We must at least acknowledge a quite separate handling of the Norman material by the writers of the twelfth-century manuscript, and when we add to this the cogent reasons offered by Hart for a pre-Conquest date for the core of the annalistic compilation, the possibility of two phases in the development of the East Anglian Chronicle presents itself. Hart's argument for the composition of the East Anglian Chronicle by Byrhtferth of Ramsey at the end of the tenth century – with its Frankish material being borrowed into a Ramsey environment via Abbo of Fleury and his entourage in the 980s – is the most coherent and economical solution. Hart demonstrated the close relationship between the East Anglian Chronicle and its Northumbrian equivalent, which Lapidge positively attributed to Byrhtferth. Hart has also demonstrated a similar close relationship between the East Anglian Chronicle and the Worcester Latin Chronicle which Lapidge also associated, in part at least, with Byrhtferth. Hart's detailed comparison suggests that the East Anglian Chronicle may be an earlier work than Byrhtferth's compilation of the precursor to the Worcester Latin Chronicle.

## The *Encomium Emmae Reginae*

Alistair Campbell demonstrated that the writer of the *Encomium Emmae Reginae* (a eulogy on Emma, the widowed queen of Cnut, who died in 1052) borrowed two glosses from the *Life* of Alfred into his text. The evidence is concise but specific and convincing, and therefore suggests that the author of the *Encomium*, who was connected with either St. Omer or St. Bertin, and who wrote *c.* 1041, had consulted either a full Cottonian-type text of Alfred's *Life* or abridgements of that text, in Flanders or perhaps in England.[121] The *Encomium* (II,8) in relating how Cnut spent a winter in Sheppey (*Sceepei*), glosses that placename with the phrase: 'that is to say in Latin *insula ovium* ['island of sheep']' (*quod est dictum Latine 'insula ovium'*).[122] In Chapter 3 of the *Life* of Alfred, Sheppey (*Sceapieg*) is also glossed: *quod interpretatur 'insula ovium'*[123] in a translation of the annal from the Anglo-Saxon Chronicle for AD 851. Similarly, the *Encomium* (II.9) glosses the placename *Aescenedun* with 'a word which we Latinists can explain as "Hill of Ash Trees"' (*quod nos Latini 'montem fraxinorum' possumus interpretari*),[124] while in Chapter 37 of Alfred's *Life*, the quite different placename *Æscesdun* is glossed: *quod Latine 'mons fraxini' interpretatur* under the annal for AD 871.[125] The Encomiast's two glosses – so obviously borrowed (out of context) from a text of the *Life* of Alfred – stand out in contrast to several other placenames in the text of the *Encomium Emmae* which are not so glossed. Campbell also claimed certainty for his opinion that the author of the *Encomium* (II.9) had access to that passage in the East Anglian Chronicle (*Annals of St. Neots*) which describes the Raven Banner of the Danish army in Devon in AD 878.[126] All three passages occur close together in the text of the *Encomium Emmae* and it is reasonable to conclude that all three items were borrowed by the author of the *Encomium* from one source. Otherwise we must accept the highly unlikely circumstance whereby this continental author was sufficiently familiar with both the *Life* of Alfred and a source such as the East Anglian Chronicle to extract such detailed information from each one. Campbell not unreasonably, for his time, concluded that the author of the *Encomium* found the passage on the Raven Banner in his copy of the *Life* of Alfred, but that is unlikely.[127] The single source used by the compiler of the *Encomium* must have been either a copy of the East Anglian Chronicle or, as Hart argued, the precursor text of the Worcester Latin Chronicle – both of which provided abridgements of Alfred's *Life*. There are problems, however, in identifying the precise source of these borrowings from the *Life* of Alfred into the *Encomium Emmae*. The unique twelfth-century Bury St. Edmunds manuscript of the East Anglian Chronicle omits the gloss on Sheppey in its version of the annal for 851 taken from the *Life* of Alfred.[128] But it does include the gloss on *Aescesdun* under 871,[129] and of course it provides the source for the Raven Banner episode at 878.[130] The abridgement of the *Life* of Alfred in the Worcester Latin Chronicle, on the other hand, includes the Sheppey and the Ashdown glosses under 851 and 871 respectively,[131] and Hart has shown that a case can be made for the compiler of the *Encomium Emmae* having had access to the Worcester Latin Chronicle's annals for the writing of his own version of early eleventh-century events. Unlike the East Anglian Chronicle, however, the Worcester Latin Chronicle lacks the account of the Raven Banner episode under the annal for AD 878. This is not such a significant omission, since the strongest evidence for the direct borrowing from a version of Alfred's *Life* into the *Encomium* rests on the Sheppey and Ashdown glosses. The Raven Banner anecdote was not necessarily textually based, and the allusion to it in the *Encomium* is vague. Its tale of the daughters of Lodbroc who had woven a magic war-banner was clearly a saga motif from an Anglo-Danish version of *Ragnars saga* which had already entered the folklore of the English Danelaw and indeed the Scandinavian homeland (in varying versions) by the eleventh century.[132] The most economical conclusion to be drawn from the evidence of the *Encomium* is to conclude that its author consulted either a version of the East Anglian Chronicle or the Worcester Latin Chronicle which included both the *Aescesdun* and *Sceapeige* glosses, and he was also aware of the Raven Banner anecdote either from his English chronicle source or from oral transmission. Byrhtferth's precursor to the Worcester Latin Chronicle has the best claim to have been that source which could have been consulted either at Worcester or in East Anglia – either at Ramsey or at Bury St. Edmunds. If that were so, then the earliest version of the Worcester Latin Chronicle must predate the composition of the *Encomium* in *c.* 1041. Alternatively, the only other reasonable conclusion to draw is that the author of the *Encomium* consulted the East Anglian Chronicle with the implication that that source also was pre-Conquest in its origin. It is highly unlikely in view of the dependence of the *Encomium* on an eleventh-century Worcester-type chronicle (including as it did the glosses from Alfred's abridged *Life*), that its author also independently consulted the *Life* of Alfred as preserved, say, in the Cottonian manuscript. It once suited Whitelock to use – with justification – the *Encomium Emmae* as proof for the existence of the *Life* of Alfred prior to the time of Bishop Leofric of Exeter, and thereby discredit Galbraith.[133] It will now have to be accepted that the same *Encomium* points to the existence of a version of either the East Anglian Chronicle or the Worcester Latin Chronicle prior to *c.* 1040.[134]

Emma (whose English name was Ælfgifu) was the daughter of Duke Richard I of Normandy (943–96) and sister of Duke Richard II.[135] She was the queen of Æthelred the Unready from 1002 until his death in 1016, and a son of that marriage was the future Edward the Confessor. A year after Æthelred's death, Emma became the queen of Cnut, whom she outlived on his death in 1035, and survived through the reign of her son, Harthacnut, dying as late as 1052. Emma was twice forced into exile during her English career – once when she retreated to Normandy during a crisis in Æthelred's reign in 1013, and later during the reign of her son, Harthacnut, when she was forced across to Flanders in the period 1037 to 1040. Emma was the Norman influence *par excellence* on early eleventh-century England. She epitomised not only the demographic links which had become firmly established in the early eleventh century between the Danelaw and Normandy on the one hand, and the Scandinavian homelands on the other, but in her dynastic and marital relationships she also personally symbolised the broadening of horizons in England's foreign policies. Emma and her immediate household had paved the way for Norman domination of England half a century before the Conquest. She lived in a time when those East Anglian monasteries which had been reconstituted by the reformers at the end of the tenth century were consolidating their position during the precarious stability of Cnut's regime. Emma herself was credited in one tradition[136] with having urged Cnut to restore Bury St. Edmunds – that place of pilgrimage of the martyred King Edmund, whose *Passio* was freely used by the compiler of the East Anglian Chronicle and of the closely related Worcester Latin Chronicle. Those two chronicles were compiled and added to by Byrhtferth at the turn of the millennium, at a time when the great monasteries of East Anglia and their rich lay patrons were most likely to want to indulge their interests in the history of England at large and of their region in particular. It was also a time when Norman and Anglo-Danish tastes in historical writing had to be ever-increasingly catered for. Emma was herself the owner of huge East Anglian estates in West Suffolk, which were used after her fall from favour in 1043 for the endowment of Bury St. Edmunds.[137] Prior to that time, a charter from Cnut in 1021–3[138] confirmed an earlier grant of privileges supposedly conferred on the abbey of Bury St. Edmunds by King Edmund (939–46).[139] In addition to Cnut's and Emma's support for Bury St. Edmunds,[140] we know that Emma and her son, Harthacnut, also enriched Ramsey Abbey, the home of Byrhtferth and his circle of writers, by granting it an estate at Hemingford in Huntingdonshire in 1040–42.[141] It is entirely in keeping with the evidence to find that a eulogy on Emma, whose continental author had associations with St. Bertin, should contain echoes of passages from a chronicle which was composed not long before that time in Ramsey. That chronicle – which happened also to contain an abridgement of the *Life* of King Alfred – provided the Continental writer with a crucial historical framework relating to the early eleventh century, which he could manipulate in his efforts to write a eulogy on Queen Emma.

### The Ramsey Annals

Lapidge rightly acknowledged the importance of Hart's pioneering study of the Ramsey Annals preserved in Oxford St. John's College MS 17.[142] For Lapidge their significance lay in the ever-mounting evidence associating Byrhtferth and his Ramsey school with an impressive compilation programme of historical works, which also embraced parts at least of the Worcester Latin Chronicle. Hart showed that this laconic set of Latin annals (called by him 'The Ramsey Annals') had been compiled at Ramsey prior to 1016 and that for their annals from 733 to 872, they drew on the Durham recension of Byrhtferth's Northumbrian Chronicle (BNC D).[143] It is abundantly clear that the compiler of the Ramsey Annals had access to a version of the *Life* of Alfred – and almost certainly to that version which is abridged in the BNC D. Not only is Alfred's birth noted under 849, but his twelfth year is marked at 860; his twenty-first in 868, and his twenty-eight-year reign as king is noted under 872.[144] All of these entries (and four others) have to derive from the chronological framework established by the author of the *Life* of King Alfred and, in the case of Alfred's age, were calculated retrospectively by that author and inserted into his crucial framework of the Anglo-Saxon Chronicle text which he used to provide the core of King Alfred's *Life*.[145] These signposts relating to Alfred's age were preserved also in Byrhtferth's Northumbrian Chronicle. The significance which the Ramsey Annals hold for any study of the *Life* of King Alfred is not for any detail they may offer us – for they are fragmentary in the extreme and contain no new information on Alfred in their own right. They are immensely significant, however, in that they provide yet another source linking the *Life* of King Alfred with Ramsey Abbey at the turn of the millennium, and with Byrhtferth in particular.

### The Life of St. Neot

The story of how King Alfred burnt the cakes is related in Chapter 53b of Stevenson's Parker-Cotton edition of King Alfred's *Life*.[146] This tale of how the king was scolded by a cowherd's wife for neglecting to prevent her cakes from burning on the fire was borrowed into the *Life* of Alfred from the East Anglian Chronicle (*Annals of St. Neots*) which otherwise included an abridgement of King Alfred's *Life*.[147] That tale of the cakes as found in the East Anglian Chronicle is acknowledged there to have been taken from the *Life* of St. Neot. It has always been assumed that the passage concerning the burning cakes was taken from the East Anglian Chronicle and inserted into Alfred's *Life* by Archbishop Parker – and this may well have been so. Parker has been demonised by scholars of the 'Genuine Asser' persuasion in their attempts to find a scapegoat to explain away the many anomalies in the printed edition of the lost Cottonian text. But Parker cannot be blamed for all the sins of the author of the *Life* of Alfred, and since it was Byrhtferth of Ramsey who almost certainly invented the legend of the burning cakes, he was quite capable of incorporating that vignette not only into his East Anglian Chronicle, but also into the *Life* of King Alfred. For Byrhtferth used fragments of textual narrative from his *Life* of St. Neot in precisely the same way as he re-used and re-moulded passages from his *Life* of King Alfred in the various editions of his Latin Chronicles.

The tale of the burning cakes first appeared in the *Life* of St. Neot, the earliest version of which was written *c.* 1000 for that monastery which had been founded beside Eynesbury in Huntingdonshire in *c.* 980. By 991, if not before, Ealdorman Æthelwine, the co-founder of Ramsey, was recognised also as patron of nearby St. Neots. Æthelwine may have been instrumental in commissioning Byrhtferth of Ramsey to write a *Life* of the saint whose relics had been taken out of Cornwall to Eynesbury at this time. The *Life* of St. Neot records only a single miracle after the foundation of the new St. Neots in Huntingdonshire, which suggests it was written soon after 980 and before *c.* 1014 when the relics of Neot had been removed for safety to Crowland.[148] The Latinity of the *Life* shows strong Byrhtferthian characteristics and its content shows it to have been invented as part of the late tenth-century Alfredian repertoire of hagiography in a parallel mode to that of the *Life* of Alfred. Neot was alleged to have been Alfred's relative or brother, yet he was born in the territory of the 'Eastern Britons (*Orientalium Britonum*)' which might – given Byrhtferth's chaotic topographical sense – mean Cornwall. He supposedly studied at Glastonbury under either Æthelwold or Ælfheah (later bishops of Winchester) and then spent seven years as a hermit at St. Neots. After going on a pilgrimage to Rome, he returned to St. Neots where he founded a community and was sought out on two occasions by King Alfred. Alfred in Neot's *Life* is not portrayed as the neurotic and pious king who in the *Life* of Alfred also visited that saint's monastery (or shrine) in Cornwall in search of a cure for one illness and for the infliction of a substitute malady. The Alfred who visited St. Neot in that saint's *Life* was a sinner in need of castigation and penance. The *Life* of Alfred and that of St. Neot are closely related texts – both of which have Alfred as a central character; both of which make crucial use of the text of the Anglo-Saxon Chronicle; and both have St. Neots in Cornwall as a place of exotic pilgrimage for Alfred.[149] Finally both texts exhibit the same distinctive arcane Latin style and special florid vocabulary which are otherwise firmly associated with Byrhtferth of Ramsey. So, while the *Life* of St. Neot does not contain any textual fragments of the *Life* of King Alfred, it is nevertheless part of Byrhtferth's Alfredian repertoire and its study has much to tell us of the historical and literary context in which the *Life* of King Alfred was composed.[150]

## Summing up the manuscript evidence

The surviving sources for the *Life* of King Alfred have crucial evidence to offer us regarding the condition of that work at *c*. AD 1000. All five abridgements or extracts from the *Life* – Byrhtferth's Northumbrian Chronicle (York and Durham recensions), the Worcester Latin Chronicle, the East Anglian Chronicle and the Ramsey Annals – can be shown to have strong Ramsey and Byrhtferthian associations. The now lost fuller Cottonian recension has long ago been dated to within a few years of AD 1000 and can be shown to have been written in a Worcester-trained hand – and Worcester was the centre from which Ramsey had been founded in 968. Although Worcester – with its centuries-old scriptorium – was still in a position to train scribes, it lacked able scholars in the late tenth century. Why else was Byrhtferth at the daughter house of Ramsey, commissioned to write the *Lives* of two Worcester saints (Ecgwine and Oswald), if Worcester had its own capable in-house hagiographers?[151] And finally the small but significant textual echo of Alfred's *Life* to be found in the *Encomium Emmae* takes us back yet again to either the East Anglian Chronicle or Worcester Latin Chronicle version of Alfred's *Life* as abridged by Byrhtferth. There is a compelling argument for saying that this sudden and unexpected burgeoning of recensions of King Alfred's *Life* at Ramsey in the time of Byrhtferth is suggestive of the birth of this work rather than its unaccountable dissemination at a supposed later stage in its development. What a strange coincidence that not a scrap of evidence for the existence of the *Life* of the king exists for the period from 893 (its alleged year of writing) until we reach Byrhtferth and his several contemporaneous abridgements in *c*. AD 1000. And after Byrhtferth's flurry of activity, we hear virtually nothing more of the work until the sixteenth century.

There may have been only one full conflated manuscript version of the *Life* of Alfred extant in the early eleventh century. That conflated version had been added to, and received alternative and revised readings from its author, Byrhtferth of Ramsey, as he returned to his narrative again and again during his ambitious programme of chronicle production. It is also possible that Byrhtferth used his *Life* of Alfred as a schoolroom project at Ramsey in an

effort to teach his pupils the uncertain art of hagiographical fiction. This
would account for the unfinished state of the work, together with the extraordinary array of conflicting aspects within the text both in regard to its
content and its arrangement of material. Abbo of Fleury, during his stay at
Ramsey, had compiled the *Life* of St. Edmund of East Anglia to provide a
prototype for the monks of the reformed monasteries of England which they
could use in their own efforts to write up the glorious deeds of their patron
saints. In Alfred, Byrhtferth found another king – a contemporary of King
Edmund – who could be held up as an example to all those who opposed the
renewed Scandinavian terror at the end of the tenth century and the beginning of the eleventh. We know that Byrhtferth compiled scientific treatises by
way of classroom manuals for his Ramsey pupils and he may well have put
the *Life* of Alfred, in its untidy and poorly edited state, to a similar use. The
Cottonian version of King Alfred's *Life* was either a very close copy of the original working draft from the Ramsey school, or it might even have been that
original Byrhtferthian manuscript itself. The lost Cottonian manuscript was
probably ultimately the text used in the Worcester Latin Chronicle[152] – a
chronicle which all parties are agreed had a definite connection with
Byrhtferth of Ramsey in the late tenth century. Hart, as we have seen,
believed that the Cotton manuscript also lay behind the extracts from Alfred's
*Life* in the East Anglian Chronicle, and Lapidge demonstrated that in one
instance at least, the Cotton manuscript could be shown to have been the
exemplar for Byrhtferth's extracts from the *Life* of Alfred in Byrhtferth's
Northumbrian Chronicle. There was also part, at least, of a text of Alfred's *Life*
available in *c*. 1041 to the pro-Danish writer of the *Encomium Emmae* who
may have been based in Flanders, and who had access to extracts from the *Life*
of Alfred in either the East Anglian Chronicle or the Worcester Latin
Chronicle. While we cannot be certain that the Cotton Otho A.xii text lies
behind all surviving versions of the *Life* of Alfred, it is equally difficult to
show that any other manuscript version was definitely involved. We can
never reach firm conclusions about manuscripts of a text which have all
perished, and so the precise relationship between the Cotton manuscript and
the original text of the *Life* of Alfred may forever elude us. Whitelock argued
that since the versions of King Alfred's *Life* in Byrhtferth's Northumbrian
Chronicle (*Historia Regum*) and in the East Anglian Chronicle (*Annals of St.
Neots*) both share the same errors in a process of miscopying from a common
exemplar, and since the Cotton manuscript has a greater number of errors
than the other two versions, then the lost Cotton manuscript was at best a
copy of a copy of the original text.[153] Even if that were true, it does not follow
that the original manuscript had to be very much older than its copies. For
Whitelock envisaged that she was dealing with several fragmentary eleventh-
and twelfth-century recensions of a ninth-century text. We now know that all

our extant abridgements date from *c*. 1000 and were all associated with the same person – Byrhtferth of Ramsey, while the Cottonian text with its Worcester (and perhaps Ramsey) associations also dates from precisely the same time. Variations in text and different ordering of events in the various recensions, therefore, may relate to Byrhtferth's own personal preferences of the moment rather than to the age or stage of copying in the relationship of one manuscript to another.

This discussion on the complicated history of the text sets the background for the debate on the authenticity of 'Asser''s *Life* of Alfred, but it also brings home to us an important point at the outset. It makes us aware of the severe limitations of textual evidence in arguments relating to the date of the work. It cannot be emphasised too often that all complete medieval manuscripts of the *Life* have perished, and the evidence as it stands cannot prove that there was ever more than one – or at the most two – fuller manuscript versions in existence in the eleventh century. Even Otho A.xii – that sole survivor of the *Life* from the pillaging of monastic libraries in sixteenth-century England[154] – tragically perished in the fire of 1731 before it could be subjected to the scrutiny of modern palaeographers. Reaching textual certainty in regard to this manuscript *Life* of King Alfred is as remote as reaching a final verdict on a report of an early eighteenth-century autopsy. Dumville[155] believed that 'at present, it seems impossible to say whether the Compiler of the Annals of St. Neots – or, indeed, Byrhtferth of Ramsey or John of Worcester – employed a text of Asser's work superior to that of the Parker-Cotton manuscript.' If, as is the case made in this study, all of the recensions referred to by Dumville stem from Byrhtferth's pen, then his view of that 'stage of transmission ancestral to the Parker-Cotton manuscript' becomes radically altered if not indeed redundant.

Dumville was suspending judgement back in 1985 until the completion of a new edition of the Parker-Cotton text of Alfred's *Life* 'in as accurate a reconstruction as the limits of the surviving evidence will permit'.[156] But the surviving evidence *is* so limited due to the loss of the Cotton manuscript, and so botched and contaminated by Parker's editorial apprentices, that any reconstruction of the text of Cotton Otho A.xii of the *Life* of King Alfred will forever remain a subjective exercise. It will never be possible for any future reconstruction of the Parker-Cotton text to carry the same authority as the lost manuscript of Alfred's *Life*. The best we can ever hope to achieve is to set out the presumed Cottonian text side by side with all other surviving abridgements – Byrhtferth's Northumbrian Chronicle (York and Durham recensions), Byrhtferth's Worcester Latin Chronicle (formerly the Florence of Worcester abridgement) and Byrhtferth's recension in the East Anglian Chronicle (*Annals of St. Neots*), and attempt a reconstruction only where alternative readings will allow. It is not until these medieval versions of the *Life* of

Alfred are accorded parity with, if not indeed primacy over, the Parker-Cotton edition that parts of the original text of the *Life* of Alfred can ever be cited with any degree of certainty.

One of the great weaknesses of Stevenson's edition was his unwritten assumption regarding the superiority of the Cottonian text of the *Life*, both in terms of age and textual readings. For in spite of editorial protestations to the contrary, he pursued a wholly arbitrary use of the abridged recensions which he pressed into service to shore up his own view regarding Asser's authorship of the work. We can never be certain precisely how much Matthew Parker added or deleted from those parts of his Cottonian manuscript source which are not supported by textual parallels from other medieval writers. And even where alternative medieval textual readings are available, we cannot be certain that Parker's variant forms derive from Cotton Otho A.xii or from Parker's own editorial 'improvements'. That is true of his transcript[157] as well as of his printed text, and Stevenson's optimism regarding the textual purity of that transcript, which was shared by Keynes and Lapidge, can scarcely be justified.[158]

A study of those passages from the *Life* of Alfred in the Worcester Latin Chronicle, the East Anglian Chronicle and Byrhtferth's Northumbrian Chronicle does allow us to exercise a limited check on Parker's edition. But that check is always only partial since the abridgements tend to concern themselves with those parts of the *Life* of Alfred which were borrowed from the Anglo-Saxon Chronicle, while summarising much of the hagiographical text and omitting the more controversial and original biographical aspects of the *Life*. As for the version in the Worcester Latin Chronicle, its editor severely edited out extensive passages in the *Life* which he may have felt were of no immediate relevance or help to that particular compilation.[159] Hart has suggested the possibility that those passages in the Cottonian *Life* ascribing the authorship to Asser, may have come late in Byrhtferth's design of King Alfred's biography and may be later than the date of the seemingly abridged recensions of the work. So, for many crucial passages in the *Life* of Alfred, we have ultimately to rely on Parker's edition, which was, on Stevenson's admission, 'filled with arbitrary alterations and interpolations, which are distinguished in no way from the readings of the original [manuscript].'[160]

### The 1574 Parker edition of the *Life* of King Alfred

Although Stevenson was aware that Parker relied a great deal on his secretaries for help with his scholarly researches,[161] he minimised the complexity of Parker's editorial teamwork and he seemed to have been unaware of the religious and ideological motivation which provided the driving-force for Parker's entire publication programme. Strype described Parker's large and diverse household at Lambeth as 'a kind of flourishing University of learned men: and his domestics, being provoked by the Archbishop's exhortations and precepts, often published to the world the fruits of their studies'.[162] We are told on Parker's authority that

> he had within his house, in wages, drawers [of pictures], and cutters [engravers], painters, limners, writers, and bookbinders.[163]

Strype goes on to inform us that the archbishop

> kept such in his family as could imitate any of the old characters admirably well. One of these was Lyly, an excellent writer, and [one] that could counterfeit any antique writing. Him the archbishop customarily used to make old books complete, that wanted some pages; that the character might seem to be the same throughout.[164]

Stevenson[165] omitted to quote the final sentence from the above passage relating to the 'completion' of old 'books' – which, from the context, must be a reference to manuscripts. Stevenson's argument that interpolations in the Cottonian manuscript (Otho A.xii), in addition to those in Parker's characteristic red ochre pencil, were in the handwriting of Parker's own time, must be questioned.[166] Since the manuscript is no longer extant, we have no way of knowing whether a man such as Lyly had tampered with it, however obvious Parker's own interpolations may have been to seventeenth- and eighteenth-century observers. Nor can we be certain as to what later medieval interpolations the Cotton manuscript may have contained. James Hill, who consulted the manuscript in 1722, shortly before its destruction, failed to distinguish between the so-called sixteenth-century Parkerian hands and medieval hands in the Cotton text.[167]

Not only did Parker run a household which was a cross between a Tudor university and a medieval monastic scriptorium,[168] but Parker was himself so busy that his role in the production of King Alfred's *Life* may not have been as immediate as is so often supposed. In the years immediately prior to the publication of the *Life*, Parker had lost his wife, and was himself in failing health.[169] He was preoccupied with the turmoil of Church and State, coping with a three-cornered struggle between Anglicans, Catholics and Puritans, and energetically monitoring (in so far as he could) the war of words between all three. Parker died in May 1575, in the year after the publication of the *Life* of Alfred. He had been responsible for ambitious building projects at Lambeth and Cambridge, and engrossed in elaborate preparations for the entertainment of his queen in Canterbury in the autumn of 1573.[170] In spite of his personal devotion to historical scholarship, Parker's role in the publication of the *Life* of Alfred in 1574 cannot have been more than that of a general editor.

We do know that the *Lives* of the archbishops of Canterbury published under the title of *De Antiquitate Britannicae Ecclesiae* were certainly compiled, if not actually completed, by John Joscelyn, the Essex antiquary, whom we might describe as Parker's chief research assistant in the 1570s.[171] The *De Antiquitate* was published by John Day in 1572 – that same publisher who gave Asser to the world only two years later.

Although Jocelyn, Parker's secretary, was a careful scholar and a man of great learning, we need to keep our assessment of that learning within the context of his day. McKisack reminded us that Jocelyn's

> methods of handling his manuscripts were much the same as Parker's. He wrote notes on them for purposes of collation, supplemented and otherwise 'improved' the text.[172]

The learned Jocelyn was also capable, like Lyly, of faking an Old English hand.[173] It is true Parker tells us in his preface to the edition of the *Life* of Alfred that it was 'exactly and literally done from the original manuscript' and that the manuscript itself (or perhaps he meant the transcript) could be collated against his printed text by anyone who wished to consult it in Corpus Christi College, Cambridge.[174] But Parker did tamper with the text of the Corpus transcript,[175] and with that of the original Cotton manuscript of Alfred's *Life*[176] and, according to Stevenson, he had elsewhere indulged in 'wanton falsification' of the Latin text of King Alfred's *will*.[177] We know, too, that Parker was responsible for an interpolation in the manuscript of the *Textus Roffensis* and for yet another in the *Black Book of the Archdeacon of Canterbury*.[178] In a letter to Cecil in 1565, Parker suggested that he would employ his gifted counterfeiter, Lyly, to add illustrations and missing text to the manuscript of a medieval psalter.[179] Parker's editorial methods were outlined in another letter, probably dating to December 1571, and written by him to a peer who is not named. In this letter it is clear that the archbishop had been sent a manuscript which he was then returning to its sender in a printed edition:

> And whereas I have been long in requiting your good will in bestowing this written story upon me, I send the same story to your lordship in print, somewhat more enlarged with such old copies as I had of other of my friends, praying for your lordship to accept it in good part.[180]

So, Parker, at the very time when he must have been planning his edition of King Alfred's *Life*, is here declaring that his editorial approach was to 'enlarge' the text of his exemplar by conflating it with related material from other sources. It was this approach which explains the presence of extensive interpolations from the East Anglian Chronicle in Parker's 1574 edition of the *Life* of King Alfred. None of this is to suggest that there was necessarily any intention to deceive. The practice of collation and conflation was no doubt viewed as a desirable procedure facilitated by the relatively novel invention of printing. But since we lack the original manuscript on which Jocelyn or his helpers left their notes, we have little idea of how those editors went about their scissors-and-paste approach. If Parker's 1571 edition of Matthew Paris's *Greater History* is anything to go by, then we must assume that the edition of the *Life* of Alfred also consisted of

> a 'mixed' text, made up ... with unbounded licence and with interpolations which belie the editor's claim [in his preface to Asser] never to have added anything to or subtracted anything from the books he published.[181]

McKisack catalogued a lengthy list of examples of defacing and altering of medieval manuscripts by Parker or his editorial assistants, which strongly suggests that were the Cottonian *Life* of King Alfred to survive today, we would find erasures and 'corrections' in a counterfeit hand, as well as 'improved' versions of the text pasted over original script, together with a multitude of marginalia.[182]

Parker was, by sixteenth-century standards, an able scholar and a bibliophile to whom we should be grateful for rescuing a vast number of medieval manuscripts from iconoclasm and ruin. To view Parker solely, however, as a renaissance scholar and antiquary would be entirely to misunderstand his publication programme. Parker was a propagandist who employed his scholarly household in a drive to justify the ideological and doctrinal position of the recently established Anglican Church. His agents ransacked the remnants of ruined monastic libraries and private book collections[183] in search of material from an elusive ancient 'British' Church – material which could be used to demonstrate a continuity with the Reformers' doctrinal position.[184] Although Parker was responsible for the collection of huge numbers of medieval books and manuscripts,[185] clearly his decision to proceed with publication was limited to only a special few of these items. That being so, we need to ask the question as to why the *Life* of Alfred was singled out for a printed edition. In his preface to his edition of Matthew Paris, Parker praised that chronicler for standing out against the usurpations and tyrannies of the papacy.[186] And the thirteenth-century manuscript, which Parker used to publish his edition of that work, has been drastically 'improved' with eight missing folios added in a counterfeit or 'restoring' hand.[187] In his *Testimony of Antiquity, showing the ancient faith in the Church of England* published in the late 1560s, Parker used Anglo-Saxon sources to attack pre-Reformation doctrine on transubstantiation.[188] The *Life* of King Alfred which Parker, following Leland,[189] firmly attributed to Asser, clearly held a special interest for the archbishop to convince him of its importance for his expensive publication programme. To begin with, Asser was regarded as an ancient 'British' – i.e. Welsh – bishop, and therefore qualified for special attention as a member of an early Church, which was seen by the Reformers as being independent of Rome. Secondly, Alfred was well known to Parker as a translator into Old English of philosophical and religious works. Parker possessed no fewer than three manuscript copies of King Alfred's translation of the *Pastoral Care*, as well as manuscripts of Gregory's Dialogues, and of the Old English Bede.[190] Alfred had therefore vindicated the Reformers' use of the vernacular, some seven centuries before the Reformation began. Finally, one of the more enduring impressions conveyed by the *Life* of Alfred was the account of how the king eagerly learnt to read and translate while discussing passages from Holy Scripture with his chaplain, Asser.[191] Alfred could be presented to the world by Parker as an Anglo-Saxon prototype and as a devout version of a Henrician Protestant king. Here was a figure who might warm the cockles of any Reforming bishop's heart – a lay ruler mulling over the Scriptures, publishing devout texts in the vernacular, and whose biography was written by a cleric from the acceptable ancient British Church. The publication of the *Life* of King Alfred was no mere antiquarian pursuit. It was a typical product of Parker's busy 'shop' – 'rough hewn by one of the apprentices' and lacking 'polishing by the foreman' who was otherwise preoccupied with the affairs of his Church and of his queen.[192]

Where does all this information leave Stevenson's lengthy discussion on the various hands of the lost Cottonian manuscript? We know that that manuscript contained glosses in Parker's hand and other glosses from his secretaries. We are also justified in concluding that Parker's editorial household worked in a tradition that was as much late medieval as it was 'modern',[193] and that in spite of his own quite reasonable protestations of editorial integrity, both Parker and his assistant scholars were capable of completing a line or finishing off a sentence without incurring any sense of guilt pertaining to modern invention or forgery.[194] Parker's Cottonian manuscript of the *Life* of Alfred included paper additions interleaved by Parker and his secretaries, which contained extracts from the East Anglian Chronicle.[195] Other interleaved material may have been inserted in the manuscript as well. The original Cottonian text was probably in two main hands, but that observation is not as relevant as it might seem since the hand of the principal scribe can be dated closely to *c.* AD 1000 and the second hand may have been contemporary or not much later. Furthermore, the principal hand, which seems to have completed all of the text down as far as Chapter 88, was exactly contemporary (on the evidence of the Long Itchington charter) with Byrhtferth of Ramsey, when Byrhtferth was at the height of his creative power.

## The task of the historian

Faced with this unsatisfactory if not indeed chaotic 'archaeology of text', the historian must turn to his rightful task – a task which would still confront him even if he had the benefit of modern palaeographical and textual criticism advising him on an extant and original manuscript. That task is to study the actual *Life* of King Alfred as it has imperfectly come down to us, and to reach an opinion regarding its consistency and plausibility, in the light of what we know as historians, of England in the ninth and tenth centuries. As we turn now to this task, of analysing the text ascribed to Asser, we are neither unmindful of the textual problems nor overawed by them. If the *Life* of Alfred had dealt with any lesser subject than the darling of early English history, it would long ago have been relegated to its appropriate place among problematical texts of doubtful origin and composition. It came to be regarded as 'one of the most important ... of the sources of our early history'[196] only because of an understandable – not to say desperate – need, on the part of nineteenth-century writers, to know more about one of England's most important kings. Compared with Bede's *Life* of Cuthbert or Eddius's *Life* of Wilfred, for instance, we shall see that the biography of Alfred reads as a sad hotch-potch of poorly wrought hagiography and translated annals. Byrhtferth's recensions of the *Life* found in the Northumbrian, Worcester and East Anglian Chronicles, when studied in their own right, shed valuable light for the first time on the nature of the fuller Parker-Cotton version. We may note, for instance, that almost all the special pleading on behalf of the biographer claiming to be an eye-witness of what he reports has been excised from the abridged versions. This may be put down to the fact that reporting in the first person would not have been appropriate for a chronicle narrative. More remarkable is the fact that all mention of Asser as the supposed author of the *Life* is absent from these shortened accounts. It is strange that never once did the editor who adapted the *Life* into its various chronicle abridgements (four in all) use any phrase alluding to Asser as his authority. We should expect to find: *as Asser says*, or *as we read in Asser's Life of King Alfred*, or the like. It is possible, as Hart has suggested, that the attribution to Asser may have been inserted at the latest stage in the clumsy compilation of a biography of King Alfred. This would also accord with the seemingly clumsy insertion of passages in the present tense in an effort to lend an air of contemporaneity to a narrative dealing with the deeds of a king who had been dead for a hundred years at the time of writing.

Much debate has centred on the possibility that either the *Life* was never finished or that it survived in a single manuscript which itself did not provide a complete transcript of a supposedly lost original and longer text.[197] The author asserts that he was writing in 893, so we may assume that not even that muddled writer would have continued his narrative beyond that date. But that fails to account for the fact that he only followed Alfred's life in chronological sequence, based slavishly on a translation of the Anglo-Saxon Chronicle, down to 887. It is now virtually certain that the author never continued his own narrative or the Chronicle translation down to 893. Had he done so, he would have translated the annals for 888 to 893 and added his usual hagiographical padding at the end of that translation – as he had done throughout the work thus far. But when we turn to the abridged accounts in the Northumbrian Chronicles, The Worcester Latin Chronicle and the East Anglian Chronicle, we find that those abridgements were based on a text whose translated annals almost certainly stopped at 887 and which contained no Alfredian hagiographical text thereafter. This must also powerfully confirm what we already know from the manuscript evidence – that the Byrhtferthian abridgements in the chronicles were extracted, if not from the Cottonian manuscript, then from a very close copy of it. Stevenson commented: 'the theory that the Cottonian manuscript was copied from an unfinished draft would account for its strange imperfections'.[198] Kirby was nearer the mark with his conclusion that the *Life* amounts to an 'imperfect conflation of several separate shorter treatises on the king, all written originally at different times'.[199] That may well have been the case, with the added proviso that it was the same author, Byrhtferth of Ramsey, who kept revisiting his own compilation as he sought to adapt it for his different chronicles at different stages in his prolific and long career as a writer. Evidence for the editor's scissors and paste is littered across the chapters of this medieval *Life*. The work consists essentially of a hagiographical narrative stitched on to translated sections of the Anglo-Saxon Chronicle. That stitched-on narrative and the Chronicle translation show definite evidence of rewriting, sometimes in the form of intrusive glosses and sometimes by way of special pleading, designed to present the author as a contemporary witness of the events he describes. Byrhtferth of Ramsey is an ideal candidate for the putting together of that compilation which we call the *Life* of King Alfred. Byrhtferth was the greatest authority which Anglo-Saxon England had ever seen on the editing and translating of manuscripts of the Anglo-Saxon Chronicle. Byrhtferth was also attached to what was perhaps the most important monastic school in early eleventh-century England, and we know that he was involved with the production of class-books for his pupils there.

We enter this discussion, equipped with some valuable information and guidelines provided by textual scholars. Clearly, parts at least of the *Life* of Alfred have to be as old as the earliest known medieval writers who made use of them. The earliest known writer who had access to the *Life* of Alfred was Byrhtferth of Ramsey, in or about the year 1000, when Byrhtferth included a summary from Alfred's *Life* in the Northumbrian Chronicle (York and

Durham recensions), the Worcester Latin Chronicle and also most probably in the East Anglian Chronicle. Byrhtferth also included chronological details from the *Life* of Alfred in his Ramsey Annals. A faint but clearly recognisable echo of Alfred's *Life* appears in the *Encomium Emmae Reginae c.* 1041, which was most probably borrowed from the Worcester Latin Chronicle.[200] The presence of lengthy abridged passages borrowed from, or based on the text of the *Life* of Alfred in so many Byrhtferthian chronicles is valuable in correcting or verifying Parker's edition of the text of the lost Cottonian manuscript. We note, too, that however unsatisfactory the facsimile of the opening lines of the Cotton text may be, it has been accepted on palaeographical grounds as dating to the very early eleventh century – a date which is in keeping with Wanley's observations on the script of the manuscript in his letter of 1721. This dating of the lost Cottonian manuscript also happens to coincide with the time when Byrhtferth was busy producing his hagiographical, historical and quasi-scientific outpourings at Ramsey, and Byrhtferth was the earliest scholar who can be shown to have been familiar with the *Life* of Alfred. It was from this same East Anglian monastic milieu within a generation of Byrhtferth's time, that the author of the *Encomium Emmae* may have been introduced to a version of the Worcester Latin Chronicle or the East Anglian Chronicle, which contained extensive extracts from the *Life* of Alfred.

The manuscript trail leads back to the turn of the millennium – to the circle of Byrhtferth of Ramsey and perhaps to a single manuscript recension of the fuller version of the *Life* with palaeographical associations with Worcester – a monastery with close Ramsey connections in the late tenth century. It was at Worcester, later in the twelfth century, that the monks Florence and then John copied out, conflated and continued Byrhtferth's Worcester Latin Chronicle which incorporated extensive sections of the text of the *Life* of King Alfred.

# 2

# The Author of the *Life*

## Unique information on King Alfred which is provided by the author

The *Life* of King Alfred offers a substantial amount of information which is not found in any other source – or at least which is not found in other records earlier than the biography of the king. We learn from the *Life* that Alfred was born in Wantage in Berkshire (Chapter 1) and that his mother, Osburh, the daughter of Oslac, was descended from the Jutish conquerors of the Isle of Wight (Chapter 2). Alfred is claimed to have gone to Rome as an infant pilgrim not just once (as in the Anglo-Saxon Chronicle) but for a second time because his father 'loved him more than his other sons' (Chapter 11). We are told of Alfred's love of learning while still an infant; of his illiteracy until he was twelve or older, and of the neglect of his education by his parents. We learn also of his skill in the hunt (Chapter 22). A competition is described in which the infant Alfred won a book prize from his mother (Chapter 23); and in the following chapter the young and precocious Alfred is said to have learnt the Divine Office and to have kept a notebook for this, for psalms and other prayers (Chapter 24). But later in the *Life* conflicting statements continue to be made regarding the king's inability to read 'anything', even when he was in his late thirties (Chapter 77). Alfred's marriage is dated to 868 and his wife is identified as being of a Mercian people called the *Gaini*, but she is not herself named. Her mother, however, is identified as Eadburh (Chapter 29). Alfred is claimed to have been joint-ruler by the time of his marriage and he is so referred to again at the time of his succession to the kingship in 871 (Chapter 42). The author ascribes a more prominent role to Alfred at the battle of Ashdown (Chapters 37–38) than is found in the Anglo-Saxon Chronicle, and he claims to have been familiar with the site of that battlefield. The famous tale of King Alfred burning the cakes while hiding as a fugitive in the cabin of the wife of a cowherd is narrated in Chapter 53a.

Received teaching on this incident is that it was inserted into the *Life* by Archbishop Matthew Parker, who edited the work in the first printed edition of 1574. The tale is acknowledged in Parker's edition of the biography of the king to have been borrowed from the *Life* of St. Neot, but it is not impossible that the borrowing from that source dates from the time of first compilation of the *Life* of Alfred. The legend of the burning cakes is not any more fantastic than several other folktales narrated in the *Life*, and indeed bears similarities in style to some of them. It is essentially a tale of reversed fortunes – of a great king reduced to being scolded by a herdsman's wife. In this it resembles another outlandish tale from the *Life* of Alfred – that of the powerful but wicked queen Eadburh, daughter of King Offa of Mercia, who once dominated Wessex and who supposedly ended up an exile and an outcast, begging in Pavia.[1] Eadburh's supposedly colourful and criminal career began with the alleged poisoning of her husband, King Beorhtric of Wessex, in 802. This was an anti-Mercian tale, which served no function in the *Life* of King Alfred other than to pad out a narrative which was bereft of reliable and original information on that king. Queen Eadburh's poisoning supposedly took place some 83 years before the author of the *Life* claimed to have met King Alfred in *c.* 885. In his attempt to make this long digression relevant, the author protests that he had heard it 'from my lord the truthful Alfred, king of Anglo-Saxons, who still often tells me about it, and he likewise had heard it from many reliable sources, indeed to a large extent from men who remembered the event in all its particulars'. The tale is inserted in the Cottonian version of King Alfred's *Life* at the account of the marriage of King Æthelwulf in 855, on the pretext of explaining why it was that West Saxons did not grant the title of *queen* to their king's wife. The abridged versions of the *Life* in the East Anglian Chronicle and the Worcester Latin Chronicle also include this irrelevant tale at the same place. Byrhtferth's Northumbrian Chronicle (BNC D), however, includes the tale under its more logical place at the death of King Beorhtric of Wessex back in 802.[2] The more appropriate location of the Eadburh legend in Byrhtferth's Northumbrian Chronicle serves to highlight the irrelevance of this digression in a *Life* of King Alfred and suggests that it may have begun life as a folktale in isolation from Alfred's biography.

In Chapter 56 we are told that Guthrum and his men, having been defeated and converted to Christianity by Alfred, were then rewarded with gifts in the form of many buildings by the king. The king's illnesses, and a hunting trip to Cornwall during his adolescence, are described in some detail in Chapter 74. Alfred's illness is also alluded to in the account of the king's childhood (Chapter 25), and again in Chapters 76 and 91. Alfred is portrayed as a saintly and neurotic invalid, who prayed for illness in order to control his sexual desires and who, when not suffering from his mysterious series of maladies, spent his days dreading their return. Alfred, the saintly super-king, established a royal prep school at his court where Latin and English studies were conducted under his personal supervision; he attended daily Mass, read the Divine Office, visited churches at night, and had the Scriptures read to him by native and visiting clergy. He engaged in aristocratic sports and was a great patron of the arts (Chapters 75–76). While Archbishop Plegmund of Canterbury and Bishop Wærfærth of Worcester are also known to have been numbered among Alfred's scholarly helpers from reliable contemporary sources, the author of the *Life* claims that Wærfærth translated the *Dialogues* of Pope Gregory for Alfred – a claim not substantiated by other independent early Alfredian records (Chapter 77). The author also adds the names of two other helpers – the Mercian priests and chaplains, Æthelstan and Wærwulf. Alfred is next said to have summoned the priestly tutors Grimbald and John, from Gaul, to his service (Chapter 78). The author (who in his dedicatory preface has claimed to be Asser) then describes his own summoning from 'the western and furthest parts of Britain' where he had been attached to the community of St. David's (Chapter 79). He describes his first meeting with King Alfred at Dean in Sussex. A bold claim is made in Chapter 80 to the effect that 'at that time (in *c.* 885 or even 873 – before the death of Nobis of St. David's) and for a long time before', all of southern Wales 'belonged' to King Alfred. The author then elaborates on this Alfredian overlordship by claiming that eventually all the leading Welsh kings, from north as well as south Wales, submitted to the Carolingian-style *imperium* of the king of the West Saxons.

The author next describes his second meeting with King Alfred at *Leonaford* after which he was loaded with gifts from the king, including the grant of two monasteries (Congresbury and Banwell) in Somerset, together with – later on – the diocese of Exeter (Chapter 81). The most dramatic and original contribution of the *Life* is the account of how the author, Asser, taught the king how to read and translate Latin in a miraculous episode on 11 November 887 (Chapters 87–89). The pious king's notebooks for collecting prayers and biblical commentary (first alluded to in Chapter 24) are now described in more detail (Chapters 88–89). Alfred is said to have founded the monastery of Athelney (Chapter 92) and a nunnery at Shaftesbury (Chapter 98), and a complicated account is given of his saintly division of his time and revenues for the service of God and his fellow man (Chapters 99–103). The king's invention of a lantern clock where time was reckoned by way of gradations on burning candles is described in Chapter 104, and the *Life* ends with an account of Alfred as the just judge (Chapters 105–106A).

The material relating to King Alfred which is exclusive to this *Life* is often vague and full of generalities, and is embellished with fantastic hagiographical and folkloric elements. Nevertheless, the sum total of unique information which the *Life* provides on the king is formidable in extent. If the *Life* is an authentic contemporary biography, it opens a window to us on the world of Anglo-Saxon England's greatest king, and sheds an unexpected and unique light on ninth-century medieval Christendom in general.

## Problems presented by the *Life* in relation to what we know independently of King Alfred's career

If the *Life* is genuine, we must revise our picture of Alfred the successful warrior as shown in the Anglo-Saxon Chronicle, and of Alfred the prolific scholar and expert on the writers of Late Antiquity, as we see him in his own writings. That picture must be reconciled with, and added to another – a portrait of a sickly over-religious man, constantly praying for illness, yet also dreading it. The Alfred of the *Life* is a saintly obsessive, preoccupied with night vigils and obsessed with devoting half of his time and resources to the service of his Christian God, night and day. Here, too, we have an illiterate Alfred whose education was ignored until he was at least twelve and who remained unable to read even English for most of his life. But Alfred the saint learnt to read and to translate Latin miraculously at the hands of the Welsh Asser when the king was 38 in November 887 and then presumably went on (even more miraculously) in the limited time left to him, to edit and translate a whole library of works from Late Antiquity. Strangely the *Life* is silent on Alfred's great personal literary output, apart from the mention of Bishop Wærferth's translation of the *Dialogues* of Gregory. Yet King Alfred, who must have the last word on the authorship of the *Dialogues*, tells us in his *Preface* to that work, that rather than one individual having translated it, the task was accomplished by his 'true friends', whom he had commissioned.[3]

The statement that Alfred was born in Wantage (Chapter 1) causes real historical problems. Wantage, even if it were within the kingdom of Wessex in 847–9, would have been on the periphery of a kingdom whose borderland in the Thames basin was plagued with Viking marauders. Such a location would have been highly unsuitable for a West Saxon king's wife to have chosen for her lying-in. Wantage was also in a border region which had been disputed between Mercia and Wessex for a century before Alfred's birth, and it had been under Mercian control until at least as late as 844. Stenton originally dated the annexation of Berkshire by Wessex to 853, but later revised that date backwards in order to accommodate (by circular argument) the birth of Alfred in Wantage in *c.* 847![4] The author names King Alfred's mother as Osburh, daughter of Oslac, but his information on her ancestry (Chapter 2) has all the appearance of genealogical invention. We are told that Oslac was a descendant of two legendary brothers, Stuf and Wihtgar, the Jutish colonisers of the Isle of Wight. The information offered on these supposed ancestors is based on a conflation of two Chronicle entries for the years 530 and 534 and no details are offered as to how Alfred's ninth-century maternal grand-father might have been connected with sixth-century legendary heroes.[5] Oslac is said in the *Life* to have been 'the famous butler (*famosi pincernae*)' of King Æthelwulf of Wessex. Even Stevenson admitted that 'there is … great difficulty about the mention of a great nobleman holding this office at the time when the burnt Cottonian manuscript of this work was written'.[6] More worrying is the fact that Byrhtferth in his Worcester Latin Chronicle (under 976) recorded the enforced exile from England, of the 'glorious ealdorman, Oslac (*uir magnificus dux Oslacus*)'.[7] This relatively rare mention of a namesake of Alfred's supposed maternal grandfather comes from that part of the Worcester Chronicle, which is acknowledged by both Hart and Lapidge to have been compiled under strong Byrhtferthian influence.[8] The tag *famosi pincernae*, applied by the author of the *Life* to Alfred's grandfather, is typically Byrhtferthian.[9] Byrhtferth was notorious for snatching names of magnates from his own contemporary scene or from genuine historical sources and applying them to the fictitious characters with which he peopled his biographies of long dead saints. So, for instance, he may have borrowed the name *Eadburh* for Alfred's mother-in-law (Chapter 29) from his tale of Eadburh, the daughter of Offa; and the wicked deeds of Æthelbald, the historical eighth-century king of Mercia, inspired the invented tale of the rebellion of King Æthelbald of Wessex (Chapter 12).[10] In the *Life* of St. Oswald, Byrhtferth invented a tutor and travelling companion on a bogus pilgrimage to Rome for the young St. Oda (later Archbishop of Canterbury), and the name he chose for that tutor was borrowed from the historical Ealdorman Æthelhelm who took the alms of King Alfred to Rome in 887 – as narrated by Byrhtferth in Chapter 86 of King Alfred's *Life*.[11] Such a ruthless forger, working as ever in a hurry, was capable of seizing on the name *Oslac* for the fictitious descendant of Jutish rulers who were far beyond the reach of genuine historical records.

The picture presented of Alfred as a saintly invalid enduring constant and dreadful pain in order to control his sexual appetite is essentially hagiographical and goes against common sense as well as what we know from contemporary sources regarding this hugely successful and active king. We are told in Chapter 74 that Alfred first contracted piles in 'the first flowering of his youth', having prayed for God to send him an affliction to control his carnal desires. This malady was later replaced by an even more debilitating scourge which lasted from the king's wedding day in his twentieth year until his forty-fifth year when his biographer was supposedly writing (Chapter 91). There are a multitude of examples from saints' *Lives* of holy men and women who endured such suffering,[12] although Alfred allegedly belonged to a more fanatical band who actually prayed for illness. The fact that Alfred was stricken with a mysterious malady during his wedding feast may suggest that the clerical biographer considered that particular illness to be a Divine punishment for the king's formal abandonment of his virginity.[13] Alfred's illnesses – and in particular his affliction with piles and his later mysterious malady contracted at his wedding – were modelled on the *Life* of the lay ruler Count Gerald of Aurillac. Just as Gerald had been punished with temporary blindness for a momentary lapse from chastity, so Alfred was punished by his puritanical biographer for abandoning his virginity on his wedding day.[14] And while Alfred was alleged to have suffered from piles, the saintly Gerald, in his *Life*, was afflicted by pustules or boils. The parallels between the *Lives* of Gerald and of Alfred are so close, and so many and specific, that there can be little doubt of the dependency of one upon the other. Both rulers, for instance, had quantities of wax turned into candles, which in turn were lit in the presence of their personal relics while they travelled abroad. Both rulers were extolled by their biographers for precisely the same virtues – being fair and conscientious judges; scholarly rulers who had books read aloud to them; men torn between desire for a life of contemplation and prayer on the one hand, and the burdens of secular office on the other. They were both pilgrims who travelled to distant Rome; and both rulers founded model monasteries, struggling to find a suitable community of monks to house in them. Both men were sufferers from illness throughout life, yet – significantly – both were concerned with avoiding a disease which would disqualify them from rule. Finally, the *Lives* of both men contain an anecdote of how a Christian ruler refused to abandon his attendance at Mass while he and his followers came under enemy attack. This rare hagiographical motif – and it is no more than that – is attributed to Count Gerald in his *Life*, and to Alfred's elder brother, King Æthelred, in the work attributed to Asser.

Professor Nelson explains the similarities between the *Lives* of Gerald and of Alfred as arising from the identical cultural milieux in which they both operated:

> the two *Lives* are similar because they draw on similar traditions, come from similar monastically-influenced milieux, and, even, describe the similar conduct of two contemporary laymen subject to similar emotional strains.[15]

But would two contemporary laymen – one in southern Francia, the other in southern England – inhabit such identical worlds that they should both be considered to have been marked off by God for affliction with specific diseases, and would the same highly specific motif concerning attendance at Mass, in the face of enemy advance, be related about Gerald of Aurillac and about Alfred's elder brother – each independently of the other? And even if we were to dismiss the numerous and sometimes compelling points of comparison between the *Lives* of both men, can we put this down solely to shared cultural and intellectual environments when in fact Alfred – unlike Count Gerald – never experienced Carolingian society at first hand? We cannot pretend – however seductive the idea may be to modern scholarship – that Alfred was either a Carolingian or that he ever lived under immediate Carolingian influence – politically, culturally or otherwise. The realities of life in Alfredian Wessex centred not on theologising the office of kingship, but on the raw business of survival in the face of a sustained and powerful Scandinavian onslaught. And while Alfred was indeed a scholarly philosopher-king who clearly tried to engage with Carolingian distance learning, the essence of what we may call the Alfredian renaissance was its *vernacular* outreach – to use the jargon of twenty-first century academic management. Everything that Alfred himself wrote – as well as the Anglo-Saxon Chronicle – declares the Alfredian emphasis to have been on the vernacular. Those who defend the Genuine Asser position have failed to answer the question as to why such a king would have allowed himself to be celebrated by a *contemporary,* and by a member of his own scholarly circle, with a biography written in obscure and pompous Latin – definitely not as Alfred himself would have wished 'in the language that we can all understand'.[16]

I am in complete agreement with Nelson's observation that King Alfred is portrayed as a man 'marked by the divine' – marked that is, by heaven-sent illness, and that he was seen by his biographer as 'a servant of God'.[17] Much past scholarly effort shied away from an analysis of the theological and hagiographical content of Alfred's biography in order to ring-fence it as an unassailable 'factual' historical source. The account of Alfred's prayer for the inflicting of an illness in Chapter 74 reveals the biographer's Augustinian theology. Here God is shown to be the agent, and man – helpless and passive – puts his hope in the gift of Divine grace which will conform him to God's will. But the essentially monastic and ecclesiastical character of this *Life* is not confined to the confused discussion of the king's illnesses in Chapter 74. In Chapter 24 we are introduced to the notion of royal discipleship, when we are told of the young Alfred's learning of the Divine Office and of his book of psalms and prayers which became his constant companion throughout his life. This theme of discipleship is clumsily inserted again in Chapter 90 by way of the gallows metaphor. Here Alfred is compared with the Good Thief who was crucified beside Jesus on Calvary. I am not suggesting that the notion of royal discipleship – so prominent in the *Life* of Alfred – was in itself either derisory or lacking in authenticity. The spiritual ideals which drove such thinking extended from the thought-world of the Irish Penitentials up to the very different milieu of Thomas More and beyond. The question to be answered is whether a *contemporary* monastic biographer who had a multitude of circumstantial details to offer on Alfred's *Life* would have confined himself so uncompromisingly to hagiographical narrative when it came to making a theological point about a royal master who was certain to read his narrative. In other words, the same argument holds good in relation to the portrayal of Alfred's military career as it does for the theological interpretation in other parts of the narrative. In both cases, we are offered nothing that brings us into close proximity with Alfred himself. Hagiographically, Alfred remains a long-dead saint, just as militarily he is a long-dead warrior, exhumed through the translated passages of the Anglo-Saxon Chronicle.

As for the 'similar monastically-influenced milieux' referred to by Professor Nelson, ninth-century England (in its pre-monastic reform mode) had little in common with the monastic thought-world of Odo of Cluny, who wrote the *Life* of Count Gerald in *c.* 940. The similarity between monastic environments lies between the Ramsey of Abbo and of Byrhtferth in late tenth-century England, and that of Fleury in Francia from where Ramsey drew its spiritual and cultural inspiration. Those scholars who point to the absence of evidence for the *Life* of Count Gerald being known in England[18] should bear in mind that evidence for links between Fleury and Ramsey in the late tenth century are perhaps stronger than for any other Frankish or English monastic house at that time, or indeed before. Abbo of Fleury – one of the greatest scholars of his age – spent two years at Ramsey from 985 to 987. Have we become so reductive in our thinking as to assume that he came carrying only those few manuscripts for which we have tangible evidence? And do not the close similarities between the motifs in the *Lives* of Gerald and of Alfred suggest in themselves the possibility of that sought-for link in the manuscript transmission? The *Life* of Gerald had been written by Odo of Cluny in the period 936–42. Odo had personally reformed the monastery of Fleury, and because of his towering influence on monastic reform in Francia and at Fleury in particular, it is virtually certain that Abbo would have taken copies of Odo's works to Ramsey – a place intended by Bishop Oswald of Worcester to emulate Fleury (and Cluny) in the production of saints' *Lives*, as well as numerous other scholarly works and chronicles. And if we are seeking a natural home for a monastic writer steeped in the ideals of royal discipleship, then surely we must at least consider the possibility of late tenth-century Ramsey, in view of its close ties with Fleury and the wider Cluniac world which had developed these same ideals throughout the tenth century.

The author of the *Life* shows that he was familiar with Alfred's introductions to his translations. That being so, he would have been familiar with the king's rhetorical references to 'earthly anxieties' (Preface to the *Dialogues*) which he claims he had to endure, or to 'the various and many worldly distractions which frequently occupied him either in mind or in body' (Prose Preface to the *Consolation of Philosophy*). A misinterpretation of such rhetoric could easily have inspired the author, in his search for a saintly king, to invent the image of a sickly Alfred patiently enduring illness or dreading its return.[19] The author of the *Life* of Alfred offers us an unusual circumstantial detail when narrating his account of the king's life-long illnesses. He tells us (Chapter 74) that sometime before Alfred's wedding in 868, 'he had gone to Cornwall to do some hunting' and as part of his enthusiasm for visiting holy shrines, the saintly youth visited the church of St. Gueriir, where, at the time of writing, the body of St. Neot was supposedly buried.[20] The reference to St. Neot is highly significant in view of the close parallels between the content and style of the *Life* of that saint and the *Life* of King Alfred. The notion of a West Saxon prince hunting in Cornwall in the 860s is improbable and anachronistic in view of the fact that Cornishmen were fielding armies against Alfred's grandfather as late as 838. Cornwall was still ruled by its own indigenous Celtic kings at least until the time of Dumgarth's death in 875 – four years after Alfred had become king of the West Saxons. Had Alfred annexed Cornish territory at that time, the Anglo-Saxon Chronicle would not have been slow to report such a triumph. It seems clear from evidence provided in King Alfred's *Will*, from the *Burghal Hidage*, and from charter evidence from the reigns of Alfred's father and brothers, that there had been little West Saxon penetration of Cornish territory prior to the reign of Athelstan (died 939).[21] Whatever the exact time of the annexation of Cornwall by Wessex, it would have been foolish as well as dangerous for a young son of the West Saxon royal house to have gone hunting in the heart of hostile and alien British territory in the 860s.

King Alfred's supposed illiteracy is described in the most contradictory terms. We are first introduced to him as a precocious infant, whose age we can deduce as being between four and six. We are invited to believe that this child beat his older brothers in a reading contest organised by their mother (Chapter 23). The tale is based on a folk-motif displaying the superiority of the youngest son, who learns to read by magic or miracle in a remarkably short time.[22] The fact that Alfred's eldest brother was already dead when this contest occurred, and that all his other brothers (excepting Æthelred) were by then grown to manhood, did not trouble the narrator. Professor Keynes lamented that 'pleasantly familiar tales' such as this had fallen prey as 'a soft target' to my hatchet-like analysis.[23] But can historical scholarship afford to allow such soft targets, indeed, to enjoy the status of half-truths? Is not the stature of the genuine Alfred enhanced when the historical record is made to shed its late tenth-century legendary accretions surrounding the memory of this great king? And do we not learn more from this analysis by concluding that the tale of Alfred's mother's book prize does have its own inherent value for what it tells us of late tenth-century English society? For if this tale tells us anything, it is surely that royal women were regarded as being personally interested, and personally involved in the education of their sons in the

England of AD 1000. The youthful Alfred's precocity in literacy is again emphasised in Chapter 24 when we are told of his prayer book containing the Divine Office and the psalms, and later in life during the period 886–7, we are shown Alfred as king reading aloud from books 'day and night' (Chapter 81). This portrait of Alfred as a highly literate infant and later as a scholar king, with its emphasis on monastic liturgical practice, is suggestive of a king who had been immersed in ecclesiastical and Latin learning from the earliest age. It comes as something of a shock, therefore, to be told by the author of the *Life* that Alfred's learning had been shamefully neglected by his parents and tutors when he was a child and that he remained illiterate until he was twelve or older (Chapter 22). The child who, in Chapter 23, is offered a book prize by his caring and educative mother is found lamenting in Chapter 25 that he had been deprived of tutors (*magistros*) in his youth. Yet in the book prize episode a special tutor (*magister*) was available to help Alfred get ahead of his brothers in the race to read a whole book and to read it aloud. And the king who later in life is shown reading aloud (*recitare*) from books in English in Chapter 76, is shown in Chapter 77 to have been incapable of understanding anything in books by himself 'because he had not yet begun to read anything' – in spite of the good offices of scholars such as Plegmund and Wærfærth. It is small wonder, therefore, that we should approach the tale of how the author taught King Alfred to read and to translate Latin in miraculous fashion on 11 November 887 with a degree of scepticism (Chapters 87–89). What is even more puzzling is that the supposedly ignorant king, who learns Latin in a moment of Divine inspiration, is already armed with his little handbook, which he kept with him day and night since childhood – crammed full of passages from the Divine Office and the psalms. Such a king was apparently ignorant of Latin and yet went on instantly to engage in biblical exegesis as well as to leave for posterity a formidable collection of translations of works from Late Antiquity. All that, we are asked to believe, was accomplished in the twelve years from 887 until Alfred's death in 899 – six or seven of which were taken up with the frantic and perilous business of Alfred's Last War.

The fiction of Alfred's struggles with illiteracy, as well as the detail of the little book from which he was never parted, although handled hagiographically by the biographer, is borrowed from Einhard's *Life* of Charlemagne. Strong echoes of Einhard's work are found at several points elsewhere in the *Life* of King Alfred, and at one point in Chapter 26, the author in an unguarded moment, refers to Alfred as *Carolus* or Charles![24] The dependence of the *Life* of Alfred on Einhard has been known for a long time and will repay further study in the future. Professor Campbell has rightly drawn attention to parallels between Charlemagne's division of his property as described by Einhard and the account of a similar process in the *Life* of Alfred.[25] Professor Nelson has drawn attention to recent suggestions that King Alfred's biographer had the 'aim all along ... to replicate the structure of Einhard's *Life* of Charlemagne'.[26] But surely if we add that evidence to the Alfredian biographer's known absolute dependence on the Anglo-Saxon Chronicle for hard information on Alfred's military career, then it strengthens rather than weakens the case for the derivative nature of this *Life*, and diminishes rather than enhances the possibility of its contemporaneous character. It was Galbraith, after all, who used dependence on Einhard as a major plank in his argument for claiming the *Life* of Alfred to have been a forgery.

In spite of the picture presented to us of Alfred as a neurotic invalid, in many ways his prowess as a warrior-ruler is exaggerated out of all recognition even of that successful king whose military career is charted in the Anglo-Saxon Chronicle. The near-contemporary Chronicle shows Alfred fighting a rearguard action against the Danes from his succession to the kingship in 871, down to 878–9, when his career almost ended in disaster as he allowed himself to be boxed in by his enemies in the Somerset marshes. Subsequently, the Chronicle shows us Alfred as master of Wessex, while exercising an unspecified overlordship over those parts of English Mercia which were ruled by his son-in-law Æthelred, and by Alfred's daughter Æthelflæd. The Alfred of the *Life*, however, is addressed in late tenth-century terms as 'king of the Anglo-Saxons and ruler of all the Christians of the island of Britain'. He is also claimed to have ruled as overlord of South Wales for a long time before 873 or 885, and to have been accepted as overlord of the whole of Wales by 893 (Chapter 80). If this were true, he would have anticipated Edgar in the later tenth century, and indeed Edward I in the thirteenth. The Alfred of this narrative who was 'warlike beyond measure and victorious in all battles' (Chapter 42) is suspiciously reminiscent of Arthur as described in Nennius – a source with which our author was familiar.[27] Not only is overlordship attributed to Alfred over all the Welsh kings and not only is he hailed as ruler of all Britain, but he is alleged by the author of the *Life* to have acted as *secundarius* ('joint ruler', or as others would argue 'heir apparent') while his brothers (plural) were alive (Chapter 42). He is earlier in the *Life* again referred to as *secundarius* at the time of his wedding in 868 (Chapter 29). This would mean that from at least as early as the reign of King Æthelberht (860–6), if not before, Alfred was regarded either as a joint-king or as heir apparent. Such a situation is impossible to accept in a society where the leading warrior aristocracy who made up the *witan*, or 'wise men' in council, would have insisted on their right to elect a king from among the royal kindred on the death of each ruler in turn. To conclude otherwise would suggest that the warriors of Wessex were willing to have their hands tied for years in advance in regard to the most crucial decision of leadership in war, upon which the future of the entire West Saxon society depended.[28] The claim that Alfred enjoyed the status of 'joint-ruler' while his older brothers were ruling as kings before him, is part of the wider apocryphal claim that King Æthelwulf loved the infant Alfred more than his other sons (Chapter 11), and that:

> he was loved by his father and mother, and indeed by everybody, with a united and immense love, more than all his brothers, and was always brought up in the royal court, and as he passed through childhood and boyhood he appeared fairer in form than all his brothers, and more pleasing in his looks, his words and his ways. (Chapter 22)

The author spells out the purpose of the tale of how the infant Alfred won his book prize as being to show that he was capable of 'forestalling his brothers who were ahead of him in years, though not in ability'. The closest parallel here is with Byrhtferth of Ramsey's description of Ealdorman Æthelwine (the joint-founder of Ramsey Abbey) at the notice of that magnate's death in the Worcester Latin Chronicle at AD 992. Æthelwine, Byrhtferth tells us:

> although younger in age than his brothers, Æthelwold, Ælfwold, and Æthelsige, nevertheless outstripped them in meekness, piety, goodness, and justice.[29]

It is helpful to have the support of Professor Lapidge in underlining the fact that this passage comes from a point in the Worcester Chronicle where the influence of Byrhtferth of Ramsey is no longer in any doubt.[30]

The record of the battle of Ashdown in the Anglo-Saxon Chronicle shows King Æthelred taking precedence over his brother, Alfred, in the order of battle. While the Chronicle attempts to promote Alfred's image during the reign of King Æthelred, by linking Alfred's name to that of his older brother in every action which is described, nevertheless the Chronicle's account of the battle is in no way supportive of the elaborate tale which is narrated in the *Life* of Alfred. Here we are told (Chapter 37) that King Æthelred insisted on his attendance at Mass until that ceremony had ended, while Alfred had to go forth on the battlefield and take on two Danish divisions on his own. The notion of King Æthelred refusing to abandon attendance at Mass on the battlefield of Ashdown (Chapter 37) is borrowed, as in the case of Alfred's supposed succession of illnesses, from the *Life* of Gerald of Aurillac.[31] In view of the apocryphal nature of the author's account of the battle of Ashdown, little credence can be given to that same author's claim to have seen a thorn tree marking the site of the engagement.

If this *Life* is genuine, then it offers us a controversial and revolutionary portrait of an early medieval warrior king whom we otherwise know from an altogether different and opposing angle of vision, provided by genuine and contemporary sources. The marvel is that in spite of the challenges presented by this text, and in spite of the urgency of the questions which it poses, scholars have fought so shy for so long of opening up a debate on the authenticity of the *Life* of King Alfred. Putting the question another way, it is fair to ask why, if the *Life* is a genuine contemporary source of information on Alfred the Great, has it not been used in a positive way to fill out our understanding of ninth-century England and Europe? Why, for instance, do we never find evidence from this supposedly genuine source, being used to show us that Eadburh, a ninth-century Mercian queen, died as a destitute and fallen woman in Pavia? Why are we not told that it was normal for West Saxon princes to hunt in what must have been a subdued Cornwall in the 860s; that King Alfred had subdued all of Wales by 893; that he was an illiterate king until he was forty; and a seriously impaired invalid for all of his life? Is it not because those generations of scholars who have defended the authenticity of the *Life* of Alfred for well over a century have been uncomfortably aware that at best they were defending only half-truths – vignettes from a hagiographical genre, rather than reliable contemporary historical testimony?

## The author's claims to being a contemporary witness

The author of the *Life* of King Alfred claims not only to be a contemporary witness, but also to have known the king intimately, to have tutored him and to have resided at his court. He mentions a four-day stay with King Alfred at Dean (Chapter 79) and an eight-month stay after a second meeting at *Leonaford* (Chapter 81). On yet another occasion (Chapter 88), on 11 November 887, the author writes of tutoring the king in his royal chamber (*in regia cambra*). Earlier in the *Life* (Chapters 24–25) he claims to have seen a book of prayers which Alfred kept with him day and night and he presents himself as a witness to Alfred's personal craving for knowledge in the midst of sustained illness. He claims (Chapter 13) to have heard the folktale of Queen Eadburh, the daughter of King Offa, from Alfred himself – 'who still often tells me about it' – and he claims Alfred heard the tale 'from men who remembered the event in all details'. He claims often to have seen the king in every kind of hunting activity (Chapter 22), and to have known King Alfred's mother-in-law 'for several years before her death' (Chapter 29). He also claims (Chapter 91) to have read letters sent to the king, although that does not necessarily imply that the writers and the reader of such letters were the biographer's contemporaries. These bold claims of writing from personal knowledge are not backed up by significant circumstantial detail at any point in the *Life*. A writer who had lived at the royal court from 885 to 893 or 899 would be expected to mention in passing at least something about the magnates or their wives who attended upon the king. Not a single name of any such secular magnate is offered which is not found in the author's translation of the Chronicle. While the author claims (Chapter 29) that Alfred's mother-in-law was a Mercian called Eadburh (perhaps a doubling of Eadburh, daughter of Offa, in the Mercian folktale in Chapters 14–15), he unaccountably fails to name Alfred's wife. And while he refers on four occasions to men who gave him information which he included in the *Life*, significantly, none of these people is ever named. There is, furthermore, great doubt surrounding the historicity of the particular anecdotes which these unnamed witnesses supposedly reported. This applies to 'the certain men' who told him the tale of Æthelbald's rebellion against King Æthelwulf (Chapter 12); to the 'many' who supposedly saw the apocryphal poverty of Queen Eadburh in Pavia (Chapter 15); to the veterans of the battle of Ashdown who related the apocryphal tale of King Æthelred praying in his tent (Chapter 37); and finally to those who reported on Abbot John of Athelney's ability as a warrior, in the tale of the attack on that cleric (Chapter 97). None of these episodes is vouched for in any other source. The accounts of the wicked Queen Eadburh and the supposed reluctance of King Æthelred to forgo his attendance at Mass in order to do battle with the Danes are both constructed from folktales and hagiographical motifs.[32] The stories regarding Æthelbald's rebellion and the attack on Abbot John can be shown to be riddled with inconsistencies and are circumstantially improbable.[33]

Against the author's special pleading in regard to his role as a contemporary witness, we have to set his worrying tendency of referring to supposedly contemporary situations in the imperfect (past continuous) tense and of lapsing from the present to the imperfect and past. We encounter such a lapse from present to past tenses in the author's account of Alfred's prowess as a huntsman (Chapter 22), when incidentally the author protests that he has seen these things for himself. The king's unknown disease is referred to in the present tense at the opening of Chapter 91 and later on in the same chapter the author's comments on the failure of the king's magnates to build fortresses as he commanded, are also written in the present. But throughout this same chapter, Alfred's achievements as a protector of his people from attacks of foreigners and his splendid building programmes are all referred to in the imperfect. The three working shifts involved in the management of the royal household are set out in complicated detail in Chapter 100 in the imperfect tense, but the author lapses back into the present with his closing sentence which summed up that arrangement. At the end of Chapter 25, the author refers to Alfred as though the king were already dead – all this in spite of his claim elsewhere in the *Life* to be writing in the king's forty-fifth year (893), which was then supposedly in progress (Chapter 91). Stevenson explained away these lapses from present to imperfect and past tenses in the narrative by arguing that no forger would have allowed this biography to enter the public domain before all such anomalies were ironed out, and he pointed out, in addition, that Thegan used the imperfect and past in his contemporary account of the emperor, Louis the Pious.[34] Stevenson suggested that such errors in tense 'may perhaps be due to the copyist [of the Cotton manuscript]'. But they could equally be due to an author who was either careless in his adherence to his role as a supposedly contemporary witness or who wrote his account of a long dead Alfred initially in the past tense and later inserted occasional references to the present to add an air of contemporaneity to his work. Several of his references to a supposedly present-day situation have the appearance of being later insertions, and indeed Keynes and Lapidge rightly identified one such possible later insertion at the end of Chapter 22.[35]

Allied to his claims to have known King Alfred are suggestions that the author may have known various places in Wessex, in Francia and elsewhere from personal knowledge. He claims to have seen a child monk of Danish parentage in the monastery at Athelney (Chapter 94); that he had seen a thorn tree growing at the site of the battle of Ashdown (Chapter 39); and his description of the fortress at Cynuit in Devon (Chapter 54) has long been taken as indicative of personal knowledge of the place.[36] His laconic descriptions or textual glosses on Reading, Wareham, London, York, Surrey, Wilton, Chippenham, Cirencester, Shaftesbury, Fulham, Athelney, Rochester, Thanet and Sheppey have also prompted admirers of the work to point to the author's original comments on these locations. His comments on Paris and Chézy have been taken by Keynes and Lapidge to be 'examples of Asser's superior knowledge of Frankish affairs'.[37] The great majority of these comments are inserted by way of glosses in the author's translation of the Anglo-Saxon Chronicle. Many of these intrusive comments fail to stand up to close scrutiny when we are in a position to check the information provided. The author's statement that London belonged to Essex was based on an outmoded antiquarian reference lifted from Bede's *Ecclesiastical History*. His comment on the meaning of the placename *Thanet* was taken from Nennius. His statement that there was a monastery (nunnery) on Sheppey in *c.* 893 (at the time when he was writing) is highly unlikely to have been true, in view of the exposed nature of that island to known Viking attack. The reference to the presence of a Danish boy in the monastery of Athelney was probably inspired by Byrhtferth of Ramsey's *Life* of St. Oswald.[38] Keynes argued that the author's reference to a causeway at Athelney linking two fortresses 'constitutes strong presumptive evidence that the author, whoever he was, knew the place well'.[39] That may have been so, but we must still take into account that descriptions of Athelney in the *Life* of St. Neot (dating to *c.* AD 1000) echo other passages in the *Life* of King Alfred; and that a key verbal reference in King Alfred's *Life* to the Somerset marshes (where Athelney lay) reveals a strong Byrhtferthian textual association. The Somerset wetlands are described in Chapter 53 of the *Life* of Alfred as being *gronnosa* or 'marshy', while in Chapter 88 the word *gronnios* is used to describe the marshes traversed by the author's metaphorical bee. That very rare word *gronna* was admitted by Stevenson to have been a Frankish import into Anglo-Latin from tenth-century Fleury. The earliest recorded instance of the word in English documents outside the *Life* of Alfred is found in King Edgar's foundation charter for Thorney Abbey. That charter was witnessed by Bishop Oswald and Ealdorman Æthelwine, who were the joint founders of Byrhtferth's monastery at nearby Ramsey.[40]

As for the author's supposed superior knowledge of Frankish affairs, all that is firmly based, as ever, on his translation of the Frankish section of the Anglo-Saxon Chronicle. And there is no added Frankish detail in his translation of the Chronicle which can match the information provided, say, in the Chronicle of Æthelweard.[41] The author does, on the other hand, mistranslate whole passages of the Frankish section of the Chronicle; shows ignorance of Carolingian topography; and follows the Chronicle in its telescoping of the dates of key Frankish events.[42] When we take a seemingly neutral gloss on the Frankish annal relating to the Danish wintering at Chézy on the Marne in AD 887 (Chapter 84), we discover a key to the author's attempts to lend an air of contemporaneity to his narrative. He comments on Chézy that it was a royal estate (*id est villa regia*). Stevenson saw this as nothing less than 'proof of the author's knowledge of Frankland',[43] while for Keynes and Lapidge it was indicative of 'superior knowledge of Frankish affairs' – with the clear implication that we are dealing with the historical Asser, as a contemporary witness. But when we take a more comprehensive view of the *Life* of King Alfred we recognise that many other places mentioned in his translation of the Chronicle are also claimed to have been royal estates and that the glossing of such placenames with words such as *id est villa regia* amounts to nothing more than a characteristic of the author's style of historical writing. Invariably this additional intrusive phrasing is added by the author to lend an air of originality to his otherwise total dependence on his translation of the Anglo-Saxon Chronicle. So in addition to Chézy, we are told that Chippenham, *Leonaford*, Reading, Sheppey, Wantage and Wedmore, were all royal estates in King Alfred's time. Some of these places may indeed have been royal estates in the late ninth century, and even more may have been so in the late tenth century and would have been known as such to the writer. But it is equally probable that in other cases the author was indulging in intelligent guesswork. Hart has linked this fondness for identifying historical places as royal estates in the *Life* of King Alfred, with the same characteristic in the writings of Byrhtferth of Ramsey which is especially prevalent in Byrhtferth's Worcester Latin Chronicle (later incorporated into the Chronicle of John of Worcester).[44] Crucially, Hart pointed to Byrhtferth's identification under annal 571 of Limbury, Aylesford, Bensington and Eynsham as royal estates (*regias villas*) captured from the Britons.[45] To describe such sites as royal villas from as far back as the sixth century was clearly anachronistic and was rightly compared by Hart with Byrhtferth's reference to Eastry in Kent as being a royal estate in the early seventh century, in Byrhtferth's account of the *Kentish Royal Legend* in The Northumbrian Chronicle.[46] Such gratuitous and anachronistic assumptions must put us on our guard against accepting an exactly similar treatment of historical locations by Byrhtferth in the *Life* of Alfred.

It remains true, of course, that the author of the *Life* – so interested as he clearly was in historical matters – may well have visited certain sites within Wessex and elsewhere. It is even more probable that this widely read scholar had some additional knowledge of many locations which was supplied by scholarly reading (especially of charters) rather than first-hand experience. But it is hazardous, if not fallacious, to argue that the additional glosses added by King Alfred's biographer to his translation of the Anglo-Saxon Chronicle afford 'proof' of his identity either as a contemporary of King Alfred or as none other than Asser, Bishop of Sherborne. On the contrary, when we take the writer's almost total reliance upon the text of Chronicle into account, and when we add in his numerous bunglings of his Chronicle translation, together with his plethora of guesswork and anachronisms, there is a formidable body of cumulative evidence pointing to an author who was entirely reliant on his Anglo-Saxon Chronicle text, onto which he grafted folktales and hagiography, the great bulk of which may have been figments of his own imagination.

## Who was the historical Asser?

King Alfred, in his *Preface* to the translation of Gregory's *Pastoral Care*, acknowledges the help of four scholars who enabled him to translate that work from Latin into Old English. These four men he lists as 'Plegmund my archbishop, Asser (*Asserie*) my bishop, Grimbald, my mass-priest and John my mass-Priest'.[47] Plegmund became Archbishop of Canterbury in 890, so the prefatory letter attached to the Alfredian *Pastoral Care* must date to after 890, although the main text of Gregory's work may have been translated some years earlier – perhaps from as early as *c*. 885. Who was this Bishop Asser who was one of King Alfred's leading Latin scholars? Did he, while being a bishop, always have charge of a diocese within Wessex – one of those bishoprics, each of which received a copy of the Alfredian translation of the *Pastoral Care*? Was Asser an Englishman – a West Saxon or Mercian perhaps – or was he one of those foreign scholars who were attracted to King Alfred's court in the years following the king's victory over the Danish Guthrum in 878? The Anglo-Saxon Chronicle tells us that 'Asser (*Asser*), who was bishop of

Sherborne', died in 909. So we know at least the bishopric where Asser ended his career and we know that he outlived King Alfred by some ten years, serving as a major figure in the service of King Edward the Elder. We do not know when Asser became bishop of Sherborne, but it seems unlikely that he was already in that post when he helped Alfred with his translation of the *Pastoral Care*. Asser's predecessor in Sherborne, Bishop Wulfsige, may have survived there until the closing years of King Alfred's reign. Wulfsige witnessed a charter of King Alfred made out in favour of Bishop Wærfærth of Worcester in 889 – a charter which is regarded as authentic in substance at least.[48] Wulfsige also appears in the witness list of a controversial charter of King Alfred in favour of his ealdorman, Æthelhelm, supposedly dating to 892.[49] Wulfsige may even have survived at Sherborne well into the 890s. His survival into the last years of Alfred's reign would seem to be confirmed by the appearance of his successor, Asser, as a witness to charters not of Alfred, but of his son, King Edward. While few if any of those Edwardian charters are genuine, it is curious that Asser's name is absent from the witness list of Alfredian charters if he were indeed Bishop of Sherborne during Alfred's reign.[50] The name of Bishop Asser is also unaccountably absent as a beneficiary in King Alfred's *Will* – unless he were one and the same as the mysterious Bishop *Esne* mentioned in that document, or unless he is referred to indirectly in the *Will* as 'to him as Sherborne'. But Esne is presumably a different name from Asser, and 'he at Sherborne' could just as easily refer to Bishop Wulfsige.[51] These, then, are the few reliable facts which we glean from contemporary sources. Bishop Asser helped King Alfred with the translation of the *Pastoral Care* and he died, as Bishop of Sherborne, ten years after the death of his royal master. There are several indications that he may not have been appointed to the Sherborne bishopric until either the end of Alfred's reign or early in the reign of Edward the Elder, and if he is indeed absent from King Alfred's *Will*, he may not have entered that king's service until after *c.* 888. 'Asser' the supposed author of the *Life* of King Alfred, however, tells us that he entered the king's service at, or very near to, 885. The author of King Alfred's *Life* claims to have been writing his biography in 893, and he finished it, in strict chronological terms, in 887. But if Asser were indeed the Bishop of Sherborne of that name who died in 909, he outlived his royal master by some ten years. Why then did he not bring Alfred's *Life* down to its close in 899, which would have allowed the writer to deal with the triumph of Alfred's Last War against the Danes and to review the king's extraordinary programme of scholarly translations?

## What the author tells us of himself

The author of the *Life* identifies himself in the opening lines of his Dedicatory Preface as 'Asser, least of all the Servants of God'. He addresses King Alfred directly in his Dedication, and later in the work (Chapters 87–89) he claims to have taught the king how to read and to translate Latin for the first time at Martinmas (11 November) 887. There is no doubt that the author wishes his readers to understand that he was the same person as the historical Bishop Asser, who was referred to and thanked by King Alfred in that ruler's Preface to his translation of the *Pastoral Care*. The crucial question is whether – in the light of all the errors and inconsistencies in the *Life* – we can accept the identity assumed by the author as the historical Bishop Asser, the contemporary of King Alfred, who had intimate knowledge of the king and his court, and who acted as his personal tutor. The author's account of his own personal background is even more astonishing than his bold claim to have been the confidant of the king. His claims to a Welsh background have been taken for granted for so long in Early Medieval English historiography that the Welshness not only of the author of the *Life* of Alfred, but also of the historical Bishop Asser of Sherborne, have entered the canon of received teaching as firmly as the Danish origins of Cnut or the Norman ancestry of William the Conqueror. The author of Alfred's *Life* tells us (Chapter 79) that he was a kinsman of Nobis, Bishop of St. David's, an important monastic centre in the kingdom of Dyfed in southwest Wales. He tells us that his people encouraged him to enter into King Alfred's service so that they might gain protection from Hyfaidd, King of Dyfed, who had attacked St. David's and who on one occasion drove out Nobis and also Asser. The author identifies unequivocally with his Welsh monastic background where he was 'brought up, trained, tonsured and eventually ordained'. He tells us (Chapter 79) he was summoned to the court of King Alfred 'from the remote westernmost parts of Wales' and that he first met the king at Dean, described as a royal estate, and probably to be identified with East or West Dean in Sussex. That first meeting took place *c.* 885. During a four-day stay at Dean, the author brokered a deal with King Alfred, the account of which is heavily influenced by a similar but earlier account in the *Life* of Alcuin of how that Northumbrian saint came to an agreement with Charlemagne. Asser from St. David's agreed to spend six months at the court of King Alfred and six months with his community in Wales, subject to the agreement of his people there. Like Alcuin, the Welsh Asser was to be rewarded with the rule of monasteries and the control of monastic wealth. The author of King Alfred's *Life* was paid for his efforts to tutor the king by being given (Chapter 81) the monasteries of Congresbury and Banwell in Somerset and eventually he was presented with the diocese of Exeter.[52] This last gift, the author of the *Life* would have seen as being in keeping with the historical Asser's standing as a bishop. That episcopal status of the historical Asser is one of the very few things about him of which we can be certain. If we interpret the Exeter passage, on the other hand, not to refer to diocesan jurisdiction, then we are faced with the further problem that the author of the *Life* makes no reference whatever to Asser's standing as a bishop.

There are several other serious problems relating to this supposedly autobiographical account by the author. Nobis of St. David's was not an archbishop in any conventional meaning of the term. His role as archbishop and supposed mentor of Asser was modelled on the relationship between the Archbishop of York and Alcuin, as found in the *Life* of Alcuin – a work which all parties are agreed was consulted by and had an influence on the author of Alfred's *Life*. Nobis died, according to the *Annales Cambriae*, in 873. The author specifically tells us (Chapter 80) that 'at that time and for a considerable time before' – when Nobis was being harassed by King Hyfaidd – 'all the districts of southern Wales belonged to King Alfred and still do'. Alfred did not become king of the West Saxons until 871 and there is no evidence apart from this statement by the author that he or any of his predecessors ever controlled any portion of south Wales. From 871 until 878–9, Alfred was under constant pressure from the Danish armies of Halfdan and later of Guthrum. As late as 878, Alfred was a fugitive hiding from his Danish enemies in the Somerset marshes. For all that remained of Alfred's reign after 879, the power of English Mercia had been broken by those Danish conquerors who occupied all of its eastern and northern territories. It was not until late in the reign of Edward the Elder that Welsh kings were forced to enter into political negotiations with the West Saxons, and even then the kingdoms of south Wales could never have been said to 'belong (*pertinebant*)' to a West Saxon king. Whoever wrote up this commentary on West Saxon and Welsh relations was writing from a late tenth- rather than a late ninth-century perspective.[53]

Several other autobiographical statements by the author of the *Life* have long prompted doubts in the minds of scholars regarding the authenticity of the work. The author refers (Chapter 79) to a year-long stay which he was forced to make at Winchester, when he was too ill to travel back home to Wales after his first meeting with King Alfred at Dean. Recent editors, following Stevenson, have massaged the text of the *Life* to read that the author lay up at Caerwent in Wales (on the way to St. David's) rather than Winchester in Hampshire. *Wintonia* however refers to Winchester[54] – that same *Wintonia* which the author correctly tells us in his translation of the Chronicle (Chapter 18) was attacked by Danes in 860. He then tells us that he and the king had to communicate with each other by letter over a whole year, in spite of the obvious importance of Winchester as a place where Alfred may have spent much of his time. And to heap confusion on an already bewildering narrative, the author – immediately before telling us of his convalescing at Winchester – informs us that he had already returned to his country (*ad patriam remeavimus*).

The original deal worked out with the king was that the author should either spend six months at his court followed by six months in Wales, or alternatively three months in Wessex followed by three months in Wales (Chapter 79). This arrangement is forgotten by Chapter 81 where we are told that on the author's second visit to King Alfred at *Leonaford*, he remained eight months with the king before eventually returning home. After that there is no further mention of rotational service or indeed of any further visits to Wales, and we are left to suppose that the author settled down in Wessex to enjoy his ecclesiastical winnings there. Chief among those winnings is the author's claim that he was rewarded by King Alfred with Exeter and all its *parochia* in Wessex and in Cornwall. If the author meant by this that he had been given a diocesan jurisdiction based on Exeter, then he is guilty of a celebrated anachronism, since Exeter was not constituted as an episcopal seat until 1050. The author's apparent claim that he had been given the bishopric of Exeter formed yet another major plank in Galbraith's argument for rejecting the authenticity of the *Life*.[55] Arguments by the 'Genuine Asser' school of historians, to the effect that since the historical Asser was already a bishop, perhaps King Alfred set him up as a suffragan at Exeter, do not stand up to scrutiny. There is no other supporting evidence for such episcopal status for Exeter either at that time or later throughout the tenth century. An alternative argument[56] claiming that the Welsh Asser would not have written of Exeter's *parochia* 'in the sense of "episcopal diocese"' but rather in the context of his own Celtic monastic organisation is equally weak. The supposed Welsh Asser had already spent eight years at the court of King Alfred by the time he had come to write the *Life* of the king in 893, and he was by then sufficiently well versed in Old English to translate the Anglo-Saxon Chronicle into Latin. The historical Asser was already a bishop in his own right when thanked by King Alfred in the Preface to the *Pastoral Care* and that same historical bishop was helping to translate Gregory's work from Latin into Old English at *c.* 890, if not from as early as 885. Such an accomplished scholar and confidant of a West Saxon king, who definitely ended his life as Bishop of Sherborne, would have known full well that to say he had received the *parochia* of Exeter from a West Saxon ruler implied episcopal authority over its diocese. That argument holds true regardless of the Welsh origins of Asser. When we bear in mind that this whole passage was modelled on Charlemagne's appointment of Alcuin to the abbacy of St. Martin's at Tours (as described in the *Life* of Alcuin), it is very difficult – not to say impossible – to accept this supposedly autobiographical narrative as an authentic late ninth-century record. From an early eleventh-century perspective, a writer such as Byrhtferth might have been dimly aware that the three dioceses of Sherborne, Wells and Crediton were a post-Alfredian creation, but he would have been vague about what had gone before. He would have known from the Anglo-Saxon Chronicle that Sherborne did possess a bishop in King Alfred's time, but that he was not Asser. He would also have seen from his several copies of the Chronicle that Exeter loomed large in the history of the Viking wars, and was so important to King Alfred that he abandoned a campaign against Vikings in Kent and Essex to return and save his West Saxon town in the far west of his kingdom. That event was recorded in 893 and the author of Alfred's *Life* was prompted to pretend that he was writing in 893 because that was the year in which one particularly early copy of the A-Text Chronicle which he had consulted, may have ended abruptly.[57] But the very last year in that copy of the Chronicle would have provided him with a record of a major Danish assault from the sea on Exeter which was successfully beaten off by King Alfred. Exeter would have been a fitting place, for a forger in Byrhtferth's position, to invent as King Alfred's gift to his favourite tutor. Indeed, the *Life* of Alfred narrated the king's gift of the *parochia* of Exeter in Chapter 81, and then immediately proceeded to swiftly bring the Chronicle translation to a close in Chapters 82–85. Having abandoned his Chronicle translation for good, the author resumed his fictional account (Chapter 87) of his relationship with King Alfred and of the miraculous tale of how the king began to read and to translate in his thirty-ninth year.[58]

If we look closely at what the author of King Alfred's *Life* tells us about his first coming to King Alfred from Wales, we find that the same inconsistencies, the similar borrowing of motifs from other sources, and a downright disregard for common sense pervade the narrative as elsewhere throughout the *Life* of Alfred. The writer tells that he was summoned by the king 'from the most westernmost part of Britain' – a phrase recalling the author's location of Athelney in the *Life* of St. Neot – and that he first met Alfred at the royal estate at Dean.[59] This narrative of the 'summoning' of Asser forms a continuation of the summoning of Grimbald and John in the previous chapter, and was based on an imitation of the notion of Charlemagne's Palace School as described by Einhard in his *Life* of Charlemagne and as also described in the *Life* of Alcuin. Indeed, the author of Alfred's *Life* borrowed verbally from Einhard's *Vita Caroli* in this very part of the *Life* of Alfred when telling us of the many gifts which King Alfred gave him.[60] When Alfred's biographer goes on to describe his reluctance to join the king's household without first consulting his *familia* at St. David's, and later when he itemises the gifts of monasteries which he received from the king, we recall that he was drawing from the Frankish *Life* of Alcuin of York. The proposed agreement between Asser and King Alfred, whereby Asser was to spend six months with Alfred and six months back in Wales, or alternatively, three months with Alfred and three months in

Wales,[61] smacks of Byrhtferth's love of symmetry and halves and quarters – as in his account of the division of Alfred's revenues.

The question has rarely if ever been asked as to whether it is likely that King Alfred would have appointed a Welshman, who until recently had been resident in Dyfed, to a major bishopric within the West Saxon kingdom. As we have seen, the author of the *Life* was himself aware that Charlemagne had appointed Alcuin, an Englishman, to high office in the Carolingian realm. Did that knowledge prompt King Alfred's biographer to recast the historical Asser as another foreigner – this time from Wales – who was promoted by Alfred to similar high office as a reward for his learning? It is true that famous bishops of the Early English Church had been drawn from among Celtic peoples – Aidan of Lindisfarne being a supreme example of the type. But Aidan and the great majority of his Celtic episcopal contemporaries in England had been Irishmen or Scots – not Welshmen. Welsh, on the contrary, was a language spoken by devils who plagued the saintly English Guthlac,[62] and the Welsh people – as Bede liked to remind his readers – were the traditional enemies of the English.[63] Besides, Aidan, together with other Irish ecclesiastical leaders in the England of his time, were rulers of a missionary church which had little option but to employ foreigners. The Synod of Whitby and subsequent developments saw to it that the English evolved their own indigenous episcopacy tightly linked to the Roman rather than to a suspect Welsh liturgical and canonical tradition. King Alfred personally celebrated that Roman dimension in English Christianity and Christian learning through his own translation programme of the works of Pope Gregory the Great, who had sent Augustine to convert the English. And indirectly Alfred celebrated that same Christian Roman theme through the compilation of the Anglo-Saxon Chronicle, which reiterated Roman connections – real and imagined – with early England and with early Wessex in particular.

Alfred may have had a real need for foreign and indeed Welsh scholars, but he had no need of a Welshman, who as Bishop of Sherborne (or indeed of Exeter) would participate in the sensitive deliberations of his *Witan* or royal councillors. All that we know of Alfred from his prolific commentaries in his translations, and not least from that king's *Will,* suggests that he was too politically astute and too vulnerable a king to put a Welsh Asser into such a high and sensitive office.[64] Plegmund, his choice for Canterbury, was a Mercian it is true. But Mercians – and especially Mercians who opposed the Danes and supported Alfred's daughter Æthelflæd – were part of the *Angelcynn* or 'English People', who accepted Alfred's rule in a greater kingdom of Wessex. We know that the historical Asser ended his career as Bishop of Sherborne under King Edward the Elder. Edward pursued a ruthless policy of expansion against the Danes of the Southern Danelaw, and he kept a wary eye out for trouble on his Welsh flank. Edward was perhaps even less likely than his father to entrust a Welsh cleric – however scholarly – with one of the most sensitive and important jobs in his kingdom. Edward was not a king who, in so far as we can judge, had any great interest in his father's scholarly programme. According to Byrhtferth of Ramsey who wrote a eulogy on Edward in what was later to become the *Chronicle of John of Worcester*, Edward was

> inferior to his father [Alfred] in the practice of letters, but his equal in dignity and power, and his superior in [military] glory.[65]

We need not necessarily believe the author of the *Life* of Alfred when he tells us that an earlier Bishop of Sherborne, Ealhstan, fomented civil war and rebellion in Wessex during the reign of Alfred's father, King Æthelwulf (Chapter 12).[66] But we do have to accept at least that the author considered such an incident plausible in a ninth- or tenth-century context. In other words, the Bishop of Sherborne was regarded as a leading magnate not only in ecclesiastical circles but in terms of court politics as well. Could a Welshman from Dyfed – however learned – be trusted with such an office in a West Saxon kingdom beset by Danish invaders, who were known on several occasions to have won over the neighbouring Cornish and other Welsh to their side?

The personal name Asser was of Old Testament origin, and although occurring in Welsh sources, it is extremely rare in a ninth-century context in spite of Keynes and Lapidge's comment that it 'is by no means a rarity'.[67] Stevenson dismissed English instances of the name in the eleventh century as being derived from Old Norse, but he could only cite two instances of the name *Asser* in Welsh sources prior to AD 900. One of those examples, relating to Asser ap Marchudd, has subsequently been shown to belong to a charter of *c.* 940,[68] leaving us with a solitary example of a ninth-century cleric, Asser, who witnessed a charter of King Hywel in favour of Bishop Cyfeilliog of Llandaff.[69] Stevenson's speculation that the author of the *Life* of King Alfred would 'have been quite at home in Caerwent' was based on a combination of textual error and gratuitous assumption.[70] It sprang from his arbitrary altering of the location of Asser's convalescing from Winchester to Caerwent, together with the assumption that the cleric Asser, whose name appears on the witness list of the Llandaff charter after that of Bishop Cyfeilliog, was the same person as the author of the *Life* of King Alfred. Precise dating of the Llandaff charters is extremely difficult and often impossible,[71] and this single charter involving the only reference to a ninth-century Welsh Asser, has been dated to *c.* 885 through a circular argument appealing to the supposed dating of the *Life* of King Alfred.[72]

The single, apparently contemporary, indication that Asser, Bishop of Sherborne was indeed a Welshman is the notice of the death of Bishop Asser in the *Annales Cambriae* under the year 908. If this is a contemporary entry, then it must almost certainly refer to the same Bishop Asser who died as Bishop of Sherborne according to the Anglo-Saxon Chronicle, in 909. This Welsh record of the death of Asser is preserved in the BL Harley MS 3859 of the *Annales Cambriae*. The manuscript dates to *c*. 1100 and since its annalistic entries stop at 954, 'it is presumed that this manuscript is a copy of a mid-tenth century compilation'.[73] Kathleen Hughes conceded that the *Annales Cambriae* might have been completed as late as 988.[74] There is no certainty that because the record ended in 954 it was completed in that year. Once that point is conceded, the entry relating to Asser might have been inserted at any time down to the end of the tenth century. It is also clear that the *Annales Cambriae,* prior to the mid-tenth century, do not provide us with a continuous set of annalistic records in the same way as either the Frankish or Irish annals do for the same early centuries. Because of this it is extremely difficult to place any entry in a contextual setting, with a view to establishing its original status as either a contemporary record of events or as a later insertion. The overall record of the *Annales Cambriae* is conspicuously sparse, with information supplied for only sixteen of the thirty years from 878 to the death of Asser in 908. Unlike contemporary Irish annals where it is usual to find twelve or more composite entries under every year during the ninth century, the *Annales Cambriae*, on the other hand, usually record one item, devoid of any accompanying detail. Of those sixteen annals between 878 and 908 in the *Annales Cambriae* which do contain a fragment of information, no less than three (878, 887, 889) deal with Irish matters,[75] while two (900 and 908) deal with English affairs.[76] This leaves only eleven years out of thirty with indigenous Welsh information, giving the decided impression that far from *Annales Cambriae* at this point being a contemporary record kept at St. David's or indeed anywhere else, what we have here is a later tenth-century compilation, which its editors were forced to pad out with information borrowed from Irish annals and the Anglo-Saxon Chronicle. The notice of the death of the Irish scholar, Suibne, for instance (889), was almost certain to have been borrowed from the Anglo-Saxon Chronicle, as could the record of the death of Asser.

On balance, it is not certain that the historical Bishop Asser of Sherborne was a Welshman. He could have been, and he could even have been the same person as the cleric Asser associated with Bishop Cyfeilliog in the Llandaff charter of King Hywel. But in the absence of convincing evidence to clinch any such remarkably precise identification, it is equally – if not more – probable that Asser, Bishop of Sherborne, was of West Saxon or West Mercian origin. It is important to distinguish between two quite distinct historical questions in this discussion. The first relates to the identity (Welsh or otherwise) of the historical Asser, a bishop in the West Saxon kingdom during the reign of King Alfred and who died as Bishop of Sherborne in the reign of his son, Edward. The second relates to the identity of the author of the *Life* of Alfred. These issues have become hopelessly confused and blurred over a century of historical debate. King Edward the Elder's Bishop of Sherborne may have been a Welshman who helped King Alfred with his translation of the *Pastoral Care*, but even if that were so, it does not entitle us to assume that he was also the author of the *Life* of King Alfred. That same assumption becomes a bold assertion in the narrative of the *Life*, but in view of the many problems, inaccuracies, anachronisms and inventions presented by its author, we ought not to accept his assertion at face value, unsupported by strong and convincing evidence from elsewhere.

## The Welsh dimension in the *Life* of King Alfred

The most serious objection to accepting Byrhtferth or one of his Ramsey associates as the author of the *Life* of King Alfred must surely be the entrenched notion that the *Life* was written by a Welshman and that it was written for a Welsh readership. The evidence that the author was Welsh – and, indeed, was a Welsh speaker – might seem, on the face of it, to be strong. Welsh etymologies are offered for the English placenames Thanet (*Ruim*), Nottingham (*Tig Guocobauc*), Dorset (*Durngueir*), Exeter (*Cairuuisc*), the Forest of Selwood (*Coit Maur*) and Cirencester (*Cairceri*).[77] Four other Welsh forms of placenames are offered – *Guilou* (River Wylye, near Wilton); *Abon* (River Avon); the fortress of *Cynuit* in Devon and the church of St. *Gueriir* in Cornwall.[78] Directional details are given in three instances in a Latinised version of the Welsh idiom, whereby 'on the right hand' (*i parth dehou*) means 'on the south side' and 'on the left hand' (*i parth cled*) signifies 'on the north side'. So, we are told the Danes at Reading constructed a rampart 'on the right-hand side (*a dextrali parte*) of the royal estate' there;[79] that the royal estate at Chippenham was in the 'left-hand part' (*in sinistrali parte*) of Wiltshire;[80] that Asser first met King Alfred 'in the territory of right-hand Saxons (*Dexteralium Saxonum*) which in English is called Sussex';[81] and during that meeting, Alfred asked Asser to relinquish 'all that I had on the left-hand and western side of the Severn' (*in sinistrali et occidentali Sabrinae parte*).[82] Finally, Asser informs us that 'all the districts of right-hand Wales (*dexteralis Britanniae partis*) belonged to Alfred'.[83]

Eleven out of fourteen of these Welsh formulae relating both to placename spelling and directions have one significant thing in common. They are all inserted in the text of the *Life* of Alfred by way of a gloss on the translation of the Anglo-Saxon Chronicle. The three exceptions consist of directional idioms which occur in Chapters 79 and 80 – one (Chapter 79) describing the 'summoning' of Asser from Wales to King Alfred's court, and the other (Chapter 80) outlining the politics of Alfredian Wales. A major characteristic of the Welsh material in the *Life* of Alfred is the fact that it either occurs in the form of intrusive glosses or it is tightly condensed into those two exclusively 'Welsh' chapters (79 and 80). In other words, the Welsh material is even less well integrated into the text of the *Life* than other hagiographical insertions in that work, such as tales of the king's childhood or accounts of his illnesses. For the Welsh material to furnish conclusive evidence of Welsh authorship of the *Life*, it would need to be much more convincingly integrated throughout that work so as to betray 'the habitual patterns of one mind expressing itself in characteristic ways' through predictable formulaic expressions.[84] But this is not the case. The author's knowledge and interest in the meaning of English placenames, show clearly that he understood Old English. We are reminded of the *Life* of Neot (another work with strong Byrhtferthian associations), whose author, in spite of his supposed knowledge of Welsh or Cornish, clearly understood the meaning of the English placename *Athelney*.[85] It would have been a remarkable feat for a man such as the historical Asser, who had come from 'the remote westernmost part of Wales' in 885, to be expounding the etymologies of Anglo-Saxon placenames when he was supposed to be writing King Alfred's *Life* in Latin, in 893. The Welsh learning displayed by the author of the *Life* of Alfred was essentially antiquarian. There is nothing spontaneous about the Welshness in the *Life*, and it is important to observe that the Welsh etymologies relate to six English rather than to Welsh placenames.[86] The 'Welshness' of those English placenames was an academic matter relating to the remote past, and in the case of Nottingham and Selwood the supposed Welsh renderings bear no relationship to later English forms. The use of Welsh directional idioms in relation to the royal estates at Chippenham and Reading may betray other anachronistic associations. Chippenham provided a location for meetings of the *witan* in the tenth century, but that in itself does not prove it was a *villa regis* as early as the reign of Alfred.[87] The same argument applies to Reading.[88] Information on the status of these places as royal estates may be compared with a similar gloss on Chézy in Francia,[89] which was probably inserted into the text as a creative guess. We have already noted that Byrhtferth conferred royal status in cavalier fashion on several plausible Anglo-Saxon locations in the Worcester Latin Chronicle and his Northumbrian Chronicle – but referring back to a time which was beyond the reach of reliable and contemporary historical documentation. It cannot be emphasised enough that Byrhtferth of Ramsey in his known works displays a powerful historical imagination and that he was capable of invention that could be as irresponsible as it was sometimes highly plausible.

The author of King Alfred's *Life* was not consistent in his use of the Welsh directional idiom. Such habits – relating to a turn of phrase so fundamental to his own language – ought to have been so ingrained as to preclude any lapses. But when he tells us that Surrey was 'situated on the southern bank of the River Thames' he chooses the conventional *meridianus* for 'southern'.[90] So, too, he tells us Wilton was on the southern bank (*in meridiana ripa*) of the Wylye;[91] Cirencester in the southern part (*in meridiana parte*) of the Hwicce;[92] Reading on the southern bank (*in meridiana ripa*) of the Thames;[93] and York on the northern bank (*in aquiloniali ripa*) of the Humber.[94] Nor can we argue convincingly that these inconsistencies in the use of directional idioms arose from the corrections of later 'improving' medieval editors, since the conventional Latin forms *aquilonalis* and *meridianus* appear in relation to the siting of York and Reading respectively in the version of Alfred's *Life* preserved in Byrhtferth's Northumbrian Chronicle.[95] These inconsistencies are very likely to go back to the original text of Alfred's *Life*. Where is the genuine and spontaneous Welshness in this? Is it not rather that the forger has nodded off, and those Anglo-Latin formulae which came naturally to betray 'the habitual patterns of his mind' have taken over from the author's self-conscious posturing as a Welshman?

The genuinely 'formulaic expressions'[96] in the *Life* of Alfred are those of Byrhtferth of Ramsey and his early eleventh-century milieu. The Welsh material, on the other hand, looks suspiciously foreign to the main text of the *Life* in every sense. The isolated structuring of the Welsh information betrays it as yet another contrived addition which was probably grafted on to the *Life* in one operation. If the author of King Alfred's *Life* were indeed 'a native speaker of Welsh', as Keynes and Lapidge insisted,[97] then we should expect a proportionately high number of Celtic borrowings spread evenly throughout his Latin text. Stevenson could point to only three words of Celtic origin – *graphium*, *gabulum* and *gronna*[98] – in the entire work, and all three of these may be shown to have come into the writer's repertoire from sources other than from Wales. *Graphium* ('charter, document') was acknowledged by Lapidge to be a Grecism[99] and it was culled by the author from his Greek glossary – a glossary most likely brought to Ramsey by Abbo of Fleury in the 980s. *Gabulum*, coming originally from Old Irish *gabul* ('a fork'), had already been borrowed into the Latin of Varro and was used by the early eighth-century Aldhelm[100] – a writer who had a major influence on Byrhtferth of Ramsey. This Aldhelmian word occurs in the text of the *Life* of Alfred[101] close to several other Aldhelmian motifs spread across Chapters 88 and 89. Significant, too, for the Byrhtferth dimension is the presence of this 'otherwise very rare [word] in English Latin'[102] in two charters of Cnut in favour of Abingdon, dating to 1032–3.[103] Abingdon, like Ramsey, was a centre for monastic reform, founded by St. Æthelwold of Winchester who had also been responsible for the refounding of Ely, Peterborough and Thorney – all within the Fenland home of Byrhtferth of Ramsey. Finally, on Stevenson's own admission, while *gronna* ('a marsh') may have begun life in Irish Latinity, 'no argument as to the nationality of the writer of the present work can be founded upon it'[104] because 'it was introduced into England, probably from Fleury, with other Franco-Celtic Latin words in the tenth century'.[105] And so the case collapses even for these three words as direct Celtic-Latin borrowings into the *Life*, and we are left with a work where the only meaningful linguistic and literary influences are either tenth-century Frankish or earlier English Aldhelmian.

While there is no conclusive proof that the writer of King Alfred's *Life* was a Welsh speaker, there is, of course, positive evidence from his treatment of English placenames, to suggest that he could at least read Old English. Those scholars who press their opinions on the Welsh origin of the author of the *Life* have failed to take into account the remarkable knowledge of Old English possessed by this man who translated the Alfredian section of the Anglo-Saxon Chronicle into Latin. More than that, he translated the Old English idiom *wælstowe gew(e)ald ahton* ('they held the place of slaughter', i.e. 'they won the battle') with a Latin rendering of *loco funeris dominati sunt*. When the author of the *Life* used that Latin phrase, describing the English victory over those Vikings who had sacked Winchester in 860, he was following his idiomatic text of the Chronicle word for word.[106] Even Stevenson, who firmly believed in the Welshness of his Asser, was forced to comment:

> It is surprising that a Welshman should have used this literal translation of an O[ld] E[nglish] phrase, for, as we are informed by Professor Rhys, no such expression is recorded in Welsh.[107]

It was one thing for a Welshman to translate an unfamiliar English idiom, word for word into Latin, when he found that idiom in his West Saxon text. But this supposed Welshman even invented the same English idiom when it was not in his original text. So, while the Chronicle simply says of the English victors at Aclea in 851 that 'they had the victory there' (*þær sige namon*),[108] the author of Alfred's *Life*, following those 'habitual patterns of one mind expressing itself in characteristic [English] ways', rendered that simple Old English sentence in Latin as *et loco funeris dominati sunt*.[109] Few aspects of the *Life* of Alfred could reveal the English mind of its author more clearly than this.

The fact that the majority of the Welsh material in the *Life* of King Alfred occurs in the form of glosses does not in itself preclude the Welshness of the author. But the Welsh material in the *Life* is invariably used to gloss English placenames and never used to explain placenames in Wales proper, as we might expect if the author had indeed come from Wales and was truly at home with the Welsh language. Nor can we argue that this was so, because he was writing exclusively for Welshmen who had no need for an explanation of their own placenames. Medieval Welsh and Irish texts abound with etymologies to satisfy the fascination which Celtic readers had for their own familiar placenames. Nor is the exclusive glossing of placenames within England in the *Life* of Alfred confined to the offering of Welsh forms of names. Etymologies in Latin are also offered on English placenames such as Sheppey, Englefield, Berkshire, Ashdown and *Aclea*. We are reminded of the comment offered by the author of St. Neot's *Life* on the placename *Selwood* ('as it is called in the language of the English').[110] The author's technique throughout the *Life* of Alfred was to give a thin gloss to the Latin translation of the Chronicle and to add his own material here and there in separate chapters. But the Welsh material is neither integrated enough nor sufficiently wide-ranging to offer proof of Welsh authorship for the *Life* as a whole. The Welsh forms offered for his placenames in England, are – precisely like those in the *Life* of St. Neot – essentially antiquarian and they are derived from book learning.

The archaic or retrospective tone of the author's Welsh information is nowhere better illustrated than in his gloss on the placename *Thanet*. He describes this as 'the island called Thanet (*Tenet*) in English and *Ruim* in Welsh'. But in the early tenth century, a genuine Welsh bard – the author of *Armes Prydein* – who referred to the English as 'the scavengers of Thanet' (*kechmyn Danet*) twice gave the Kentish island its contemporary English name.[111] That patriotic Welsh poet, who was striving to rouse the Welsh kings to battle against the English and hoping to drive the English off old British lands back into the sea at Sandwich, might well have used a Welsh form for Thanet, had he access to it. But clearly the conventional and contemporary usage for tenth-century Welsh writers was to refer to Thanet by its English name. Knowledge of the obsolete word *Ruim* for Thanet on the part of the author of King Alfred's *Life*, did not stem from any Welshness on his part; it owed its existence to his familiarity with Nennius's early ninth-century *Historia Brittonum*. Nennius also provided him with information on the worship of the Old English ancestor-god, Geat.[112] This evidence for the author's book learning in relation to Welsh information may have implications for his other glosses relating to things Welsh. The notion that Nottingham was called *Tig Guocobauc* in Welsh and *Speluncarum Domus* ('House of Caves') in Latin – a name that bears no relationship to the English *Snotengaham* – must also have come from a written source.[113] Nottingham, unlike Cirencester (*Cairceri*), Dorset (*Durngueir*) or Exeter (*Cairuuisc*), was far removed from Wales or Cornwall, and even further removed in time from when it was under British rule. The author's interest in Nottingham as a placename is exactly paralleled by the late tenth-century Ramsey author of St. Neot's *Life* and his antiquarian treatment of Brittonic or Old Welsh forms of the East Anglian placenames – Ely, Wells and the River Ivel.[114] The archaic and bookish learning revealed by the Welsh forms applied by the author of the *Life* of St. Neot to those three East Anglian placenames, combined with the impression he may have been trying to convey of not being an Englishman, strongly recalls the most controversial feature in the *Life* of King Alfred. The *Life of King Alfred* also presents us with some ten Welsh or British forms of English placenames, and just as the author of St. Neot's *Life* renders *Wella* as *Guella*, so too the author of King Alfred's *Life* calls the River Wylye in Wiltshire *Guilou*[115] rather than giving its English form of *Wilig*, or the like. Similarly, while the author of Neot's *Life* writes of that island 'which in English is called Athelney and which we refer to as "Athelings' Isle"', so, too, the *Life* of Alfred describes a fort at *Cynuit* or Countisbury in Devon fortified by 'ramparts thrown up in our fashion'.[116] The reader is being invited in both the quoted examples to view his author as something other than English. The Welsh element in the *Life* of King Alfred is more prominent than anything we can detect in that of St. Neot, if only because the author of King Alfred's *Life* proclaims himself to be Asser, a Welsh cleric from St. David's.

At first sight, there seems nothing odd about a supposedly early medieval Welsh writer of a *Life* of King Alfred, referring to the Severn by its classical name of *Sabrina*.[117] Ninth-century Frankish annalists and biographers regularly referred to the Seine, for instance, by its classical name *Sequana*. The Welsh historian Nennius used the classical *Sabrina* for the Severn throughout his work,[118] and the form *Sabrina* was also used by the compiler of the *Annales Cambriae*.[119] But while Nennius used the classical *Sabrina* in his *Historia Brittonum*, he also – in contrast to the *Life* of Alfred – sometimes referred to the Severn by way of the vernacular *Habren*.[120] What is remarkable is that while the *Life* of Alfred used the same word for the Severn as Ptolemy, Gildas and Bede, it comes up with a contemporary Frankish word, *Signe*, for the Seine, in preference to the classical *Sequana* of ninth-century Frankish writers.[121] Few things could more clearly demonstrate where the most powerful contemporary cultural influences on the author of King Alfred's *Life* were coming from, than this. When a ninth- or tenth-century author writes of the Welsh *Sabrina*, he shows he has been consulting his antiquarian books. When he writes of the Frankish *Signe*, he shows that he is either a Frank, or else that he is someone writing under the strongest of contemporary Frankish influences. Such a man was Byrhtferth of Ramsey, the pupil of the learned Abbo of Fleury.

Recognising the book learning that lies behind so much of the Welsh information in the *Life* of Alfred, it is quite feasible that a scholar with an antiquarian outlook such as that certainly possessed by Byrhtferth of Ramsey, may have acquired the modest amount of Welsh nomenclature and sporadic use of Welsh directional idioms as displayed in the *Life* of Alfred, from books consulted either at Ramsey or in the library at Worcester, which was also accessible to Byrhtferth. An alternative explanation suggests itself in the form of a Cornish or Welsh monk of the community of St. Neot's in Huntingdonshire, who provided Byrhtferth or one of his circle with the necessary knowledge of Brittonic which enabled him to experiment with those forms in the *Life* of Neot and eventually to develop the more ambitious idea of presenting the *Life* of Alfred as the work of the Welsh bishop, Asser. But it is doubtful if St. Neots in East Anglia had preserved any meaningful contacts with the Cornish house from which the relics of the saint had been stolen. Indeed, the evidence would point in the other direction. To deprive a monastic house of the relics of its founding saint in the early Middle Ages was to rob it of its spiritual and economic *raison d'être*, and the only connection between the two St. Neot monasteries may have been that a dominant English community had deprived a house in a conquered Cornish territory of the bones of its patron saint.[122]

Whatever the precise route through which their Welsh antiquarian material was received, it is nevertheless legitimate, in view of all the evidence, to attribute the *Lives* of Alfred and of St. Neot to Byrhtferth of Ramsey. We know that Byrhtferth was personally interested in the etymology of placenames, as witnessed by his lengthy digression on the derivation and meaning of the word *Ramsey* in his *Life* of St. Oswald.[123] Once he had embarked on the experiment of writing King Alfred's *Life* in the person of a Welsh bishop, Asser, he was then committed to injecting some plausibly Welsh-looking material into his work. The material most useful and most accessible to a non-Welsh medieval researcher would have been of an etymological nature and written in Latin in the format of a glossary. Such a work could have been consulted by Byrhtferth in precisely the same way as he culled pretentious words from his Greek lexicon. At the time when Byrhtferth and his associates were writing at Ramsey, Latin works from Wales were circulating among English monastic libraries, and at Glastonbury in particular. We need only point to the Anglo-Latin 'Vatican' recension of Nennius's *Historia Brittonum* to appreciate how interested tenth-century English scholars had become in Welsh historical works.[124] That English recension of the Cambro-Latin text of Nennius was compiled as early as *c*. 944 in the reign of Edmund, and is suggestive of a new antiquarian interest in things Welsh on the part of Anglo-Saxon scholars, which can only have increased as the tenth century advanced and as Wales was brought ever closer into the English political sphere.

The second of the two so-called Welsh chapters – Chapter 80 of King Alfred's *Life* – contains a brief discussion, consisting of only 151 words. But it contains a narrative densely packed with political and dynastic information on late ninth-century Wales. The narrative opens with the bold statement:

at that time and for a considerable time before then, all the districts of southern Wales belonged to King Alfred, and still do.[125]

This statement is patently not true. We note first of all the plea for contemporaneity of writing in the phrase 'and they still do belong to him' (*et adhuc pertinent*) – always a suspicious element in the forger's text, striving to impress on his readership that he is ever the genuine Asser. Common sense suggests that if the Cornish peninsula survived under the rule of its own kings into the reign of Alfred and perhaps down to the time of his grandson, Athelstan, then the much more isolated territories of South Wales remained free of West Saxon overlordship for at least as long. The southern Welsh rulers of Dyfed, Brycheiniog and Glywysing were cut off by the great expanse of the Bristol Channel from all contact with Wessex, whose own northern coasts along that Channel (in Devon and Somerset) formed a virtually impassable frontier of forest and marsh. The author of the *Life* himself informs us that the army of the brother of Halfdan and Ivar attacked north Devon from a winter base in Dyfed in south-west Wales in 878, and from then until the reign of Edward the Elder in 914 the Bristol Channel was clearly a major entry point into western Britain for Viking marauders. The Viking invasion of 914 shows that while Edward was largely successful in protecting the coast of Wessex along the Bristol Channel 'from Cornwall east as far as Avonmouth' there were raiding parties which broke through his defences along that coast, and Viking fleets also ravaged at will around southern Wales.[126] Such accounts show that South Wales and the Bristol Channel lay dangerously exposed to sea-borne raiders – not only from Scandinavia, but also from Brittany and Ireland. We cannot seriously entertain the idea, therefore, that Alfred or his immediate predecessors 'for a considerable time before then' were either in a position to subdue the southern Welsh physically, or indeed to reach them with effective aid in any military crisis. Added to all this was the reality that Alfred and his older brothers and their father, Æthelwulf, had more than enough on their plates to ward off Danish attacks on the West Saxon heartlands. They were in no position to embark on dangerous adventures in South Wales at a time when Mercia still retained its independence, under King Burgred, until 874. The only evidence we have for a West Saxon expedition against the Welsh proper is the record of King Æthelwulf's raid back in 853. But the Chronicle makes it clear that the initiative for that raid came from Burgred and his Mercian *witan*, and that Æthelwulf joined in as Burgred's ally in order 'to help him [i.e. Burgred] to bring the Welsh under subjection to him'.[127] So if any portion of Wales had been brought into a tributary position to the English 'for a considerable time before' Alfred's reign (or before the death of Nobis of St. David's in 873), it was surely subject to Mercia rather than to Wessex. The earliest evidence we have for West Saxon overlordship in Wales proper comes from the end of the reign of Edward the Elder and from more plausible accounts of submissions on the part of Welsh rulers to King Athelstan in *c.* 927 as recorded in the Anglo-Saxon Chronicle and later by William of Malmesbury.[128]

The author, having told us of the subjection of southern Wales to King Alfred, proceeds to supply us with a *Who's Who* of rulers in the region. This may be set out as follows:

Hyfaidd, with all the inhabitants of the kingdom of Dyfed
   [driven by the might of the six sons of Rhodri (Mawr) submitted to King
   Alfred]
Hywell ap Rhys, king of Glywysing and
Brochfael and Ffernfael, sons of Meurig and kings of Gwent
   [driven by the might and tyrannical behaviour of Ealdorman Eadred
   (*sic*) and the Mercians, sought King Alfred's protection]
Elise ap Tewdwr king of Brycheiniog
   [driven by the might of the same sons of Rhodri (Mawr) submitted to
   King Alfred]
Anarawd ap Rhodri and his brothers
   [abandoned his alliance with the Northumbrians and submitted to King
   Alfred in person].

Most of the Welsh rulers mentioned in this short and compact chapter can be shown from Welsh annals and other fragmentary sources to have been active in the 880s and 890s in their respective kingdoms in Wales. As a list of late ninth-century Welsh rulers, this chapter from the *Life* of Alfred would seem to supply us with genuine information, and so it may well be the most valuable section in the entire work. This information stands out among the 106 chapters of Stevenson's edition of King Alfred's *Life* for its density of information, the consistency of its Welshness and the consistency of content in regard to dynastic information. All this stands out in stark contrast to the remainder of this vague and derivative biography. It is a remarkable fact that King Alfred's biographer supplies us with the names of six Welsh rulers – Hyfaidd, Hywell, Brochfael, Ffernfael, Elise and Anarawd – together with names of four territories – Dyfed, Glywysing, Gwent and Brycheiniog – as well as the names of four kings' fathers – Rhys, Meurig, Tewdwr and Rhodri [Mawr]. It could, of course, be argued that this furnishes undoubted proof of the Welsh origins of the biographer of King Alfred. Yet that same biographer, who alleged he was a confidant and tutor of the king, offers us not one single name of a follower of Alfred or of a member of his household who is not mentioned in the Anglo-Saxon Chronicle. So ignorant was he of Alfredian Wessex and of the king's household, that he failed even to give the name of

King Alfred's wife, and in this very chapter on Welsh rulers, he confuses the name of King Alfred's son-in-law, Æthelred of Mercia, with that of Eadred.[129] The explanation for the relative wealth of information on Wales – as compressed into Chapter 80 – in contrast to the poverty and glaring ignorance in the rest of the *Life*, may not be that the author was a Welshman, but that he used a genuine Welsh source on late ninth-century Welsh history, and inserted it *en masse* into this short chapter. What the author of the *Life* may well have used was an historical source equivalent to the medieval Irish synchronisms or a set of king-lists setting out contemporary Welsh rulers from the late ninth century. This he then used for his own purposes, transforming it from a mere list – accurate though it may have been – into a political commentary to enhance the reputation of King Alfred. And in claiming that all of these Welsh kings submitted to Alfred, he achieved two goals at once: he glorified the subject of his biography and he also provided his forgery with a powerful semblance of authenticity for its Welsh authorship, which has proved impervious to historical criticism.

The author claimed that all the rulers in his list submitted to King Alfred. In this optimistic account of things, not only did the southern Welsh princes submit, but their northern Welsh persecutors from Gwynedd – the sons of Rhodri, who were overlords of Powys and Ceredigion, also came into Alfred's camp. In short, the whole of Wales was at King Alfred's feet. Had all that really happened before the author was supposed to have written in 893, is it possible that the Anglo-Saxon Chronicle would have ignored the most momentous development in Anglo-Welsh relations since the *adventus Saxonum* back in the fifth century? It is simply not possible that the Chronicle, in which the military and political career of King Alfred was one of the prime concerns, would have ignored a triumph which anticipated the achievements of Edward I in the thirteenth century. It would have been a triumph, too, which had massive repercussions for the progress of the Danish Wars, which were also at the centre of the Chronicle's theme. The Chronicle does touch briefly on Welsh help given to the English in their victory over the Danes at Buttington 'on the bank of the Severn' in 893. But the Chronicle is significantly vague on what that Welsh help consisted of. It comprised 'some portion of the Welsh people'.[130] We are not told which Welsh, how many, or from where. They might have been levies from within English districts along the Welsh borders, or they might have been Welsh warriors from a Welsh kingdom. But for the writer of the Chronicle, the Welsh were still a distant people whose affairs scarcely impinged on the concerns of Wessex. It was not until the reign of Alfred's son Edward, and later in the reign of his grandson Athelstan, that Welsh submission to the House of Alfred began to become an issue of some importance for the West Saxons. To a writer such as Byrhtferth of Ramsey, who was writing several decades after the submission of the Welsh to King Edgar at Chester in 973, it seemed natural to project such events back into Alfred's time. But as Davies reminded us, the nature even of tenth-century Welsh submissions remains obscure, and evidence for the appearance of Welsh kings at the English court most certainly belongs to the tenth century rather than to the ninth.[131] From 928 to 956 kings of Dyfed, Gwynedd, Brycheiniog and Gwent-Glywysing occasionally witnessed English charters. Welsh submission to the House of Wessex followed on from the West Saxon conquest of the Danelaw and consequent West Saxon unification of England under Alfred's immediate descendants. Welsh submissions followed those momentous Anglo-Danish events of the tenth century; they did not drive them. It is unsafe to use the doubtful testimony of the *Life* of King Alfred as evidence for a Welsh coalition organised by Alfred, which in turn helped him in his struggle with the Danes. The opposite was, in fact, the case. Welsh independence was more secure while Wessex was kept busy with a dangerous Danish enemy. As the power of Wessex grew *vis-à-vis* the Danes, a Welsh bard in his poem *Armes Prydein* read the signs of the times correctly, and begged his countrymen to join a Norse alliance in order to keep either Athelstan or his successor and brother, Edmund, in their place.[132] That alliance failed, and the submission of Welsh rulers to Wessex was a continuing and inevitable consequence. For as the English – i.e. West Saxon – frontier was pushed relentlessly northwards through the Danelaw, and as Mercia, too, became subsumed into the new English realm, it was inevitable that Mercia's old enemies, the Welsh, should be forced to respond to West Saxon claims of overlordship. Those were the political realities of the time of Alfred's grandsons and great-grandsons of the later tenth century. All of that was far into the future, when in the late ninth century, Alfred was fighting for his life and for the survival of Wessex. We search in vain to find royal Welsh witnesses to the charters of King Alfred, and not even industrious forgers of a later age unearthed names of Welsh witnesses from now lost genuine documents, to add to their own bogus lists.

One piece of information which the *Life* of Alfred provided in the Welsh chapter has been the subject of close scrutiny. He tells us that Hyfaidd, along with 'all the inhabitants of the kingdom of Dyfed, driven by the might of the six sons of Rhodri, had subjected himself to [Alfred's] royal overlordship'. Stevenson expressed some disquiet in 1904 that the reference by Alfred's biographer to 'the six sons of Rhodri Mawr' did not tally with information available from other sources, which seemed to identify only four sons.[133] Dumville's investigation into the number of Rhodri's sons yielded little comfort to those who had put their faith in the Genuine Asser. Stevenson's four sons of Rhodri were those mentioned in the *Annales Cambriae* – one of whom, Gwriad, was slain by the Saxons (*a Saxonibus*) in 877. Yet, the time when these sons were supposed to have submitted to Alfred must, on

Dumville's own ruling, have been between 878, after Alfred had overcome Guthrum, and 893, the year in which 'Asser' was supposed to have been writing.[134] With Gwriad already dead, that left only three sons who were politically active in contemporary Welsh records. Matters become yet further complicated when we turn to thirteenth- and fourteenth-century genealogical collections, of which one mentions seven sons of Rhodri and another gives us eight.[135] When all the sons mentioned in these later medieval genealogical tracts are added up, we arrive at a total of ten sons in all. Dumville was compelled in the face of these difficulties to abandon altogether the notion of the Parker-Cotton reading of 'Six sons of Rhodri', on the grounds that the text at this point was corrupt. In spite of Dumville's admission that 'Here Stevenson's text [of the *Life* of Alfred] depends directly on no witness earlier in date than the second half of the sixteenth century',[136] this did not deter him from inventing 'the best available approximation to Asser's [*sic*] words'.[137] Without any alternative readings to guide him – from Byrhtferth's version of Alfred's *Life* in the *Historia Regum*, from the East Anglian Chronicle or from John of Worcester – Dumville amended Parker's text of *sex filiorum Rotri vi compulsus* ('driven by [fear of] the might of the six sons of Rhodri') to read: *filiorum Rotri vi compulsus* ('driven by the might of the sons of Rhodri').[138] Dumville could then declare that 'Rhodri's six sons may thus be banished by some quick strokes of the editorial pen',[139] and by a subjective route, we arrive at a 'reconstructed text' of the *Life* of King Alfred. Dumville's reconstruction – admitted to be founded on supposition[140] and conjecture[141] – goes against what little evidence we have of the original manuscript reading. The Early Modern edition of the *Life* of Alfred, together with the surviving sixteenth-century transcripts, all read: *sex filiorum* for the 'six sons' of Rhodri. Wise reported *sex* to have been the reading of the lost Cotton manuscript.[142] The alteration of Parker's *sex filiorum Rotri vi compulsus* to reconstruct a supposed original *ui filiorum Rotri compulsus* requires that two changes rather than one, were made to the original manuscript reading.[143] But why should Parker be blamed for inventing the 'six sons of Rhodri'? It would seem that in the absence of other medieval textual readings from this section of the *Life* of Alfred, any uncomfortable aspects of this chaotic text can be conveniently blamed on a sixteenth-century archbishop.

Even if we were to abandon the notion of the elusive 'six' sons of Rhodri in this passage in the *Life*, we are still left with serious historical anomalies in its account of late ninth-century Welsh politics and political geography. The *Annales Cambriae* record that in 895, 'Anarawd came with the English (*cum Anglis*) to lay waste Ceredigion and Ystrad Tywi'.[144] By this time – supposedly two years after 'Asser' had written – Anarawd ap Rhodri and his brothers had abandoned their hostility against the south Welsh kingdoms and had, supposedly, submitted to King Alfred in person. What was the sense, therefore, in this

Alfredian ally attacking Alfred's other and older allies in Ceredigion and Ystrad Tywi? Dumville offered the suggestion that Anarawd 'was enjoying a military benefit of the new alliance' with Alfred. But Anarawd and his brothers already controlled all of North Wales from Anglesey to the far south of Ceredigion and Powys. Alfred was a wise enough king to have known that if he supported Anarawd in his conquests further south in Wales (even if, say, Ceredigion had rebelled against Alfred), it would have been foolish to allow Anarawd to dominate the whole of Wales from the inaccessible north. By Dumville's own reckoning, Anarawd's attack on Ystrad Tywi in 895 was directed against territory which the author of the *Life* of Alfred had declared had 'belonged to King Alfred for a long time before'.[145] Dumville was, understandably, confused by the account in the *Life* of Alfred of things in Wales during the period 878 to 893. If, as its author claimed, the sons of Rhodri – be they three, four, six, seven, eight or ten – had been harrying Dyfed and putting such pressure on its king, Hyfaidd, to rush into an alliance with Alfred, then why as late as 895 were Rhodri's sons still only trying to control Ceredigion – a kingdom which lay between them and Dyfed? A perplexed Dumville asked: 'Had the Scandinavians taken control?' The only conclusion we can agree with from Dumville's investigation is that 'our knowledge of the political structure of Wales in the year around 900 is lamentably deficient' and that being so, we should refrain from inventing a history for a country that is based on the evidence of a text which elsewhere can be shown to be riddled with inconsistency, invention and – sometimes – deceit. Anarawd's English allies in 895 were more likely to have been Mercian than West Saxon. We know little or nothing of Scandinavian involvement in local Welsh politics, but we may assume that as in remoter parts of Ireland, transitory coastal Viking settlers took sides in inter-tribal wars, without ever being able to dominate any one faction or any one territorial kingdom.[146] There is no evidence whatever – apart from the *Life* of Alfred – to suggest that Alfred ever enjoyed an overlordship over the northern Welsh kingdoms of Gwynedd or Powys, and it is highly unlikely that either he or his son, Edward, ever even considered that South Wales 'belonged' to the West Saxon dynasty in any meaningful sense.

Among the many unjustified assumptions found in the literature on King Alfred that have eventually been firmed up into 'facts', is the belief that the *Life* of the king was not only written by a Welshman, but that it was also intended for a Welsh readership. What began with Whitelock's tentative support for Schütt's thesis of a Welsh readership ('I think that he had in part Welsh readers in mind')[147] developed later on – on no further evidence – into a definite statement by the Penguin translators of King Alfred's *Life* that its author's provision of the Welsh forms of eleven English names was 'a sure sign that he was writing with a Welsh audience in mind'.[148] Elsewhere, these same commentators claimed:

It is evident that the *Life of King Alfred* was written principally for the benefit of readers (and listeners) in Wales.[149]

We may well ask what benefit Welsh 'listeners' would have derived from a garbled translation of the Anglo-Saxon Chronicle, written, on its editors' own admission, in a bombastic and atrociously convoluted Latin which defies the scrutiny of modern scholarship. We might ask, too, what Welsh listeners – or indeed the few Welsh 'readers' who were capable of reading Latin – would have made of the neologisms, Grecisms and archaic Latin words deliberately inserted in the text to confuse and to impress the most erudite scholars. As for Welsh princes, they had other and infinitely superior forms of literary entertainment to while away evenings in their halls, rather than being assailed with a garbled story in unintelligible Latin of a Welsh monk who had gone over to the hated Saxons to be rewarded with pots and pans in Congresbury and Banwell. Welsh princes were very unlikely to warm to a West Saxon tale of how in 853 King Alfred's father, Æthelwulf,

> assembled an army and went with King Burgred [of Mercia] to Wales, where immediately on entry he devastated that race and reduced it to Burgred's authority.[150]

One can only hope for the sake of the personal safety of the reader of the *Life* of Alfred, that his sentence *gentem illam devastans, dominio Burgredi subdit* was either lost on an uncomprehending audience, or else drowned out in derision along the benches of the halls in Glywysing and Gwent. There is little or nothing in the *Life* of King Alfred which was either written for, or of interest to, a Welsh audience – apart from the material in Chapter 80 which was borrowed from a Welsh source. There was, on the other hand, plenty in the *Life* which might have given offence. There may have been little in the *Life* which was of interest even to the English warrior aristocracy of the later Anglo-Saxon era, since that work of hagiographical fiction portraying a pious and neurotic king was essentially the product of early eleventh-century English monastic reformers who were experimenting with a genre which had been brought to them from Fleury and from elsewhere in Francia.

The unchallenged assumption that the *Life* of Alfred was essentially Welsh in origin has given rise to a penumbra of unscholarly comments on this text, which have served only to enmesh the subject yet further in a tangle of half-truths. Take, for instance, the author's description of Alfred fighting 'like a wild boar' (*aprino more*) against the Danes at Ashdown.[151] Williams,[152] followed by Keynes and Lapidge,[153] believed that this simile was inspired by the vocabulary of early Welsh poetry where the word 'boar' is synonymous with brave warrior. But the early medieval Welsh – and indeed Celtic peoples generally – did not possess a monopoly on boar similes. The valour of the wild boar provided clichés for a wide variety of warrior societies throughout the Middle Ages. Boar-crested helmets are described in *Beowulf*, and an actual specimen of just such a seventh-century Anglo-Saxon helmet from Benty Grange in Derbyshire may be seen in the Sheffield City Museum.[154] When Geoffrey le Baker referred to Edward, the Black Prince, as 'the boar of Cornwall' (*aper Cornubiensis*) in his account of the campaign at Poitiers in 1356,[155] was he also alluding to the valour of a Celtic boar? And when Geoffrey changed his metaphor a few lines further on to describe how 'the prince of Wales charged into the enemy with the wild courage of a lion',[156] was he then abandoning his encoded Celtic imagery and moving on to some Plantagenet motif? It is only when scholars have fallen prey to the Welshness of the *Life* of Alfred that Celtic boars are seen to emerge from the undergrowth of its sub-text.

# 3
# The Author's Latin Style

We begin with the *Life* of Count Gerald of Aurillac in the French Auvergne. Gerald was almost the exact contemporary of King Alfred. He was born in 855 and died, most probably, on 13 October 909 – coincidentally in the same year as the historical Bishop Asser of Sherborne. His *Life*, written by Odo, Abbot of Cluny, in *c*. 940, is a near-contemporary work compiled by one of the founding fathers of the Cluniac monastic reform movement. Its purpose was to demonstrate not only the sanctity of Gerald, but to show to monks and recalcitrant canons in Francia that even high-born laymen were capable of achieving great sanctity while immersed in worldly preoccupations. Hagiographical this work may be, but its author interviewed several witnesses who had personal knowledge of Count Gerald, some of whom were monks and some were aristocratic laymen. It tells an idealised tale of a saintly magnate of Aquitaine who grew up with a sweetness and modesty of mind, but whose parents neglected his education – to the extent that in Gerald's case he was only allowed to study the Psalter.[1] It was most likely here, in this account of Gerald's early education, that Alfred's biographer first hit on the notion that Alfred's education had also been neglected by his parents (Chapter 22) and yet the young Alfred is shown mastering the psalms and Divine Office (Chapter 24). Like Alfred, too, Gerald's adolescence was spent in aristocratic pursuits with his hunting dogs, archery and falcons. Gerald was plagued by sickness in early youth and just as Alfred was tormented by piles, so too Gerald was covered by pustules (*pustulis*) or boils which rendered him unsuited to worldly affairs and enabled him to return to study. He mastered Gregorian chant and grammar, and like Alfred he performed the Divine Office and prayed in chapel alone at night. Gerald recited the psalms and learnt a whole series of the Scriptures which put his contemporary 'clerical smatterers' to shame.[2] Like Alfred, too, Gerald struggled to preserve his chastity and after a partial succumbing to temptation he was stricken with blindness from a cataract for more than a year. Just as Alfred prayed for a disease which 'would not be outwardly visible on his body', so as to render him useless for public office, so too the long-suffering Count Gerald had his blindness concealed 'with the greatest care' by his followers 'from the peering eyes of strangers'. Gerald succeeded to his father's office but accepted his responsibilities as a reluctant ruler, torn by the tensions between worldly rule and the cultivation of the inner life.[3] So too the saintly Alfred, although allegedly far better qualified for kingship than his older brothers, did, according to his hagiographer, come eventually to rule 'almost unwillingly'.[4] Alfred was also, exactly like Gerald, beset by tensions caused by the demands of his worldly office – tensions which were in conflict with the king's natural desire for study and contemplation.[5]

Gerald, like Alfred, was a conscientious judge who upheld the cause of the poor and the weak, and who fasted before presiding over his law court,[6] and although he did not himself write or publish works of learning, he was portrayed none the less as a great scholarly ruler. Like King Alfred, Count Gerald had works read aloud to him, and he divided his time between prayer and contemplation on the one hand, and a busy life of a secular lord and administrator on the other. Gerald's hall was transformed into a seminar where meals were taken listening to readings or to commentaries on readings by those so qualified in learning. Like Alfred, Gerald carefully planned the building of a model monastery which he found difficult to staff with suitably spiritually-minded monks, and like Alfred, he carefully provided for the church and the poor during his life and in his *will*. Gerald was a lover of pilgrimage journeying to Tours and to Limoges, and like Alfred he visited distant Rome.[7] For Professor Lapidge, who is convinced only by evidence of direct textual borrowing, such parallel motifs are dismissed with a contempt worthy of arguments which rely on the shared initial 'M' in Macedon and Monmouth.[8] But a detailed study of Odo's *Life* of Gerald suggests that it did indeed provide Alfred's biographer with material for the life of that English king. While Carolingian royal biographies had an obvious influence on Alfred's biographer, nevertheless Alfred's *vita* was essentially hagiographical. As such, the *Life* of Alfred belongs to a genre which is spiritual rather than secular, and it displays few of those pretensions to Roman imperialism which are the hallmark of its Carolingian counterparts. Gerald's tenth-century *Life* provided an obvious model for a monastic biographer who wished to invest Alfred with the saintly qualities of royal discipleship. For Gerald, although a saint, was remarkable also for being, like Alfred, a secular lord. Not only did the overall picture of the sickly and saintly scholarly ruler provide what may be described as the major 'original contribution' to the *Life* of Alfred, but numerous details in the *Life* of Count Gerald have been replicated in Alfred's *Life*. We have already encountered the same rare motifs in both works, such as that of the ruler who risked capture or death at the hands of his attacking enemies rather than abandon his presence at Mass during the attack. There are many other detailed points of contact between these two works.

Odo who wrote the *Life* of Gerald had been abbot, first of Baume and later of Cluny in Burgundy. As second abbot of Cluny he was the successor of Berno (910–26) who, under the auspices of Duke William of Aquitaine, began the whole reforming process of Frankish monasteries.[9] The most important monastery near Cluny, which Odo reformed and ruled as abbot, was Fleury on the Loire. Fleury boasted of being the custodian of the relics of St. Benedict of Monte Cassino, the father of western monasticism – a fact alluded to by Byrhtferth in his Northumbrian Chronicle.[10] Later in the tenth century, Fleury's monastic school was ruled by Abbo, one of the finest scholars of his day. With Fleury and its brilliant scholar, Abbo, we arrive at the connection between the *Lives* of Count Gerald of Aurillac and his biographer, Odo of Cluny on the one hand, and the English environment which produced the *Life* of King Alfred on the other. England's connection with the house of Fleury went back into the second quarter of the tenth century in the person of Archbishop Oda of Canterbury (941–58). Oda, perhaps independently of St. Dunstan, was one of the first ecclesiastical reformers in tenth-century England who laid the foundations not only of monastic reform but of the rebuilding of an English Church, badly mauled by the Viking wars of the previous century. He went to Francia in 936 as one of Athelstan's ambassadors to Hugh, Duke of the Franks, and it was at Fleury, probably in 936, that Oda (then Bishop of Ramsbury) took his vows of obedience to the Rule of St. Benedict. In 952 Oda sent his nephew, Oswald, to study at Fleury for six years and that same Oswald was later to become Bishop of Worcester (961) and eventually Archbishop of York (971).[11] In August 968, Bishop Oswald of Worcester raised the battle-standard of the *milites Dei* in the Danelaw with his founding or refounding of the monastery of Ramsey in Huntingdonshire with the help of his friend and patron, Ealdorman Æthelwine of East Anglia.[12] The founding of Ramsey was one of the major turning points in early English religious and cultural history. Neither Canterbury, York nor Winchester could rival this isolated monastic settlement in its educational achievement. Ramsey, more than any other centre, was responsible for the consolidation and dissemination of a distinctly English scholarly and monastic culture which was to endure the second wave of Danish conquest under Cnut, and whose legacy was to survive the Norman Conquest as well.[13]

Not long after the founding of Ramsey, its role as a leading centre of scholarship and Latin learning in England was assured by the arrival of Abbo from Fleury who spent two years there from *c.* 985 to 987.[14] Abbo was already an established scholar by the time he arrived at Ramsey, having studied at Rheims and at Paris and being by now head of the monastic school at Fleury. While at Ramsey, Abbo compiled works on astronomy, a poem on Ramsey and a treatise on grammar. More significantly, he composed the *Passio* or *Passion* of the saint and king, Edmund of East Anglia – a contemporary of King Alfred – who had been slain by the Danes in 869. Personal edification was not the sole function of this production. Abbo's biography of King Edmund – compiled with only a kernel of historical material – was designed to show would-be English hagiographers how spiritual biography could be used as a tool to further the aims of ecclesiastical reformers. The *Passion* of St. Edmund was to provide inspiration for a much more comprehensive biographical collection designed to provide an ideology and a sense of purpose to the entire programme of monastic and spiritual regeneration. As that movement entered on its secondary phase, when the age of its saintly founders – Oda, Dunstan, Æthelwold and Oswald – was past, Abbo's *Passion* of St. Edmund was joined by the *Lives* of St. Dunstan, St. Æthelwold and St. Oswald, as well as *Lives* of earlier figures which were forged or invented at this time, as part of a great literary drive to shore up the spiritual and cultural recovery of the Anglo-Saxon soul in the aftermath of the Viking onslaught. One of those inventions was Byrhtferth of Ramsey's *Life* of St. Ecgwine – the biography of a shadowy early eighth-century Bishop of Worcester. Another such bogus production was the *Life* of King Alfred. And closely associated with the *Life* of Alfred was yet another saintly biography from Byrhtferth's hand – that of Alfred's friend and supposed relative, Neot. St. Neot's relics had been taken from Cornwall to be housed at a new monastery with close Ramsey connections, which enjoyed the patronage of Ramsey's protector, Ealdorman Æthelwine. St. Neot could not be compared in stature with the reforming bishops Oswald or Æthelwold, but his saintly bones, purloined from the conquered Cornishmen, more than compensated for the obscurity of Neot when in life. A Ramsey biography for St. Neot helped to bridge the credibility gap between the unknown Cornish saint hijacked by West Saxon conquerors, and the new upstart foundation in East Anglia which bore his name. A spurious connection with King Alfred, alluded to in Alfred's *Life* and elaborated upon in the *Life* of Neot, helped to underline crucial West Saxon royal support for the new monastic foundations in the Ramsey sphere of influence.

Abbo of Fleury's time at Ramsey constitutes a milestone in the history of Anglo-Latin biography and hagiography. For Abbo's pupil, Byrhtferth of Ramsey, was to follow his Frankish master's lead and make biography a characteristic genre of the second generation of monastic reformers in late tenth- and early eleventh-century England. Byrhtferth of Ramsey is known for his mathematical and astronomical work in his *Manual* or *Enchiridion* which was intended as a handbook to the *Computus*, written partly in Latin and partly in English.[15] He was identified long ago by Crawford as the author of the *Life* of St. Oswald who founded Byrhtferth's house at Ramsey and of whom Byrhtferth had personal knowledge.[16] Lapidge first identified Byrhtferth as the author of the *Life* of St. Ecgwine, the third bishop of Worcester, who ruled that diocese in the early eighth century and who was supposed to have founded the monastery of Evesham.[17] Hart and Lapidge independently demonstrated that the Northumbrian Chronicle, which makes up the first five sections in the *Historia Regum* attributed to Symeon of Durham, was also compiled by Byrhtferth of Ramsey.[18] That work contains a summary of the *Life* of King Alfred. Hart (again endorsed by Lapidge) has identified Byrhtferth's key role in the compilation of tenth-century sections of the Worcester Latin Chronicle, and Hart has made a convincing case for Byrhtferth as the compiler of the East Anglian Chronicle – both works also containing abridged, but nevertheless extensive versions of King Alfred's *Life*. The greatest Frankish influence on Byrhtferth's career must have been that of his teacher, Abbo. Byrhtferth inherited from Abbo his obsession with elementary mathematics, astronomy and natural science generally. But he also absorbed a passion for hagiography and biography which must have been fired by Byrhtferth's own vivid historical imagination. That historical imagination was to induce Byrhtferth to overstep the bounds of historical writing and take on, in the case of the *Life* of Ecgwine, the role of a forger. It also inspired in Byrhtferth an all-pervading interest in the career of King Alfred, not only leading to his compilation of the *Life* of that king and the related *Life* of Neot, but also to his use of abridged versions of Alfred's *Life* in a whole series of Latin chronicles which formed part of Byrhtferth's monumental programme of annalistic compilation in early eleventh-century England.

So many key people at Ramsey had had personal contacts with Fleury or had been trained there as monks and scholars, that Byrhtferth, his contemporaries and pupils, must have had access not only to Frankish tutors, but also to the many books which those tutors had brought as essential equipment in their baggage. Books and learning were at the heart of Cluniac and related reform movements. John of Salerno informs us that St. Odo of Cluny took 100 volumes from the library of the monastery of Tours to help equip the monastic school at Baume in Burgundy.[19] St. Oswald is said to have presented books to Ramsey,[20] and books taken by Fleury monks to Ramsey could have included not only Einhard's *Life* of Charlemagne and the *Life* of Alcuin, which were used by the author of Alfred's *Life*, but also the writings of Odo of Cluny, and particularly Odo's biography of the saintly Count Gerald of Aurillac and perhaps John of Salerno's *Life* of Abbot Odo. For Odo of Cluny, even more than the founding abbot, Berno, was viewed by his successors as the instigator and apostle of Monastic Reform, and it was Odo rather than Berno who had taken Fleury in hand, and given it back its monastic way of life.[21] Odo's literary works must have been dear to Abbo of Fleury, and they provided him with models for the task ahead in England – namely the writing up of the *Lives* of those English holy men and robust Christian kings, which in their turn would provide an inspiration to the disciples of Monastic Reform among the Anglo-Saxons. It is incumbent on Latinists to take the historical background to this debate into account, for Anglo-Frankish cultural links in the late tenth century cannot be evaluated solely on the basis of a crude manuscript count which is itself dependent on cultural upheavals which destroyed so much evidence from those same societies in the sixteenth and late eighteenth centuries.[22]

Odo of Cluny is of interest not only for his sanctity and role as a reformer. He was also the exponent of a newly developing style of Latin writing – a style with roots in the Late Antique and Early Medieval past, but one which developed its own abstruse qualities in early tenth-century Francia. The main features of this hermeneutic style were 'the ostentatious parade of unusual, often very arcane and apparently learned vocabulary'.[23] The characteristic hallmarks of that vocabulary were archaisms – even by the standards of classical writers, neologisms or made-up words, and loan-words – especially words culled from Greek lexicons or Greek glossaries. Archbishop Oda of Canterbury, who may well have had personal knowledge of Odo of Cluny – and who certainly studied with members of his community – was a leading practitioner of the hermeneutic style of Latin in mid-tenth-century England,[24] while St. Oswald (the founder of Ramsey) who had studied for even longer at Fleury must also have known and practised this style of writing. Ramsey, from the time of Abbo of Fleury's teaching there, had become the major centre of the hermeneutic school of Latinists in England, as the writings of its star performer, Byrhtferth, amply demonstrate.

If the *Life* of King Alfred were written in a late tenth- or early eleventh-century Ramsey milieu, we should expect that work to contain Frankish loan-words of that time, and also to exhibit many, if not all, the characteristics of the hermeneutic style. This can indeed be shown to have been the case. Stevenson itemised some ten or so distinctively Frankish words in the *Life* of King Alfred which he considered to have been borrowed by the historical Bishop Asser either through his own personal contact with Francia or through 'foreign clerks in Alfred's service' – no doubt in Stevenson's mind, the elusive Grimbald and John, whose apocryphal careers have caused so much distortion in the historiography of ninth-century England.[25] Remarkably, Stevenson suggested that three of the Frankish borrowings in the *Life* of Alfred – *indiculus* ('letter'), *gronnosa* ('marshy, swampy'), and *famina* ('words, conversation') were tenth-century Frankish borrowings into Anglo-Latin writings – in spite of the fact that such an admission argued against his own sustained thesis for a ninth-century date for the *Life* of Alfred.[26] Furthermore, Stevenson believed that the Frankish-Latin *gronna* and *gronnosa* had been imported from the Fleury school of writers – the same which enjoyed such influence in late tenth-century Ramsey.[27] And in the case of *famina* Stevenson

observed that although this word had been used by Aldhelm, its most prevalent English context was the late tenth century 'when it came into use again
… with other Frankish-Latin words'.[28] The implication must be that, in
Stevenson's view, there was no continuity of use in regard to such a word by
English writers of Latin, and therefore if the word were indeed reintroduced
in the tenth century, we ought not to expect to find it in genuine ninth-
century texts. *Famen* occurs in a charter of King Edgar for AD 964; and in
Frithegod's *Life* of St. Wilfrid. It also appears in the *B* Life of St. Dunstan, in
the *Chronicle* of Æthelweard, and in the *B* author's letter to Archbishop
Æthelgar of Canterbury.[29] These are mostly the works of late tenth- or early
eleventh-century writers. Frithegod, who was the earliest of this group of
authors, was the disciple of Archbishop Oda of Canterbury, and was steeped
in the hermeneutic style of tenth-century Anglo-Latin.[30] The *B* author of
Dunstan's *Life*, who wrote *c.* AD 1000, was also a leading exponent of the
hermeneutic style.[31] *Famen* was not only a Frankish borrowing or reintroduc-
tion into English tenth-century Latin, but like the adverb *oppido* ('very much,
exceedingly') it was also an archaism in the text of the *Life* of Alfred. That
same archaism, *oppido*, appears also in Byrhtferth's *Life* of St. Oswald.[32]

The evidence from English charters is strongly against any argument for
continuity between earlier so-called hisperic forms of Anglo-Latin usage and
the hermeneutic style proper, of later tenth-century England.[33] Clearly,
Alfred's *Life* belongs to a different genre from that of Anglo-Latin charters, but
when viewed against the Latin usage of charters, the *Life* of Alfred would be
conspicuously out of place in a ninth-century English context, and entirely at
home in a late tenth- or early eleventh-century English environment. To argue
otherwise demands an explanation for why a work of such profound significance as the *Life* of Alfred had so little stylistic influence on late ninth- and
early tenth-century Anglo-Latin writing – including charters – and why its
identical Latin style was reintroduced into England at the end of the tenth
century. For were it not for their insistence on linking Alfred's *Life* to the
historical Asser, Anglo-Latin scholars from Stevenson onwards would, by their
own definition, have instinctively consigned that work, on textual grounds, to
the turn of the millennium rather than to the later part of the ninth century.

The words *castellum* ('castle or fort'); *fasellus* (or *vasselus*) and *satelles* for
'thegn', and the title *senior* (Modern French *Seigneur*) for 'lord' – all of which
appear in the *Life* of King Alfred – are not only Frankish borrowings, but these
words are all found in St. Odo's *Life* of Count Gerald of Aurillac. *Satellites*,
*seniores* and *castellum* also occur in Byrhtferth of Ramsey's *Life* of St. Oswald.
And while Campbell rightly argued[34] that such words are found in the ninth
century in their native Carolingian context, I contend, nevertheless, that it is
as tenth-century Frankish borrowings we encounter them in an English
setting. Fleury is acknowledged by Stevenson, Crawford and subsequent

scholars to have provided a major source of influence for the introduction of the hermeneutic style of Latin writing into late tenth-century England.[35] One of the characteristics of that convoluted style was the inevitable inclusion of tenth-century Frankish vocabulary. Frankish loan-words in the *Life* of Alfred, therefore, fit perfectly within a late tenth-century Ramsey context and do not of themselves require any special pleading involving premature transmission of such vocabulary by way of Frankish clerks at Alfred's court. Nor need we speculate on the possibility of the historical Asser having studied in Francia in an earlier life, for which there is not a shred of evidence apart from the Frankish literary and linguistic influence within the *Life* of Alfred.[36] It is not impossible that King Alfred's clerks were influenced by contemporary Frankish Latin. Alfred's grandfather, Egbert, had been a refugee at the Carolingian court before becoming king of the West Saxons, and his father, King Æthelwulf, employed a Frankish clerk as one of his secretaries,[37] and was himself married to Judith, daughter of Charles the Bald. But King Alfred and his scholarly circle were committed to translation into the vernacular – the very opposite to the cultivation of arcane Latin so evident both in the *Life* of Alfred and in late tenth-century writers in Anglo-Latin. Indeed, King Alfred was clearly against obscurantism of any kind, and he himself gives as the *raison d'être* for his translation programme 'that we should turn into the language that we can all understand certain books which are the most necessary for all men to know'. Is it credible, or even possible, that such a king – himself a master of communication in the vernacular – should have allowed his own biography to be written in a disorganised and bombastic style of difficult Latin, exuding what Keynes and Lapidge have admitted to be a 'baroque flavour',[38] and which Stevenson described as a 'highly rhetorical' display of 'recondite words' whose author's 'meaning is obscured by a cloud of verbiage'?[39]

Unreal distinctions can be made by Latinists between what they see as a definitive hermeneutic Anglo-Latin style of the late tenth century and earlier English Latin works based on a style of Aldhelmian prose. Because the late tenth-century hermeneutic school of English writers included keen students and admirers of Aldhelm, it is often difficult to decide on stylistic evidence alone, whether a work such as the *Life* of Alfred belongs to the ninth century or to the late tenth or early eleventh. Since the later hermeneutic style in England owed so much to Frankish influence, coming by way of monastic reform, then clearly evidence for Frankish borrowings in vocabulary provides one of the major indicators for lateness of date of an Anglo-Latin text. Late tenth-century Anglo-Latin writers cultivated a style involving repetitive, esoteric, if not positively arcane vocabulary, embedded in a convoluted syntax. That style took its inspiration from two distinct sources – the one indigenous and tracing its origins back ultimately to Aldhelm and his school, the other dependent on powerful and novel Frankish influences, most notably from writers at Fleury as they were known and admired at Ramsey in the late tenth century. The indigenous or Aldhelmian strain was not necessarily part of a continuous tradition. Any late tenth-century writer at Winchester, Canterbury, Ramsey or elsewhere, was capable of reading Aldhelm in the original and incorporating his style into his own writings, without being dependent on intermediaries in any way. We know that Byrhtferth and the late tenth-century Anglo-Latin school were fully conversant with Aldhelm's works.[40] It is rather the case, that the two late tenth-century hermeneutic streams – Frankish and English – were inextricably related, in that Frankish scholarly and literary influences on late tenth-century England, encouraged Anglo-Latin writers to draw on their own earlier arcane Aldhelmian tradition. But the impetus was essentially Frankish, stemming from the movement for monastic reform. The English scholarly reversion to the Latin of Aldhelm may not have been driven so much by a desire to impress stylistically as to imitate Frankish models which were associated in the minds of scholarly English monks with the reforming principles of their Frankish mentors at Fleury and elsewhere. The great majority, if not indeed all the exponents of the Frankish hermeneutic style in England, were themselves steeped in the ideals of monastic reform. Given the indigenous and ongoing Aldhelmian element, therefore, which pervades the earlier and later stages of the English hermeneutic tradition, it is the presence of Frankish-Latin borrowings in Anglo-Latin texts such as the *Life* of King Alfred that provides us with crucial evidence to indicate a date of composition later than the middle of the tenth century.[41]

Campbell's grasp of the history of Anglo-Saxon Latinity is still unrivalled for its clarity and its validity. He pointed to two parallel and contemporaneous strains of Anglo-Saxon Latinity, divided into two chronological phases. The strains were classical and hermeneutic, and they spanned an earlier phase which was pre-Viking, or up to *c.* AD 800, and a later which was post-Viking from *c.* 930 onwards.[42] In the earliest phase, Campbell pointed to Bede as an example of the classical style, and to Aldhelm for the hermeneutic, while for the post-Viking period, he saw Ælfric's *Life* of Æthelwold in the classical tradition and the *Life* of Oswald (by Byrhtferth of Ramsey) in the hermeneutic. An essential element in Campbell's view of the history of Anglo-Latin writing was the hiatus caused 'by the barren years of the Danish wars'.[43] It is into this hiatus that those who hold to the Genuine Asser thesis would place the *Life* of King Alfred. But by so doing, they make a work which, as we shall see, exhibits the closest ties to late tenth- and early eleventh-century Anglo-Latin writing, stand alone and without context in a period otherwise renowned for its emphasis on the vernacular.[44] The ninth-century hiatus identified by Campbell was real, and it was not confined exclusively to linguistic or literary matters, for it was rather the symptom of a much greater phenomenon.

The ninth-century Viking wars had accelerated the decline of monasticism – not to speak of the annihilation of many great English monasteries – thereby creating a need for reconstruction at the end of the tenth century. That decline and revival of monasticism is reflected in the development of Anglo-Latin literature. The argument relating to the date of Alfred's *Life* is exacerbated by the fact that the ninth century presents us with a hiatus in Latin works in England – the Alfredian renaissance after all being a vernacular phenomenon. Since we know even less about ninth-century Latin in Wales than we do about middle and late ninth-century Anglo-Latin texts, the claim that the biographer of King Alfred was indeed the historical Welsh Bishop Asser, is incapable of proof on textual grounds. This is so, because we have no other substantial text to compare it with. Far from prompting caution in linguistic circles, this conspicuous lack of evidence has not deterred a century of commentators from holding the view that, on stylistic grounds, the *Life* of Alfred was indeed written by Asser, and from pointing to this supposedly unique work to demonstrate, by circular argument, the quality of Latin in ninth-century Wales and England. So, for instance, Keynes and Lapidge decided that because the Old Latin version of the bible was quoted twice by the author, and because the author was clearly the historical Asser, then all this indicated 'that St. David's (where Asser was supposedly trained) was a cultural backwater'.[45] But if the historical Bishop Asser really had been invited to lead a team of scholars at King Alfred's court, it is difficult to understand how such a shrewd and knowledgeable king as Alfred clearly was, would ever have summoned a cleric from a Welsh backwater.[46]

The *Life* of Alfred contains the topos of Alfred who, like the busy bee, dutifully crammed his little handbook with an anthology of exegetical class-studies – 'those flowers which had been gathered from various masters'. We note the remarkable name which the author chose to call the king's notebook:

> This book he used to call his *Enchiridion*, that is 'hand book' (*Quem enchiridion suum, id est manualem librum, nominari voluit*).[47]

This exceedingly rare word in Anglo-Latin texts is borrowed from the Greek (τὸ ἐγχειρίδιον) meaning 'handbook', but it is, remarkably, the very same Greek word used by Byrhtferth of Ramsey to describe his *Manual*:

> We have set down in this *Enchiridion*, that is *manualis* in Latin, and *handboc* in English (*enchiridion, þæt ys manualis on Lyden 7 handboc on Englisc*), many things about the computus, because we wished that young men should be able the more easily to understand the Latin and speak with greater freedom to old priests about these things.[48]

The Greek word and its gloss reveal an intimate connection between the text of Byrhtferth's *Manual* and that of the *Life* of Alfred. There is nothing remarkable in this, since we now know that Byrhtferth as the summariser of the *Life* of King Alfred in his Northumbrian Chronicle, the East Anglian Chronicle and the Worcester Latin Chronicle clearly had access to the text of Alfred's *Life*. Lapidge was willing to speculate that Byrhtferth may have borrowed the idea of the *Enchiridion* for his *Manual* from King Alfred's *Life*.[49] But we must now be prepared to envisage the possibility of the borrowing in the other direction. The author of Alfred's *Life* informs us that it was not Bishop Asser, but rather King Alfred himself who wished his class-book to be called *Enchiridion*. There is no evidence whatever to suggest that King Alfred knew any Greek or that he had access to, or an interest in, Greek lexicography. Although his biographer did have access to Einhard, who made extravagant claims for Charlemagne's knowledge of Greek, he was not tempted to transfer those claims to King Alfred. Knowledge of Greek flourished among a select band of Carolingian scholars in the later ninth century, led by the Irishman John Scotus Eriugena, who died *c.* 877. Lecture notes explaining Eriugena's Greek words and phrases subsequently provided pedantic Frankish writers with poorly understood Greek vocabulary, with which they embroidered their ostentatious Latin prose.[50] Those English writers who, in imitation of their Frankish masters, posed as *savants* of Greek, flourished not in the ninth, but rather – as Lapidge pointed out[51] – in the second half of the tenth century. The use of Greek words, culled from lexicons, accompanied the bombastic Latin hermeneutic style which first made its appearance in the charters of King Athelstan in the 930s and which came to full bloom in the late tenth century, and of which Byrhtferth of Ramsey was the prime exponent. If we concede – as we must – that the naming of King Alfred's handbook and of Byrhtferth's *Manual* are a related phenomenon, and if we bear in mind that the invention of Alfred's handbook was inspired by Einhard's account of Charlemagne's 'writing-tablets and notebooks' (*tabulasque et codicellos*),[52] it is possible that the title *Enchiridion* was invented not by King Alfred, nor even by the historical Bishop Asser, but by Byrhtferth of Ramsey or one of his circle. These Ramsey writers were otherwise known to be avid collectors of abstruse Greek vocabulary, and in the case of Byrhtferth, made use of this very Greek term in his own writings.

The significant *enchiridion* does not stand alone as a Greek borrowing in the text of King Alfred's *Life*. We also find *graphium* ('charter' or 'document') in Chapter 11, *eulogii* ('Scriptural text') in Chapter 91, and *zizania* ('darnel weed') in Chapter 95. These Greek borrowings in the *Life* of Alfred may not compare in their frequency with those in some of Byrhtferth's other works, but there are reasons why this should be so. The great bulk of the text of the *Life* of Alfred – unlike Byrhtferth's *Life* of St. Oswald or his *Life* of St. Ecgwine

– followed a close translation of the Anglo-Saxon Chronicle which left little scope for experimentation with vocabulary. Nor did the *Life* of a king present its author with the same scope for the borrowing of technical terms from the Greek as did Byrhtferth's study of the computus and the natural sciences. What is important is that Greek borrowings *do* occur in the *Life* of Alfred and that they are otherwise a hallmark of late tenth-century Anglo-Latin writers and – in the case of the very special *enchiridion* – of Byrhtferth of Ramsey in particular. Byrhtferth's summary of the *Life* of Alfred significantly includes at least three more Grecisms – *onoma*,[53] *hypocrissima*[54] and *pentecontarchus*,[55] which are absent from the Parker-Cotton text as edited by Stevenson. Stevenson observed how Florence (*alias* John) of Worcester had carried out editorial 'improvements' on his copy of the *Life* of Alfred in the Worcester Latin Chronicle[56] and how that twelfth-century editor excised a Frankish Latinism from his exemplar of the *Life* on the grounds that it was 'evidently considered as pleonastic'.

The exotic plural *zizania*, which occurs in Chapter 95 of Stevenson's edition of the *Life* of King Alfred, leads us to a remarkable conclusion in relation to the authorship of the *Life*. *Zizania* is ultimately also of Greek origin (τὸ ζιζάνιον) – being the diabolically inspired tare or darnel which was sown among the wheat, as narrated in the Gospel story of Matthew 13: 25. The author of Alfred's *Life* with his love of arcane vocabulary and of Grecisms could not resist using such a word, and he aptly applied it to the tale of the wicked monks who tried to slay Abbot John at Athelney. He excused and explained his lurid tale of monastic violence with the comment:

> throughout Scripture, the foul deeds of the unrighteous are sown among the holy deeds of the righteous, like darnel and tares in the crop of wheat (*sicut zizania et lolium in tritici segetibus interseminantur*).[57]

Keynes and Lapidge observed[58] that the author of the *Life* of Alfred was here 'interestingly' conflating two different weeds from two different sources. He was conflating his biblical darnel weeds – *zizania* in the midst of St. Matthew's wheat – with Vergil's crops (*Georgics* I, 152–4) which were overcome by the 'wretched tare (*infelix lolium*)'. What is remarkable about all this is that Byrhtferth of Ramsey in his *Life* of St. Oswald, repeats this very conflation. He tells us that while the saintly Oswald was studying at Fleury, he drove out 'the brambles, thorns, and *zizania* (*vepres et spinas et zizania*)' from his heart, and clothing himself in his baptismal garment (i.e. the monastic habit) he began to tear up by the root the cockle and nettles of sin (*lolium et urticas exstirpare*).[59] So, not only is this exotic word *zizania* found in the *Life* of King Alfred and in Byrhtferth's *Life* of Oswald, but it is used in both works in association with *lolium* and in such a specific way as to suggest that we are dealing with the mind of the same writer in each case.

In addition to Grecisms, Lapidge itemised the use of Latin diminutives and unusual agentive nouns in *-or* as being a distinct characteristic of Byrhtferth's Latin style. Among the latter he cites *bellator* as turning up in the *Life* of St. Oswald and in Byrhtferth's Northumbrian Chronicle in the *Historia Regum*.[60] But Byrhtferth also writes of *bellatores* in his *Life* of St. Ecgwine[61] and *bellatores* are mentioned at least twice in the *Life* of King Alfred.[62] As for other examples of this usage in the *Life* of Alfred, we find *operator* ('workman');[63] *administrator* ('administrator'), *coadiutores* ('assistants') and *inspector*;[64] *rector* ('ruler, regent');[65] *habitator* ('inhabitant');[66] *ductor* ('leader, guide'),[67] and *gubernator* ('ruler').[68] The author's fondness for using *gubernator* and its related forms *gubernaculum/gubernacula* and *guberno*, is found throughout the text of Byrhtferth's Northumbrian Chronicle (outside the summary of the *Life* of Alfred), as well as in his *Manual*, and in the *Life* of St. Ecgwine and the *Life* of St. Oswald. With the more usual *gubernator*, we may compare Byrhtferth's use of *gubernatrix* in his *Life* of St. Oswald,[69] and just as the author of the *Life* of Alfred delighted in what Lapidge described elsewhere as 'verbal playfulness'[70] – playing with word repetition and in varying his word forms as in *semel regni gubernaculum, veluti gubernator praecipuus* – so too, Byrhtferth wrote in his *Manual*: *penetrando circumdat et circumdando adimplet et adimplendo gubernat et gubernando*.[71] As for Byrhtferth's known fondness for diminutives, these turn up also in the *Life* of Alfred as evidenced by *servulus* ('young slave');[72] *campulus* ('piece of ground');[73] *latrunculus* ('bandit, desperado');[74] *foliuncula* ('sheet of parchment')[75] and *opusculum* ('short work'),[76] as well as seeming diminutives such as *patibulum* ('gallows').[77]

One of the more definitive hallmarks of Byrhtferth's Latin is his use of uncommon polysyllabic adverbs ending in *-iter*, and it was the identification of those particular adverbs which formed the main plank in Lapidge's argument for attributing authorship of the *Northumbrian Chronicle* in the early sections of the *Historia Regum* as well as the *Life* of St. Ecgwine to Byrhtferth of Ramsey.[78] Elsewhere Keynes and Lapidge, although upholding Whitelock's thesis for the Genuine (ninth-century) Asser, nevertheless recognised precisely the same tenth-century features in his Latin as those exhibited by Byrhtferth:

> Above all Asser seems to have been obsessed with a love of polysyllabic adverbs, to the point that scarcely a sentence lacks one.[79]

That statement repeats verbatim what Lapidge wrote of Byrhtferth of Ramsey:

Yet another aspect of this same lexical predilection is revealed in the use (it is virtually an abuse) of polysyllabic adverbs terminating in *-iter*. Although adverbs of this sort are used sparingly by most medieval Latin authors, they occur so frequently in the two works [i.e. Byrhtferth's *Life* of Ecgwine and the *Life* of St. Oswald] that there is seldom a sentence which does not have one.[80]

Here is a scholar who, like Byrhtferth the subject of his study, revealed the 'ingrained mental habits' of a writer 'where he is too lazy or too much in a hurry, to pay close attention to the wording of a ... phrase',[81] but by his own judgement, Lapidge identified the hand of Byrhtferth of Ramsey in the composition of the *Life* of King Alfred. A more detailed study of those Latin adverbs occurring in the text of the *Life* of King Alfred, set alongside the other known works of Byrhtferth, reveals a significant sharing in rare vocabulary.[82] Witness, for instance, a rare word such as *incommutabiliter* which occurs in the *Life* of King Alfred and resurfaces in the *Life* of St. Neot.[83] Lapidge's survey of Byrhtferthian vocabulary, confined as it was to, say, adverbial or adjectival use of particular words, was inappropriately mechanical and unrealistically schematised when applied to an author's use of language. For instance, if we take the adverb *affabiliter* which occurs in Byrhtferth's *Life* of Oswald, we may note that this is absent from the *Life* of Alfred, but equally we need to register the presence of *affabilitate* in the latter text.[84] We might compare *amabiliter* which appears to be unique to Alfred's *Life*[85] with *amicabiliter* in the *Life* of St. Oswald. We may compare *immisericorditer* common to the *Lives* of Oswald and Ecgwine and to Byrhtferth's *Northumbrian Chronicle*, with *misericorditer* which occurs in the *Life* of Alfred, and again in the *Lives* of Oswald and Ecgwine. The instance of the more unusual *pigriter* ('slothful') in the *Life* of Ecgwine[86] may be set alongside the *pigritia populi* ('sloth of the people') of the *Life* of Alfred,[87] while *venerabiliter* of the *Northumbrian Chronicle* needs to be compared with the ubiquitous *venerabilis* and *venerabilissimae* of the *Life* of Alfred.[88]

Lapidge drew attention to Byrhtferth's fondness for polysyllabic superlatives in general and for their use in modifying the word *rex* in particular. He noted how the form *famosissimus ... rex* appears no less than twice in the *Life* of St. Ecgwine,[89] but precisely the same phrase is applied to Charlemagne in the Parker-Cotton edition of the *Life* of Alfred (*Karolum illum famosissimum Francorum regem*), and also in Byrhtferth's version of that text in his Northumbrian Chronicle at that same place in the Eadburh tale.[90] But it also occurs elsewhere in Byrhtferth's Northumbrian version of Alfred's *Life sub anno* 883 where it is applied to King Alfred,[91] and Byrhtferth uses it in his Northumbrian Chronicle outside his summary of the *Life* in relation to the Frankish king, Carloman *sub anno* 771[92] – all of which suggests that there is little or no distinction between the style of Byrhtferth's Northumbrian Chronicle as a whole and that of the summary version of the *Life* of Alfred which is contained within it. Byrhtferth may well have borrowed the usage from the opening lines of Einhard's *Life* of Charlemagne where that writer refers to Charlemagne as *excellentissimi et ... famosissimi regis.*[93] The author of the *Life* of Alfred is also known to have borrowed, sometimes verbatim, from Einhard's work, and it is no coincidence that both the superlatives *famosissimus* and *excellentissimus* are used by him in his *Life* of Alfred.[94] Byrhtferth refers, in his *Life* of St. Oswald, to King Edgar who was the patron of the monastic reformers, as *piissimus rex*,[95] and he uses *piissimae* yet again in his tale of the martyrdom of the Kentish princes Æthelberht and Æthelred.[96] In the Worcester Latin Chronicle, at the notice of King Alfred's death under 901, Byrhtferth refers to Alfred's father, Æthelwulf, as *piissimus rex* which echoes the reference in the Dedication of the *Life* of King Alfred to that *Domino meo venerabili piissimoque omnium Brittanniae insulae Christianorum rectori, Ælfred, Anglorum Saxonum regi.*[97] The regnal titles accorded to Alfred in this Dedication reflect later tenth-century usage rather than that of the ninth.[98] We note the personal mark of Byrhtferth in the reference to Alfred as *piissimus rex* in the dedicatory words at the opening of Alfred's *Life*, and we note, too, that Byrhtferth in his version of the *Life* of Alfred in the Northumbrian Chronicle[99] referred to Guthrum's baptism 'at the hand of the most pious king [Alfred] (*sub manu piissimi regis*)'. In the *Life* of St. Ecgwine, that saint, supposedly writing in the first person – precisely as Asser is made to do in the *Life* of King Alfred – refers to his supposed friend Cenred, as *rex famosissimus mihique dilectissimus amicus.*[100] The *Life* of Alfred, as we have seen, uses the superlative *famosissimus*, but it also uses *dilectissimus* in relation to King Alfred's 'thegns [who were] most dear to him' (*dilectissimos suos ministros*).[101] The text of the *Life* of Alfred is indeed littered with polysyllabic superlatives characteristic of Byrhtferth's Latinity. A systematic study of these words will no doubt show more exact parallels with Byrhtferth's other works, but it may be noted that in addition to *famosissimus* and *dilectissimus*, we also find *munitissima*,[102] *nobilissimos*,[103] *prudentissima*[104] and *pulcherrima*[105] – all of which appear in Byrhtferth's Northumbrian Chronicle, independently of the summary of the *Life* of Alfred also found in that work. *Pulcherrimus* is also used in the *Life* of St. Oswald,[106] while *turpissimus* is common to the *Life* of Alfred[107] and to Byrhtferth's *Life* of St. Ecgwine.[108] Two further superlatives from the same phrase in the *Life* of Alfred – *opinatissimum atque opulentissimum*[109] – also appear in Byrhtferth's short *Epilogue*.[110]

Let us return to Lapidge's observation regarding Byrhtferth's fondness for qualifying the word *rex* with a polysyllabic superlative. The compiler of the East Anglian Chronicle (*Annals of St. Neots*) – identified by Hart as Byrhtferth of Ramsey – refers to King Offa of Mercia as *perfidissimus* ('most treacherous') and to King Alfred, by contrast, as *religiosus atque sapientissimus*.[111] It is clear that Byrhtferth's anti-Mercian sentiments derive from the attack which the Mercians under Ealdorman Ælfhere threatened to mount against the monasteries of East Anglia in the immediate aftermath of the death of King Edgar in 975. Indeed Byrhtferth sets out for us in detail in the Worcester Latin Chronicle how the wicked Mercians planned the destruction of the East Anglian monasteries in 975, and how the devout Ealdorman Æthelwine of East Anglia defended his monasteries with an armed band.[112] That same champion, Ealdorman Æthelwine, had been the co-founder of Ramsey along with Bishop Oswald of Worcester. If we consider, then, those two hyperbolical adjectives applied by the compiler of the East Anglian Chronicle to Offa on the one hand and to Alfred on the other, we can see how two major themes were developed in the *Life* of King Alfred. Alfred the *religiosus* was given a biography to suit a saint – who was a founder of model monasteries, who devoted half of all his time, night and day, to God, and who prayed for illness to ensure his eternal salvation. Offa 'the most treacherous' (*perfidissimus*) inspired an elaborate tale of treachery woven about the name of his daughter, Eadburh, who supposedly poisoned her royal West Saxon husband. And to drive the point home about the ill-advised nature of West Saxon kings marrying Mercian women, Alfred's biographer chose the wedding feast of that king and his Mercian bride as the time when – due to witchcraft or otherwise – Alfred was supposedly stricken with his most terrible and long-lasting disease.

In comparing the Latinity of the *Life* of Alfred with that of Byrhtferth and his circle of Ramsey writers, we need to distinguish between particles or other Latin parts of speech which are immutable, and those which turn up in a variety of substantival, adjectival or adverbial forms. So, the emphatic *immo* which turns up frequently in the *Life* of Alfred also appears (although less often) in the *Lives* of St. Oswald, St. Neot and St. Ecgwine.[113] In cases such as *immo* we can proceed with a mechanical listing of the word. But it is possible to arrive at unreal if not misleading conclusions by analysing various parts of speech found in ninth- and tenth-century texts in a too rigorous grammatical or syntactical isolation from each other. It would be wrong to ignore the obvious relationship which exists in the *Life* of Alfred and in the other works of Byrhtferth, between polysyllabic adverbs and superlatives on the one hand, and polysyllabic adjectives with the prefix *in-* and suffix *-bilis* on the other. These adjectives – seen in their separate category – were also identified by Lapidge as characteristic of Byrhtferth's style, and he cited *inedicibilis* from the Northumbrian Chronicle as an instance of a rare form in this class.[114] Lapidge has observed that a characteristically rare Byrhtferthian polysyllabic adverb such as *inedicibiliter* is not found in the *Life* of Alfred.[115] But the related form *inedicibilis* is found in Byrhtferth's abridged version of the *Life* of Alfred in his Northumbrian Chronicle.[116] We note the form *indicibilis* found in

Byrhtferth's contribution to the Worcester Latin Chronicle (AD 1001). By the same analogy, we need to connect Byrhtferth's use of *ineffabiliter* in his *Lives* of Oswald and of Ecgwine with his use of *ineffabilis* again in the *Lives* of Oswald and of Ecgwine, and in his *Epilogue*. But *ineffabilis* also appears in the text of the *Life* of Alfred.[117] We note the occurrence of *incomparabiliter*[118] in the *Life* of Alfred, and compare it with *incomparabilis* as found earlier on in that same work.[119] The form *incomparabilis* also occurs in Byrhtferth's Northumbrian Chronicle outside of the summary of the *Life* of Alfred,[120] and these forms must be taken together in any analysis, in the same way as we note the alternation between *incessabiliter* and *incessabilius* within the text of the *Life* of Alfred elsewhere.[121] We might cite the author's use of the more common *laudabiliter*[122] along with *laudabilis* in the *Lives* of Oswald and of Ecgwine.[123] There are, of course, more direct comparisons between polysyllabic adjectives which we can make, as in the case of *innumerabilis* used by Byrhtferth in his *Lives* of St. Oswald and of St. Neot,[124] as well as in the Worcester Latin Chronicle,[125] and which occurs at least six times in the *Life* of Alfred.[126] Byrhtferth was not unique in resorting to polysyllabic adjectives with *in-* and *-bilis*, but that usage which was only one of several distinctive features of the hermeneutic style, was essentially characteristic of the school of writers belonging to the later tenth-century English Monastic Reform. Archbishop Oda of Canterbury, for instance, uses the rare word *intransmeabilis* ('impassable') in his short mid-tenth-century *Preface* to Frithegod's *Life* of St. Wilfrid.[127] That same rare word is used by the author of Alfred's *Life* to describe the topography of Athelney in Somerset.[128] Oda's vocabulary generally has close similarities with that of the *Life* of Alfred and the works of Byrhtferth of Ramsey, which suggests yet again that the *Life* of King Alfred is textually at home in the later tenth and early eleventh century rather than in the ninth. It is an easy matter for a medieval Latinist to latch on to individual items of vocabulary such as *breviter*, *feliciter* or *pariter* and dismiss my entire argument on the grounds that such words 'are common coin and their occurrence in any Latin work cannot be used as a criterion of authorship'.[129] But the cumulative effect of such words may be significant and scholars in their quest for attributing authorship of the *Life* of Alfred must address the issue of the excessive use of common adverbs as well as the presence in the *Life* of rare and distinctive vocabulary which is clearly at home in late tenth-century hermeneutic Latin.

When recognising the close similarities between the text of the *Life* of King Alfred and the known works of Byrhtferth of Ramsey, we are not dealing solely with a matter of comparing the same Latin words, or words used as specific parts of speech. The author of the *Life* of Alfred and Byrhtferth of Ramsey gloried in piling up polysyllabic adverbs, adjectives and superlatives within the same sentence, frequently playing on variations of the same Latin root. When we compare passages from the *Life* of Alfred with other known works of Byrhtferth, we are not necessarily looking for word-for-word similarities – though these do occur – or for evidence of direct borrowing. We are looking primarily for similarities in the use of language and in style, and for the similar manipulation of vocabulary. A striking feature of the text of the *Life* of Alfred is the author's love of word-play – *irrationabiliter – irrationabilius*; *utiliter – utilius*; or sometimes just the repetition within a sentence of the same polysyllabic adverb – as in the case of *honorabiliter* (Chapter 19) or *multipliciter* (Chapter 99).[130] Lapidge drew attention to Byrhtferth's use throughout his writings of the rhetorical question to achieve emphasis, and to Byrhtferth's use of compounds based on *nuntio, expedio, enarro* or *edico*.[131] In an example quoted in note 130 above, from the *Life* of Oswald, the formula used is that of *quis annuntiet?* The precise formulae used by Byrhtferth when employing this rhetorical device vary considerably, and in addition to his use of those forms cited by Lapidge we may also point to his piling up of rhetorical questions in the sentence *Quid restat? Quid superest? Quid moramur? Cur non dicimus quae restant?* in the *Life* of Ecgwine,[132] or to *Quid dicam? Quidve referam?* in the *Life* of St. Oswald.[133] The passage beginning *His sollemniter finitis* quoted in note 130 above from the *Life* of Oswald may also be compared in its rhetorical *quis annuntiet?* in relation to the church of Ramsey, with the author's similar rhetorical question in relation to King Alfred's building achievements:

> *Quid loquar de ... civitatibus et urbibus renovandis et aliis, ubi nunquam ante fuerant, construendis? De aedificiis aureis et argenteis incomparabiliter, illo edocente, fabricatis? De aulis et cambris regalibus, lapideis et ligneis suo iussu mirabiliter constructis?* [What of the cities and towns he restored, and the others, which he built where none had been before? Of the buildings made by his instructions with gold and silver, beyond compare? Of royal halls and chambers constructed admirably in stone and timber at his command?']134

The adverb *mirabiliter* from this passage in King Alfred's *Life* occurs in at least three of Byrhtferth's known works, in at least nine instances.[135] The author's use of *incomparabiliter* in this same passage may be set against the adjectival form, *incomparabilis*, which appears elsewhere in the *Life* of Alfred,[136] and which reappears in Byrhtferth's Northumbrian Chronicle.[137] That particular passage in Chapter 22 of the *Life* of Alfred is resonant with echoes from the writings of Byrhtferth:

> *Sed, proh dolor! indigna suorum parentum et nutritorum incuria usque ad duodecimum aetatis annum, aut eo amplius, illiteratus permansit. Sed Saxonica*

*poemata die noctuque solers auditor, relatu aliorum saepissime audiens, docibilis memoriter retinebat. In omni venatoria arte industrius venator incessabiliter laborat non in vanum; nam incomparabilis omnibus peritia et felicitate in illa arte, sicut et in ceteris omnibus Dei donis, fuit, sicut et nos saepissime vidimus.* [But alas, by the unworthy carelessness of his parents and tutors, he [Alfred] remained ignorant of letters until his twelfth year, or even longer. But he listened attentively to Saxon poems by day and night, and hearing them often recited by others committed them to his retentive memory. A keen huntsman, he toiled unceasingly in every branch of hunting, and not in vain; for he was without equal in his skill and good fortune in that art, as also in all other gifts of God, as we have ourselves [very] often seen.][138]

This passage – so dependent in its ideas on St. Odo's *Life* of Gerald and Einhard's *Life* of Charlemagne – contains the rhetorical lamentation *proh dolor* which recurs several times throughout the *Life* of King Alfred. Crawford identified *heu pro dolor* as a characteristic feature of Byrhtferth's Latin in both his *Manual* and the *Life* of St. Oswald.[139] Stevenson, on the other hand, identified *eo amplius* as a hallmark of the textual style of the *Life* of King Alfred.[140] Remarkably, the combination of *proh dolor ... eo amplius* occurs in close proximity in the passage quoted above from Chapter 22 of Alfred's *Life* and the combination recurs yet again in Chapter 74.[141] Precisely the same combination of phrases occurs within a single passage in a section of Byrhtferth's Northumbrian Chronicle referring to AD 792, and therefore prior to Byrhtferth's summary of the *Life* of Alfred in that work.[142]

Yet another phrase in that passage from Chapter 22 of King Alfred's *Life* is *die noctuque* ('by day and by night') which occurs at least eleven times in that work.[143] Lapidge was at pains to point out that this archaism does not occur in the known works of Byrhtferth who always uses *nocte* or *noctibus*.[144] Lapidge chose not to comment on the significance of the occurrence in Chapter 74 of the *Life* of King Alfred of *diuturnitas*,[145] a word described by him as a 'rare abstraction', which for Lapidge was a diagnostic word in the repertoire of Byrhtferth of Ramsey.[146] *Diuturnitas* occurs in Byrhtferth's Northumbrian Chronicle at the end of his account of the Kentish hagiographical legends.[147] The text of the *Life* of Alfred is replete with phrases relating to night and day, which is what we should expect if its author were Byrhtferth, who was an expert on the measurement of time, and who devoted a large part of his *Manual* to discussing the divisions of day and night. We have in the *Life* of Alfred *diuturna et nocturna*,[148] *diuturna die noctuque*[149] and *diurno ... ac nocturno*,[150] and *nocturnarum horarum ... et diurnarum*.[151] We may compare the phrase *diurnus ... et nocturnus* in the Northumbrian Chronicle,[152] or *peractis nocturnalibus mysteriis* in the *Life* of St. Ecgwine.[153] The majority of these phrases relating to time would be commonplace in any medieval Latin narrative, but it is the frequency with which they are repeated, and their variety of form in the *Life* of King Alfred, which links those phrases to the works of Byrhtferth of Ramsey – that master of time studies in his *Manual*.

Lapidge drew attention to Byrhtferth's characteristic use of continuity phrases which he saw as ultimately deriving from Bede.[154] Such borrowings may not always have involved deliberate cloning of phrases on the part of Byrhtferth, whose intense study of writers such as Bede and Aldhelm must have implanted techniques and turns of phrase in his own subconscious repertoire as a writer. Approaching this subject from an analysis of the text of the *Life* of Alfred we find that it, too, makes extensive use of continuity passages:

> I think we should return to that which particularly inspired me to this work ... I consider that some small account ... of Alfred ... should briefly be inserted at this point (*ad id, quod nos maxime ad hoc opus incitavit, nobis redeundum esse censeo, scilicet aliquantulum ... de Ælfredi, moribus hoc in loco breviter inserendum esse existimo*).[155] In order that I may return to that point from which I digressed ... I shall, as I promised, undertake with God's guidance, to say something albeit succinctly and briefly ... about the life ... of Alfred (*ad id, unde digressus sum, redeam ... aliquantulum quantum notitiae meae innotuerit, de vita ... Ælfredi ... Deo annuente, succinctim ac breviter ... ut promisi, expedire procurabo*).[156]

We may compare the author's *digressus sum redeam* with a related passage from Byrhtferth's *Life* of St. Oswald:

> *Digressi sumus paulisper ab ordine narrationis ... sed etiam tempus esse dinoscitur ut ad viam nostri sermonis redeamus,*[157]

or with

> *extra viam paulatim digressimus, sed redeamus ad viam quae nos reducat ad callem justitiae*

from that same saint's *Life*.[158] Returning to the *Life* of King Alfred, the phrase: Now that I have related these things, let us return to the proper subject' (*His ita relatis, ad incepta redeamus*),[159] may be compared with Byrhtferth's *His strictim dictis, ad ordinem revertamur narrationis* in his Northumbrian Chronicle[160] and with the same writer's *His dictis, redeamus ad nos ipsos* in his *Manual*[161] or *His dictis, redeamus uenusto animo unde discesseramus mediocri alloquio,*[162] and *ad ordinem ... redeamus propriae relationis* in the *Life* of St. Oswald.[163] Byrhtferth's desire in his known writings to return *ad ordinem* reminds us of the author's admission of his inability to handle the chaotic account, as he presented it, of King Alfred's illness:

> For, if I may speak succinctly and briefly although I set things out in the reverse order (*Nam, ut ... succinctim ac breviter, quamvis praeposterato ordine, loquar*).[164]

The author is telling us quite literally that he is presenting his narrative, or 'order', back to front!

Several of the continuity phrases in the *Life* of Alfred are couched as announcements for the inclusion of a specific narrative, or apologies for leaving it out as in Chapter 92:

> At this point I do not think that I can profitably bypass ... the intention and resolve of his most excellent enterprise (*De voto quoque et proposito excellentissimae meditationis suae ... praetereundum esse hoc in loco utiliter non existimo*).[165]

Byrhtferth makes similar statements throughout his works as in this passage from the *Life* of Oswald:

> *Rem breviter narrare desidero, quam praeterire non libet ob inertiam desidiae torporis.*[166]

The author of Alfred's *Life* also excuses himself from going into detail:

> It is not necessary to mention the other details of his bequests to men in this short work, for fear its readers or those wishing to listen to it should find its verbosity distasteful (*Nam cetera, quae ad humanam dispensationem pertinent, in hoc opusculo inserere necesse non est, ne fastidium prolixitate legentibus vel etiam audire desiderantibus procreaverit*).[167]

Here we have the writer's excuse that he does not wish to bore his readers and indeed his hearers. Significantly, Byrhtferth panders to his hearers (*audientes*) in a similarly apologetic vein in his *Manual*:

> We refrain at this point from discoursing of [the numbers] sixty, seventy, eighty and ninety, lest we should disturb our hearers. (*De sexagessimo et septuagessimo et octuagesimo, nec non et nonagesimo supersedimus hoc in loco sermocinari, ne forte perturbemus audientes*).[168]

We may compare Byrhtferth's

we have no desire to treat these subjects further, lest it should prove tedious to educated priests (*nu ne lyst us þas þing leng styrian, þelæspe hyt beo æpryt gelæredum preostum*),[169]

or that same writer's excuse for terminating his long digression in his *Manual* on figures of speech:

We could say a great deal on these things, but we are afraid that scholars may hate our speaking so fully about their mysteries.... But I am eager [to return] to pursue the study of the computus.[170]

This formula may be compared with the other announcements of Byrhtferth:

Let these words suffice at this point (*Hoc in loco sufficiant h(a)ec dicta*).[171]

Or:

Let us pass over these in this place because we wish to come to more important matters (*de his hoc in loco taceamus, quia ad necessiora cupimus peruenire*).[172]

No less than three of these continuity passages of Byrhtferth of Ramsey are linked to the continuity text in Chapter 92 of the *Life* of Alfred (quoted above) by the key formula *hoc in loco*.

The author of King Alfred's *Life*, like Byrhtferth, also makes announcements for the benefit of ignorant readers:

And because many do not know, I suspect ... I think I should explain it a little more fully (*Et quia, ut opinor, multis habetur incognitum ... paulo latius mihi videtur intimandum*).[173]

We may compare this with Byrhtferth's plea in his *Manual*:

Time presses us to speak concisely of the number one thousand – beseeching those who have the knowledge not to be annoyed with what is our pleasure to set forth for those who are ignorant (*Nunc tempus instat ut de millenario strictim loquamar, scientes obsecrans ut oneri non sit quod ignorantibus placet traducere*).[174]

Lapidge cited a closely related passage from the *Life* of St. Ecgwine.[175] Similarly, in the *Life* of Alfred, the author protests that he does not itemise the gifts which he received from the king out of vanity:

I call God to witness that I have not done so [out of vanity], but only to make clear to those who do not know (*nescientibus*) [the king] how profuse is his generosity.[176]

The author's 'those who do not know' (*nescientibus*) may be compared with a similar class of readers who 'do not know' (*nescientes*) and who consequently were in need of Byrhtferth's instruction in the Northumbrian Chronicle and elsewhere in his writings.

Other closer verbal similarities may be found between the text of the *Life* of Alfred and other known works of Byrhtferth of Ramsey. The author in his account of how Alfred first learnt to read and to translate, tells us 'I gave immense thanks, although silently, to Almighty God, with hands outstretched to Heaven' (*immensas Omnipotenti Deo grates, extensis ad aethera volis, tacitus quamvis, persolvi*).[177] The passage echoes another in Byrhtferth's *Life* of St. Ecgwine: *Salvatoris gratia concedente propriis arvis redditi sumus, immensas ei grates rependentes, erectis digniter palmis ad aethera.*[178] It may indeed be argued that both passages are derived ultimately from Aldhelm[179] – and all parties are agreed that the author of Alfred's *Life* and Byrhtferth had studied Aldhelm – but what is remarkable is that precisely these same phrases should be borrowed by the author and by Byrhtferth who have hitherto been regarded as living a whole century apart. Crawford, as long ago as 1929, observed as 'noteworthy ... the fact that in both the *Manual* and the *Vita Oswaldi* [of Byrhtferth of Ramsey] we never find *in hoc loco*, but always *hoc in loco*'.[180] Indeed Crawford used this 'marked characteristic' to help show that Byrhtferth was none other than the author of the *Life* of St. Oswald – a fact now generally accepted. We find this same distinctive Byrhtferthian usage of *hoc in loco* ('in this place') throughout the *Life* of Alfred, two examples of which have been cited in the continuity passages above.[181] Witness the celebrated passage where the biographer informs us that King Alfred rewarded him with Exeter and all its *parochia*:

besides innumerable daily gifts of all kinds of earthly riches, which it would be tedious to enumerate here, lest it should cause weariness to the readers. But do not let anyone think that I have mentioned such gifts in this place out of any vain glory or in flattery, or for the sake of gaining greater honour (*quae hoc in loco percensere longum est, ne fastidium legentibus procreent. Sed nullus existimet, pro vana aliqua gloria aut adulatione aut maioris honoris quaerendi gratia, me talia hoc in loco dona commemorasse*).[182]

The passage may be borrowed in part from Einhard – as are other announcements by the author that he does not wish to bore his readers. Nevertheless, the repeated use of *hoc in loco* in this single passage is – *pace* Howlett – peculiar to the author and to Byrhtferth of Ramsey.[183]

The author of Alfred's *Life* and Byrhtferth of Ramsey fell back on the same devices to excuse their scissors-and-paste technique of writing. They each made excessive use of signposting and apologising to their readers, and both writers too often resorted to 'continuity formulae' which appear in the *Life* of King Alfred and throughout all the major works of Byrhtferth: 'I think I should return to my main subject ...' , 'Having said these things, let us return to the main narrative ...', 'Having digressed from the main narrative, let us return ...' or simply 'as I have said'. We also encounter signposting of an apologetic or explanatory variety: 'Because many do not know, I think I should explain this more fully' or alternatively, 'it is not necessary to mention other details for fear of boring readers'. There are, as we might expect, points of difference between the texts of the *Life* of Alfred and those of the other known works of Byrhtferth of Ramsey. We cannot expect such a prolific author, writing perhaps over half a century in time, to display the exact same characteristics in all his writings. Other scholars have noted variations in Byrhtferth's use of vocabulary and style across the range of his works.[184]

A study of the metaphors employed by the biographer of King Alfred shows that they bear a remarkable similarity to those found in the writings of Byrhtferth of Ramsey. On three occasions in the *Life* of Alfred, the biographer uses a nautical image – twice[185] referring to himself as a ship's pilot and to his work as a ship holding its course and seeking a safe harbour, and a third time referring to King Alfred himself as the pilot guiding his treasure-laden ship of state (the kingdom) to that same metaphorical safe harbour. The nautical metaphor was a literary commonplace, and King Alfred in his own writings made frequent use of it. Alfred was probably influenced in this, as in so much else, by his great knowledge of some of the works of Gregory the Great.[186] But the nautical metaphors in the *Life* of Alfred are quite different from those used by Alfred in his own writings and bear a close relationship to those of late tenth- and early eleventh-century writers. As early as 1877, Howorth observed that the author of King Alfred's *Life* may have borrowed his nautical metaphors from the late tenth-century *Chronicle* of Æthelweard.[187] The notion was contemptuously dismissed by Stevenson with the comment:

> This argument would equally prove that Cicero also borrowed from Æthelweard.[188]

But Cicero and Æthelweard were separated by a millennium, whereas Æthelweard and the biographer of Alfred, who both worked on Latin translations of the Anglo-Saxon Chronicle, had more in common than Stevenson was willing to admit. The fact that the nautical metaphor had established itself as a topos in the writings of Jerome, Fortunatus or Eriugena – and among earlier English writers such as Aldhelm and Alcuin – cannot *per se* invalidate the possibility that the same metaphor was borrowed by King Alfred's biographer from Æthelweard, or – more realistically – that it might date from the same late tenth-century literary milieu as that of Æthelweard and his contemporaries. The author of Alfred's *Life* tells us he had:

> entrusted the ship to waves and sails, and having sailed quite far away from the land – among such terrible wars, and in year by year reckoning (*inter tantas bellorum clades et annorum enumerationes*), I think I should return to that which particularly inspired me to this work: in other words I consider that some small account (as much as has come to my knowledge) of the infancy and boyhood of my esteemed lord Alfred, king of the Anglo-Saxons, should briefly be inserted at this point.[189]

Later on, in Chapter 73, he repeats his hollow pledge:

> to return to that point from which I digressed – and so that I shall not be compelled to sail past the haven of my desired rest as a result of my protracted voyage – I shall as I promised, undertake, with God's guidance, to say something ... about the life, behaviour, equitable character and, without exaggeration, the accomplishments of my lord Alfred, king of the Anglo-Saxons.[190]

For the author, his ocean was in part the relentless following (by way of translation) of the Anglo-Saxon Chronicle, while the safe haven from this boring digression beckoned in the form of elusive details relating to Alfred's own life – about which the author knew so little. What is remarkable about the parallel use of this same metaphor by the chronicler Æthelweard is that it is used in precisely the same context by that late tenth-century writer. At a point in Book Four of his *Chronicle*, Æthelweard brings his narrative down to the death of his own ancestor, King Æthelred I (the older brother of Alfred) in AD 871. At this point in his work, Æthelweard turns aside to address his German cousin (for whom he was compiling his *Chronicle* in the first instance):

> Having just retraced my steps, O revered cousin Matilda, I will begin to give you confirmation with added clarity. Just as a ship which has been carried through the turmoil of the waves for great distances, which she has explored on her careful voyage, comes at last to port, so we enter [port] as if in the manner of sailors.... So setting aside my less even style, I will speak of the sons of Æthelwulf. The brothers were five in number. The first was Æthelstan who had taken up government at the same time as his father. The second was Æthelbald, who was also king of the West Saxons.

The third was Æthelbyrht, king of the people of Kent. The fourth was Æthelred who succeeded to the kingdom after the death of Æthelbyrht, and who was my great-great-grandfather. The fifth was Alfred successor of all the others to the entire kingdom, who was your great-great-grandfather. Accordingly, sweet cousin Matilda, having gathered these things from remote antiquity, I have made communication to you, and above all I have given attention to the history of our race as far as these two kings, from whom we derive our descent.... Therefore let us return to our neglected subject and the death of the above-mentioned King Æthelred.... When these things had happened, Alfred got the kingdom after the death of his brothers.[191]

So, for Æthelweard too – like the author of Alfred's *Life* – the translation of earlier sections of the Anglo-Saxon Chronicle was a preliminary but necessary chore – an ocean leading to a safe harbour – essentially that same harbour which was being sought by the pseudo-Asser, namely the account of King Alfred's career. It was quite mistaken of Stevenson to assess Æthelweard's *Chronicle* as 'merely a brief version of the history of England with no personal details'.[192] On the contrary it was designed as a work showing King Alfred's central role in the history of the House of Wessex and in demonstrating the connection between Matilda, abbess of Essen (the recipient of the work) with King Alfred and the West Saxon dynasty. The ship's voyage was used by Æthelweard as a central metaphor to make the connection between King Æthelred and his brother Alfred on the one hand, and the relentless annalistic narrative of English history on the other. Howorth argued that had Æthelweard known of the biography of King Alfred he would most certainly have supplied his cousin with details from that colourful narrative, and concluded, therefore, that it was the biographer of King Alfred who had borrowed his nautical metaphors from Æthelweard.[193] That argument, after more than a century, returns to centre-stage – not necessarily to demonstrate any direct borrowing of one author from the other, but to show how Æthelweard may indeed have been a contemporary of King Alfred's biographer, and how these two writers, inhabiting the same thought-world, shared very similar perceptions of West Saxon history.

As it happens, the nautical metaphor is also used by Byrhtferth of Ramsey in an even more elaborate form near the beginning of his *Manual*:

We have stirred with our oars the waves of the deep pool. We have likewise beheld the mountains around the salt sea strand, and with outstretched sail and prosperous winds, we have succeeded in pitching our camp on the coasts of the fairest of lands. The waves symbolise this profound art [of computation], and the mountains, too, symbolise the magnitude of this

> art.... These things we found at Ramsey, by the merciful grace of God.... We have touched the deep sea and the mountains of this work.[194]

Byrhtferth's ocean waves represent the art of computation, while for Alfred's biographer the waves were the *annorum enumerationes* and for Æthelweard, 'the turmoil of the waves over the great distances' represented also the history of the English down to the reign of King Alfred. Indeed, for the author of Alfred's *Life* as for Æthelweard, the ocean represented the translation of the Anglo-Saxon Chronicle into Latin, and the harbour at journey's end represented the central role of King Alfred in English history, as both men perceived that rôle at the end of the millennium. Paradoxically, both Alfred's biographer and Æthelweard, who held King Alfred in such awe, were busy reversing that ruler's cultural achievement in the vernacular. For they both translated the powerfully direct and laconic West Saxon prose of the Anglo-Saxon Chronicle, which had been written in Alfred's reign, into a garbled and pretentious Latin of a sort that Alfred would have most certainly disapproved.

Byrhtferth's metaphor of the pilot on his ocean voyage mixes in other images which that writer developed with regularity in his other known works. In describing the metaphorical journey's end in his pursuit of the art of computation, Byrhtferth not only identified the place with his own monastic home at Ramsey, but he described it as a land of flowers and sweet-tasting honey. It was a place:

> Where we perceived the blossom of the lily – that is the beauty of computation – there we scented the perfume of roses – that is we perceived the profundity of reckoning. In that place the noble plain provided us with honey sweet and pleasant to taste. In that place we received myrrh, ... and 'gutta' that is a drop, sweet as honey ... and *thus*, that is incense. These things we found at Ramsey by the merciful grace of God.[195]

This vision of the land of honey is closely related to yet another of Byrhtferth's metaphors of the honey-bee which he used as a symbol for the scholar toiling with his work or browsing through the 'flowers of Scripture', or for learning in general. Later in his *Manual*, Byrhtferth, in striving to explain the devilishly complicated routine for calculating the correct date of Easter, encourages his pupils to persevere with their calculations in these words:

> Behold the chaste bee very often visits far and wide the beautiful flowers for so long that her rough thighs become heavily burdened. And fierce winds meet her and vex the poor thing, so that she can scarcely reach home. When she has ascended her throne in this dazed condition, she is

constrained with such gladness in her heart, that she has no hesitation in singing a pleasant song.[196]

Byrhtferth uses the bee metaphor yet again in his *Epilogue*[197] and also in his *Life* of St. Oswald, where he compares the studies undertaken at Fleury on the 'flowers of the Scriptures' by the Winchester monk Germanus with the work of a honey-bee.[198] The author of Alfred's *Life* uses the bee metaphor twice in his *Life* of King Alfred. He tells us that Alfred, unable to find scholars within his own kingdom, was inspired by divine promptings to seek them from outside:

> Forthwith, like the prudent bee, which arises in the summer-time at dawn from its beloved cells and, directing its course in swift flight through the unknown ways of the air, alights upon many and various blossoms of herbs, plants and fruits, and finds and carries home what pleases it most.[199]

Later, in his celebrated passage describing how he taught King Alfred to read and to translate, the author relates that the eager king began searching daily for interesting passages in the Scriptures which might be transcribed into his notebook:

> like a most productive bee, travelling far and wide over the marshes in his quest, he eagerly and unceasingly collected many various flowers of Holy Scripture, with which he densely stored the cells of his mind.[200]

Stevenson, followed by Keynes and Lapidge, stressed that the bee metaphor in the *Life* of King Alfred was derived from the writings of the late seventh-century Aldhelm.[201] But Aldhelm, as we have seen, had a profound influence on hermeneutic writers of late tenth- and early eleventh-century England. Stevenson recognised that the bee metaphor also enjoyed popularity in the late tenth century (although he did not identify it with Byrhtferth of Ramsey), but his judgement was already constrained by his conviction that the *Life* of Alfred was a ninth-century production. The late tenth-century writer of the *B* Life of St. Dunstan likened that saint's studies at Glastonbury to the labours of the honey-bee,[202] and that same author of Dunstan's *Life*, writing *c.* 988–90 to Archbishop Æthelgar of Canterbury, informed the prelate in his letter that he was on his way to Winchester to study the works of Aldhelm. Even in that selfsame letter, he employs the metaphor of the 'obedient honey-bee' (*apis obediens*).[203] The question hinges, then, not on whether the bee metaphors in the *Life* of Alfred derive from Aldhelm, because ultimately most if not all such English imagery may well derive from that early West Saxon scholar. The question is, rather, do the bee metaphors in King Alfred's *Life* date to the late ninth century, where they would then stand in a conspicuously isolated English context, or do they belong to a significant body of closely related literary *topoi* used by Anglo-Latin writers of the late tenth and early eleventh centuries? To answer this question we must take into the account the fact that Byrhtferth of Ramsey and the author of the *Life* of Alfred have this significant point in common: they both made extensive use of the ship's pilot *and* the honey-bee metaphors. We note, too, that the biographer of Alfred likened the supposedly saintly king to a honey-bee searching 'far and wide over the marshes' in his thirst for biblical knowledge. The image of a bee searching for honey in extensive marshland would be more appropriate to a Fenland context in East Anglia than to the prosperous downlands of Alfredian Wessex. The word used by Alfred's biographer for those metaphorical 'marshes' traversed by his scholarly bee was *gronnios*[204] and elsewhere he uses *gronnosa* or 'marshy' to describe the wetlands of Somerset where Alfred retreated during his Athelney campaign.[205] That rare word *gronna* ('marsh' or 'fen') was – as we have seen – a Frankish import from tenth-century Fleury[206] and its earliest occurrence in England, outside the *Life* of Alfred, is in King Edgar's foundation charter for Thorney Abbey, dating to 973.[207] John Leland, the sixteenth-century antiquary, claimed that Byrhtferth of Ramsey had once been a monk at nearby Thorney.[208]

The author of the *Life* of Alfred narrated that king's sudden ability in middle age to read and to translate in terms of a conventional miracle story. It is clear too, how Alfred, whose own well-documented translation programme centred on historical or philosophical and largely non-Scriptural themes, was nevertheless portrayed by his biographer as a saint translating passages from Scripture and indulging in biblical exegesis. The bee metaphor in his *Life* reinforces the image of Alfred as the saintly monk – a true *religiosus* – collecting 'the various little flowers of Holy Scripture' (*multimodos divinae scripturae flosculos*).[209] The *Life* again refers to these flowers (*flosculos*) 'of the rudiments of Holy Scripture' which Alfred collected in that king's supposed *Enchiridion* or handbook.[210] Byrhtferth wrote of Germanus at Fleury, for instance, studying just those very same 'flowers of the Scriptures' (*flores Scripturarum*).[211] The entire context of the account of King Alfred's learning to read and to pursue a scholarly life, is cast in a late tenth-century monastic mould. And if we need any further confirmation that the imagery of the *Life* of Alfred belongs not to the ninth century, but to the era of the monastic reformers at the end of the tenth, then we need turn only to the text of the *Regularis Concordia Monachorum* of King Edgar, where we find there, in the very charter of the monastic reformers, an instance of the bee metaphor used to describe the *vita regularis* in terms reminiscent both of the letter to Archbishop Æthelgar and of Byrhtferth's *Epilogue*.[212]

There we are told that a Winchester synod of reforming clergy, encouraged by King Edgar,

> gathered from their praiseworthy customs [of Fleury and of Ghent] much that was good and thus, even as honey is gathered by bees from all manner of wild flowers and collected into one hive, so also the said monastic customs ... were, by the grace of Christ ... embodied in this small book.

Byrhtferth of Ramsey, as a hagiographer, writing in that monastery which was a flagship of Oswald's monastic reform, was steeped in the sentiments of the *Regularis Concordia*. It would have been natural for such a man, writing the biography of a supposedly saintly King Alfred, to have transferred the metaphor of the monastic bees and the all-important 'little book' (*codicellus*) of the *Rule*, to the scholarly Alfred collecting 'flowers' or notes on biblical exegesis into his little handbook (*manualem librum*) or *enchiridion*.

# 4

# The Author's Use of the Anglo-Saxon Chronicle

## A framework for the *Life*

The Anglo-Saxon Chronicle was used by the author of the *Life* of King Alfred to provide the basic framework for his entire narrative. Having decided on AD 849 as the year of Alfred's birth, the author took the Anglo-Saxon Chronicle, and used every entry covering the period from 849 to 887 to fill in the many gaps in his knowledge of that period of the king's life. Although the author suggests that he has written his account in 893,[1] he provides no specific historical information either of his own creation, or borrowed from the Chronicle, or from annals other than the Chronicle text, on Alfred or his times, for the interval from 887 to 893 (the supposed time of writing). Yet that was the very time when he claims to have been a contemporary witness residing at the court of the king. We may never know why the author ceased to follow the Anglo-Saxon Chronicle text after 887, but having decided to do so, he also ceased offering his readers any specific historical information, which is amenable to verification from other sources. He also failed to provide information drawn from other chronicles or annals, suggesting that his dependence on the Anglo-Saxon Chronicle as an historical source was well-nigh total, and that his account of King Alfred's life was essentially retrospective and antiquarian. The *Life* of King Alfred provides us in effect with a Latin translation of yet another version of the Anglo-Saxon Chronicle covering the period 849 to 887. The actual span of translated entries runs from 851 to 887, because the version of the Chronicle used by Alfred's biographer contained a dating sequence identical to that of the Parker manuscript (the A-Text).[2] When we set the sequence of Chronicle entries provided by Alfred's biographer alongside the Parker text, a number of remarkable points become clear. Alfred's biographer began his narrative of Alfred's life with the Chronicle's entry for 851 dealing with the victory of the men of Devon over a heathen army at *Wicanbeorg*. The author would of course have begun at 849 (his calculated year for Alfred's birth), had his Chronicle text provided him with an entry for that year. But in the A-Text of the Chronicle, the years 849 and 850 are blank, which left our author bereft of historical material for those same two years. He made good this loss by inserting the genealogy of Alfred's father, King Æthelwulf, which he lifted from the Chronicle at AD 855 together with an irrelevant digression on Geat, a legendary ancestor of West Saxon kings whom the author confused with a character from Latin comedy (Chapter 1).[3] This is followed by legendary material on Alfred's mother borrowed from Chronicle entries at AD 530 and 534 (Chapter 2). Having translated virtually word-for-word the five separate items which he found in the annal for 851 in the Chronicle (taking him from Chapter 3 to the end of Chapter 6), the author continued in Chapter 7 with his word-for-word translation of the Chronicle's entry for 853. We are told nothing of events for 852, because that year was blank also in the Version *A*-type sequence which he found in his Chronicle exemplar. So too we find that the author of the *Life* of Alfred offers us no information on the years 854, 856, 857, 858, 859, 861, 862, 863 and 864[4] because those years also were devoid of entries in his *A*-type Chronicle text. Conversely, his information for the years 851, 853, 855, 860 and 865–87 is firmly dependent on the Chronicle narrative. While on a few occasions he adds what may appear to be additional information by way of an intrusive gloss on those events which he borrowed from the Chronicle, he never once adds a discrete Chronicle-type annal which is not now to be found in a surviving Chronicle text. This lack of annalistic information for a specific number of years which is peculiar to the biography of King Alfred and the A-Text of the Anglo-Saxon Chronicle shows the all-embracing dependence of a supposedly late ninth-century writer on his Chronicle source, and provides – as we shall see – one of the most compelling arguments for rejecting the medieval *Life* of King Alfred as a contemporary narrative which was written by an intimate of the king who shared in the life of the royal court.

The beginning of each narrative sequence in the *Life* of King Alfred which is borrowed from the Anglo-Saxon Chronicle is not only given its AD date as in the Chronicle A-Text, but each year is also identified with whatever age Alfred was assumed to have been at that time – based on a year of birth for the king in 849. Frequently, the only connection the narrative has with King Alfred is the statement that this was 'the *x*th year since the birth of Alfred'. The full text of Chronicle entries is given even though all the entries prior to AD 868 (with the exception of the doubtful account of the infant Alfred's pilgrimage to Rome under 853) contained no direct information on Alfred at all. The author's harping on the fact that, say, when in 867 'the Pagan Army went from East Anglia to the city of York' that was 'the nineteenth year from the birth of Alfred' is an obvious ploy to keep Alfred in the forefront of a narrative borrowed from the Chronicle, and where originally the king had no place whatever. Allied to this point is the crucial fact that the author of the *Life* does not in effect begin his account of Alfred's life until the Chronicle itself commences to offer us a continuous series of substantial biographical and annalistic details on the king from 868 onwards. The author tells us that in 868 Alfred joined his brother, King Æthelred I, on an expedition to Nottingham. But this too – and all the historical information that follows down to 887 – is derived verbatim from the Chronicle, which suggests that the author knew nothing of Alfred's life prior to when the Chronicle began its continuous account of the career of the king in 868.[5]

The author's own biographical contribution on the supposedly contemporary Alfred (after 868) remained as thin as his information on the king prior to 868 – apart from what his copy of the Chronicle had to offer. This was so much the case that it was necessary for him to continue to include the translation of the entire Chronicle text from 868 to 887 – even incorporating a great mass of irrelevant detail on Danish inroads in Francia from 880 to 887. The Anglo-Saxon Chronicle included that Frankish material because it had taken as its central theme, the progress of King Alfred's military career *vis-à-vis* the Danish invaders. That Frankish interlude in the Chronicle from 880 to 892 constituted a retrospective insertion on the part of the original compilers of the Chronicle which was designed to establish continuity between Alfred's triumph over the Danes at the end of his Second War in 878 and the beginning of his Last War in 892. The significance of the retrospective nature of this material in the Chronicle has the most profound implications for the dating of the *Life* of King Alfred.[6] If the Frankish entries in the Chronicle from 880 to 891–2 had constituted a contemporary and cumulative record put together by an English compiler, year by year as they occurred, we should expect them to differ substantially in content and in sequence from the genre of Frankish annals which so clearly provided a textual base for them. That Frankish Latin textual base for this entire series of Frankish entries is most evident in the account, for instance, of the division of the Frankish kingdom in 887 as recorded in the Annals of Fulda.[7] It was clearly a Fulda-type text which eventually provided the Frankish material for the West Saxon chronicler. If the Frankish entries in the Anglo-Saxon Chronicle were strictly contemporaneous and of English origin, we should expect – because of the time-lag created by difficulties of communication between Wessex and Francia – to find that some Frankish events at least were dated in the Chronicle later than their true year of occurrence. The opposite is in fact the case. Frankish events of 889 are recorded by the Anglo-Saxon chronicler two years before they actually occurred in 887! Sawyer was the first to observe that the Anglo-Saxon chronicler's relentless following of the Danish army in Francia from 880 to 891–2 was done in the certain knowledge that it would return to Kent in 892.[8] We can go even further and say that an English chronicler who borrowed this Frankish-based material into his chronicle had done so in the equally certain knowledge that this same Danish scourge had been finally defeated by King Alfred in 896. In other words, the compilation date for the Anglo-Saxon Chronicle coincided with the closing years of Alfred's life in the period 896–9. That being so, a biographer of the king who was supposedly writing in 893 could not have had access to a Chronicle whose text he translated down to 887, which had not itself been compiled before 896. Because the forger of King Alfred's *Life* was writing 100 years after the king's death, he was not to know that this Frankish material he had lifted from the Anglo-Saxon Chronicle had not been put in place there until at least three years after he alleged to have been writing, and that some of that material was itself wrongly dated by two years.

For the author of the *Life* of Alfred, his Frankish digression was particularly irrelevant – not least, because, unlike his original Anglo-Saxon Chronicle text, Alfred's biographer cut his narrative short in 887 and thus never dealt with King Alfred's Last War, where the true significance of the Scandinavian invasion of Francia might have become clear. The Anglo-Saxon Chronicle contains information on Frankish affairs for every single year from 881 to 892.[9] The author included all that Frankish material in his translation of the Chronicle down as far as AD 887. He shows in his slavish copying of Frankish events dated erroneously by the Anglo-Saxon Chronicle to 887, that he was not aware he was bringing the Frankish record down in reality as far as 889, although he had cut off his English historical narrative at 887. For the author's account (translated from the Anglo-Saxon Chronicle) of Danish activity on the Yonne (Chapter 84) and of civil wars in Lombardy (Chapter 85), although recorded retrospectively in the Chronicle under 887, refers in reality to events of 888–9. That material, which had nothing whatever to do with King Alfred, was pressed into service by his biographer to cover the nakedness of his narrative on the king, when at that very time – from 885 onwards – 'Asser' informs us that he had first joined the king's household. So at that very time when the author should have been making his most original contribution to the *Life* of his supposed royal patron and friend, we find him slavishly translating irrelevant Frankish annals. This is the point in the *Life* when its compiler has least to say on King Alfred's activities within Wessex – apart from his vague and garbled account of the king's illiteracy. Even the undated and generalised account of the supposed submission of the Welsh kings to Alfred is said to have happened 'a considerable time before' the arrival of Asser at the West Saxon court in *c.* 885.[10] The reason for this dearth of information on Alfred and on Wessex in the 880s is not difficult to seek. Between 880 and 891, the Anglo-Saxon Chronicle contains seven years which are completely devoid of any information on King Alfred or the internal affairs of Wessex.[11] All that the Chronicle offers by way of Alfredian home news from 881 to 887 is the meagre record of Alfred's minor naval battle in 882; a Danish attack on Rochester in 885, Alfred's attack on East Anglia (whose Danes had broken their truce with him), in the same year; his taking of London in 886; and the sending of Ealdorman Æthelhelm to Rome in 887. The author of the *Life* was totally reliant on this material and added nothing to it of any significance. He followed the Chronicle in recording the movement of the Viking army from Fulham to Ghent in 880 (Chapter 61), and from Chapters 62 to 72 and from Chapters 82 to 86 he faithfully transcribed the Chronicle's Frankish material into the Latin of his *Life* of King Alfred where it is completely out of place in that work. At this point in the *Life*, it is fair to say the biography degenerates into the slavish transcription of a Latin translation (from Old English) of large chunks of a completely irrelevant Chronicle text. And all that the author can offer us by way of information on Alfred are those poverty-stricken islands of information which he gleaned from the Chronicle for that very time when the Chronicle also has least to say about the king – Alfred's naval battle (Chapter 64); the Viking siege of Rochester (Chapter 66); Alfred's attack on Danish East Anglia (Chapter 67); and the East Anglian breaking of the truce (Chapter 72); Alfred's restoration of London (Chapter 83) and the sending of Ealdorman Æthelhelm to Rome in 887 (Chapter 86). Everything is derived from the Chronicle and nothing original is offered to us, even though the author supposedly joined the king's court in or around AD 885.

It is in this context – of the author's complete reliance on the Chronicle even when that record is itself deficient on Alfredian matters – that we need to get the so-called additional material offered by the author of the *Life* into a proper perspective. For instance, he identifies Ealdorman Æthelhelm's ealdormanry as being that of Wiltshire, in his translation of the Chronicle's annal for 887 (Chapter 86). He adds that there was a nunnery at Condé in his translation of the Chronicle's brief account of Viking activity in Francia in 883 (Chapter 65), and he claims – when translating the Chronicle annal for 887 – that Chézy was a royal estate (Chapter 84). He correctly names the Carolingian ruler who died in a boar hunt before Christmas in 884 as Carloman and not as Charles – the name incorrectly given both by the Anglo-Saxon Chronicle and by the Annals of Fulda (Chapter 68). The author also correctly adds the name Louis to identify the brother of that Carloman who was slain by the boar (Chapter 68) and he correctly identifies Charles the Fat as king of the 'Alemmani' or Germans (Chapter 70). We note first, that the only item in this list relating to Wessex is the identification of Ealdorman Æthelhelm with Wiltshire – an association which is recorded elsewhere in the Chronicle under AD 897 and which could easily have been written as a marginal gloss in the author's copy of the Chronicle alongside the entry for 887. The remainder of the additional material relates to Francia – a curious misplacement of detail by an author whose task ought to have been to write about Alfred of Wessex. All these additions are by way of glosses on the Chronicle text (or its ultimate Frankish source at this point)[12] rather than additional discrete items of information offered by Alfred's biographer. Nor should such additional information – be it the insertion of a correct ruler's name or a gloss on the placename *Condé* – be necessarily taken as evidence for a ninth-century date for the author of King Alfred's *Life*. These sparse and laconic glosses relating to Frankish affairs – and not remotely connected with the career of King Alfred – must be assessed alongside the author's other treatment of Frankish matters, which is either patently incorrect or betrays a careless handling of the original Chronicle narrative. He accidentally omitted the Chronicle's Frankish annal for 884, which recorded the movement of the Northmen up the Somme to Amiens, and he then went on to misplace the Chronicle's record of events for AD 885 under 884 (Chapter 66).[13] In one of his supposedly helpful glosses, he erroneously assumed that Saxony – the home of his 'Old Saxons' – was not in Germany proper (Chapter 69), and although he correctly identified Charles the Fat as king of the Alemmani or 'Germans', he misunderstood that very same 885 annal in the Chronicle by referring nonsensically to a 'bay of the sea which lies between the Old Saxons and the Gauls' (Chapter 70). This reference was almost certainly prompted by a misunderstanding, on the part of the author of the *Life*, of a mention in the original Chronicle text of the Mediterranean. And to add to all the confusion, while none of this Frankish material related to Alfred, it did not deter his biographer from providing an age for the king for each of those same years from 880 to 887 which was three years too little for a year of birth, wrongly computed in the first instance by the author himself, as being in AD 849. None of this can give us any confidence in an opinion which would claim that the author of King Alfred's *Life* had either first-hand information on Frankish matters or that he was a contemporary observer of Frankish events in the 880s.[14]

An example of the author's handling of the Chronicle is well illustrated in his account of Alfred's taking of London in AD 886. The Anglo-Saxon Chronicle's version and that of the *Life* of King Alfred are set out below:

ANGLO-SAXON CHRONICLE
AD 886: That same year King Alfred occupied London; and all the English people that were not under subjection to the Danes submitted to him. And he then entrusted the borough to the control of ealdorman Æthelred.
*LIFE* OF KING ALFRED
Chapter 83: In the same year [886], Alfred, king of the Anglo-Saxons, restored with honour the city of London and he made it habitable – after the burning of cities and the slaughter of people. He entrusted it to Æthelred, ealdorman

of the Mercians. To this king [i.e. to Alfred], all the Anglo-Saxons – those who had formerly been dispersed everywhere or who were not in captivity with the Pagans – turned voluntarily and submitted themselves to his rule.

Clearly, Chapter 83 of the *Life* of King Alfred provides us with a worked-over version of the Anglo-Saxon Chronicle's annal for 886. The author's account of Alfred's 'restoration' (*restauravit*) is an accurate translation of one meaning of the Old English *gesettan* ('build, restore, occupy a conquered territory'). His use of the additional adverb *honorifice* ('honourably') is typical of the verbose style of this author, and the same word is frequently found in the writings of Byrhtferth of Ramsey where it is employed to qualify actions pertaining to saints. The designation 'king of the Anglo-Saxons' attributed to Alfred, as opposed to the simpler *cyning* ('king') which describes him in the near-contemporary Chronicle, is once again typical of the anachronistic tone of the *Life* where Alfred is frequently so described. Whitelock took the additional phrase in the *Life* of Alfred to the effect that London was taken 'after the burning of cities and the slaughter of people' as evidence that the city was 'obtained by warfare' from the Danes. This was an assumption which could only be justified were scholars absolutely satisfied that the *Life* of Alfred is as reliable a source as the Anglo-Saxon Chronicle itself. The vague imagery of destruction embodied in the phrase *burning of cities and slaughter of people* is a cliché which might be found in any account of the Viking wars by any writer in the Christian West at any time from the mid-ninth to the mid-eleventh century. The important point about this entry – and the only significant point – is that in all its essential details – Alfred's taking of London, his handing of it to Æthelred of Mercia and the submission to him of those English who were not under Danish rule – all this is based firmly on the Chronicle narrative. This passage in the *Life* of Alfred owes everything of substance to the Chronicle annal of 886 just as surely as the absence of any mention in the *Life* of the encampment of an English army against the Danes at London in 883 was also based on a Chronicle text. For the omission in the *Life* of any reference to an English action against Danes in London in 883 was due to the fact that the author was following (for his 883 annal) a version of the Chronicle similar to the A-Text and to the version used by Æthelweard, where all reference to the London siege of 883 was also omitted.

Those scholars whose view of ninth-century Anglo-Saxon history was driven by a 'contemporary Asser' thesis, inadvertently promoted a climate of scholarship in which the *Life* of Alfred came more and more to be studied in isolation from other sources of its kind, such as the Worcester Latin Chronicle (later attributed first to Florence and then to John) or the Latin version of the Anglo-Saxon Chronicle which was translated by Æthelweard. Sensitivities surrounding the authenticity debate came to obscure the fact that the *Life* provided yet another version of the Alfredian Chronicle which was worthy of study for its own sake.[15] When, for instance, the *Life* of Alfred provides vague additional information on the siege of Paris in 886 (Chapter 82) or when it tells us that there was a nunnery at Condé (Chapter 65), such information has been hailed as evidence for its author displaying 'a good knowledge of Frankish affairs'[16] with the explicit notion that this information might derive from personal knowledge on the part of a contemporary ninth-century observer. When Æthelweard (at *c.* AD 1000) translated his Chronicle account of the Viking campaign on the Meuse in AD 882, he added that the Northmen encamped at *Escelun* or Elsloo. Here we are offered a precise location – unique to Æthelweard's version of the Chronicle text – which was very unlikely to have been invented and which was very probably ultimately derived from a version of a Fulda-type annal. Æthelweard's addition of a key placename is surely as important as, if not more important than, the gloss in the *Life* of Alfred to the effect that Condé was a nunnery – for the placename *Cundop* (unlike Æthelweard's *escelum*) already existed in the Anglo-Saxon Chronicle for the author of the *Life* of Alfred to copy. Yet no scholar thus far has ever suggested that we must treat the early eleventh-century Æthelweard as a contemporary source for ninth-century annals. The additions in the *Life* of Alfred on the siege of Paris in 886 are not matched by Æthelweard, whose particular version of the Chronicle in company with the A-Text even omitted the name of Paris from their brief account of this incident. But Æthelweard's account of the attack on Rochester by a Danish warband from Francia does provide an opportunity for comparison, and supplies far more original and specific material than the account given in the *Life* of Alfred. The Chronicle's account of this incident runs as follows:

> AD 885: In this year the aforesaid army divided into two, one part going east [i.e. into East Francia], the other part to Rochester, where they besieged the city and made other fortifications round themselves. And nevertheless the English defended the city until King Alfred came up with his army. Then the enemy went to their ships and abandoned their fortification, and they were deprived of their horses there, and immediately that same summer they went back across the sea.
>
> That same year King Alfred sent a naval force [from Kent] into East Anglia.

The author of the *Life* of Alfred in his translation of this annal (Chapter 66) adds the mention of East Francia as the specific destination of one part of the Viking army which had divided into two and he states additionally that the Pagans constructed their fortress at Rochester 'in front of the gate (*ante portam*) of this place'. He describes the outcome of this Danish siege in what is essentially an inflated version of what he found in the Chronicle:

> Then the Pagans, leaving their stronghold and abandoning all the horses which they had taken with them from Francia as well as the greater part of their captives, fled immediately to their ships on the sudden arrival of the king. The Saxons at once seized the spoil of captives and horses which had been abandoned by the Pagans. And thus the Pagans compelled by great necessity returned to Francia in that same summer.

Whitelock's assessment of this passage was that 'Asser's account is fuller [than that of the Chronicle] and sounds genuine'.[17] The only addition of substance in the text of the *Life* of Alfred, however, is the reference to captives – an insertion which may have been added by the author. Any writer familiar with Scandinavian slave-raiding in late tenth- and early eleventh-century England could easily have added the notion of captives as being part of the English booty. It is when we compare this account of the Rochester siege in the *Life* of Alfred with the treatment of this same annal in the *Chronicle* of Æthelweard, that we realise how superior Æthelweard's treatment of the Chronicle's text is to that of the author of King Alfred's *Life*. Æthelweard tells us that the section of the continental Viking army which went east, headed for Louvain – once again a specific placename is added. He also shows that at first only a section of the defeated Northmen at Rochester headed back across the Channel to Francia in the summer of 885. Another section of the invaders made peace with Alfred and eventually encamped at Benfleet, having twice broken their treaty by raiding south of the Thames. Æthelweard tells us these invaders from Francia were aided by Danes already settled in East Anglia – information which makes sense of Alfred's expedition against East Anglia as reported in the Chronicle immediately after the account of the siege of Rochester. Eventually, more of the Benfleet Danes – having quarrelled with their allies – also departed across the Channel.[18] Whether or not this information was once part of an early version of the Chronicle now lost,[19] we search in vain throughout the pages of the *Life* of Alfred to find such a series of additional and specific annalistic information of this sort.

Elsewhere in his translation of the Alfredian section of the Chronicle, Æthelweard adds a whole corpus of substantive detail which is conspicuously lacking in the garbled narrative of the *Life* of Alfred. Æthelweard tells us of the death of Eanwulf, ealdorman of Somerset in 867, and of his burial in Glastonbury; of how Guthrum's army built booths in the town of Gloucester in 877; how Ealdorman Æthelnoth of Somerset held out against the Danes in 878 and had a share with King Alfred in the baptismal rites of Guthrum and his men; how Ealdorman Odda of Devon led the native defence against the brother of Ivar and Halfdan in the same year; and Æthelweard reports a Frankish victory over the Danes in 881. The author of the *Life* of Alfred has no such detail to offer because unlike Æthelweard, he either did not have access to any hard historical information other than what he found in his particular versions of his Chronicle texts, or if he had such, he chose not to use it. Indeed, it is ironic that it is Æthelweard who provides us with those few additional scraps of substantial information on the life of King Alfred which are absent from the Chronicle proper and which are so lamentably lacking in the *Life* of that king written by someone who claimed to have been his personal tutor. We have already encountered Ealdorman Æthelnoth of Somerset who, according to Æthelweard, supported Alfred in his hour of need on Athelney and who later turned up at Guthrum's baptism. An even more interesting personal vignette is Æthelweard's mention of Alfred's attendance at the funeral of his brother, King Æthelred, in 871. How can it be that a Chronicler such as Æthelweard, who we know was writing in the early eleventh century, provides us with more detailed and substantial fragments of historical information on King Alfred than a biographer supposedly writing in 893 who claimed to have enjoyed the company of the king in his own royal chamber?

The narrative of the Anglo-Saxon Chronicle (if we exclude the Frankish interlude in the 880s) from 835 to 900 is almost exclusively preoccupied with the West Saxon (and later with King Alfred's) struggle against the Danes. A biographer of King Alfred who was genuinely writing in *c.* 893 would be expected to generously supplement that very restricted Chronicle theme and supply us with substantial historical information on many other aspects of the king's life. For instance, the account in the *Life* of Alfred of the king's movements throughout Wessex and of his location at any one time within the kingdom are almost entirely dependent on the Chronicle narrative. That narrative, unlike contemporary Frankish annals, offers us very meagre information on Alfred's royal itineraries. Yet we know that all ninth-century rulers were constantly on the move in an age when all government was personal and when a king needed to be seen by his great men in the regions, as a leader capable of enforcing his will through the administration of justice, collection of taxes, presiding over church synods or the dispensing of favours through charters and other means. The charter evidence relating to Alfred, together with his immediate predecessors, and descendants, shows how much the West Saxon court was on the move and pinpoints places where the magnates attended upon the king. We know, for instance, that in 875 Alfred was in the eastern corner of his kingdom – most probably at Canterbury – when he witnessed a transaction relating to land in the Romney Marsh in Kent. He was accompanied then by Æthelred, Archbishop of Canterbury, by Oswald, Alfred's nephew (or illegitimate son), two of the king's ealdormen and thirteen of his thegns.[20] One of the earliest genuine historical references to Alfred in a charter occurs in a grant by his older brother, King Æthelberht, to the church of Sherborne in Dorset, in 864, in which that West Saxon king associated his younger brothers, Æthelred and Alfred (who was then about 16) in the grant.[21] We search in vain for such circumstantial detail – so crucial in validating a contemporary account – in the hagiographical inventions of the author of the *Life*. He adds nothing to the meagre Chronicle account of Alfred's journeys and he shows no knowledge of specific locations for the king within Wessex at any time, with only two exceptions. He tells us in Chapter 79 that when he was first summoned to King Alfred 'from the western and furthest parts of Britain', he met the king at Dean, a royal estate in Sussex, perhaps sometime in AD 885. We are told in Chapter 81 that when the author returned to King Alfred after a long illness which the author endured at Winchester, he next found the king at an unidentified royal estate called *Leonaford*. These two isolated examples are not enough to justify the claim that this author was the confidant of the king, whom he supposedly tutored in Latin and with whom he presumably moved, along with his itinerant court, across the kingdom. We do not read of one single Alfredian itinerary across Wessex or Kent which is not mentioned in the Chronicle – and in that source such information is confined exclusively to the Danish wars. Yet Alfred must have been constantly on the move in times of peace, when his chaplains and tutors would have accompanied him. Such men would have gone with him to Canterbury, London, and even occasionally to the Mercian towns of Worcester or Gloucester. Paradoxically, King Alfred himself, while immersed in explaining St. Augustine's *Soliloquies*, provides a far more vivid and reliable contemporary glimpse of life at his primitive court than anything which his biographer could invent a whole century after Alfred's death. King Alfred invites us to consider how the magnates of a region converge on a royal farm when the king arrives there:

> Some come from very far away, and have a lengthy journey on a very bad and difficult road; some have a very long journey but a very direct and very good road.... Some have a very short journey which is nevertheless rough, difficult and filthy.... It is likewise with the estates of every king: some men are in the chamber, some in the hall, some on the threshing-floor, some in prison.[22]

The *Life* contains nothing to match the raw simplicity or the eye for detail which Alfred himself brought to bear – albeit in passing – on conditions for visitors at his own royal estates. We hear nothing of such travellers in the *Life* of King Alfred. We are not offered a scrap of additional information on Winchester, which was clearly a major centre of Alfredian power. We are told nothing of Wimborne in Dorset, the site of an important nunnery and another key centre of West Saxon influence. Alfred's brother Æthelred was buried there, and Æthelweard tells us that Alfred (as we might expect) attended the funeral. Nor are we offered any additional information on Sherborne in Dorset, where the author was himself supposedly bishop for at least a decade prior to the death of the historical Asser in 909 and where two of Alfred's older brothers and predecessors in the kingship of Wessex were buried.

Allied to the poverty of geographical information is the lack of mention of the countless magnates who must have attended on Alfred as he moved about his kingdom. A contemporary writer who had known the king intimately between the years 885 and 893, would surely be expected to have mentioned some of the king's leading ealdormen and thegns in a context other than that which he gleaned from the Anglo-Saxon Chronicle. But the Chronicle proper tells us far more about King Alfred's leading men in its annals dealing with the years 893 and 896 (when it becomes strictly contemporary)[23] than we shall ever learn from the so-called contemporary Asser for the years immediately before. Alfred's biographer has nothing to tell us of those 'best king's thegns' who ended their lives in 896 – Swithwulf, Bishop of Rochester, Ceolmund, Ealdorman of Kent, Brihtwulf, Ealdorman of Essex, Wulfred, Ealdorman of Hampshire, Ealhheard, Bishop of Dorchester, Eadwulf, a king's thegn in Sussex, Beornwulf, town-reeve of Winchester, and Ecgwulf, the king's Marshal. Although these men died at or soon after the author of the *Life* claims to have written in 893, they and many others like them must have dominated the Alfredian court throughout the 880s. We search in vain through the *Life* of Alfred to find a single reference to such men, whom a contemporary biographer writing at court would certainly have met and would have had cause to mention. These were the loyal followers upon whom King Alfred relied for his *witan* or 'wise men' – men who attended his councils and who witnessed his charters. And would not a Welshman, that historical Bishop Asser – had he really written this biography – not have made mention somewhere in his narrative of men such as Wulfric the king's 'Horse Thegn' who was also his 'Welsh (or Cornish) Reeve'? Such a magnate would have been of special interest to Bishop Asser, if – as has been argued by Keynes and Lapidge[24] – he were writing the *Life* of Alfred with a view to winning over Welsh rulers to Alfred's side. Nor does the author of the *Life* introduce us to wandering Irishmen such as Dubslane, Mechbethu and Maelinmum who made a sensational visit to King Alfred's court in 891 about two years before the king's biography was supposedly written, and we hear not a word of the king's Frisian advisers who are mentioned by name in the Chronicle under 896. No doubt if the author had continued translating his Chronicle text down beyond 887, he would have slavishly repeated the information on all those people that we find mentioned there after that year. In other words, the *Life* of Alfred was never a spontaneous and contemporaneous account of a ninth-century king. It was essentially a source-based, historical chronicle compiled in the same mould as, say, Byrhtferth's Northumbrian Chronicle – of which, significantly, it forms an integral part. A crucial issue here is that for the period 880 to 887, when the Chronicle narrative was preoccupied with Frankish affairs, the *Life* is also bereft of that kind of detailed and circumstantial West Saxon material which the later, strictly contemporary Chronicle offers us in the 890s. It was during those years and months leading up to 11 November 887 that Alfred's biographer alleges to have nursed the illiterate king through a crash course in Latin – a time when, on his own testimony, he shared the Frankish-style *cambra* or chamber with the king (Chapter 88). Yet all he can tell us of life during those days spent at the very heart of the West Saxon court is what he copied from the Anglo-Saxon Chronicle's eccentric digression on Viking inroads in Francia.

Finally, we come to the complex matter of which precise version of the Anglo-Saxon Chronicle was used by the author in his preparation of the translation of the Alfredian annals from 851 to 887. Stevenson's views in his 1904 edition of the *Life* of Alfred – which dominated Alfredian scholarship throughout the twentieth century – may be summed up as follows. The exemplar of the Anglo-Saxon Chronicle used by the author of the *Life* was different from any extant version, but bore a close relationship with the A-Text and also with versions B and C.[25] The *Life* agrees with the A-Text, for instance, in omitting the mission to India in 883 and in omitting all mention of the Raven Banner captured by the West Saxons from the Danish army in 878. But Stevenson correctly noted that the Alfredian annals in the *Life* of Alfred frequently contain earlier or more correct readings of placenames than the oldest surviving A-Text, and that on several occasions a B-C-type version of the Chronicle was being followed – as in the case of the West Saxon genealogy in Chapter 1. In particular he pointed to the position of Chapter 6 in the *Life*, which records a victory by King Æthelstan over a Danish fleet at Sandwich in 851. This incident is reported at the end of a long entry in Versions B and C of the Chronicle,[26] but in the A-Text it is inserted as the second item under 851, immediately after the battle of *Wicanbeorg*. If the author of the *Life* had been following the A-Text or A-Text Precursor, on the other hand, he would have inserted the Sandwich episode in his Chapter 3. The A-Text fails to name Paris as the location of the Danish winter camp in 886, but the *Life* of Alfred (Chapter 82), following a B-type version, does identify the place on the Seine as Paris. For Stevenson, all this was grist to his mill in constructing his Genuine Asser thesis, for he argued that 'the copy used by the author cannot have been far removed from the archetype of the Chronicle' which 'was, to all appearances drawn up' in the author's own lifetime.[27] Stevenson, followed by Whitelock and Keynes, Dumville and Lapidge, subscribed to a compilation date of *c.* 891–2 for the Chronicle archetype. That would leave an extremely tight but convenient timetable for the author of the *Life* to have translated the Alfredian annals for his biography of King Alfred, supposedly written in 893.[28] But such a hypothesis – and it was never anything more than that – fails to explain why a Chronicle supposedly created in 891 or 892 should already by 893 exhibit what can only be described as a labyrinthine textual history in the first twelve months of its existence. For if the *Life* of Alfred truly dated to 893 then it has to be argued that either its Alfredian annals constitute a translation of the archetypal Chronicle text, or alternatively that twelve months into its existence, there were ancestral prototypes of Versions A, as well as B, and C, already in existence.

There is, however, a more economical explanation of the relationship between the *Life* of Alfred and the later extant versions of the Anglo-Saxon Chronicle. In 1982 Hart argued that the home of the B-Text of the Anglo-Saxon Chronicle was Ramsey Abbey and not Abingdon as Plummer had long before proposed.[29] Hart also believed that the compiler of the B-Text was none other than Byrhtferth of Ramsey, who acting on the instructions of Bishop Oswald of Worcester, acquired a copy of the A-Text and A-Text Precursor from Winchester in order to provide the reformed monasteries of Mercia and the Danelaw with an updated copy of a collection of national annals. Hart's views on the B-Text were given unexpected but dramatic endorsement by Lapidge, who in 1996 conceded 'the possibility that the B-Text of the *Anglo-Saxon Chronicle* was at Ramsey by *c.* 1000'[30] – when, as Hart argued, Byrhtferth was the only plausible computistical scholar working at Ramsey who can have been responsible for chronicle production there. Hart's views on Byrhtferth's authorship of the B-Text appeared some thirteen years before my identification of the authorship of the *Life* of Alfred with the Ramsey School at *c.* 1000. If we accept Byrhtferth's authorship of the *Life* of King Alfred at that time, then the influence of the A-Text as well as the B-Text Precursors on that *Life* falls into place. For Hart, supported by Lapidge, has identified Ramsey as the very place where the B-Text was compiled also in Byrhtferth's time. And just as we have to envisage several (abridged) versions of Byrhtferth's *Life* of Alfred being prepared – sometimes perhaps simultaneously – for different versions of his Latin Chronicle programme, so too we must envisage different versions of the vernacular Anglo-Saxon Chronicle being continued and compiled at Ramsey on the basis of the A-Text or A-Text Precursor which arrived there from Winchester. And what once seemed to Stevenson and others to be ancestral relationships between the A-Text and the B–C-Texts in the *Life* of Alfred, may be due to Byrhtferth's synthesis and manipulation of his translation of the Alfredian annals which he put together by largely following the A-Text, with judicious alterations and additions drawn from his own compilation of the B-Text.[31] For if the B-Text came into existence, as is believed, in *c.* 977, it would be earlier than the *Life* of Alfred. It goes without saying that the *Life* of King Alfred was compiled by someone with a chronicler's obsession with chronology – the translated version of the Alfredian annals, together with the calculation of Alfred's age for each year throughout the *Life*, is a witness to that. In other respects the *Life* of Alfred is constructed along precisely the same lines as Byrhtferth's Northumbrian Chronicle – as a pastiche of existing annals onto which are grafted hagiographical and legendary anecdotes.

## The author's miscalculation of King Alfred's age

The author of the *Life* of Alfred declares in Chapter 1 that Alfred was born in AD 849 – a statement which is at variance with the earliest extant version of the West Saxon king-list as preserved in the genealogical preface attached to the A-Text of the Anglo-Saxon Chronicle. There we read that Alfred was already past 23 when he succeeded to the kingship of the West Saxons.[32] And since that same A-Text of the Chronicle tells us that Alfred succeeded to the kingship after Easter in 871, then we deduce that he was born in 847 or 848. Having declared that Alfred was born in 849, his biographer proceeds to build a narrative on a Latin translation of the Anglo-Saxon Chronicle for those years covering Alfred's life from his birth down to 887. Few historians have commented on this highly unusual structure which underpins the *Life*. Not only did its author graft a hagiographical narrative on to a framework provided by the Chronicle, but he calculated for that framework the year of Alfred's birth, and also the king's age for each annal which he translated from the Chronicle thereafter. At first sight Alfred's age in any given year seems to be calculated only sporadically in 26 out of a total of 106 chapters in Stevenson's edition of the *Life*. But on closer inspection we realise that the author, in slavishly following the Chronicle layout, had the opportunity of translating only 27 years of annals from that text over the period 849 to 887 (the remaining years being blank in the Chronicle), and of those years he accidentally omitted the Chronicle's annals for 877 and 884.[33] Yet for each of the twenty-five annals which he did include, with the exception of the annal for 865, he calculated Alfred's age for each year. Interestingly, in the case of that exceptional year 865, the author misplaced the annal under 864 which happened to be a blank year in the Chronicle. For any early medieval hagiography or biography of any sort, this annalistic framework, together with regular calculations of the age of the subject of the *Life*, is exceptional in the extreme. It is clear that the author of King Alfred's *Life* – regardless of what century he wrote in – had not only a keen interest in the Anglo-Saxon

Chronicle whose ninth-century annals he translated from the vernacular into Latin, but he was also hugely interested in chronology. Byrhtferth of Ramsey was just such a writer. He was responsible not only for the B-Text of the Chronicle which he produced in late tenth-century Ramsey, and for the Ramsey Chronicle; but also for the production of four Latin Chronicles which had various versions of the Anglo-Saxon Chronicle at their core.

The author's calculation of Alfred's age in those annals which depend on the Anglo-Saxon Chronicle survive in the Cottonian version of the *Life* as well as in Byrhtferth's abridged version in the Northumbrian Chronicle and in very fragmentary form in the Ramsey Annals. We find that in these versions Alfred's age for any given year is frequently miscalculated, arriving at a figure which was at variance even with the author's own initial statement that the king was born in 849. So, if 849 was supposedly Alfred's first year, then 851 was correctly identified by the author in Chapter 3 as being Alfred's third year. But AD 853 is wrongly identified in Chapter 7 as the infant king's eleventh year! This was a one-off error in the Cottonian version of the *Life* which is not repeated in the version preserved in the Northumbrian Chronicle, confidently attributed to Byrhtferth of Ramsey. Alfred's age – based on a supposed year of birth in 849 – is correctly given down as far as AD 869, where the king is said to have been in his twenty-first year (Chapter 31). But in Chapter 32 (for AD 870), the king's age is repeated as his twenty-first year – an error which appeared in the now lost Cotton manuscript as well as in the version preserved in Byrhtferth's Northumbrian Chronicle. King Alfred's age is then given as one year short for a calculation based on a birth in 849 from Chapter 32 (for AD 870) through Chapters 35 (for AD 871); 44 (for AD 872); 45 (for AD 873); 46 (for AD 874); and 47 (for AD 875). When we reach Chapter 49 (for AD 876) things become even more confused. The author in the Cotton manuscript version gave AD 876 as Alfred's twenty-sixth year – repeating his miscalculation given under 875, and so produced a figure which was now two years short of the correct age based on a year of birth in 849. Chapter 51 – covering events in the Anglo-Saxon Chronicle for AD 877 – was almost certainly omitted in error by the author of the *Life* of Alfred. A note in the Corpus Christi transcript of the *Life* indicates that this annal was missing from the Cotton manuscript, and it is also absent from Byrhtferth's Northumbrian Chronicle.[34] The result of this omission was that, in Chapter 52, the author labelled the year 878 as Alfred's twenty-seventh year – producing now a cumulative error of three years in Alfred's supposed age in AD 878. The three-year error is repeated through Chapters 57 (for AD 879); 60 (for AD 880); 62 (for AD 881); 63 (for AD 882); and 65 (for AD 883). Chapter 66 wrongly ascribes material from the Chronicle under 885 to the year 884, and 884 is given in the Cotton version of Alfred's *Life* as the king's thirty-third year. This produced a one-off error of four years in the king's age in the

Cottonian and Northumbrian Chronicle versions of the *Life*. When Alfred's age is next given in the Cotton version in Chapter 82 (for events of AD 886) the king's age is given as his thirty-fifth year, and finally in Chapter 84 (for AD 887) Alfred's age is given as his thirty-sixth year. Byrhtferth's Northumbrian Chronicle keeps in step with the errors of the Cottonian manuscript at this point. So the author's error in misdating 885 material to 884 has not made any change to his earlier miscalculation of Alfred's age which continues as three years too little to the end of the work.

Stevenson disingenuously made light of these errors by claiming they were 'parallel with those that occur in innumerable chronicles, and must be due to the same cause, the carelessness of the copyist and not of the author'.[35] Keynes and Lapidge dismissed the errors in the calculation of Alfred's age as 'purely mechanical'[36] and silently corrected them in their translation of the *Life*. Even less excusable was the belief of those same editors that 'presumably [the author of the *Life*] knew he was writing in 893 ... [and] it would be perverse to imagine that Alfred's age is the primary dating criterion'.[37] That comment showed a remarkable lack of understanding of an author who was obsessed with chronological and numerical calculations and whose own trust-worthiness had been challenged by numerous reputable scholars for more than a century. We can agree with Stevenson that it was normal for chroni-clers to miss out an annal when transcribing a text – especially when transcribing from a text such as the Anglo-Saxon Chronicle where many of its years were bereft of any material. There is strong evidence to suggest, however, that the miscalculations of Alfred's age in the *Life* of that king go back to the lost precursor manuscript of the *Life* and were not due to a care-less later copier. Let us return, for instance, to Chapter 47, where – when translating the Chronicle's annal for 875 – the author claims Alfred as being in his twenty-sixth year. In fact, it ought to have been the king's twenty-seventh year, if he had been born in 849 as the author supposed. When the author comes to translate the next annal for 876 in Chapter 49, he repeats Alfred's age as being in his twenty-sixth year – thereby falling two years behind the correct age. The author accidentally omitted the next year (877) and when we reach Chapter 52, translating the Chronicle's annal for 878, we find Alfred's age given as for the king's twenty-seventh year – instead of for his twenty-eighth year as we might expect. We may therefore conclude that the omission of the Chronicle annal for 877 was due to the author and not to a copyist – otherwise the author and the copyist would have moved Alfred's age forward to his twenty-eighth year in 878. Second, we can say that the miscalculations of Alfred's age are not suggestive of errors by later copyists working in a hurry. These errors have their own inherent logical sequences which have all the appearances of having been built in to the earliest version of the *Life* by a compiler who was indeed working at great speed. Lastly, the

Durham version of Byrhtferth's Northumbrian Chronicle also misses out the annal for 877, putting the material for 878 under 877 in error. This means that from 879 onwards, Byrhtferth's Northumbrian Chronicle marches in step with the cumulative error of the Cottonian version of the *Life* in being three years behind a calculated year of Alfred's life, based on a year of birth in 849. Earlier, Byrhtferth's Northumbrian Chronicle shares an error of one year in the calculation of Alfred's age with the Cottonian manuscript for the years 870 to 876 inclusive.

There may be several explanations for the phenomenon of shared errors in the calculation of Alfred's age between the Parker-Cotton edition and the abridged recension in Byrhtferth's Northumbrian Chronicle. One explanation is that these two versions are not just two closely related, early eleventh-century copies of a ninth-century text, but rather that they are two early recensions of the same work, originally written by Byrhtferth of Ramsey, and intended to serve two different purposes. The decision to calculate the king's age goes back to the earliest version of the *Life*, and cannot be attributed to Byrhtferth acting as, say, an editor in a much later age. The calculation of the year of Alfred's birth and the related calculations of the king's age form an integral part of the overarching framework of this biography, and those calculations and their inbuilt errors must be the product of the mind of the original compiler. Tied in with some of the miscalculations is the question of missing annals from the Anglo-Saxon Chronicle which the compiler of the *Life* failed to translate and incorporate into his work. The fact that the missing out of these annals in King Alfred's *Life* was mostly caused by the presence of blank years in adjoining parts of the author's A-Text manuscript of his Chronicle exemplar again strongly suggests the Chronicle omissions (and the consequent miscalculation of the king's age) to have been original to the text of the *Life*.

What may be crucially significant in helping to point to the authorship of these calculations of Alfred's age is a small series of entries in the Ramsey Annals. This is a text composed at Ramsey at *c.* 1016 and containing a laconic annalistic summary of events from 538 to 1016.[38] Hart has shown[39] that these collections of annals were entered as marginal notes on a set of Easter Tables (for the years 532 to 1421) originally kept at Ramsey and which in turn formed part of a scientific compendium assembled by Byrhtferth in the early eleventh century. Although the annals appear as marginal notes on Easter Tables in the classic early format of annalistic compilations, these annals – prior to the late tenth century at least – were never entered contemporaneously (at Ramsey) with the events they describe. They are rather the result of a Ramsey compiler's editorial labours – being dependent from 538 to 729 on a set of Northumbrian Latin annals as well as southern annals which were also used by the compiler of the A-Text of the Anglo-Saxon Chronicle. The section from 733 to 872 was probably the same source as that used by Byrhtferth to compile that same section of his Durham recension of the Northumbrian Chronicle. The third section from 900 to 1016 was based on a text close to, or identical with the prototype of the D-Text of the Chronicle.[40] Although these annals are in the main derivative, it is instructive to see what their compiler considered important to incorporate into this epic Cook's Tour of Anglo-Saxon History, and what he chose to leave out. We find entries relating to Colum Cille (the Irish missionary saint); and to Pope Gregory's sending of Augustine. We read of the mission of Paulinus; of Bishop Felix among the East Angles; of Archbishop Theodore, Abbess Hilda, and of Cuthbert, Wilfrid and Bede. Here too are fleeting notices of the great warlords of early English history – Edwin, Oswald, Wulfhere, Penda, Aldfrith, and many others. What we have here – for the most part – is a conventional summary of Anglo-Saxon history with most of the major players referred to in passing.

What is remarkable from the standpoint of Alfredian studies is that these annals contain only twelve entries (under separate years) for the entire period from 801 to 900. Yet there are 37 entries for the period 600 to 700; 27 for the period 700 to 800; and twelve entries for the very brief sixteen-year period from 1000 to 1016 – as many as for the entire ninth century. And of those twelve ninth-century annals, no less than eight deal with King Alfred. Even more remarkable is the fact that three or four of the Alfredian entries in turn deal with calculations regarding the king's age – Alfred's birth in 849 and his age for the years 860 and 868 are calculated for us, while we are also told that he reigned for twenty-eight years after his accession. Alfred's age of twelve as calculated for 860 agrees with the Cotton text of his *Life* and with the version in Byrhtferth's Northumbrian Chronicle, while his age of 21 at 868 is one year older than that given in the two versions of his *Life*. Clearly the compiler of these annals was very interested in the career of King Alfred. But the question must be asked, given that the compiler of the Ramsey Annals had all of Alfred's career down to 887 or 893 to choose from (in his abridged version of the *Life* found in the Northumbrian Chronicle), why did he concentrate on calculations relating to the king's age? Why in a Chronicle sketching the great events of England's national past – in the briefest of summaries of a saga stretching from Æthelberht of Kent at 600, down to Æthelred the Unready – did the compiler bother to tell us that Alfred was born in 849, that he was twelve years old in 860, that he was twenty-one in 868, and that he reigned for twenty-eight years after his accession in 872? And why did he choose to tell us all this when he ignored Alfred's two pilgrimages to Rome or his great and historical victories at Ashdown in 871 and Edington in 878 – victories which we know were recorded in the text of the Northumbrian Chronicle which lay before the compiler of the Ramsey Annals? The answer surely lies in the fact that the compiler of the Ramsey Annals had a deep personal interest in those very calculations – a compiler identified by Hart as Byrhtferth of Ramsey. Lapidge, too, has endorsed Hart's work on the Ramsey Annals, pointing to their composition around AD 1000 at Ramsey, as leading to the possibility that Byrhtferth was also responsible for the compilation of the tenth-century sections of the Worcester Latin Chronicle – where yet another extensive abridgement of King Alfred's *Life* is also to be found.[41] Can it be that two Anglo-Saxon scholars separated by a century of time could have shared a unique interest in calculating Alfred's age at various stages in his life – both based on what was almost certainly an erroneous date of birth in 849? And can it be that the later of these two scholars shared that interest with a supposed ninth-century author of King Alfred's *Life*, to the exclusion of other kings, saints and scholars – to whom he might also have applied such calculations – across 500 years of early English history in his collection of annals? The reason why these bizarre details of Alfred's age appear in the Ramsey Annals is because they were calculated in the first instance by the compiler of King Alfred's *Life* who was that same Byrhtferth of Ramsey who chose to highlight them in his summary annals as part of his scientific compendium.

## Errors in the author's treatment of the Anglo-Saxon Chronicle

### Chapter 1 (AD 849)

The omission of the names of Wig, Freawine and Freothegar in the West Saxon genealogy may have arisen from the author's accidentally skipping a whole line in the pedigree which he had before him under the annal 855 in his version of the Anglo-Saxon Chronicle.[42] The author's omission of Esla between Elesa and Gewis may be due to no more than a confusion between similar looking names. The Chronicle version used by the author of King Alfred's *Life* – as far as the West Saxon genealogy was concerned – was closer to the B-Text than to the A-Text. The author follows the B-Text, for instance, in including the name Creoda between those of Cynric and Cerdic, whereas the A-Text omits Creoda altogether. And while the A-Text skips from Hathra directly to Noah, the author of the *Life* correctly follows a B-Text version of the pedigree by including Hwala, Bedwig and Seth. The author identifies Seth son of Noah with Sceaf.

### Chapter 3 (AD 851)

The author erroneously records the first wintering of the Pagans on Sheppey. Manuscripts *B, C, D* and *E* of the Chronicle name Thanet as the correct location. Even if the author's exemplar of the Chronicle lacked the location of the

Viking camp – as did Manuscript *A* – his guess that it was Sheppey was not only wrong, but was in conflict with his A-Text Chronicle record, which told him that the first wintering on Sheppey took place in 855 (Chapter 10).

### Chapter 4 (AD 851)

The author of the *Life* accidentally omitted the Chronicle's record of the Danish attack on London. Versions *D, E* and *F* of the Chronicle also omit mention of London, but London is mentioned in the A-Text and, besides, the author goes on to give an erroneous account of London's location which shows that his omission of the place was his own error.[43] The statement that London belongs to the East Saxons (Essex) was anachronistic from the time of the Mercian supremacy in the eighth century down to the early tenth century, when the town was under the control of Mercian rulers. The author's association of London with the defunct East Saxon kingdom was derived from his book-learning and from Bede in particular.[44] It was an antiquarian observation which was in conflict with the reality of late ninth-century English politics.

### Chapter 11 (AD 855)

The *Life* of King Alfred is the sole authority for the infant Alfred's second journey to Rome. The Anglo-Saxon Chronicle, followed by the author of the *Life* (Chapter 8), records Alfred's first pilgrimage to Rome in 853. The historicity even of the first journey is in doubt, but the notion that King Æthelwulf took his infant boy to Rome for a second journey in 855 'because he loved him more than his other sons' is a fiction which is in keeping with other episodes in the *Life* designed to elevate the infant Alfred above his older brothers.[45]

### Chapter 18 (AD 860)

The statement that on the death of King Æthelbald, his brother Æthelberht 'added Kent, Surrey and also Sussex to his dominion' is wrong. Æthelberht was already ruling Kent, Surrey and Sussex during King Æthelbald's reign. In 860 Æthelberht took charge of the kingdom of Wessex proper. The author, in his haste, misread the Chronicle's last annal under the previous entry at 855 where it is stated that Æthelberht ruled Kent, [Essex], Surrey and Sussex, but at a time when King Æthelbald ruled the West Saxons proper.

### Chapter 20 (AD 865)

This chapter which is based on the Chronicle's entry for 865 is misdated by the author of the *Life* to 864. Keynes and Lapidge pointed to the fact that the Anglo-Saxon year in the 860s was reckoned to begin in the autumn and so some incidents which took place late in the year 864 of our reckoning were dated to 865 by Anglo-Saxon chroniclers. The real reason, however, why the author of the *Life* misdated the events of this chapter was because the Chronicle which he was translating had no entries for the years 861, 862, 863 and 864, and he became confused by so many successive blank years. This dating error in the *Life* is shared by the abridged versions in the East Anglian Chronicle (*Annals of St. Neots*) and by the Worcester Latin Chronicle.

### Chapter 21 (AD 866)

The author made two if not three major errors in his translation of the Chronicle's account of the arrival of the 'great heathen army' in England in 866 which wintered in East Anglia. He claimed that the great Pagan fleet arrived in Britain (*Britanniam*) rather than England; that it wintered in the kingdom of the East Saxons (Essex – *in regno Orientalium Saxonum*), which is confused with East Anglia (*quod Saxonice 'East Engle' dicitur*), and that it came from the Danube. His derivation of the Danish invaders from the Danube was based on a late tenth-century literary conceit of Norman origin.[46] His confusion of East Saxons with East Angles also reflects the political situation in eastern England at the turn of the first millennium.[47] The version of the *Life* in the Worcester Latin Chronicle follows the Cottonian account by bringing the Danes from the Danube to Britain, but shows no confusion between East Angles and East Saxons. The East Anglian Chronicle's abridgement of the *Life* omits any mention of the Danube, *Britannia*, or of the East Saxons.

### Chapter 26 (AD 867)

The Cotton manuscript originally gave AD 867 as the nineteenth year since the birth of Charles (*Karoli*) revealing the author's dependence on Charlemagne as his model for the *Life* of King Alfred and echoing his dependence elsewhere in his text on Einhard's *Life* of Charlemagne.[48]

The author informs us that York 'is situated on the northern bank of the river Humber'. This is not so. York is located on the banks of the Ouse more than 30 miles upstream from the western, or inland end of the Humber estuary.

### Chapter 28 (AD 867)

The statement that Bishop Ealhstan of Sherborne had ruled his bishopric 'honourably' (*honorabiliter*) and that he was buried 'in peace' (*in pace*) in Sherborne are two very typical Byrhtferthian additions by the translator of the Chronicle's text, which stand out in sharp contrast to his earlier vilifying of Ealhstan of Sherborne for stirring up rebellion against Alfred's father, King Æthelwulf, in *c*. 856 (Chapter 12). Professor Keynes's attempt to show that there is 'an implicit exoneration of the bishop' in Chapter 12 cannot be sustained.[49] There is no exoneration, implicit or otherwise. We are told first that King Æthelbald, Bishop Ealhstan and Ealdorman Eanwulf of Somerset were involved in 'a certain infamous thing which was contrary to the practice of Christian men'. This is followed by the statement that 'very many people ascribe this misfortune, unheard of in all previous ages, to the bishop and to the ealdorman alone, and it was on their advice that the deed was proposed. There are also many who attribute the deed solely to the royal insolence [of King Æthelbald]'. If the author had been attempting to exonerate Bishop Ealhstan, we should have expected that bishop to have been singled out as the possible innocent party, but he is, on the contrary, twice named as a conspirator. It is only King Æthelbald who is singled out – not as an innocent party, but as a possible culprit acting on his own. Elsewhere Keynes and Lapidge suggested that King Alfred's biographer, in his benign glossing of the account of Bishop Ealhstan's death, may have been 'defending one of his predecessors from the charges of complicity in the plot against King Æthelwulf'. But if 'Asser' were trying to exonerate Bishop Ealhstan in Chapter 28, then why did he *twice* accuse him of treason against his king in Chapter 12 – for which that same 'Asser' is our sole witness? And even Keynes and Lapidge are agreed that it is uncertain that the historical Asser was Bishop of Sherborne at the time of writing.[50]

### Chapter 40 (AD 871)

The author omitted the Chronicle's account of the battle of *Meretune*. This error must go back to the earliest version of the *Life*. It is common to the East Anglian Chronicle and the Northumbrian Chronicle as well as to the Cottonian manuscript. Although the account of the battle of *Meretun* appears in the Worcester Latin Chronicle, it was very probably added in there by a twelfth-century editor, directly from the Anglo-Saxon Chronicle.[51]

### Chapter 42 (AD 871)

The author refers to eight battles which the West Saxons fought against the Danes in this year in place of the 'nine' referred to by the Chronicle. He may have emended the number he found in his Chronicle text to tally with his omission – accidental or otherwise – of the battle of *Meretune* in his Chapter 40. Significantly, the Worcester Latin Chronicle also mentions only eight battles, which suggests that the source also originally omitted all mention of *Meretune* in keeping with other versions of the *Life* of Alfred.

### Chapter 48 (AD 875)

The author gives the number of ships which King Alfred fought against in this year, as six. The Anglo-Saxon Chronicle puts the number of enemy ships at seven. Byrhtferth's version of the *Life* of Alfred in the Northumbrian Chronicle and the Worcester Latin Chronicle agrees with the Cotton version in putting the number of ships at six. The version of the *Life* preserved in the East Anglian Chronicle (*Annals of St. Neots*) agrees with the correct and original Chronicle reading of seven ships.

## Chapter 49 (AD 876)

The Chronicle's account of Alfred's negotiations with the Danes at Wareham shows that the invaders 'swore oaths to him on the holy ring – a thing which they would not do before for any nation – that they would speedily leave his kingdom'. The author of the *Life* either failed to recognise the 'holy ring' (*halgan beage*) as a Norse cult object or more likely found it too repugnant as a monk in the Monastic Reform tradition of *c.* 1000 to accept that the Christian Alfred would recognise a Norse oath taken to Norse gods on a heathen ring. So he mistranslated the Chronicle passage thus:

> They also swore an oath on all the relics in which the king placed most confidence after God – and on which they had never before been willing to swear for any race – that they would most quickly depart from his kingdom.

Originally, the only object referred to in the Chronicle's account was the holy ring. This was the ring of Thor which, according to *Eyrbyggja saga* and other later Old Icelandic accounts, Northmen wore as an arm-ring and which was displayed as a cult-object for oath-swearing in their temples.[52] The Cotton manuscript, the Worcester Latin Chronicle and the East Anglian Chronicle all shift the emphasis from the heathen ring to King Alfred's relics. The East Anglian Chronicle alone supplies a reference to the holy ring – but only after a verbatim account of Alfred's relics as described in the Cotton version of the *Life*. This passage provides yet one more example of how the author of King Alfred's *Life* misunderstood or deliberately misconstrued his Chronicle text.

## Chapter 51 (AD 877)

The whole of the Anglo-Saxon Chronicle's annal for 877 was omitted by the author of the *Life*. It is very unlikely that it was absent from his versions of the Chronicle, and much more likely (see below) that he omitted it himself.[53] This chapter is also missing from the Corpus Christi College transcript of the *Life*. It is clear from a study of the versions of the *Life* preserved in the Northumbrian Chronicle and the Worcester Latin Chronicle that the 877 annal was missing in those versions.[54]

## Chapter 52 (AD 878)

The author wrongly brought the Danish army from Exeter directly to Chippenham. This is a sequence of events which is not to be found in any accurate surviving version of a Chronicle text, since the Anglo-Saxon Chronicle takes the Danes from Exeter in 877 first to Mercia, and in the following year (878) they are reported to have returned to Wessex again from Mercia and to have attacked Alfred at Chippenham. The reason why the author had to take his Danes on a direct route from Exeter to Chippenham was because he had either omitted the 877 annal from his translation of the Chronicle or else he had muddled the correct sequence of Danish movements. Stevenson was correct[55] in pointing to the conflation, by the author of the *Life*, of the Chronicle text of the entries in 876 and 877. Under 876 the author (Chapter 49) tells us that the Pagan army 'gave him [i.e. Alfred] as many selected hostages (*electos obsides*) as he alone chose (*nominavit*)' before they departed from Wareham. This clearly echoes the Chronicle's text for 877 where we are told the enemy 'gave him preliminary hostages there [at Exeter] as many as he wished to have' (*7 hie him þær foregislas saldon swa fela swa he habban wolde*).[56] But the Chronicle's account of the Wareham negotiations in 876 differs from that of the *Life* of Alfred. All references to hostages are absent from the A-Text, while the B-Text version uses a different turn of phrase. At Wareham, according to the B-Text of the Chronicle, Alfred was given hostages 'who were the most important men next to their king in the army' (*þe on þam here weorðoste wæron, to þæm cinge*).[57] The author of the *Life* of Alfred clearly ran the accounts of the hostage exchange at Wareham and Exeter together in his version of the 876 annal, most likely because his A-Text exemplar of the Chronicle had no reference to hostages under 876. Having borrowed the reference to hostages from the A-Text annal for 877, and having inserted it wrongly under 876, he then omitted the annal for 877 under its proper place. Keynes and Lapidge assumed that 'the annal for 877 was carelessly omitted in Asser's copy of the *Chronicle*',[58] and that the ninth-century Asser should be given points for trying 'to lend continuity to his narrative' by taking the Danes directly from Exeter to Chippenham, because his faulty Chronicle source had no mention of any intervening stay in Mercia.[59] In view of the careless as well as the unfinished appearance which permeates the whole of the *Life* of Alfred, it is unwarranted to shift blame from the author of that *Life* to his Anglo-Saxon Chronicle source. On the contrary, the textual evidence suggests that the author did indeed have access to the original Chronicle annal for 877 and it was he who omitted that annal in his own cavalier treatment of the Chronicle translation. We know that he used one version of the Chronicle which was very close to the surviving A-Text. As it happens MS *A* omits the phrase 'they gave him hostages, who were the most important men next to their king in the army', though the phrase does occur in other Chronicle manuscript versions of events at Wareham in 876.[60] To sum up: the author of the *Life*, finding no mention of hostage-giving in his Chronicle's account of those Wareham negotiations, borrowed a phrase from the hostage-giving at Exeter in 877, and then most likely decided to leave out the 877 annal altogether.

## Chapter 54 (AD 878)

The *Life* of Alfred gives the number of men who were slain in the army of 'the brother of Ivar and Halfdan' as 1,200 men. Versions *A, D* and *E* of the Chronicle put the number of Danish slain at 840 men, while *B* and *C* have 860. The discrepancy between *A*'s *.dccc. + .xl.* and *B*'s *.dccc. + .lx.* is easily accounted for. The *Life*'s 1,200 is well out of line with these figures from the author's Chronicle exemplar. Stevenson admitted that it was not likely that a Chronicle reading of *D.CCC* would have given rise to *M.CC* and went on to offer a highly implausible explanation:

> It is possible that it [i.e. the account of the Danish attack on Devon as given in the *Life* of Alfred] was drawn up from information gathered in the neighbourhood, and that the Danish losses had been gradually magnified by the inhabitants of the locality during the time that had elapsed between the battle and the time when it was related to the author of the life.[61]

## Chapter 55 (AD 878)

The Chronicle informs us that when the enemy army 'came stealthily' (*bestel*) to Chippenham in January 878,

> it occupied the land of the West Saxons and settled there and drove a great part of the people across the sea (*ofer se*), and conquered most of the others; and the people submitted to them except King Alfred.

Later in the same annal, when describing how the men of Wessex rallied to Alfred's banner at Egbert's Stone, east of Selwood, in the seventh week after Easter, the Chronicle lists the king's allies as:

> all the people of Somerset and of Wiltshire and of that part of Hampshire which was on this side of the sea.[62]

So, it seems clear that the sea – in the mind of the Chronicler – separated parts of Hampshire rather than separating Wessex from, say, Francia on the other side of the Channel. It is, of course, possible that some of King Alfred's magnates in Western Wessex possessed sufficient resources to escape to Francia. But such a move would have risked abandoning all their estates and possessions to the invader, while a more prudent course of action would have been to escape across Southampton Water towards Chichester or Winchester which, as centres of Alfredian power, must by then have been fortified to withstand a Danish attack. The Chronicle at any rate is explicit in its association of 'this side of the sea' with a part of Hampshire. The author's treatment of this annal takes no account of the Hampshire link. His interpretation of the Chronicle's reference to West Saxon refugees asserts that the Pagan army

> compelled many of that race through poverty and trepidation to sail overseas (Chapter 52),[63]

and later on (Chapter 55), he tells us that among the men who rallied to Alfred at Egbert's Stone were

> all the inhabitants of the district of Hampshire, who had not sailed overseas for fear of the Pagans.[64]

But why was it that only people of Hampshire had fled overseas and not some of those also who lived in Somerset and Wiltshire? It seems as though the author of the *Life* of Alfred was, in this instance, not only slavishly following the Chronicle but also failing to understand it.[65]

### Chapter 56 (AD 878)

The Chronicle tells us that after the baptism of Guthrum along with thirty of his magnates at Aller, followed by the unbinding of the chrism at Wedmore, Guthrum 'was twelve days with the king, and he honoured him and his companions greatly with gifts'. The author of the *Life* renders this passage thus:

> He Guthrum remained with the king for twelve nights after his baptism, and the king bountifully bestowed many and excellent buildings on him and on all his men.

The 'gifts' (*feo*) of the Chronicle, which might have consisted of money or lands as well as treasure, have been transformed by the author into the incongruous *aedificia* or 'buildings'. The reading was massaged by Stevenson to read *beneficia* ('gifts') for which there is no support from any surviving version of the text. Subsequent editors were happy to follow Stevenson's lead,[66] even though the reading *aedificia* is supported by the Worcester Latin Chronicle and by the East Anglian Chronicle. That same word *aedificia* was repeated in Chapter 91 of the *Life* to describe the 'buildings of gold and silver incomparably made at his [i.e. Alfred's] instructions'. In this last case, there is little doubt that 'buildings' – however fictional – were meant, since the word is used between one reference to the building of towns (*de civitatibus et urbibus*

... *construendis*) and another to the construction of royal halls and chambers (*de aulis et cambris regalibus ... constructis*).[67]

### Chapter 58 (AD 879)

The author tells us that 'a great army of Pagans sailing from overseas parts came into the river Thames and united with the former army, but nevertheless wintered in a place which is called Fulham beside the River Thames'. We are being clearly told that the Danes, who had arrived at Fulham, joined forces with Guthrum's army which was based at Cirencester. Keynes and Lapidge translated this passage to mean that the newly arrived Fulham Danes 'made contact with the army further upstream'.[68] But *adunatus est* means 'was united', just as when the author used the same phrase back in Chapter 36 to describe how King Æthelred and his brother Alfred united their forces (*adunatis viribus*) to attack the Reading Danes.[69] As for the *superiori exercitui*, it has to refer to 'the earlier army' at Cirencester rather than to the army 'further upstream' of Keynes and Lapidge. We are being told that the new army at Fulham joined forces with Guthrum's army which was then at Cirencester – over 130 miles upstream from Fulham and close to the source of the Thames. Cirencester is only 20 miles from the Severn Estuary. There is no evidence in the Chronicle for the uniting of these two armies, and the idea may have been suggested to the author of the *Life* by his earlier statement (Chapter 40) that the Summer Army which arrived in 871 'joined itself' (*se adiunxit*) to the company of the Great Army which was already active in Wessex. The Chronicle entry for the following year (880) shows that the Fulham army had retained its separate identity:

The army which had encamped at Fulham went overseas.

### Chapter 59 (AD 879)

The author translates the account in the Chronicle of an eclipse of the sun which occurred by the Chronicle's reckoning in AD 879. The true date of this eclipse was 29 October 878, which would have fallen within the Anglo-Saxon year (beginning sometime in September/October) 879. The Chronicle states that the solar eclipse lasted 'for one hour of the day', but fails to provide the month, day, date or time of day, which is consistent with the view that the Chronicle does not provide a strictly contemporary record of events prior to the 890s.[70] The author of the *Life* replaced the Chronicle's time of duration of this solar eclipse with the statement that it occurred 'between Nones and Vespers but nearer to Nones'. But like his Chronicle source, he also failed to provide month, day or date. His timing of the event to the Nones side of the half-way mark between Vespers and Nones would locate his place of observation of this remarkable total solar eclipse to somewhere on the borders of eastern Germany or well within Poland.[71] Stevenson seriously mishandled the astronomical calculations regarding the time of this eclipse. He saw the record of it by the author of the *Life* as the major plank in his argument for showing the *Life* of King Alfred to be an authentic and contemporary work. Stevenson boldly stated that 'If it could be proved that the time of the day assigned for the eclipse is accurate, it would be a conclusive proof of the authenticity of the *Life*.'[72]

Stevenson went on to devote seven pages of dense astronomical commentary in his edition of the *Life* in an attempt to prove his 'Asser' right. Whitelock, too, saw this passage as providing crucial evidence for authenticity.[73] Yet a close scrutiny of the account of this eclipse as reported in the *Life* of Alfred shows it to conform to the author's vague and sloppy treatment of the Anglo-Saxon Chronicle which pervades the rest of his work. The notice of the eclipse is basically a Latin translation of what was little better than a dim memory of the event by the Anglo-Saxon chronicler – lacking any indication of day of the week, date or month. Contemporary Irish and Frankish annals, by contrast, dated the phenomenon to 29 October 878, with an accurate indication of the local time on that Wednesday. The author of the *Life* of King Alfred was not content, however, to leave the vague information in the Chronicle as he had found it. Typically, he intruded his own gloss on the event by adding that the eclipse took place 'between Nones and Vespers, but nearer to Nones'. The comment was a nonsense in so far as it failed to identify the day and the month when this supposedly detailed timing occurred. It was rather like telling someone you would meet them at 3 p.m. in the year 2000, without specifying which day and month. Keynes's attempt to get his Genuine Asser off the hook simply will not do.[74] He attributes the timing either to 'the author's own imprecise memory'; or by way of information received at second hand; or due to poor weather conditions 'in different parts of northern Europe'. But when weather is poor and the memory is dim, it is the broad detail of an astronomical event which survives – such as the month in the year and perhaps the day in the month. But in this case, the broad detail is absent (as it was from the Chronicle) and a detail of precise timing is added. This account of the eclipse resembles a multitude of other intrusive comments in the translated text of the Chronicle in the *Life* of Alfred, some of which – like the account of the death of Bishop Ealhstan – contradict what was said before. To make matters worse, if the time of day dreamt up by the author is subjected to astronomical calculation, then that author had to have observed this eclipse somewhere near Zary in western Poland. The converse of Stevenson's dramatic statement regarding the veracity of the account of this eclipse must also hold true, and the author's account of it therefore may provide a cogent argument against the contemporaneity of his *Life* of King Alfred.[75]

### Chapter 66 (AD 884 recte 885)

The author's translation of the Chronicle accidentally omitted the Chronicle annal for AD 884 (the Danish occupation of Amiens). This resulted in a further error in the author's text by his dating Chronicle events which properly belonged to 885, in Chapter 66, to AD 884.

### Chapter 67 (AD 885)

The author put the number of East Anglian Pagan ships which Alfred's fleet encountered at the mouth of the river Stour at thirteen. Either he or a copyist misread *xvi* of the A- and B-Texts of the Chronicle to read *xiii*. The Worcester Latin Chronicle's version of the *Life* gives the correct number of sixteen ships. But the error was not peculiar to the Cottonian manuscript, for it was repeated in Byrhtferth's summary of the *Life* of Alfred in the Northumbrian Chronicle.[76]

### Chapter 67 (AD 885)

The Chronicle tells us that when 'they' – King Alfred's ships which had attacked East Anglia – 'turned homeward with the booty, they met a large naval force of Vikings and fought against them on the same day, and the Danes had the victory'. The author of the *Life* rendered this passage thus:

> When the victorious royal fleet was about to go to sleep, the Pagans who inhabited the region of the East Angles, gathering ships from every quarter, confronted the royal fleet ... in the mouth of the same river. When a naval battle was joined the Pagans had the victory.

The author of King Alfred's *Life* mistranslated the Chronicle's *þa hie þa hamweard wendon* ('When they turned homewards')[77] to read *cumque inde victrix regia classis dormiret* ('when the ... fleet was about to go to sleep') – a reading confirmed by the *ubi dormiebant somno inerti* of the version of the *Life* of Alfred summarised by Byrhtferth of Ramsey in his Northumbrian Chronicle.[78] This suggests, as Stevenson pointed out, that the original reading of the *Life* of Alfred ought to have read: *domum rediret* or *domum iret* – a reading suggested also by the Worcester Latin Chronicle.[79]

### Chapter 69 (AD 885)

By telling us that the Pagan army 'came from Germany (*de Germania*) into the region of the Old Saxons which is called *Eald Seaxum*' the author reveals that he was not aware that Saxony was a part of *Germania*.

## Chapter 70 (AD 885)

The author of the *Life* misinterpreted the Anglo-Saxon Chronicle's account of the extent of the kingdom of the Carolingian ruler, Charles the Fat. The Chronicle, which was itself drawing from a set of near-contemporary Frankish annals of the Fulda type, tells us that Charles the Fat:

> succeeded to the Western Kingdom and to all the kingdom on this side of the Mediterranean and beyond this sea, as his great-grandfather [Charlemagne] had held it except for Brittany.[80]

The author of the *Life* translated this passage thus:

> Charles king of the Alemmani, with the voluntary consent of all, received the kingdoms of the Western Franks which lie between the Mediterranean and that bay of the sea which lies between the Old Saxons and the Gauls, with the exception of the kingdom of Brittany.

Charles the Fat was crowned emperor in Rome in 881. He had consolidated his hold over the German territories of the Carolingian empire from 876 onwards. He had become king of Italy in 879. The Chronicle was correct, therefore, in following its Frankish source by stating that Charles the Fat had become ruler of Charlemagne's old lands north of the Mediterranean as well as those territories 'beyond' it to the south in Italy. The author of the *Life*, however, confused what was a second reference in the Chronicle to the Mediterranean ('this sea') with the mouth of the Rhine – hence 'that bay of the sea which lies between the Old Saxons and the Gauls', showing, yet again, his ignorance regarding the location of Saxony *vis-à-vis* the Carolingian Empire and showing also his lack of understanding of the Italian conquests of Charles the Fat.[81] Yet, in the face of this textual chaos and geographical ignorance, Stevenson used this passage to argue that the author of King Alfred's *Life* had 'knowledge of the continent'. Keynes and Lapidge followed Stevenson.[82]

The *Life* of Alfred follows the Chronicle's version of the genealogy of Charles the Fat, but when it reaches the name of Louis the Pious, the Cotton text reads: 'Louis in truth was the son of Pepin or Charles (*filius Pipini sivi Caroli*)'. The version of the *Life* in the Worcester Latin Chronicle shares this confusion with the reading: 'Louis was the son of Pepin.'[83] Louis the Pious was the son of Charlemagne and the grandson of Pepin. The East Anglian Chronicle (*Annals of St. Neots*) gives the correct reading in its abridged version of the *Life* of Alfred. Hart argued that the compiler of the East Anglian Chronicle borrowed the correct reading on Louis the Pious directly from the Anglo-Saxon Chronicle to correct the Cottonian manuscript of the *Life* which he was otherwise following.[84] The author of the *Life* of Alfred translated the Alfredian Chronicle down to the annal for AD 887, and to the end of Chapter 86 in the *Life*. In effect, however, the author unwittingly translated Frankish annalistic material (via the Anglo-Saxon Chronicle) relating to events down as far as 889.

## Other errors and inconsistencies in the author's text

### Dedication

The author addresses Alfred as 'king of the Anglo-Saxons' and 'ruler of all the Christians of the island of Britain'. It is not impossible for King Alfred to have been addressed as 'king of the Anglo-Saxons' by a contemporary biographer wishing to flatter his master.[85] The Anglo-Saxon Chronicle describes Alfred in AD 886 as enjoying rule over 'all the English people (*Angelcyn*) that were not under subjection to the Danes'. The treaty between Alfred and the Danish leader, Guthrum – drawn up around that time – associates King Alfred with 'the councillors of all the English race (*ealles Angelcynnes witan*)'. By the late 880s, West Saxon political thinking – closely directed by Alfred himself – was edging close to the idea that since Alfred was the sole surviving English king, then he could be described as king of all the English who were not under Danish rule, and by extension as 'king of the Angles and Saxons' – even if his territorial base was no larger than Wessex and English Mercia.[86] At the notice of Alfred's death in the Chronicle, we are told: 'He was king over the whole English people (*Ongelcyn*) except for that part which was under Danish rule' – a monumental understatement, considering that the Danes ruled the greater part of England. Although it is true that the notion of the *Angelcyn* or 'English people' as a unified political group under one kingship had its origin in late Alfredian times, it took a whole century for that concept to develop into a political reality.[87] At no point, however, does the Chronicle ever style Alfred 'king of the Anglo-Saxons', and neither in his charters nor on his coins did he dare assume the title 'king of the Mercians'. Contemporary evidence from Alfred's own extensive writings – including the king's own *Will* which was probably revised several times in his lifetime – confirms that Alfred referred to himself as 'king of the West Saxons by the grace of God' or simply as 'king'.[88]

Novel claims associating Alfred with the kingship of all the English, therefore, are conspicuous for their novelty in the contemporary sources. The few reliable surviving charters of King Alfred confirm the evidence from his own writings, for he is referred to in those charters as 'king of the West Saxons', 'king of the Saxons', 'king of the West Saxons and of the Men of Kent', or simply as 'king'. It is only the obvious and agreed forgeries which refer to

Alfred as 'king of the Anglo-Saxons', or 'king of the English'. What is worrying about the use of the title 'king of the Anglo-Saxons' in the *Life* of Alfred is the frequency and prominence with which it appears – at least ten times – beginning with the Dedication, and reappearing in Chapters 1, 13, 21, 64, 67, 71, 73, 83 and 87. In some instances (Chapters 13 and 87) the title is used in a context where the author is supposedly referring to the king as his contemporary, while in others (Chapters 71) the novel title is superimposed on the translation of the Anglo-Saxon Chronicle where the original Chronicle text had 'king of the West Saxons'[89] or where the Chronicle simply refers to Alfred as 'king' (Chapters 64 and 83). The author refers to Alfred as 'king of the Anglo-Saxons' (Chapter 87) in association with the notorious and supposedly intimate account of how the king learnt to read in Chapter 88. This frequency of use of the style 'king of the Anglo-Saxons' in the *Life* of Alfred, and its intrusion into the otherwise workmanlike translation of the Chronicle text, would seem to betray a strongly anachronistic tone set by a writer who was familiar with late tenth-century royal titles. There is a crucial factor in the application of the title 'king of the Anglo-Saxons' to King Alfred by the author of his *Life* in relation to his interpretation of the vernacular Chronicle. Although in the Chronicle entries for 885 and 886, Alfred is referred to as 'king of the West Saxons' and as 'king' respectively, both entries do contain a reference to the novel term, *Angelcyn* or 'English people' in passages referring to King Alfred. In the 885 entry, there is a reference to the English quarter (*Ongelcynnes scole*) – or the *Schola Saxonum* – in Rome which had been freed from taxation by Alfred's friend, Pope Marinus, while in 886 we are told that 'all the English people' who were not under Danish rule submitted to King Alfred.[90] In the late ninth century when the Chronicle was first compiled, Alfred had not yet tailored the precise terms of his kingship to embrace all the *Angelcyn*, or 'the English people' at large. But to a translator of the late tenth or early eleventh century, when West Saxon kings had extended their kingship over all of England, that was a natural connection to make. Hence the author of King Alfred's *Life* tampered with his original vernacular Chronicle text at this point and inserted the notion of Alfred being 'king of the Anglo-Saxons' into his Latin translation under influence of the adjacent and ambiguous word *Angelcyn* in his Chronicle exemplar.

One of the more obvious forgeries of an Alfredian Charter involving a grant of land at Worthy in Hampshire, which was supposedly issued by King Alfred in favour of the thegn, Heahferth, refers to Alfred as 'king of all Britain (*rex tocius Bryttanniæ*)'.[91] Alfred is also flamboyantly described in this forgery as *basileus* or 'emperor of the English and of all peoples round about'. The use of the Greek word for emperor in that fraudulent charter for Heahferth betrays the hermeneutic Latin tastes of writers such as Byrhtferth of Ramsey at the end of the tenth century – Byrhtferth who, incidentally, also used the anachronistic *rector* to describe a late seventh-century king in his *Life* of St. Ecgwine.[92] The actual date of Alfred's supposed grant to Heahferth is AD 939 – some forty years after that king's death!

While the notion of Alfred being a king of the Angles and Saxons had a vague political basis in the face of the Danish occupation of all the other early English kingdoms, the idea of a writer addressing Alfred as *rector* in the context of 'ruler of all the Christians of the island of Britain' is – *pace* Keynes – not compatible with a ninth-century Anglo-Latin historical text.[93] The use of *rector* as applied to English kings in the context of rulers of Britain appears in charters from the reign of Alfred's grandson, Athelstan, onwards. The notion of the English king being regarded (in West Saxon eyes) as the ruler of all Britain is a concept which we find especially associated with the reign of kings such as Eadred and Edgar in the later tenth century. Eadred (946–55) was a king who had not only united all the English under his rule, but had finally seen off Eric Bloodaxe from Norway and several other Hiberno-Norse contenders for the kingship of Scandinavian York. He was not king of the Scots or Strathclyde Britons, or of the Norsemen of the Isles, but he had treated with Scottish and other Scandinavian rulers. The pompous reference therefore to Eadred in his charters as a king guiding 'the government of the diadems of the Anglo-Saxons with the Northumbrians, and of the pagans with the Britons' who was 'orthodoxly consecrated king and ruler to the sovereignty of the quadripartite rule', while not setting out the true facts of his kingship, was at least striving to embellish and exaggerate existing political realities. But for an author to have addressed Alfred in 893 as 'king of the Anglo-Saxons and ruler of all the Christians of the island of Britain' would have been to insult the intelligence of England's wisest of kings and to have mocked at the modest jurisdiction which Alfred in reality precariously enjoyed. Alfred was a king whose very existence was probably unknown among his contemporaries in Strathclyde and Scotland, not to mention the Isles beyond. It is salutary for insular historians to bear in mind that while Alfred's father (Æthelwulf) and his brother (Æthelbald) are both mentioned in the Annals of St. Bertin, we seek in vain for any reference to Alfred in that same Frankish source. His two kinsmen would never have been mentioned there had they not been married in their turn to the Carolingian Judith. The compilers of the precursor text to the Annals of Ulster took a keen contemporary interest in the major political players on the mainland of Britain. They noted, for instance, the crucial Saxon victory over the Danes at Buttington in 893 – with no mention of Alfred who was not present. And while they did note the death of King Æthelwulf in 858 they made no mention of the passing of his son, Alfred, in 899. By contrast, the Annals of Ulster did note the death of Donald II, King of Scots in 900. All this suggests what is abundantly clear from a close scrutiny of contemporary English sources, namely that Alfred could not have been regarded in his own lifetime – and certainly not before 892–3 – either as a great warrior or successful leader in battle.[94] Alfred the patient tactician and Alfred the wise scholar was no Offa. He was capable of snatching a crucial victory out of the jaws of defeat, but Alfred was not the stuff of which Bretwaldas were made. It was the low cunning and reckless heroism of a warrior breed which brought overlordship to Penda and Offa, not contemplation of the works of Pope Gregory. All of which should sound a note of caution for those of us who would rush to embrace the extravagant political rhetoric used by the author of King Alfred's *Life* as contemporary realities. The opening lines of the Dedication in that *Life* suggest that it is the product of a late tenth- or early eleventh-century writer.

### Chapter 1 (AD 849)

The author confuses *Geat*, a supposed distant ancestor in Alfred's West Saxon royal genealogy, with *Geta*, a character in Terence's Roman comedies *Adelphoe* and *Phormio*. There was no connection whatever between the two characters. The error was most probably wilful since it afforded the author of the *Life* an opportunity to quote an irrelevant poem by Sedulius and thus fill out his narrative on the early years of King Alfred, about which he otherwise knew little. Byrhtferth of Ramsey cites Sedulius elsewhere in his *Life* of St. Oswald and in his *Manual*. Unusually for a medieval writer, the author of the *Life* of Alfred, and Byrhtferth elsewhere in his works, not only quotes from Sedulius but cites him by name.[95]

### Chapter 11 (AD 855)

The author of the *Life* declares that:

> King Æthelwulf freed a tenth part of his entire kingdom from all royal service and taxation and by a perpetual written grant he gave it over to the One Trinitarian God on the Cross of Christ for the redemption of his soul and [the souls] of his ancestors.

'Few things', wrote Stevenson,[96] 'in our early history have led to so much discussion as the famous Donation of Æthelwulf.' The great bulk of Stevenson's discussion consists of special pleading to defend the implausible account of this donation. While the author understood King Æthelwulf's grant to have embraced the lands of a tenth 'of his entire kingdom (*totius regni sui*)', the Chronicle text which lay behind this extravagant claim suggests that Æthelwulf gave up only a tenth of his own personal land holdings:

> King Æthelwulf conveyed by charter the tenth part of his land throughout all his kingdom to the praise of God and to his own eternal salvation.

The author of the *Life* understood Æthelwulf's all-embracing gift as going exclusively to the Church. A closer reading of the Chronicle would have shown him that Æthelwulf's generosity, while aiding his salvation, was not necessarily confined to churchmen, and that 'the tenth part of his land throughout all his kingdom' (*teoþan dęl his londes ofer al his rice*) did not necessarily refer to lands other than Æthelwulf's own estates and may not even have included lands belonging to the royal fisc. As long ago as the time of Kemble and Stubbs, those scholars were uneasy at the prospect of Æthelwulf's grant embracing a tenth of the entire kingdom of Wessex, while even Stevenson recognised that 'the author of the Life has overlooked the restriction of the grant to the king's own lands'.[97]

## Chapter 11 (AD 855)

The statement in the *Life* that when King Æthelwulf 'journeyed to Rome with great honour' he took the infant Alfred 'with him on that same journey for a second time' should be treated with great caution. The Chronicle claims that King Æthelwulf sent Alfred to Rome in 853, and that King Æthelwulf went on the Rome pilgrimage himself in 855. The Chronicle has no mention of Alfred in the account of the second journey. The author's assertion that the infant Alfred was chosen to accompany his father because Æthelwulf 'loved him more than his other sons' is a crude attempt to condition the reader into accepting the inevitability of Alfred's ultimate succession to the kingship of Wessex and his superiority in that kingship over his brothers who reigned before him. Later (Chapter 22) the author tells us that Alfred 'was cherished by his father and mother, and indeed by everybody with a universal and immense love more than all his brothers.' The infant Alfred is shown to outwit his duller brothers in the competition for the book prize (Chapter 23), although 'they were senior to him in age though not in grace'. The idea is exactly mirrored in Byrhtferth of Ramsey's account of the death of Ealdorman Æthelwine in the entry for 992 in the Worcester Latin Chronicle.[98] We are told (Chapter 42) that had he wished to do so, Alfred could have taken over the kingship from his brother Æthelred 'for without a doubt he was superior to all of his brothers together, both in wisdom and in all good habits'. So, Alfred's supposed second journey to Rome with his father was designed by the author of the *Life* to underline the notion that Alfred, although younger than all his brothers, was nevertheless destined to succeed them all, and surpass them all, as king. The historicity even of Alfred's first visit to Rome in 853 as described in the Chronicle is beset by problems. The Chronicle's statement that Pope Leo consecrated Alfred as king in 853 cannot be accepted. The doubling of the infant Alfred's Rome visit by the author of the *Life* has no sound evidence to support it, and it runs counter to common sense.[99]

## Chapter 12 (AD 855–8)

The author of the *Life* describes the rebellion of Æthelbald, son of King Æthelwulf, against his father, during which Æthelbald initially supposedly tried to prevent Æthelwulf's return to the kingdom of Wessex after Æthelwulf's pilgrimage to Rome and his marriage to the Carolingian Judith. There is no substantial evidence to support any idea of a rebellion on the part of Æthelbald. He had ruled the kingdom of the West Saxons in the absence of his father in 855–6 and when he died in 860, the Chronicle ascribed a five-year reign to him, implying that his reign began back in 855 and that he ruled as sole over-king of Wessex from Æthelwulf's death in 858. The Chronicle's statement that when:

> Afterwards he [i.e. Æthelwulf] came home to his own people, they were glad of it

might seem to suggest that when King Æthelwulf returned from Rome in 858 he found the kingdom in turmoil during that supposed rebellion by his son as described in the *Life* of Alfred. But this provides very weak support for the author's tale of rebellion. The compilers of the Anglo-Saxon Chronicle placed great emphasis on Æthelwulf's reign, as their inclusion of the elaborate genealogy of that king amply demonstrates. As the father of King Alfred who figures more prominently than any other member of the House of Wessex within the Chronicle, Æthelwulf occupied a special and central place in the compilation. The statement, therefore, that his people 'were glad of it' when King Æthelwulf returned was intended as a compliment to Æthelwulf, and indirectly as a compliment to his son, Alfred, during whose reign and under whose influence the Chronicle was compiled. In the absence of other evidence to the contrary, this statement on Æthelwulf cannot be used as a hostile comment on Æthelbald. Indeed, it could be argued that it was the Chronicle's comment on King Æthelwulf's return which was misconstrued by the author of the *Life* and which prompted him in turn to invent the tale of Æthelbald's rebellion. The entire story of Æthelbald's rebellion and of his supposed wickedness in marrying his young stepmother on King Æthelwulf's death in 858, may be nothing more than a fabrication.[100] It was most likely prompted as part of the author's ongoing attempt to promote the standing of Alfred at the expense of his older brothers, and it may have been concocted from a wilful confusion of King Æthelbald of Wessex with his royal namesake, King Æthelbald of Mercia, who was castigated by St. Boniface in *c.* 747 for a life of fornication. There is a further inconsistency in the author's handling of this tale of Æthelbald's rebellion. One of the conspirators (in Chapter 12) who supposedly egged on Æthelbald to rebel against his father, was Bishop Ealhstan of Sherborne. Yet that prelate who was numbered among those 'traitors' who 'tried to perpetrate so great a villainy as to banish the king from his own kingdom' and who in so doing was responsible for an 'infamous thing which was contrary to the practice of all Christians' (Chapter 12), is later given an honourable mention by the same author in Chapter 28. In Chapter 28, the author informs us that on Ealhstan's death in 867, he 'was buried in peace in Sherborne after he had ruled the bishopric honourably for fifty years'. The embellishments *in peace* (*in pace*) and *honourably* (*honourabiliter*) were the author's additions to his Chronicle translation. Arguments to the effect that the author of the *Life* of Alfred was trying to exonerate one of his own predecessors in the bishopric of Sherborne will not stand up.[101] If the historical Asser were trying to exonerate Bishop Ealhstan, then why did he twice implicate him in a traitorous rebellion of which Asser is our only witness? Besides, it is extremely unlikely that the historical Asser had become bishop of Sherborne by the time the *Life* of King Alfred was allegedly written in 893, and the author of that *Life* – whoever he was and whenever he wrote – never once claims to have been bishop of Sherborne.

## Chapter 16 (AD 855)

The author of King Alfred's *Life* tells us that on King Æthelwulf's return from Rome he drew up a document or *will* in which he arranged for a division of the kingdom between his two eldest sons in order to prevent quarrelling over the succession on his death. Æthelwulf would not have been empowered to dispose of the kingship of Wessex in any *will*. King Alfred's *will*, which survives in its entirety, makes no mention of any attempt on his part to dispose of the kingship of Wessex. The kingship, although confined within a royal kindred, was elective, and kings were chosen by their *witan* or councillors. But even if the author's account of Æthelwulf's disposing of the kingdom by *will* were true, it goes against almost everything which we have been told before. Æthelwulf on his return to Wessex was forced, according to the author of the *Life*, to concede the kingship of Wessex proper to his son, Æthelbald, while Æthelwulf had to remain content with the eastern portion of the kingdom – Kent, Surrey, Sussex and Essex. That portion on the author's own admission was regarded as the less important part of the kingdom of Greater Wessex. The author alleges that Æthelwulf acceded to this arrangement to avert civil war. But whatever the reason, if there were any shred of truth in this account, it would be suggestive of serious weakness on the part of the father. Such a king was in no position to unilaterally dispose of the kingship by means of a *will* – written or otherwise.

## Chapter 25

There is a reference in this chapter to the death of King Alfred as an event which may have already taken place. Stevenson arbitrarily placed the embarrassing phrase in square brackets, while Keynes and Lapidge allowed it to stand but massaged the translated text to convey the sense of the king's death being at some future time.[102]

## Chapter 74

The author tells us that Alfred, sometime during his adolescence and prior to his marriage in 876, went hunting around the St. Neots area in Cornwall. It is highly unlikely that Alfred would have ventured into Cornish territory – then still ruled by its own British king.[103] Later, in Chapter 102, Cornwall is acknowledged to be *de facto* foreign territory to Alfred, where it is listed alongside Wales, Gaul, Brittany, Northumbria and Ireland as an exotic region which benefited from Alfred's charity, during his reign as king. The region was not assimilated into Wessex proper until the reign of Alfred's grandsons.[104]

## Chapter 75

The author informs us that Alfred's children, Edward and Ælfthryth 'were always brought up in the royal court ... and indeed they remain there to this day'. But the author was writing supposedly in 893 – the very year in which Edward the Elder was leading an army in his own right against Danish invaders at Farnham in Surrey. The Chronicler Æthelweard ascribes a prominent role to the 'prince (*clito*)', Edward, in that battle which rivals anything the Anglo-Saxon Chronicle has to say of King Alfred's activities as a warrior.[105] Clearly, by 893, Edward's days as a diligent schoolboy in the care of his father's court were long past. He is styled 'king (*rex*)' in the witness list of a problematic charter of AD 898,[106] which may suggest that by then he was acting as a sub-king under his father. Six years after the author of the *Life* wrote of him as a schoolboy constantly studying in his father's prep school, Edward succeeded Alfred as king of the West Saxons, in 899.

## Chapter 77

The author twice refers to Plegmund as archbishop (of Canterbury) which shows that the *Life* had to be written after 890 – the year in which Plegmund became Metropolitan. The author refers anachronistically to Plegmund twice as archbishop in a context which clearly relates to a time prior to November 887, when King Alfred was supposed to have learnt to read and to translate on his own account (Chapter 87).

## Chapter 93

The author tells us that King Alfred could not find any native novices for the monastic life 'apart from infants (*infantes*) who, because of the tenderness of their unsuitable age, were unable either to choose good or reject evil'. Yet in the next chapter we are told that when Alfred failed to recruit a sufficient number of Gaulish monks he also pressed Gaulish infants (*infantes*) into the service of Abbot John's monastery at Athelney. So while English infants were deemed unsuitable for monastic life, their Gaulish equivalents were encouraged to join up. Byrhtferth of Ramsey, who had read Bede's *Life* of St. Cuthbert, would have known from that source that infancy was regarded as ending in the eighth year, after which boyhood commenced.[107]

## Chapter 94

There is the implication in this chapter that John 'the Old Saxon' was of 'the same Gaulish nation' as other monastic recruits at Athelney. This tallies with an even stronger assumption on the part of the author, back in Chapter 78, that John the Old Saxon had been summoned by King Alfred along with Grimbald, who also came from Gaul. This confusion in the author's mind between Saxons and 'Gauls' (presumably Western 'Franks') is echoed also in Chapter 69 where Old (or continental) Saxons are seen as not being part of Germany. In Chapter 76, the author lists Franks as a distinct people from 'Gauls'. The author seems to be very confused, and indeed ignorant, on continental affairs.

# 5
# Why Was the *Life* of King Alfred Written at Ramsey in *c*. AD 1000?

The Danish conquest of northern and eastern England had a particularly devastating effect on organised Christianity in East Anglia and the southern Danelaw. Even in Northumbria where the bishoprics at York and Lindisfarne managed eventually to negotiate a way through the Viking mayhem, other historic sees at Hexham and Whithorn were not so fortunate. In the southern Danelaw, the collapse of Christian organisation was more marked. Episcopal succession at Lindsey, Leicester, Dunwich and Elham was either disrupted or destroyed, while early English monasticism in the region was virtually wiped out. Eastern England had been trampled underfoot for fourteen years by the Great Army of Danes in the 860s and 870s. It had been colonised by settlers from Scandinavia in the later ninth and early tenth centuries, and had been regularly fought over by West Saxon and Norse kings of Dublin and York throughout the first half of the tenth century.[1] At the time when the West Saxon ruler, Eadred, succeeded the last Danish king of York in 954, many parts of the southern Danelaw must by then have reverted to being a pagan society. Such a region was in need of evangelisation – as far as its new ruling class was concerned – on a scale which was comparable with that of Francia in the time of Clovis. The tenth-century Christian evangelisation programme in East Anglia had its own cohort of saintly founders who were, if anything, more effective than their predecessors who led the Roman mission to England in the early seventh century. Neither Oswald, Bishop of Worcester, nor Æthelwold of Winchester, were men who – like Paulinus, Mellitus or Justus – were likely to quit. In addition to its saintly founders, the conversion of the southern Danelaw also had its exotic missionaries from overseas. Oswald, because of his prolonged stay at Fleury, was in that sense a foreign missionary among the pagan Danes of East Anglia. But it was Abbo of Fleury and his entourage who represented the true Roman presence (as interpreted by the monastic rites of Fleury) at the Ramsey monastic mission station. Abbo's role may not have been quite as clear-cut as that of an Aidan of Lindisfarne or

Augustine of Canterbury in earlier centuries. The tenth-century conversion programme was intellectually led and was rooted in a monastic power base. The brief of Abbo and his followers was to transplant a liturgical, prayer-driven and scholarly programme from the best monastic practice of Francia into the heart of the English Fens. And the man who commissioned this programme in the first instance was Oswald of Worcester, who had founded Ramsey with the backing of the lay magnate, Ealdorman Æthelwine, in c. 968.

Oswald's plan for Ramsey embodied the notion of a Christian cultural powerhouse in what had hitherto been a wilderness held in the grip of Danish warlords. At the heart of that plan lay the foundation of a great monastery with its Benedictine liturgy and Rule, and with its uniquely endowed library and scriptorium where books would be gathered from those cathedral churches (such as Winchester, Worcester, Canterbury and York) which had escaped the worst of the Viking terror. At Ramsey, the documentary history of English Christianity would be rescued, reassembled, and if need be, rein-vented, before being copied and disseminated back across the Anglo-Saxon nation. This plan involved nothing short of a revolution in the historiogra-phy of Anglo-Saxon England – the rewriting and reinvention of England's past. It was a plan whose implications have gone almost unnoticed by modern historians. It was this ambitious design of Oswald which led Byrhtferth – the leading English scholar of his time – to assemble the earliest English annals at Ramsey and from that collection of scattered sources, Byrhtferth welded together a series of Latin and vernacular chronicles which provided a basis for most, if not all, future historical writing on the Anglo-Saxon centuries in later medieval England. Byrhtferth's sources consisted of the works of Bede and fragmentary Northumbrian and southern annals; as well as the A-Text of the Anglo-Saxon Chronicle which was brought from Winchester to Ramsey in the late tenth century. The transfer of that precious but neglected A-Text must have been facilitated by cooperation between Bishop Æthelwold of Winchester and his colleague Oswald of Worcester – both of whom shared the agenda for the conversion of the southern Danelaw and the restoration of its monastic houses.

Byrhtferth's intense familiarity with the A-Text of the Alfredian Chronicle – which he copied, edited and continued down to his own time as the B-Text – must have made him acutely aware of the key role ascribed to King Alfred by the compiler of the original Chronicle. Byrhtferth would have been keenly aware of Alfred's portrayal in the Chronicle as a champion in the Danish wars who persevered against his enemies and who eventually overcame them, first at Edington in 878 and later in his Last War in 896. Byrhtferth and his Worcester diocesan masters, Bishop Oswald and later Bishop Wulfstan, were living through an age which, from the 980s onwards, was again under constant threat from a Danish invader and when a strong and determined

West Saxon king was conspicuously lacking. This was the England of Æthelred the Unready. It is easy to see how it would have occurred to Byrhtferth – the greatest expert on the Anglo-Saxon Chronicle – to compile a *Life* of King Alfred based on a Latin translation of the Alfredian section of the A-Text. He may well have been commissioned to produce that royal biography by either Oswald, who died in 992, or by his successor, Bishop Wulfstan. It is also probable that Ealdorman Æthelwine, Ramsey's lay co-founder who died in 992, may also have been a patron of the *Life*. As Byrhtferth's career moved towards the 990s, Alfred's reign had become a dim memory in a land troubled by invasion and relentless warfare. Alfred's vernacular works – and the educational ideals which they represented – were by then well-nigh forgotten, and the details of Alfred's life and career had been irretrievably lost apart from that precious, albeit partisan, record of the king's life preserved in the A-Text of the Chronicle. As it happened, a *Life* of Alfred was also a necessary part of the Ramsey programme as established by the scholarly Abbo of Fleury. Abbo had shown the way, while staying at Ramsey in 985–7, by compiling a *Life* of Alfred's contemporary, the martyred king Edmund of East Anglia. The *Life* of Edmund was a pastiche of pious legend, hagiographical motifs and a few scraps of genuine historical and topographical information. It was designed, as was Byrhtferth's *Life* of Alfred, to hold up a mirror to Christian kings and their warrior aristocracies at the turn of the millennium, to show how their saintly and robust predecessors stood up to pagan hordes from Scandinavia. In the case of Edmund, he paid for his heroism with his life, obtaining a martyr's crown, while his relics (eventually housed at Bury St. Edmunds) provided a rallying point for Christian revival in East Anglia. The Worcester Latin Chronicle records the hostility in 1014 of the Danish conqueror, Swein Forkbeard, to the monks of Bury and of Swein's personal hatred of the potency of King Edmund's relics there.[2] It may even be that the account of Swein's ranting against St. Edmund was written up for that Chronicle by the ageing Byrhtferth himself.

The writing of Alfred's *Life* carried an even more immediate political message than that of St. Edmund. In Alfred, Byrhtferth found his ideal West Saxon king – the very ancestor of Æthelred the Unready – who waged relentless and successful war against his pagan foes and who triumphed in the face of overwhelming odds. Alfred had been a great scholar and must have been especially dear to the heart of that bookish Ramsey community, which was committed to the restoration of English Christianity through learning and liturgy. The saintly Alfred, according to his biographer, had supposedly endured unending illness which he – again supposedly – had wilfully sought from Heaven in an effort to curb his passions. In Alfred, Byrhtferth invented a chaste king who founded model monasteries at Shaftesbury and Athelney, where – as at Ramsey – the *regula* of a reformed Benedictine lifestyle was observed.[3] Significantly, when Byrhtferth came to describe the fictional details of life in Alfred's monastery at Athelney from a century before, he chose to fill that community with 'Gauls' – those same people (i.e. Franks) who provided the impetus for the very foundation of Ramsey itself and for the genuine restoration of the Danelaw monasteries in Byrhtferth's own day.

Saintly biographies were part of the propaganda with which Fenland abbeys like Ramsey consolidated their spiritual and political gains among the half-Christian Anglo-Danish magnates of eastern England. In this they were supported not only by their ecclesiastical superiors in the bishopric of Worcester but also by lay magnates such as Ealdorman Æthelwine, the son of Athelstan 'Half-King' and a close friend of King Edgar. In his *Life* of St. Oswald and in his Worcester Latin Chronicle, Byrhtferth took a swipe at the wicked Mercian ruler, Ælfhere, who in 975 had supposedly tried to destroy the monastic reform programme so carefully fostered by King Edgar. And Byrhtferth lost no opportunity to praise his own lay patron, Ealdorman Æthelwine, who had protected Ramsey and other reformed houses by resisting the Mercian backlash. That anti-Mercian feeling is abundantly clear in the *Life* of King Alfred. The tale of Eadburh, the Mercian poisoner of West Saxon kings (Chapters 14–15), and the association of King Alfred's mysterious illness with his wedding feast when he, too, married a Mercian woman (Chapter 74), are clear evidence of that. The *Life* of Alfred also contains noticeable moralising against civil war – in the case of the Northumbrian power struggle of 867 (Chapter 27) and in the case of the invented civil strife between King Æthelwulf of Wessex and his son, Æthelbald in 855 (Chapter 12). In one case (Chapter 12), Byrhtferth saw dynastic strife as posing an 'irremedial' threat to the stability of a kingdom, and in the other (Chapter 27) he digressed to say that rebellion against the rightful king was inspired by the devil. Byrhtferth was well aware of the evils of civil unrest which he himself chronicled in the aftermath of King Edgar's death in 975, followed by the murder of Edgar's son, Edward, at Corfe in Dorset in 978. Edward's murder was supposedly engineered at the command of his step-mother, Queen Ælfthryth, and Ealdorman Ælfhere (the sworn enemy of Ramsey Abbey) may also have been involved. The murder of Edward ushered in the reign of his half-brother, Æthelred the Unready. King Alfred's biographer comes closest to lecturing his readers on the evils of his own day, when in Chapter 91 he fulminates against those magnates who through laziness or because they 'scorned the royal commands' failed to carry out necessary fortifications against Pagan inroads. The author of King Alfred's *Life* may have been prompted into this tirade by reading the notice in the Anglo-Saxon Chronicle of an unfinished fortress in Kent which was overrun by Hæsten's Danish army in 892. But Byrhtferth used that incident in his *Life* of King Alfred to lecture readers of his own day on the catalogue of treachery and disloyalty on the part of the magnates towards

Æthelred the Unready, in that ruler's largely fruitless campaigns to stem the Viking advance in the 990s.

There are several reasons to conclude that the *Life* of King Alfred may have been compiled early in Byrhtferth's writing career. First, since Byrhtferth inserted abridged versions of his biography of King Alfred into his series of Latin chronicles – the Northumbrian Chronicle, the East Anglian Chronicle and the Worcester Latin Chronicle – then clearly his *Life* of Alfred pre-dates those works. Second, it is noticeable that although the Danish invaders are consistently referred to in Alfred's *Life* as 'Pagans' (*pagani*), they are not treated with the same developed hostility in that work as Byrhtferth metes out to those same enemies in his Northumbrian Chronicle or in the Worcester Latin Chronicle. That might be suggestive of a date for the compilation of Alfred's *Life* which was prior to the deepening crisis that engulfed England in the years from, say, 1006 onwards. Although the earlier Danish wars from the era of the Great Army form a central theme in the *Life* of King Alfred in so far as that material was lifted wholesale from the Anglo-Saxon Chronicle, nevertheless, the main editorial comment in that work concentrates more on the role of Christian kings who befriended the Church. That, of course, was the understandable preoccupation of a writer who was obsessed with monastic dependency on the patronage and support of late tenth-century Christian kings and other lay magnates. We are told in Chapter 12 of his *Life* that Alfred's father, King Æthelwulf, alienated 'a tenth part of his whole kingdom' essentially for the benefit of the Church – 'for the redemption of his soul and those of his predecessors'. That extravagant and inaccurate statement was based on a mistranslation of the Anglo-Saxon Chronicle's account of the same episode.[4] No sane medieval king would have even attempted to diminish the resources of his kingdom and the inheritance of its ruling class in such a way, and hope to have stayed in office. As for Alfred himself, his biographer made even more outlandish claims regarding his unbounded generosity to the Church. 'Wishing to surpass the practice of his predecessors', Alfred supposedly promised 'to give to God one half of his service, both by day and by night, and one half of all the riches ... which accrued to him during the year' (Chapter 99). These, and the other more detailed and unreal measures which Alfred allegedly took to fulfil his financial duties to God and to his clergy (Chapter 102), were clearly inspired by a monastic writer who had seen his own monastery brought to the brink of ruin by Ealdorman Ælfhere of Mercia. Ælfhere had tried – no doubt for pressing economic reasons – to dissolve the monastic endowments of King Edgar. But according to the author of King Alfred's *Life*, half that saintly king's revenues were divided into four equal shares and given to the poor, to his monasteries at Athelney and Shaftesbury, to his school, and finally to the monastic houses of Wessex and Mercia generally, and sometimes to monasteries in foreign parts. Significantly, the Master of that celebrated School at Ramsey fantasised that King Alfred bequeathed one eighth of his entire royal revenue to just such a *schola* as Byrhtferth himself was running. Indeed, much of what Byrhtferth wrote of Alfred's royal prep school where 'books in both languages – Latin and English – were carefully read' may have been prompted by the writer's own preoccupation with his Ramsey school. The foundation of a monastery at Athelney may well be post-Alfredian, and Byrhtferth may have assumed its origin to have been Alfredian solely on the evidence of the Chronicle's account of Alfred having built a fort there in 878. The author's interest in the nunneries at Wareham (Chapter 49) and at Shaftesbury (Chapter 98) may have been inspired by the association of those houses with the murdered king, Edward, who was probably slain by Ealdorman Ælfhere's anti-monastic party in 978 – a deed vividly described by Byrhtferth in one of his typical digressions in his *Life* of St. Oswald. Edward's body was taken to Wareham for temporary burial after his murder. He was reinterred in the nunnery in Shaftesbury in 980 and his relics were translated into a shrine there in 1001.

Relics and the resting places of saints were central to the thought-world of Byrhtferth of Ramsey, and their place in that world was as much political as it was spiritual. When the House of Alfred established itself from the reign of Athelstan (died 939) onwards, as a new unifying native kingship for the whole of Anglo-Saxon England, the cult of English saints took on a special significance. On the one hand, English saints and their relics could be used as a focus for rallying resistance to the pagan Scandinavian invaders, and in this respect the relics of both King Edmund of East Anglia and of Cuthbert of Lindisfarne were primary examples. But such relics and saints' cults could also be used to help consolidate the West Saxon hold over its newly conquered neighbours – be they Scandinavian pagan or Old English. So, Athelstan asserted the West Saxon right of patronage over the shrine of Cuthbert at Chester-le-Street for the first time in 934, and Archbishop Oda of Canterbury seized the relics of St. Wilfrid from Ripon and carried them back in triumph to Canterbury not long after. As the new monastic churches of the Fens sprang up in the wake of the West Saxon conquest of the southern Danelaw, there too, relics and the cult of saints were used to consolidate the hold of new Christian masters over a conquered land. And the enshrined remains of holy men and women that had once been destroyed and looted by the hated Dane, back in the 860s, had to be replaced by other invented, and – if need be – by stolen relics. To set the seal on these prestige ritual acquisitions, the *Lives* of the saints associated with such remains had to be written up in the remarkable Ramsey scriptorium, where the indefatigable Byrhtferth worked tirelessly on their production. Byrhtferth wrote his account of the martyrdom of the royal Kentish princes Æthelberht and Æthelred, who were slain at

Eastry in East Kent in the seventh century, but whose bodies were translated to Ramsey in the reign of Æthelred the Unready.[5] That Ramsey acquisition had been brought about by its lay patron and co-founder, Ealdorman Æthelwine, 'Friend of God'. The same powerful ealdorman became the patron of the recently founded monastery at nearby St. Neots sometime between *c.* 980 and 991. It seems clear that Æthelwine must also have been instrumental in helping the unnamed West Saxon king[6] and Bishop Æthelwold of Winchester to purloin the relics of Neot from his Cornish monastery and establish them at the heart of a new community in East Anglia. In this case, the newly annexed Cornish kingdom was being plundered for its ritual treasures in the drive to lend prestige – if not a false sense of antiquity – to a newly-founded monastery in the Danelaw. And it was Byrhtferth again, or one of his scholarly team at Ramsey, who sold the Neot legend to the Anglo-Danish community of eastern England by writing up a *Life* which had even less by way of an historical kernel than his creation for King Alfred. He did, however, again make use of the Anglo-Saxon Chronicle as his core text for Neot, and he produced an alternative version of the Alfred–Neot relationship, this time with a twist in which the saintly Neot helps to reform Alfred the Sinner, and assists Alfred from the grave in that king's war against the Danish Guthrum. So, here the Ramsey writer reminds his West Saxon royal masters that Alfred's victory over Guthrum – on which all subsequent West Saxon conquests were based – was due to crucial supernatural assistance from a holy man whose relics were now preserved within the Ramsey monastic sphere of influence. In effect, this was a powerful statement against those magnates who would encourage Æthelred the Unready to unravel the lucrative endowments which his father, Edgar, had settled on the Fenland abbeys.

The editors of the earliest Latin *Life* of Neot at first considered the likely date of that work to have been sometime between the foundation of the church at Eynesbury in *c.* 980 and the removal of the relics of Neot out of the path of marauding Danish armies into the safety of Crowland *c.* 1004–1013.[7] Having been led by the evidence of the *Life* to consider that Byrhtferthian date, the editors subsequently backed off in favour of a later eleventh-century date of writing because of one particular glaring historical error in the *Life*.[8] That error centred on the author's claim that Neot (the supposed contemporary of King Alfred) had studied at Glastonbury in the time of Æthelwold, the later Bishop of Winchester, who died in 984. To allow such an egregious error, however, to sway their judgement against other more compelling internal textual evidence, was to attribute to Byrhtferth a sense of responsibility as an historical writer, which Lapidge himself had never accorded him. The hallmark of Byrhtferth's frantic rewriting of England's past at the turn of the first millennium was its almost total disregard for historical truth; together with the juxtaposition of authentic historical records, such as the Anglo-Saxon

Chronicle and Bede's *History*, alongside folklore, hagiography, and wilful invention. Byrhtferth was a great expert not only on the Chronicle but also on the works of Bede. But by weaving a narrative based on those reliable sources – frequently using passages completely out of their historical context – interspersed with fraudulent invention, he wove an obscurative web of deceit around an entire corpus of eleventh-century English historiography. When Whitelock introduced Byrhtferth's *Life* of St. Oswald in her 1955 edition of *English Historical Documents*[9] she might have been forgiven for stating that the work contained 'important information on political history'. Byrhtferth had, after all, known Oswald as his superior throughout his career at Ramsey and he must have been present on several occasions when Oswald visited that place. It is also highly likely that Oswald personally commissioned several of Byrhtferth's writings – not least the *Life* of King Alfred. Yet in spite of that, Byrhtferth's biography of Oswald contains numerous irrelevant digressions, names of people plucked out of the air, and serious errors relating to well-known and major events of Byrhtferth's own time – the year of St. Dunstan's death, confusion as to the identity of Ælfthryth, step-mother of Edward the Martyr, as well as what Lapidge described as the fabrication of a supposed eye-witness account of the coronation of Edgar. Lapidge formed so low an opinion of Byrhtferth's biography of his own contemporary, St. Oswald, as to warn his readers: 'I should urge that extreme caution be applied by anyone wishing to use the *Vita s. Oswaldi* as a record of tenth-century history.'[10]

While Byrhtferth played fast and loose with his historical narrative when describing events of his own time, he allowed his imagination free rein when it came to describing more distant eras. In the case of his *Life* of Ecgwine – an eighth-century Bishop of Worcester who founded Evesham – Byrhtferth unscrupulously cobbled together an invented biography from a combination of forgery and the misappropriation of genuine historical material, interspersed with folklore and hagiography. The *Life* of Ecgwine contains a spurious charter – almost certainly invented by Byrhtferth – and the saint is made to write in the first person, so as to lend an authentic air to an otherwise fraudulent work. Byrhtferth adopted that same 'first-person' mode in his biography of King Alfred, when he took on the persona of Bishop Asser. The *Life* of King Alfred, then, forms part of a much larger portfolio of late tenth- and early eleventh-century monastic propaganda which sought to provide Christian England with a past of which it had been largely robbed by Viking marauders of the ninth century. It formed part also of a monastic ritualistic and scholarly strategy to provide the re-established churches of the Danelaw with a gallery of heroic Christian kings and holy men.

By writing up the *Lives* of men such as King Alfred and his supposed kinsman, Neot, Ramsey Abbey was not just supplying a need for edifying tales of Christian living. It was also serving its own political purposes as well as those of its West Saxon masters. And West Saxon masters were not as far removed from the Fens as we might imagine. Local magnates like Ealdorman Æthelwine, the lay founder and protector of Ramsey, represented the interests of the king of Wessex throughout the southern Danelaw. Æthelwine's father, Ealdorman Athelstan, had ruled such a vast territory from the Thames to the Welland, that he was known as the 'Half King'. The future king, Edgar, had been reared in Athelstan's household, and grew up there with the young Æthelwine. When Ealdorman Æthelwine, 'Friend of God', died in 992 he was buried in Ramsey Abbey. Byrhtferth of Ramsey wrote of his patron, Æthelwine, in the Worcester Latin Chronicle, in precisely the same terms as King Alfred had been described in his biography – a man younger than all his brothers, but superior to them in ability and virtue. A powerful magnate such as Ealdorman Æthelwine would have made a fine patron for the writing of the *Life* of King Alfred.

# Notes

## Introduction

1. *Asser's Life of King Alfred*, ed. W.H. Stevenson (Oxford reprint of 1904 edn.), p. vi.
2. Ibid., p. vii.
3. S. Keynes, 'It is Authentic', *The Times Higher Education Supplement*, 8 December 1995, p. 17.
4. S. Keynes, 'On the Authenticity of Asser's *Life* of King Alfred', *Journal of Ecclesiastical History*, xlvii (1996), 529–51.
5. M. Lapidge, 'A King of Monkish Fable?', *The Times Higher Education Supplement*, 8 March 1996, p. 20.
6. Cf. J. Nelson, 'Waiting for Alfred', *Early Medieval Europe*, vii (1998), 121–2, where the argument is put more cogently.
7. A.P. Smyth, 'King Alfred's Issue Carries on Burning', *The Times Higher Education Supplement*, 29 March 1996, p. 13. I leave it to others to judge the merits of Mr Howlett's contribution in the *English Historical Review* – D.R. Howlett, review of *King Alfred the Great* by A.P. Smyth, in *English Historical Review*, cxii (1997), 942–7.
8. Nelson, 'Waiting for Alfred', pp. 120–2, 124.
9. E. Christiansen 'The Rescue of a Great English Ruler', *The Spectator*, 13 January 1996, p. 32.
10. J. Campbell, 'Alfred's Lives', *The Times Literary Supplement*, 26 July 1996, p. 30.
11. R. Abels, *Alfred the Great: War, Kingship and Culture in Anglo-Saxon England* (London and New York, 1998), pp. 318–26.
12. P. Stafford, *Queen Emma and Queen Edith: Queenship and Women's Power in Eleventh-Century England* (Oxford and Malden, 1997).
13. Alistair Campbell's excellent edition of the *Encomium Emmae* has been reissued as a Camden Classic with a supplementary introduction by Simon Keynes. A. Campbell ed. (with introd. by S. Keynes), *Encomium Emmae Reginae* (Roy. Hist. Soc. Cambridge, 1998 reprint of 1949 edn.).
14. M. Lapidge, 'Byrhtferth and Oswald', in *St. Oswald of Worcester*, eds. N. Brook and C. Cubitt (Leicester, 1996), p. 78.

## Translation of the *Life* of King Alfred

1. The exaggerated form of address used in the opening lines of this text echoes the language of charters issued in the names of Alfred's grandsons and great-grand-sons in the later tenth century. See pp. 194–6.
2. The author's statement that Alfred was born in 849 is at variance with the earliest versions of the West Saxon king-list which claim that Alfred was 23 when he succeeded to the kingship of Wessex in 871. See p. 176.
3. This genealogy is based on that of Alfred's father, King Æthelwulf, which appears in the composite annal in the Anglo-Saxon Chronicle for 855–58. There is nothing in the genealogy of Æthelwulf as given by the author of the *Life* of Alfred which does not appear in the overall surviving manuscript tradition of the 855

annal of the Chronicle. There are, on the other hand, two omissions – the name of *Elsa* between Elesa and Gewis, and the three names *Wig, Freawine* and *Freothegar* between Gewis and Brond. It is always unsound to base any argument for originality in a text on evidence for omission of material which might well have been left out in error.

4. The author of the *Life* may have accidentally omitted a line here from his copy of King Æthelwulf's genealogy in the Anglo-Saxon Chronicle. See Smyth, *King Alfred the Great*, pp. 173–4, and Keynes and Lapidge, *Alfred the Great*, n. 4, p. 228.

5. Sedulius is here, unusually, cited by name as the author of the *Carmen Paschale*. Byrhtferth of Ramsey also cites Sedulius in his *Life* of Oswald and in his *Manual*.

6. The idea that Geata was once worshipped as a god is borrowed from Nennius' *Historia Brittonum* (*Nennius: British History and the Welsh Annals*, ed. and transl. J. Morris (London and Chichester, 1980), p. 26). The author's confusion of Geata in the West Saxon pedigree with Geta, a character from classical Roman comedy, was probably a wilful device which enabled him to introduce the irrelevant poem of Sedulius in order to pad out his thin narrative.

7. Literally 'Nilotic (*Niliacis*) books'. A reference to pagan writings on papyri, perhaps, as opposed to medieval Christian Latin texts written on skins.

8. Oslac the so-called cup-bearer of King Æthelwulf, is known only from this passing reference in the *Life* of Alfred. See pp. 95–6.

9. I follow Stevenson in translating the Frankish *comes* ('count') as *ealdorman*. It is clear from the author's translation of the Anglo-Saxon Chronicle that this is correct. The word *comes* is also applied by the author to Danish leaders as in Chapter 33.

10. This passage on the legendary history of the Isle of Wight relies on the Anglo-Saxon Chronicle's annals for AD 530 and 534.

11. The name of the island is missing from MS *A*. The author of the *Life* inserts Sheppey in error. The correct location was Thanet, which is also the location given in the Chronicle of Æthelweard. The Anglo-Saxon Chronicle specifically tells us that 'heathen men' wintered on Sheppey for the first time in 855.

12. The monastery on Sheppey is referred to as though it were still a going concern, which would have been well-nigh impossible because of intense Viking activity from the 860s onwards in the later ninth century.

13. *et Londoniam* was omitted from the Cotton manuscript according to Wise. Mention of London is also absent from MSS. *D, E, F* of the Chronicle. But the author of the *Life* must have known of its inclusion in the earliest Chronicle entry since he goes on to give (inaccurate) details of London's location.

14. The statement that such a well-known and important town as London belonged to Essex shows that this *Life* cannot be a contemporary late ninth-century account of King Alfred. London, under the Mercian supremacy, was a key Mercian emporium and it continued to be so down to Alfred's reign under King Burgred. The Chronicle's statement that King Alfred entrusted London to Æthelred, ealdorman of the Mercians in 886, and that on Æthelred's death in 911 London fell under the control of King Edward the Elder, shows that London was still identified as a Mercian town when the author of the *Life* was supposedly writing in 893.

15. The author's phrase *loco funeris dominati sunt* ('they were masters of the place of slaughter') is repeated many times in his translation of the Anglo-Saxon idiom *wælstowe geweald ahton* found in the Anglo-Saxon Chronicle. Cf. Chapters 18, 33, 35, 36, etc. Significantly, the author uses the Latinised form of the Anglo-Saxon idiom here, where it is absent from the Chronicle's annal for 851. Cf. note 109

below. Stevenson, ed., *Life of Alfred*, pp. 178–9. For the significance of the phrase in helping to identify the cultural origins of the author see p. 120.

16. This record of the battle at Sandwich is inserted in MS A of the Chronicle after events at *Wicganbeorg* as recorded under this year. MS *A* originally had the Sandwich episode under annal 845, but it was later erased. The author follows the B Text of the Chronicle in entering it here at the end of 851.

17. The Anglo-Saxon Chronicle, unlike the author, gives Athelstan his title of 'king'. He was eldest known son of King Æthelwulf and he had been king of Surrey, Sussex, Kent and Essex since 839. He died in or shortly after 851.

18. The Cotton manuscript gave the year of Alfred's life as *undecimo* or 'eleventh' in the year 853. Byrhtferth's version of the *Life* of Alfred preserved in his Northumbrian Chronicle gave the correct reading of 'fifth' year (*Historia Regum*, ed. T. Arnold (Rolls Ser. London, 1882–85), ii, 70). This error in the Cotton manuscript would imply that Alfred was born in 842–3 rather than in 849 as the author himself had initially calculated. The author's assessment of Alfred's age begins to go wrong again for the year 870 in Chapter 32, and his Alfredian age-reckoning continues to present problems from then until the end of the work.

19. *Britannia* in this case means Wales.

20. The claim that Alfred was anointed king during his infancy cannot be accepted. See p. 197 and cf. Keynes and Lapidge, *Alfred the Great*, p. 232, n. 19.

21. The information that the Brittonic name for the Isle of Thanet was *Ruim* was borrowed from Nennius' *Historia Brittonum* where it occurs in the same chapter (31) as the statement that Geta was worshipped as a god – information also borrowed by the author of the *Life* of Alfred (*Nennius*, ed. and transl. Morris, pp. 26, 67). Keynes and Lapidge (*Alfred the Great*, p. 69) translate *Britannico sermone* as 'Welsh'. It could refer to any form of early medieval Brittonic, including Cornish.

22. For Chippenham as a royal estate, see pp. 107, 118.

23. According to the Anglo-Saxon Chronicle, this was the first viking wintering on Sheppey, but the author of the *Life* does not translate that statement because he had earlier erroneously placed the first wintering on Sheppey back in AD 851. See note 11 on p. 212 above.

24. The Anglo-Saxon Chronicle more realistically claims that Æthelwulf gave over a tenth part of his 'land' rather than of his kingdom (*totius regni*) for his own spiritual benefit. That in effect is confirmed by the author when he returns to report on King Æthelwulf's bequest for a second time in Chapter 16. Because of the author's mistranslation of the 855 annal from the Chronicle, and because of his doubling of the record of King Æthelwulf's bequest, historians have been led into accepting that Æthelwulf may have made two separate 'decimations' of his lands – hence the so-called First Decimation supposedly dating to November 844 (from Winchester) and a Second Decimation, issued at Wilton in 854. Early forgers of Anglo-Saxon charters were not slow in capitalising on the author's garbled account of these events. The Latin phrasing used by the author to describe this supposed extravagant grant of King Æthelwulf echoes the language of the mostly spurious Second Decimation charters of King Æthelwulf. It is, of course, possible that some genuine charters did reflect the wishes of King Æthelwulf as briefly outlined in the Chronicle annal of 855, where we are told that: 'King Æthelwulf conveyed by charter the tenth part of his land throughout all his kingdom to the praise of God and to his own eternal salvation.'

25. Stevenson interprets *graphium* as 'land secured by deed as private inheritance', but it is important not to lose sight of the overall devotional sense of this

passage with echoes of Col.ii. 14 and echoes also of the penitent thief in Chapters 89 and 90. The author was, after all, a monk steeped in the devotional literature of his time.

26. The statement that the infant Alfred went twice to Rome is peculiar to this author, and was almost certainly his invention. See Smyth, *Alfred the Great*, pp. 12–17.

27. This is part of a widespread attempt on the part of the author to demonstrate Alfred's superiority over his older brothers. See p. 197.

28. The account of this rebellion by King Æthelbald against his father, King Æthelwulf, is found only in the text of the *Life*. For the possible origin of this tale, based on a confusion of Æthelbald of Wessex with his eighth-century namesake, King Æthelbald of Mercia (716–57), see pp. 198–9.

    There are serious contradictions in the author's narrative. On the one hand we are told that Æthelbald had the backing of all his *witan*, together with a powerful bishop and an ealdorman. Yet we are also told that the 'nobles' of Wessex prevented Æthelwulf from being banished from his own kingdom, although he supposedly had to remain content with ruling the sub-kingdoms to the east of Wessex. And while Bishop Ealhstan is vilified as a traitor for his part in this rebellion, we are later told (Chapter 28) that he was buried with honour at Sherborne.

29. This passage reveals the author's personal dislike of civil war. Cf. Chapters 13, 17.

30. The author, like Byrhtferth of Ramsey, was notorious for snatching names of historical figures at random from other sources and then using those names to invent historical fictions. The chronicler, Æthelweard, links the names of Bishop Ealhstan of Sherborne and Ealdorman Eanwulf of Somerset under the year 867 – for the very good reason that they happened to die in that same year. Such a record may have prompted the author to press the names of these magnates into service in his tale of revolt against King Æthelwulf. The coincidence is striking.

31. *Saxoniae*, 'of Saxony'. This is the author's usual term for the kingdom of the West Saxons (Wessex).

32. C.R. Hart has suggested with good reason that the author of King Alfred's *Life* based his notion of King Æthelwulf's exclusion from Wessex and his improbable confinement to Kent and the eastern kingdoms, on a garbled reading of annal 825 of the Anglo-Saxon Chronicle (MS *A*). That annal reads:

    'Then he [King Egberht of Wessex] sent from the army his son, Æthelwulf, and his bishop, Ealhstan, and his ealdorman, Wulfheard, to Kent with a large force and they drove King Bealdred north across the Thames. And the people of Kent and of Surrey and the South Saxons and the East Saxons submitted to him because they had been wrongfully forced away from his kinsmen.' (*E.H.D.*, ed. Whitelock, i, 185)

    We may note that Bishop Ealhstan also figures in this account of the campaign of 825, which may well have supplied the unscrupulous author of King Alfred's *Life* with ideas for the same bishop's role in the fictitious rebellion against Æthelwulf.

33. The description of King Æthelwulf of Wessex as a *senior* in the sense of 'lord' is a characteristic Frankish usage displayed by this author. The title *senior* is also applied to John, the supposed abbot of Athelney in Chapter 97.

34. The author again shows his abhorrence of dynastic strife within a kingdom.

35. This statement was almost certainly prompted by the statement in the *Annals of St. Bertin* (*sub anno* 856) to the effect that King Æthelwulf 'formally conferred on her [Judith daughter of Charles the Bald] the title of queen, which was something

not customary before then to him or to his people'. See Smyth, *Alfred the Great*, pp. 177–8.

36. Stevenson's note on *Theotisci*, the author's collective name for the Germanic peoples of Early Medieval Europe, contains an over-tight and specious argument in which he endeavoured to show that the use of this word indicated the *Life* of Alfred had been written 'at some date earlier than the date of the Cottonian manuscript'. *Life of Alfred*, ed. Stevenson, pp. 202–4. The word could easily have found its way to late tenth-century Ramsey via the writings of Abbo and his Frankish colleagues from Fleury.

37. *Ælfredo veredico* ('Alfred, the truth-teller'). Note the reference to 'reliable witnesses' (*veredicis referentibus*) within the same sentence.

38. *Britanniam*, i.e. Wales. The author is not consistent in his use of *Britannia* through-out this work. In this case he is referring to Wales. Later in Chapter 21, he confuses *Britannia* with England.

39. The marriage of the historical Eadburh of Mercia to the Beorhtric of Wessex was a political phenomenon designed to consolidate Mercia's hold over Wessex and designed also to exclude the future House of Alfred (under his grandfather, Ecgberht) from the kingship of Wessex. That marriage took place in 789 and was among the few such unions recorded by the Anglo-Saxon Chronicle. This marriage between Eadburh and Beorhtric was mentioned in the Chronicle not once but twice – in 789 and in 839. The 839 annal highlights Eadburh's complicity in the exile of King Alfred's grandfather:

> 'Before he became king, Offa king of the Mercians, and Beorhtric king of the West Saxons, had driven him [Ecgberht of Wessex] from England to France for three years. Beorhtric had helped Offa because he had married his daughter.'

It was this annal and the notice of the marriage of Eadburh to Beorhtric of Wessex back in 789 which prompted the author to include his cocktail of invention and folktale regarding the misdeeds of the hated Eadburh into the *Life* of King Alfred.

40. Charles i.e. Charlemagne.

41. The reference to Charles as a 'king' (*Karoli regis*) may be anachronistic. Charlemagne had been crowned emperor by 800, and King Beorhtric of Wessex had died 802, after which event – according to the tale narrated in the *Life* of Alfred – Queen Eadburh emigrated to the court of Charlemagne.

42. Pavia was a plausible place to send Eadburh to die. The author would have read in his copy of the Chronicle under the year 888, that King Alfred's sister, Æthelswith, died in Pavia then. The notion of Eadburh being reduced to penury before her death is a common folk-motif involving the reversal of roles. See Smyth, *King Alfred the Great*, pp. 176–7.

43. It is likely that King Æthelwulf secured the agreement of his *witan* or royal coun-sellors before his departure for Rome in 855 to have his son Æthelbald recognised as king of Wessex in his absence and to have his son Æthelberht recognised as sub-king of Kent and the south-east. The notion, however, that any king could unilaterally bestow the kingship on a successor by means of a 'will' cannot be accepted. The West Saxon kingship (although confined within a royal kindred) was elective and controlled in effect by the *witan*. No *will* of Æthelwulf has survived in full, but neither the *wills* of King Alfred nor of King Eadred make any mention of the disposal of the kingship as such. Not even the author included the infant Alfred in King Æthelwulf's settlement of the succession in 855, although he lost no opportunity in according Alfred special status as the best loved of

Æthelwulf's sons and (later on) as *secundarius* (heir-apparent or joint-ruler?) during the reign of his older brother Æthelred. This has not deterred scholars from indulging in speculation to the effect that King Æthelwulf may have secured the kingship on the infant Alfred from as early as 855. There is not a shred of evidence in this *Life* to support such an idea. See Smyth, *King Alfred the Great*, pp. 403–9, 415–17.

44. *in hoc opusculo* 'in this little work' – an example of the author's fondness for diminutives.

45. The desire not to bore readers is borrowed from the *Preface* of Einhard's *Life* of Charlemagne (*Einhardi Vita Karoli*, ed. R. Rau, in *Ausgewählte Quellen zur deutschen Geschichte des Mittelalters*, V, i, 164).

46. This mention of King Æthelwulf's bequest of one tenth of 'all his hereditary land' (*per omnem hereditariam terram*) refers back to Æthelwulf's bequest as outlined in annal 855 of the Anglo-Saxon Chronicle and as mistranslated earlier by the author in Chapter 11 above. Here the bequest was confined to the hereditary lands of the king.

47. Stevenson (*Life of Alfred*, p. 211) rightly questioned the notion that King Æthelwulf could enjoin on his heirs for ever an annual payment of 300 mancuses for Rome. This was indeed 'a great sum of money' by ninth-century standards – no less than 42 pounds.

48. Keynes and Lapidge (*Alfred the Great*, p. 73) omit to translate that the offering sent to Rome annually, was for the benefit of Æthelwulf's soul (*pro anima sua*).

49. The statement that Æthelwulf was buried in Winchester appears in the Corpus transcript of Otho A.xii. According to Wise it did not appear in Otho A.xii (Stevenson, p. 16, notes). King Æthelwulf was most probably initially buried in Steyning in Sussex as mentioned in the East Anglian Chronicle (*Annals of St. Neots*), but his body was afterwards moved to Winchester – perhaps before the compilation of the Anglo-Saxon Chronicle in the late ninth century. (Cf. D. Whitelock, *The Genuine Asser*, p. 9.)

50. This was not true. Marriage with a step-mother was widespread practice across Early Medieval Europe. The author's comment was prompted by Bede's disapproval of the marriage of Eadbald of Kent (*c.* 616–18) with his step-mother and of Bede's mistaken belief that it was *inter gentes inaudita* (*Venerabilis Bedae Historiam Ecclesiasticam* [II.v], ed. C. Plummer (Oxford, 1969, reprint of 1896 edn.), i, 90; ii, 88. *Bede's Ecclesiastical History*, eds. Colgrave and Mynors, pp. 150–1 and p. 151, n. 5). The author's statement that King Æthelbald's conduct was 'contrary to the custom of all pagans' echoes not only Bede on King Eadbald but also the sentiments of a letter from St. Boniface and his fellow German bishops to King Æthelbald of Mercia written in 747. In that letter, Boniface claimed that fornication 'was held not only by Christians, but even by the pagans as a reproach and a shame'. Byrhtferth of Ramsey had used both Bede's account of Eadbald and the letter from Boniface to King Æthelbald of Mercia, to fabricate an episode in the fictitious *Life* of St. Ecgwine which Byrhtferth also wrote. Byrhtferth had noted the juxtaposition in Bede of a reference to a letter from Pope Boniface IV (608–15) written to King Æthelberht of Kent, and Bede's account of the subsequent marriage of Æthelberht's son, Eadbald, to his father's widow – together with Bede's disapproval of that incestuous marriage. This prompted Byrhtferth (while concocting his 'life' of Ecgwine) to invent a letter from a pope, Boniface – presumably Boniface V (619–25) – to King Eadbald of Kent. Only the opening and closing lines of this 'papal' letter are quoted by Byrhtferth, but it was clearly never written

by any Pope Boniface, nor sent to King Eadbald of Kent. It was, rather, written by Boniface the English archbishop of Mainz to King Æthelbald of Mercia in 747. Byrhtferth of Ramsey, in his *Life* of King Alfred, was also prompted by this same letter to mentally identify Æthelbald of Mercia with his namesake in ninth-century Wessex and so transferred the evil reputation of the eighth-century Mercian king to the son of Alfred the Great. See Smyth, *Alfred the Great*, pp. 309–11.

51. Judith was the daughter of Charles the Bald, granddaughter of Louis the Pious and great-granddaughter of Charlemagne. The Alfredian Chronicle ignored the marriage of Judith to King Æthelbald because of the obvious prestige such a Carolingian union conferred on Alfred's older brother. It is very probable that the author of the *Life* had access to a version of the *Annals of St. Bertin* where Æthelbald's marriage to Judith is recorded, without comment, in 858. See Smyth, *King Alfred the Great*, pp. 193–4.

52. The Chronicle gives five years for Æthelbald's reign. The *Annals of St. Neots* explains the two and a half years offered by the author of the *Life* of Alfred with the phrase:

> 'Æthelbald, his son, reigned two and a half years after him, and he previously reigned two and a half years with his father.'

53. It can be seen from the author's text how he filled out the laconic Chronicle narrative with his own character assassination of King Æthelbald.

54. This chapter was considered by Stevenson to have been inserted into the original text of the *Life* of Alfred in a later hand. He attributed the passage to a borrowing from the East Anglian Chronicle (Annals of St. Neots), from whence he believed Archbishop Matthew Parker had added it to the text of 'Asser' (Stevenson, *Asser's Life of King Alfred*, pp. 16, 215).

55. The correct age for King Alfred is given in this supposedly interpolated chapter, based on a year of birth in 849, and thus conforming with other chapters in this earlier section of the *Life*. See pp. 176–81.

56. The author is in error here. Æthelberht was already king of Kent, Surrey, Sussex – and indeed Essex. It was Wessex which he had now inherited from the deceased king, Æthelbald. The author of the *Life* made this error by carelessly reading the annal above at the end of the composite entry under the years 855–58 of his version of the Chronicle, where he read that on the death of King Æthelwulf,

> 'Æthelberht succeeded to the kingdom of the people of Kent, and the kingdom of the East Saxons, and of the people of Surrey, and to the kingdom of the South Saxons.'

It is notable that King Alfred's biographer in misplacing this passage from the Chronicle, omitted the reference to the kingdom of the East Saxons (Essex) which is also omitted by Version *C* of the Chronicle.

57. This pagan army had come from Francia. See Smyth, *King Alfred the Great*, p. 20.

58. The Anglo-Saxon Chronicle records this material under the year 865.

59. Unusually, Alfred's age is not given for this year.

60. The Chronicle notes that the army of Danes came to England (*Angelcynnes lond*) rather than to Britain (*Britannia*).

61. For the statement that the Danes arrived in England from the Danube, see Smyth, *King Alfred the Great*, pp. 304–6, where it is argued that the writer of the *Life* of Alfred had access to early eleventh-century Norman pseudo-histories which

sought to invent a Dacian or Danubian ancestry for the founders of the Norman colony.

62. The notion of Essex (*Orientalium Saxonum*) being the same as East Anglia (*East-Engle*) derives from the political conditions in East Anglia at *c.* AD 1000. See Smyth, *Alfred the Great*, pp. 303–4.

63. This is one of the more blatant attempts by the author to demonstrate Alfred's superiority over his older brothers – four of whom were kings, and three of whom preceded him in the kingship of Wessex. See Smyth, *Alfred the Great*, pp. 149, 180, 185.

64. The author's claim that Alfred was always brought up at the royal court mirrors the statement in Chapter 75 that Alfred's own children – Edward and Ælfthryth – were always brought up at his royal court. While these statements are quite plausible, they were most probably prompted by Einhard's account of Charlemagne's children:

> 'He paid such attention to the upbringing of his sons and daughters that he never sat down to table without them when he was at home, and never set out on a journey without taking them with him.' (Einhard, *Life* of Charlemagne, III. *Two Lives of Charlemagne*, transl., Thorpe, p. 75)

65. This statement about the neglect of his education by Alfred's parents makes a nonsense of the next chapter, where his mother is shown conducting a reading class and setting up a reading competition.

66. The statement that Alfred remained an illiterate (*illiteratus*) until his twelfth year is flatly contradicted by the anecdote of the book prize in the next chapter. There Alfred is said to have read the contents of an entire book and then to have read it aloud at a time when he was aged somewhere between 3 and 8. We are then told (Chapter 24) that the precocious Alfred mastered the psalms and Divine Office and that he kept a notebook on his person which contained these and other private devotions. Even if we were to accept the statement that Alfred was an illiterate until he was twelve, we are still faced with a further contradiction in Chapter 77, where we are told that the king 'had still not begun to read anything', and had to be read aloud to by his tutors. That was supposed to have been shortly before 'Asser' met King Alfred for the first time in *c.* 885, when by the author's own reckoning the king was 36.

67. Einhart in his *Life* of Charlemagne (Book III. transl., Thorpe, pp. 64–7, 72) tells us that Charlemagne listened to the recitation of sagas during meals and he directed 'that the age-old narrative poems, barbarous enough, it is true, in which were celebrated the warlike deeds of the kings of ancient times, should be written out and so preserved'.

68. This is one of several places in the *Life* where the author protests that he had either personal knowledge of the king or of some of the events he describes. Cf. Chapters 29 and 39. The author lapses into the present tense in this passage, which may have been a later insertion.

69. This chapter was constructed around two folk motifs – one being the tale of *The Younger Brother who alone succeeds on a Quest* and the other being a hagiographical motif of the saint or infant saint *Learning or Reading in a remarkably short time by Magic or Miracle* (see Smyth, *Alfred the Great*, pp. 181–5). Whitelock and others have treated the tale as though it were near-contemporary historical narrative. It is riddled with historical contradictions and its purpose was to glorify Alfred while denigrating his brothers.

70. Alfred's eldest known brother was Athelstan, sub-king from as early as perhaps 839 and who died sometime between 851 and 855. Æthelbald, the next in line, was old enough in 851 to have fought alongside his father at *Aclea*, while Æthelberht was also old enough to be ruling a section of the kingdom from at least as early as 855.

    In spite of the emphasis on Alfred's brothers (plural), the only brother eligible for this competition would have been Æthelred.

    For Alfred's mother, Osburh, to have been able to supervise the competition, it must have taken place prior to 855 when her husband, Æthelwulf, headed off for Rome and for the acquisition of a second spouse. Alfred was then only six or less, according to the author's own reckoning. If we were to assume the competition took place in Alfred's twelfth year (as the previous chapter might suggest), then the mother was a step-mother, Judith, and the year would have been 861–2. By then, Æthelbald had already succeeded his father, married his step-mother and died. And the twice-widowed Judith would by then have returned to Francia! Since the tale is entirely apocryphal, it is folly to attempt a serious scholarly analysis.

71. The meaning is that Alfred's brothers were ahead of him in years but not in regard to the favour (*gratia*) in which he was held – especially perhaps – by his mother. This statement is yet another of the many attempts by the author to elevate the reputation of Alfred above that of his brothers.

72. The primary meaning of *recitare* is 'to read aloud'.

73. *legit* of the text clearly indicates that Alfred *read* the book. Attempts by Keynes and Lapidge (*Alfred the Great*, p. 239, n. 48) to massage the meaning of this passage to be that Alfred either 'absorbed the contents' of the book, or (following Stevenson) to hold that it was the tutor who read it rather than Alfred, carried little conviction. Stevenson's commentary on this chapter (*Life of Alfred*, pp. 221–5) was an attempt to sustain the hypothesis for a 'genuine Asser' against all evidence to the contrary.

74. *cursum diurnum*, literally 'the daily course', but in this context of the services of the hours and psalms can only mean the Divine Office (Niermeyer, *Mediae Latinitatis Lexicon Minus*, p. 292).

75. The idea of the infant Alfred's handbook or personal notebook was inspired by the account of a similar though more celebrated notebook in Einhard's *Life* of Charlemagne:

    > 'He [Charlemagne] also tried to learn to write. With this object in view he used to keep writing-tablets and notebooks under the pillows on his bed, so that he could try his hand at forming letters during his leisure moments.' (*Vita Caroli*, III, transl., L. Thorpe, *Two Lives of Charlemagne: Einhard and Notker the Stammerer* [Harmondsworth, 1969], p. 79)

    King Alfred's lifelong attachment to this notebook is described later on in the *Life* in Chapters 88 and 89.

    The author's confusion and endless contradictory statements on Alfred's ability to read and on his supposed adult illiteracy were partly triggered by Einhard's account of Charlemagne's inability to read and write into old age. The notion that Alfred's education was neglected by his parents, but that he somehow mastered the Psalms and Divine Office, was most probably inspired by the *Life* of Gerald of Aurillac, whose education was also neglected by his parents and who was only allowed to study the Psalter. See Smyth, *King Alfred the Great*, p. 272.

76. This comment on the lack of 'readers' (*lectores*) in Wessex was inspired by Alfred's own comments in his Introductory Letter to the *Pastoral Care* on the inability of West Saxon scholars to read Latin. The word *lectores* then, ought to be translated in its primary meaning as 'readers' rather than 'scholars'.

77. *dispendia* translated as 'burdens, trials or hindrances' by other editors.

78. This claim that Alfred lacked tutors (*magistri*) when he was young, together with the claim (Chapter 22) that he remained illiterate because of the 'unworthy neglect of his parents' contradicts the tale of the book prize (Chapter 23), where we see Alfred's mother involved in the provision of a personal tutor (*magister*) who was immediately at hand to provide Alfred with a crash-course in reading!

79. *legere non poterat* clearly translates 'he was not able to read'. Whitelock, followed by Keynes and Lapidge, translated: 'he was not able to study' (*E.H.D.*, ed. Whitelock, i, 267; Keynes and Lapidge, *Alfred the Great*, p. 76).

80. *and as I believe up until his death*: Stevenson (*Life of Alfred*, pp. xlix, 22) placed this phrase quite arbitrarily within square brackets in his edition of the *Life*, because of the obvious embarrassment caused by the author's apparently posthumous reference to King Alfred, who is otherwise supposed to have been alive and in his 45th year. Keynes and Lapidge (*Alfred the Great*, p. 76) allowed the passage to stand, but silently inserted a future tense for which there is no evidence in the Latin text – their version then reading:

> 'Just as he did not previously desist from the same insatiable desire, among the difficulties of the present life, from infancy right up to the present day (and will not, I dare say, to the end of his life), so too he does not yet cease to yearn for it.'

Howorth commented on this passage as long ago as 1876:

> '[It was] most clearly the phrase of an after compiler who has been napping, and has forgotten for the nonse that he should have known nothing of Alfred's death.' (*Athenaeum*, 2 September 1876, p. 307)

81. Words in square brackets added by editor.

82. The confusion between the names of Alfred and Charles reveals the strength of influence which Einhard's *Life* of Charlemagne exerted on the mind of King Alfred's biographer.

83. The statement that York was situated on the northern bank of the Humber is incorrect. York lies 23 miles north-west of the head of the Humber on the Ouse. The author has mistranslated the original Chronicle text which stated that the heathen army had moved 'across the Humber estuary' (*ofer Humbre muthan*) to York.

84. The author has not mentioned anything about the expulsion of Osberht before this point in his narrative.

85. The phrase *tunc adhuc* suggests that by the time the author was writing, the walls of York had been put back into commission.

86. Byrhtferth of Ramsey makes a very similar reference to the walls of York in his *Life* of St. Oswald. See Smyth, *Alfred the Great*, pp. 313–14.

87. The author's insertion of the words *honorabiliter* ('honourably') and *in pace* ('in peace') to his translation of this entry from the Chronicle is in flagrant contradiction of his attack on the character of Bishop Ealhstan in Chapter 12.

88. Niermeyer translates *secundarius* as 'joint king' which is most probably the meaning which the author intended for that word he chose to describe Alfred

during the reign of his brother Æthelred (J.F. Niermeyer, *Mediae Latinitatis Lexicon Minus* [Leiden, 1976], p. 951). The notion of Alfred being 'joint-ruler' would have been strongly conveyed to the author by the Anglo-Saxon Chronicle which invariably links Alfred's name to all the actions of his brother, King Æthelred, during the reign of that king. Cf. *Life of Alfred,* ed. Stevenson, p. 227. 'Heir apparent' is the meaning preferred by Keynes and Lapidge, *Alfred the Great,* p. 77) – a preference inspired by the belief that Alfred may have been chosen from his infancy for the kingship by his father.

89. The author at no point in his narrative names King Alfred's wife. Yet he names her father and mother, and while giving no information whatever on the wife, he provides a small eulogy on the mother-in-law. The choice of *Eadburh* as a name for Alfred's mother-in-law, together with her supposed Mercian origin, may have been inspired by nothing more than the tale of Queen Eadburh which is narrated in Chapters 14 and 15.

90. Despite much speculation by scholars from Stenton onwards, we know nothing of the supposed *Gaini* and nothing of any certainty about the identification of Æthelred *alias* Mucill. There were several magnates of this name witnessing charters in ninth-century Mercia and Wessex. Ironically, the three important things we know with certainty about King Alfred's wife, are details of which the author may have been ignorant. The first two are that she was called Ealhswith and she died in 903. The third is that she had a brother who was an ealdorman called Æthelwulf, who died in 901. She and her brother may have been Mercians, but they might well have been West Saxons. See Smyth, *Alfred the Great,* pp. 24–8.

91. The author protests his standing as a contemporary witness of the events he describes. Cf. Chapters 22, 39, etc.

92. The Old Welsh *Tigguocobauc* may translate into Latin as *Speluncarum Domus,* but neither of these forms explains the meaning of the placename *Snotengaham* as the author claims.

93. *suppliciter obsecrantes* ('humbly imploring'). The author's additional words in his translation of the Chronicle were flattering to the West Saxons.

94. This should read as Alfred's twenty-second year based on the calculation of a year of birth in 849. Alfred's age is given as one year too little from here until Chapter 47, when a further error creeps in. See pp. 176–81.

95. *atrociter* ('fiercely') was added by the author to his translation of the Chronicle's text. Such gratuitous adverbial intrusions were typical of his late tenth- and early eleventh-century Latin style. The author of the *Life* failed to pick up the Chronicle's point that King Edmund fought against the Danes in winter – a fact which ties in with his feast day being held on 20 November. Although Edmund's death is entered in the Chronicle (followed by the author) under 870, he was actually slain in November 869, the Anglo-Saxon year having begun at that time in autumn. See Smyth, *Scandinavian Kings in the British Isles,* pp. 170–1, 205, 227, 233–4.

96. The information that Archbishop Ceolnoth was buried in Canterbury also occurs in Æthelweard's Chronicle and may not therefore have originated with the author of the *Life* of Alfred.

97. 'in that district' (*in illa paga*). The author uses *paga* instead of the conventional *pagus* to translate 'district' or 'shire'. See *Life of Alfred,* ed. Stevenson, p. 155.

98. *comites,* 'counts' probably refers to Norse jarls or earls.

99. This detail regarding the division of the Scandinavian army relies on the Anglo-Saxon Chronicle and can be vouched for in other sources. See Smyth, *Alfred the*

*Great*, p. 34; ibid., *Scandinavian York and Dublin*, i, 93–4.

100. This is the point in the author's narrative where he attempts to rob King Æthelred of the credit for this victory by inserting an anecdote, which while not actually denigrating Æthelred, was calculated to glorify the exploits of his younger brother, Alfred.

101. The motif of the pious ruler who would not abandon his attendance at Mass in the face of an on-coming enemy, occurs in the *Life* of Count Gerald of Aurillac, written by Odo of Cluny in *c.* 940. See Smyth, *King Alfred the Great*, pp. 188, 272–4. This particular episode has hitherto been treated with the respect accorded to an eye-witness account. A stock hagiographical device has been inserted here to allow Alfred to take credit for one of the few victories of the First War against the Danes.

102. See *Life of Alfred*, ed. Stevenson, pp. 238–9, on the meaning of *sumere debere sciret*. The phrase is repeated in the Worcester Latin Chronicle's version of the *Life* (*Chronicle of John of Worcester*, eds. Darlington and McGurk, ii, 288).

103. *secundarius* ('joint-ruler'), see n. 88, pp. 220–1.

104. This sentence is added in the Worcester Latin Chronicle (*Chronicle of John of Worcester*, eds. Darlington and McGurk, ii, 290–1). The addition was made either by the author of the *Life* or by a later editor to reconcile the author's hagiographical tale of Æthelred's distraction at Mass with the absence of any mention of this in the Chronicle's near-contemporary account of the same battle.

105. The author protests his standing as a contemporary witness. Cf. Chapters 22, 29, etc.

106. The verb (*pugnarent*) is imperfect – literally, 'were fighting'.

107. Ashdown cannot be described as *campester* ('level countryside'). Its landscape exhibits classic southern English downland terrain.

108. This incoherent sentence, which was part of the original text, was omitted by Parker. Stevenson considered it to be a sentence left unfinished by the author and to provide evidence that the *Life* as a whole survives as an unfinished draft. The Latin sentence read: *Quibus cum talia praesentis vitae dispendia alienigenis perperam quaerentibus non sufficerent.*

109. This is an example of where the author of the *Life* adds his own Latinised version (*loco funeris dominati sunt*) of the English idiom: 'they held the place of slaughter' i.e. they were victorious. The author adds in the idiom here although he did not find it in his text of the Chronicle.

110. This was the Summer Army which arrived perhaps just before, or during Easter in 871. Guthrum may have been one of its leaders. See Smyth, *Scandinavian Kings in the British Isles* (Oxford, 1977), pp. 240–6. The author does not tell us that this new army came to Reading (also omitted by MS *A* of the Chronicle), but Reading is the implied destination in his statement that it joined up with the warband which was already attacking Wessex. The author has also left out the Chronicle's account of the West Saxon defeat at *Meretun* where Bishop Heahmund of Sherborne 'and many important men' lost their lives. The conflict at *Meretune* occurred between the fight at Basing and the arrival of the Summer Army.

111. Easter fell on Sunday, 15 April, in 871.

112. *secundarius* ('joint ruler'), see n. 88, pp. 220–1.

113. The phrase *cum summa omnium illius regni accolarum voluntate* reminds us of the related cliché *voluntario omnium consensu* ('with the voluntary consent of all') which the author uses to describe the accession of Charles the Fat to the kingship of the Franks in Chapter 70 of the *Life*. See n. 209, p. 230.

114. The author's assertion of Alfred's superiority over all his brothers is a prominent feature of the *Life* and is reiterated elsewhere in Chapters 11, 12, 17, 22, 23, 37–8. See Smyth, *Alfred the Great*, pp. 180, 182, 185–96.

115. The phrase *victor prope in omnibus bellis erat* ('he was victorious in almost all battles') echoes what Nennius wrote of Arthur – *et in omnibus bellis victor extitit* (*Nennius: British History and the Welsh Annals*, ed. J. Morris (London and Chichester, 1980), p. 76). We know that the author of King Alfred's *Life* had access to Nennius' *British History*. See n. 21, p. 213 above.

116. The imperfect, *pugnarent* ('they were fighting') is used here as in Chapter 39.

117. *peraudacitatem persequentium decipientes*. The text in the East Anglian Chronicle (*Annals of St. Neots*) reads: *paucitatem persequentium despicientes* ('despising the small number of pursuers').

118. The Anglo-Saxon Chronicle gives the number of battles as nine. The author had earlier omitted the battle of Meretune in error from the original Chronicle list, and he now adjusts his Chronicle total down from an original nine to eight.

119. *populariter* ('in great numbers'). This adverbial use is typical of the author's style.

120. *duces*, 'commanders' or 'earls'.

121. *duces*, translated here as 'ealdormen'.

122. *ministri*, 'thegns'. The word *minister* is not found to denote 'thegn' in Anglo-Saxon charters before the middle of the tenth century.

123. Northumbria is described as a *regio* ('region') and Lindsey as a *paga* ('district'). The Anglo-Saxon Chronicle (MS *A*) adds that the Danish army wintered at Torksey in Lindsey. The author's assertion that 'they spent the winter there (*ibi*)' suggests that he considered Lindsey to be a part of Northumbria.

124. *Schola Saxonum*. For the meaning of this term and its military significance, see *Life of Alfred*, ed. Stevenson, pp. 243–7.

125. *commendaverunt* ('they entrusted') may be a Frankish term relating to feudal practice within the Carolingian empire in the ninth and tenth centuries.

126. This king, spelt *Godrum* in MS *A* of the Anglo-Saxon Chronicle, is rendered as *Gothrum* or *Godrum* by the author of King Alfred's *Life*.

127. The Chronicle adds: 'with a great army'. The detail may be important because it was part of that same 'great army' which wintered in Cambridge in 875 which attacked Wareham in Wessex in the following year.

128. The Chronicle gives the number of enemy ships as seven, and places the incident in the summer time.

129. The age of Alfred based on a year of birth of AD 849 has now fallen two years behind.

130. Æthelweard alone of other versions of the Chronicle notes that it was the Cambridge army which attacked Wareham.

131. *castellum* ('fortress'). Perhaps the author is thinking of a tenth-century Anglo-Saxon *burh*.

132. Dorset is described as a *paga* ('district').

133. *Durngueir* is the Old Welsh for Dorchester, not Dorset.

134. The author provides a garbled version of the Chronicle's account here. The Chronicle states that Alfred persuaded the Danes to swear an oath on their own sacred ring. See pp. 185–6.

135. *omnes equites* is a corrupt reading. Keynes and Lapidge emended the text to read *obsides*, the meaning then being that the Danes slew their (West Saxon) hostages. Keynes and Lapidge, *Alfred the Great*, n. 91, p. 246. The sense of the original text is far from clear.

136. The *illius partis* surely refers back to the *altera pars* into which the Pagan army had been divided at Repton as described in Chapter 47. Keynes and Lapidge took the passage here to refer to 'part of the Northumbrians'. Keynes and Lapidge, *Alfred the Great*, p. 83.

137. Stevenson (*Asser's Life of Alfred*, pp. 253–4) was adamant that this passage relating to Rollo of Normandy was interpolated by Archbishop Parker. Whether or not Chapters 50B and 50D were originally part of the *Life* is doubtful, but it is not beyond the realms of possibility. The issue is important for our understanding of the transmission of the text of the *Life* of Alfred and of the East Anglian Chronicle. Unfortunately, the conflation of the East Anglian Chronicle by Parker and by other early editors and annotators has rendered the complete restoration of the original text of the *Life* of Alfred impossible. Modern editors, anxious to separate the East Anglian Chronicle text from 'Asser' as far as possible (not least because they have erroneously supposed the East Anglian Chronicle to have been compiled much later than 'Asser', and to have been compiled by unrelated authors) are unwilling to accept either the passage from Chapter 50B or 50D as part of the 'Asserian' canon. They may be mistaken.

138. *dux* ('duke').

139. The confusion of *antiqua Britannia* ('Old Britain') with *Anglia* or 'England' may be significant. The author makes a similar confusion in Chapter 21, where the reference to the Danube as the homeland of the Danish invaders also betrays a knowledge of early eleventh-century Norman material. While Chapter 50B is based on the East Anglian Chronicle, it derives ultimately from Norman Annals.

140. Chapter 50D like that of 50B is also dependent on the East Anglian Chronicle. Ultimately, it probably derives from the Anglo-Saxon Chronicle. Again, it is quite unclear as to what stage material from this chapter became incorporated into the text of the *Life* of Alfred. Arguments that 'Asser's text of the Chronicle lacked the annal for 877 (and so 'Asser' omitted all the 877 material from his text) are not sustainable (See however Keynes and Lapidge, *Alfred the Great*, n. 94, pp. 246–7). The author was aware of the contents of the 877 annal from the Chronicle, since he incorporated phrasing from that annal into his account of events in 876. See pp. 186–7.

141. Chapter 51. The material in this chapter covers the last section of the entry in the Anglo-Saxon Chronicle under AD 877. We cannot be certain that this material formed part of the original text of the Cotton MS of the *Life* of King Alfred. The Corpus transcript of the *Life* shows that the translation of annal 877 was missing from that recension (MS 100, f. 339r.). That in itself does not *prove* that all or part of annal 877 was missing from the Cotton manuscript. Material from the 877 annal, printed here under 50B, 50C, 50D and 51, all formed part of the main text of the Otho transcript. Wise, writing in 1722, noted that 50B, 50C and 50D were not in the 'old' Cotton manuscript. But he seems to have regarded 51 as part of the original text. It may be significant that the material for 50C was inserted into the Corpus transcript on a separate slip. This material from Roger of Wendover is significantly later than that in sections 50B, 50D and 51.

142. MS *A* of the Chronicle says 'in harvest time'. According to Byrhtferth of Ramsey, the harvest season began on 7 August (*Byrhtferth's Enchiridion*, eds., Baker and Lapidge, p. 77).

143. The use of the term *minister* for 'thegn' in this passage is typical of the terminology used by the author of the *Life* throughout this work. The phrase *cuidam insipienti regis ministro* ('a certain foolish king's thegn') translates the Chronicle's

reference to Ceolwulf as an *unwisum cyninges thegne*. But the Chronicle's reference occurs under the year 874 (*Life* of Alfred, Chapter 46) and was not repeated under the annal 877 which is translated here in Chapter 51.

144. This entry on the division of Mercia between the Danes and their tributary king, Ceolwulf, is the last item in a much longer Chronicle entry – none of which was included by the author of the Corpus transcript of the *Life* of King Alfred. That entry in the Chronicle read in full:

> 'In this year the enemy army from Wareham came to Exeter; and the naval force sailed west along the coast and encountered a great storm at sea, and 120 ships were lost at Swanage. And King Alfred rode after the mounted army with the English army as far as Exeter, but could not overtake them before they were in the fortress where they could not be reached. And they gave him preliminary hostages there, as many as he wished to have, and swore great oaths and then kept a firm peace.
>
> Then in the harvest season the army went away into Mercia and shared out some of it, and gave some to Ceolwulf.' (*E.H.D.*, ed. Whitelock, i, 179)

145. The version of the text preserved by Byrhtferth of Ramsey in the *Historia Regum I* gives this as Alfred's twenty-eighth year (*Historia Regum*, ii, ed. Arnold, p. 83). The proper reckoning based on the internal chronology of the *Life* ought to read 'the thirtieth year' of King Alfred's life. *Trigesimo* was in fact substituted by Stevenson (*Life of Alfred*, p. 40).

146. The author of Alfred's *Life* takes the Danes directly from Exeter to Chippenham, leaving out the Chronicle's account of the Danish withdrawal from Exeter to Mercia during harvest time in 877, when the Danes shared out that kingdom with Ceolwulf. So, while the Chronicle takes Guthrum and the Danes back into Wessex from Mercia (and – if we are to believe Æthelweard – from the Gloucester region), the author of King Alfred's *Life* – ignoring the settlement of Mercia – takes the Danes direct from Exeter to Chippenham.

147. The Chronicle adds that the Danish army came 'stealthily' (*bestæl*) to Chippenham 'in midwinter after Twelfth Night (6 January)'. The author does not quite translate the Chronicle here, which latter claims the enemy 'occupied' or 'settled' the land. The author's claim that the enemy 'wintered' at Chippenham was probably based on the Chronicle's statement that the Danes attacked in midwinter.

148. For the author's misunderstanding of this phrase, see p. 187.

149. Wiltshire is described as a *regio* or 'region'.

150. *cum militibus et fasellis* ('with knights and vassals'). The Frankish terminology seems anachronistic for ninth-century England.

151. *gronnosa*. See pp. 137–8, 160 and *Life of Alfred*, ed. Stevenson, pp. 255–6.

152. Somerset is described as a *paga* or 'district'.

153. Matthew Parker inserted the tale of King Alfred and the burning cakes at this point in his 1574 edition of the *Life* of King Alfred.

154. The tale of how Alfred burnt the cakes is most probably an interpolation borrowed from the East Anglian Chronicle (*Annals of St. Neots*). The tale is not so much later than the *Life* of Alfred as was once thought. The story of the burning cakes originated in the *Life* of St. Neot, and as such began life in the late tenth century – precisely the time, and in the same literary and hagiographical milieu of Ramsey, as when the *Life* of Alfred came into being. From the point of view of manuscript transmission, folklore motifs, Latinity and geographical context, this tale of the

burning cakes is inextricably bound up with the author's text which provided it with a home from the sixteenth century if not from the eleventh. See Smyth, *Alfred the Great*, pp. 325–67, and pp. 79–81.

155. The tale of how King Alfred burnt the cakes relies for its central motif on the image of a great king who is down on his luck and disguised as a menial. As yet another manifestation of the *reversal of roles* motif, it is no better and no worse than the folktale of Queen Eadburh narrated in Chapters 14 and 15 above.

156. The reference to Alfred 'who waged so many wars against the Pagans and who gained so many victories from them' (*qui tot bella gessit contra paganos, tantasque victorias accepit de eis*) echoes the author's claim in Chapter 42 that Alfred was superior to all his brothers 'because he was warlike beyond measure and victorious in almost all battles' (*quod nimium bellicosus et victor prope in omnibus bellis erat*). The correspondence between these two extravagant claims is striking because the historical Alfred is on record for having won few pitched battles. On the contrary, prior to 878 he had lost far more battles than he had won, and by 878 he was on the verge of total defeat. The point is important, because hitherto medieval scholars have been anxious to distance the *Life* of King Alfred from the fictional *Life* of St. Neot, from which the burning cakes story derives. For the very probable influence of Nennius on the author's text, see n. 115, p. 223 above.

157. MS. *A* of the Chronicle reads: 'And the same winter, the brother of Ivar and Halfdan was in the kingdom of the West Saxons in Devon.' The Chronicle has no mention of the attack on Dyfed or of the siege of *Cynuit*.

158. This brother is not named in the Chronicle. He may or may not have been Ubbe. See A.P. Smyth, *Scandinavian Kings in the British Isles*, pp. 248–9, 269–70. Smyth, *Alfred the Great*, pp. 58–9, 78–9.

159. While the *A*-Text of the Chronicle simply relates that the 'brother of Ivar and Halfdan **was in** Devon', the author translates: 'the brother of Ivar and Halfdan **sailed to** Devon'.

160. Dyfed is described as a *regio* or 'region'.

161. *arx* 'a fortress', literally 'a citadel'.

162. The A-Text puts the number of Norse slain at 840; B, C put the number at 860. See p. 187.

163. Keynes and Lapidge (*Alfred the Great*, p. 84) translate *moenia* as 'earthworks'. The word may relate to any type of walls or defences and in classical Latin it might even refer to the walled town itself.

164. 'after our custom' has been taken by Stevenson and by those who subsequently copied him, to refer to Welsh practice. It is also possible that the fort was of West Saxon construction. It was situated within Devon and was defended by Alfred's men. Its Brittonic name does not guarantee a Welsh origin. The author of Alfred's biography had a flair for giving antiquarian 'Welsh' names to well-known English locations. His assertion that he himself had seen the place may count for little. His description of the secure nature of its position 'on every side except on the east' could very possibly answer the location of Countisbury Head. On the other hand, the author's topographical detail in this case is suspiciously similar to his description of Wareham ('sited in the most secure position … except on the western side') which he gave in Chapter 49. There also seems to be a typical inherent contradiction in the author's account of this action. If the fort where the West Saxons had sought refuge were indeed 'unprepared and altogether unfortified' and if indeed it were vulnerable on its eastern side, then why was it that the Danes 'did not try to break into it'? And why tell us of the poor state of its defences, if it

were otherwise naturally impregnable? Æthelweard, as ever, gives us more specific detail than the author by naming Ealdorman Odda of Devon as the leader of the West Saxon defence during this siege. Æthelweard also named Ealdorman Æthelnoth of Somerset as a magnate who helped King Alfred construct the fort at Athelney in this same year. It seems likely that the attack on north Devon was part of a Danish pincer aimed at dislodging Alfred and his remaining supporters from their newly fortified refuges in Somerset and Devon. We have in this 878 campaign a marked reversal of policy on behalf of the West Saxon defence. Prior to AD 878, the Chronicle shows that it was the Danes who availed of the protection of fortified sites, while the West Saxons invariably relied on pitched battles and imprudently tried to dislodge their enemies from fortified positions. This must surely be the real significance of the Athelney and north Devon episodes in 878, as we gather from the Chronicle account. But all strategic significance was lost on the author of Alfred's *Life*, whose late account of the siege of *Cynuit* reeks of antiquarism in a vague narrative devoid of substantial or relevant detail.

165. The author has no mention of the capture by the men of Devon of the Raven Banner which Versions *B, C, D* and *E* of the Chronicle include in their account of the defeat of the brother of Ivar and Halfdan. The A-Text – which the author seems to have followed here – does not include this banner episode and Æthelweard also omits it.

166. Easter Sunday fell on 23 March 878.

167. The seventh week after Easter was 4–10 May 878.

168. The author has mistranslated the Chronicle here, whose text reads: [There came to meet him all the people of Somerset and of Wiltshire] 'and of that part of Hampshire which was on this side of the sea' – i.e. the folk who lived in Hampshire west of Southampton Water. See pp. 187–8.

169. Iley Oak near Warminster in Wiltshire.

170. *nominatos* 'named' or perhaps 'well known'.

171. Whitelock's comment (*E.H.D.*, i, p. 196, n. 7) on this passage that it 'is fuller' than that of the Anglo-Saxon Chronicle does not stand up to scrutiny. The author's account of Alfred's hostage negotiations after Edington is replete with cliché if it is not a nonsense. It was most likely inspired by the exaggerated comment of the Chronicle regarding the exceptional nature of the Danish oath-swearing during Alfred's negotiations at Wareham in 876 (see Chapter 49).

172. *suatim utens*. The phrase recurs in Chapters 74 and 106.

173. This was not the case. The Chronicle has no word to match the *citissime* ('very quickly') of the author's translated account, and in fact we gather from the Chronicle that the Danes hung about in Chippenham from May until October 878 if not indeed much later, when in the Anglo-Saxon year 879 they retired to Cirencester.

174. The number of weeks is supplied by the Chronicle text.

175. The Chronicle assumes the number was thirty *including* Guthrum. See *E.H.D.*, ed. Whitelock, i, p. 148, n. 5; p. 180, n. 13.

176. *aedificia* 'buildings'. Stevenson substituted *beneficia* (*Life of Alfred*, ed. Stevenson, p. 47 and cf. ibid., p. 279). Cf. Chapters 76, 91 and 101. Keynes and Lapidge, *Alfred the Great*, p. 85, translated the word as 'treasures'. Ibid., n. 114, pp. 249–50.

177. The text ought to read 'thirty-first year' of Alfred's life and was so emended by Stevenson and silently copied by Keynes and Lapidge (*Alfred the Great*, p. 85).

178. The territory of the Hwicce included what is now Gloucestershire, Worcestershire and parts of Warwickshire and Oxfordshire. The original kings of the Hwicce were

ousted by the ruling dynasty of Mercia in the eighth century, when members of the Mercian royal kindred ruled the Hwicce as sub-kings of the Mercians. By *c.* AD 1000, at the time when the author was writing, the Hwicce had their own ealdorman within Mercia.

179. This is one of the two rare instances in the Alfredian Chronicle where the Danish invaders are referred to as 'Vikings'. The other reference occurs in annal 885. The author as always refers to the invaders as *pagani*, which Keynes and Lapidge invariably mistranslate as 'Vikings'.

180. The statement that the new army at Fulham united (*adunatus est*) with Guthrum's army which was based on Cirencester is contradicted by the Anglo-Saxon Chronicle and even by Chapters 60 and 61 of this *Life*. Keynes and Lapidge's phrase 'made contact with' fails to convey the force of the original *adunatus est* which clearly suggests union (Keynes and Lapidge, *Alfred the Great*, p. 85). *superiori exercitui* surely refers to the 'former' or 'earlier army' rather than 'further upstream' as translated by Keynes and Lapidge (ibid.). Cirencester is over 130 miles 'upstream' from Fulham and near the source of the Thames. It is within 20 miles of the Severn Estuary.

181. This was the total solar eclipse of Wednesday, 29 October 878. The author of the *Life* provides the wrong time of day for this eclipse, which by his reckoning was more appropriate for an observer located in eastern Germany or Poland. It is the author's gloss on the Anglo-Saxon Chronicle's reporting of the 878 eclipse which now helps to confirm the early eleventh-century date for his forgery. See pp. 189–90.

182. By the author's reckoning, this ought to be Alfred's thirty-second year.

183. East Anglia is described as a *regio* ('region').

184. It seems clear from this account – which relies totally on that of the Chronicle – that the author has already forgotten or disregarded his throw-away remark in Chapter 58 that the Fulham army had supposedly united with the army of Cirencester.

185. This was the thirty-third year of Alfred's life by the earlier reckoning of the author.

186. The Latin of the *Life* is entirely reliant on the original text of the Chronicle at this point (*Anglo-Saxon Chronicle*, ed. Bately, p. 51). The phrase *contra quem Franci pugnaverunt* – translating *þa Francan him wiþ gefuhton* – makes the Franks and not the Danes the subject of this narrative. This may suggest that the account is borrowed from a Frankish annalistic source which described the action from a Frankish point of view.

187. This was Alfred's thirty-fourth year according to earlier calculations of the author.

188. The author's *tanto longe* ('much further') translates the 'far' of MS *A* of the Chronicle – showing how close the author's translation is, in this instance, to the *A* Text.

189. The author describes the enemy vessels as 'Pagan ships' (*paganicas naves*), translating 'four crews of Danish men' of the Anglo-Saxon Chronicle.

190. AD 883 was Alfred's thirty-fifth year according to the author's earlier reckoning.

191. The cliché *praefatus exercitus* is ambiguous. The last time the author mentioned *paganicas naves* was in the context of a naval battle off the West Saxon coast.

192. The remainder of this annal from all versions of the Anglo-Saxon Chronicle – except the A-Text – was not included by King Alfred's biographer at this point. The later versions of the Chronicle here record the sending of wood from the Holy Cross by Pope Marinus to King Alfred; the taking of alms to Rome and to India; and the encampment of the English army before London. The *Life* of Alfred,

Æthelweard, and the A-Text all omit this material.

193. All of the material recorded by the author under Chapter 66 and dated by him to 884 belongs in fact to AD 885. This error arose from the author's omission of annal 884 from the Chronicle text which he followed. That entry, if it were in his version of the Chronicle, would have read:

> '884: In this year the army went up the Somme to Amiens, and stayed there a year.'

194. AD 884 was Alfred's thirty-sixth year according to the author's earlier reckoning. The error in the calculation of King Alfred's age has now fallen three year's behind, due to the author's omission of the Chronicle annal for 884.

195. *castellum firmum* ('a strong fortification'). The author later refers to the structure as an *arx*.

196. The author is here translating from the Anglo-Saxon Chronicle. It would seem clear from the Chronicle's account that the (Roman) walls of Rochester had been put in a sufficient state of repair so as to withstand a Danish siege.

197. The Anglo-Saxon Chronicle gives the number of ships as 16. *xvi* of the Chronicle text was misread as *xiii*. Keynes and Lapidge (*Alfred the Great*, p. 87) translate *tredecim naves paganorum* as 'thirteen Viking ships' rather than 'thirteen Pagan ships' of the Latin text. Significantly the text of the Anglo-Saxon Chronicle in this rare instance does use the word *wiceng* twice in this annal – referring to *xui scipu wicenga* ('sixteen viking ships'), and *hie micelne sciphere wicenga* ('a large Viking fleet'), but Alfred's biographer preferred to translate *wiceng* as *paganus*, here in this passage and earlier in his translation of the Chronicle text for 879 (Chapter 58).

198. The text reads *dormiret* – a reading confirmed by the *ubi dormiebant somno inerti* of the version of the *Life* preserved elsewhere by Byrhtferth of Ramsey (*Historia regum*, ed. Arnold, ii, 87). The Chronicle account, however, of which both these Latin versions constitute a mistranslation, reads: *þa hie þa hamweard wendon* 'when they turned homewards' (*Anglo-Saxon Chronicle MS A* (*sub anno* 885), ed. Bately, p. 52). This, as Stevenson pointed out, suggests that the original reading of the *Life* of Alfred ought to have read: *domum rediret* or *domum iret* (*Life of Alfred*, ed. Stevenson, p. 291).

199. See Stevenson's note on *singularis* ('boar': Modern French *sanglier*) in *Life of Alfred*, p. 292. This may be yet another of the many examples of Frankish Latin influence in the *Life* of Alfred.

200. King Alfred's biographer gives the name of this Frankish king correctly as *Carloman* and not *Charles* of the Anglo-Saxon Chronicle account. The Chronicle's reading of *Charles* shows that source was following a Fulda-type version of Frankish annals. Our author also correctly describes Carloman as king of the Western Franks, but he may well have based that statement on the fact that his version of the Chronicle claimed his [i.e. Carloman's] brother 'also held the western kingdom.'

201. Louis III died in AD 882.

202. Louis the Stammerer, king of the Franks, died on 10 April 879.

203. The solar eclipse actually took place in October 878, but was recorded in the Anglo-Saxon year 879. See Chapter 59 above.

204. Charles the Bald died in AD 877.

205. The Chronicle has 'a large naval force'.

206. The Old Saxons were – by any reckoning – already living in Germania. The author's knowledge of continental geography was poor in the extreme. See

Smyth, 'The Solar Eclipse of 29 October, 878' in Roberts, Nelson and Godden (eds.), *Alfred the Wise*, p. 207.

207.  The Cotton MS reads *ibi* for *bis* with the meaning that the Saxons and Frisians 'fought courageously there in that one year' (*Life of Alfred*, ed. Stevenson, p. 52). But the subsequent phrase *in quibus duobus bellis* clearly suggests that an earlier *bis in uno illo anno* was the original reading, which in turn was dictated by the Chronicle text which the author of Alfred's *Life* was following here.

208.  Charles the Fat was deposed in 887 and died in the following year.

209.  *voluntario omnium consensu* ('with the voluntary consent of all'). A similar cliché was used by the author, when recording King Alfred's accession to kingship in Chapter 42 of the *Life*. See n. 113, p. 222.

210.   The Chronicle entry reads:

> 'That same year Charles succeeded to the western kingdom and to all the kingdom on this side of the Mediterranean and beyond this sea ... except for Brittany.'

The Chronicle's reference to 'this sea' would seem (as Plummer rightly believed) to refer back to the Mediterranean and indicate those lands in Italy which belonged to the Carolingians. The author is confused here. See pp. 192–3.

211.  Louis the German, who died in 876.

212.  Charles the Bald, who died in 877.

213.  Louis the Pious, who died in 840.

214.  The text of the Cotton manuscript of the *Life* may be corrupt here. But it is entirely in character that the author should confuse Charlemagne's relationship to his father Pepin. The East Anglian Chronicle has the better reading:

> 'The two brothers were the sons of Louis [the Pious]. Louis in truth was the son of the ancient and most wise Charles the Great, [who was] himself the son of Pepin.'  *Hlodowicus vero ille [filius Karoli magni, et antiqui atque sapientissimi, qui etiam] fuit filius Pipini.*

The Latin text within square brackets was absent from the Cotton manuscript of the *Life*. (Cf. *Life of Alfred*, ed. Stevenson, p. 53, and Keynes and Lapidge, n. 135, pp. 253–4.)

215.  The Anglo-Saxon Chronicle text, on which the author relied so heavily, described Alfred as 'king of the West Saxons'. The Chronicle does not refer to Alfred as 'King of the Anglo-Saxons'.

216.  See Keynes and Lapidge, n. 137, p. 254.

217.  The Chronicle describes this force as 'the Danish army'. The author, as ever, sees the campaign in terms of a religious war between Christians and pagans.

218.  Alfred's wife is first introduced in Chapter 29, but in spite of being 'aforementioned' (*praefatam*) she is nowhere named by the author.

219.  This passage is based on Einhard's *Life* of Charlemagne. Cf. Chapters 16 and 81.

220.  Whitelock, clearly embarrassed by what she rightly judged to be 'a confused account' of King Alfred's illnesses, chose not to include this key chapter in her abridged translation of the *Life* of King Alfred, detracting as it did from her 'Genuine Asser' thesis. *E.H.D.*, ed. Whitelock, i, 267, n. 1.

221.  The association in the author's mind between the onset of Alfred's mysterious illness and his marriage is stressed in no less than three places in this chapter. The model for Alfred's personal affliction was provided by the *Life* of Count Gerald of Aurillac, who like Alfred endured two separate illnesses – the first an outbreak of

boils in his youth, and the second a bout of blindness which lasted for more than a year and was sent by Heaven as a punishment for a momentary lapse of chastity on Gerald's part. Alfred is supposed to have first contracted piles in adolescence, when at his own request he prayed for a malady which might control his lust. But Gerald, unlike Alfred, resisted marriage and persevered as a lay ruler with monk-like chastity to the end. So when the author came to record King Alfred's marriage, he was prompted to invent a punishment from Heaven for his hero who had failed to live up to those standards of chastity expected of a saint. See pp. 132–4.

222. The phrase *inter innumerabiles utriusque sexus populos, sollemniter celebrat* echoes the phrase *ad eum multitudo utriusque sexus populi conflueret* from the *Life* of St. Neot – a work very closely connected with the *Life* of Alfred. The phrase *populusque utriusque sexus innumerabilis* was used yet again by Byrhtferth of Ramsey in his description of the Danish sack of Canterbury in AD 1011 in the Worcester Latin Chronicle (*Chronicle of John of Worcester*, eds. Darlington and McGurk, ii, 468).

223. *favore et fascinatione circumstantis populi*. It is difficult to reconcile *favor* ('applause' or 'favour') with *fascinatio* ('witchcraft') as the supposed cause of Alfred's illness, unless as Stevenson suggested, the adulation of the crowd were seen by the author as attracting the unwelcome and demonic attention of the 'evil eye' (*Life of Alfred*, ed. Stevenson, pp. 55, 294–5). Keynes and Lapidge (*Alfred the Great*, n. 140, p. 254) suggested *fauore* of the lost Cotton manuscript should have read *furore* meaning '"inspired frenzy", and hence ... "spell"' which makes better sense, but for which we have no evidence.

224. *infantia* ('infancy' or 'early childhood') had a broader meaning in Latin than its English equivalent. It is nevertheless erroneously translated by Keynes and Lapidge (*Alfred the Great*, p. 89) as 'youth'. The mistranslation is significant because it was intended to silently circumvent one of the numerous contradictions in this account of Alfred's illnesses. Here we are told that Alfred had endured piles from infancy. But later in the same chapter Alfred is shown to have contracted piles as an adolescent – 'in the first flowering of his youth before he married his wife'.

225. *suatim* 'on his own initiative' or 'in his own way'. *suatim utens* 'acting on his own initiative'. This is the reading of the Corpus transcript of the *Life*. The British Library transcript and Parker's 1574 edition have the reading *sublevatus est* (*Life of Alfred*, ed. Stevenson, p. 298, n. 1).

226. It is no coincidence that the *Life* of St. Neot claims that King Alfred was befriended by St. Neot in AD 878 and that in the *Life* of Alfred, its author alleges that Alfred visited a Cornish church where Neot would be buried at some future time. The *Lives* of Alfred and of Neot are both Ramsey productions, written under the influence of Byrhtferth *c.* AD 1000. According to Neot's *Life*, that saint and Alfred were contemporaries. Later development of the cult suggested that Alfred and Neot were brothers! See pp. 79–81.

227. Stevenson (*Life of Alfred*, pp. 296–7) regarded the phrase *et nunc etiam Sanctus Niot ibidem pausat* as an interpolation, Keynes and Lapidge (*Alfred the Great*, n. 142, p. 254) rightly regarded it as original to the text. It is highly implausible that the youthful Alfred ever ventured into the hunting grounds of Cornwall. The West Saxons were still in conflict with Cornishmen in the time of Alfred's grandson, King Athelstan in the 930s. The author later lists Cornwall and its monasteries as being among foreign lands in Chapter 102.

228. The fear of contracting visible marks of infirmity or disability on the body, which would make one unsuitable for rulership, is modelled on the same concerns which exercised the mind of Count Gerald of Aurillac. See pp. 132–3 and cf. Smyth, *Alfred the Great*, p. 209.

229. *metuens* ('fearing') was missing from the Cotton text.

230. The author was influenced by Einhard who tells us that Charlemagne was also an inveterate church-goer, attending early morning Mass and the late Night Hours. Odo's *Life* of Gerald – also available to the biographer of King Alfred – portrayed a Frankish count who was (like Alfred) devoted to the Night Office and who regularly prayed for long periods and alone in churches at night. Smyth, *Alfred the Great*, pp. 200–2, 206.

231. See note 228 above.

232. So unhealthy was Alfred's desire for chastity and penitence, that according to the author he prayed for illness. Smyth, *Alfred the Great*, p. 205.

233. Alfred's forty-fifth year would have been 893 – based on the author's own reckoning.

234. The author nowhere mentions the name of King Alfred's wife.

235. Either the name of a supposed child of King Alfred or the number of those of his children who died in childhood is missing here. Cf. Chapters 35 and 56 where other numerals have been lost or omitted from the text. Wheeler, 'Textual Emendations', *Eng. Hist. Rev.*, xlvii (1932), 87.

236. *Eadred* is an error for *Æthelred* – an error repeated in Chapter 80. Eadred is described as a *comes* or 'count', translated here as 'ealdorman'.

237. *monasticae vitae regulis* – a phrase which reflects the early eleventh-century writer's concern with the *regula* or *Rule* of reformed monasteries. The author returns to the subject of Æthelgifu in Chapter 98.

238. 'reading and writing': literally 'the discipline of letters' (*literariae disciplinae*).

239. Cf. Chapter 22, where we are told that Alfred also was always brought up at the royal court. King Alfred's solicitude for the education of his children – both boys and girls – and the notion that they were always brought up at court were modelled on Einhard's account of Charlemagne's concern for his imperial offspring:

> 'Charlemagne was determined to give his children, his daughters just as much as his sons, a proper training in the liberal arts which had formed the subject of his own studies. As soon as they were old enough he had his sons taught to ride in the Frankish fashion, to use arms and to hunt.
>
> He paid such attention to the upbringing of his sons and daughters that he never sat down to table without them when he was at home, and never set out on a journey without taking them with him. His sons rode at his side and his daughters followed along behind.' (Einhard, *Life of Charlemagne*, III, *Two Lives of Charlemagne*, transl. Thorpe, pp. 74–5)

240. This supposedly contemporary description of the prince, Edward, as a diligent and obedient schoolboy is anachronistic for an account claimed to have been written in *c.* 893. In that very year according to the chronicler, Æthelweard, Edward was leading an army in his own right against the Danish invaders at Farnham. Such a warrior son would, by then, have left his schooldays – 'before he had the strengths suitable for manly skills' – long behind him.

241. The author's interest in education and his description of this ideal class-room reflect the concerns not of the ninth-century Asser but of Byrhtferth, master of the school at Ramsey, a whole century later.

242. Niermeyer (*Mediae Latinitatis Lexicon Minus*, p. 10), citing only the *Life* of King Alfred as his authority, renders *accipitrarius* as 'falconer'. But the author of the *Life* has already mentioned Alfred's *falconarios* in this same list of craftsmen and hunting specialists belonging to the king. 'Hawk-handlers' seems a reasonable translation, since the word derives from *accipiter* 'the sparrow-hawk'.

243. This is a catalogue of medieval aristocratic pursuits. The *Life* of Gerald of Aurillac may have provided the model even for this standard material.

244. The statement that Alfred used 'to read aloud' (*recitare*) from 'Saxon books' is in direct contradiction to what we are told of that king's complete adult illiteracy in Chapter 77. This passage, however, was most probably inspired by what Einhard has to say of Charlemagne who 'directed that the age-old narrative poems, barbarous enough, it is true, in which were celebrated the warlike deeds of the kings of ancient times, should be written out and so preserved.' Einhard also tells us that 'stories would be recited for him [Charlemagne], or the doings of the ancients told again' (*Vita Caroli*, III, transl., Thorpe, *Two Lives of Charlemagne*, pp. 78, 82).

245. *divina ministeria* probably relates to sacraments or worship rather than the Divine Office proper, which is covered by *horas diurnas et nocturnas* lower down the formidable list of 'Saint' Alfred's devotions.

246. This passage relies heavily on Einhard's account of Charlemagne's piety which involved attendance at morning Mass and the late-night hours. Smyth, *Alfred the Great*, pp. 200–1. The *Life* of Gerald of Aurillac relates that Gerald too was devoted to the Night Office and to the Mass, and that he regularly prayed for long periods alone in churches at night. Ibid., p. 206.

247. Stevenson amended the original *de se nugebat* of the Cotton manuscript to read: *se iungebat* (*Life of Alfred*, ed. Stevenson, p. 60).

248. It is no coincidence that this list of foreigners who benefited from Alfred's generosity is positioned in the author's text alongside the king's alms-giving or *eleemosyna*. The passage is modelled closely on Einhard's *Life* of Charlemagne, where that author stresses the significance of the same *eleemosyna*:

> 'He [Charlemagne] was most active in relieving the poor and in that form of really disinterested charity which the Greeks call *eleemosyna*. He gave alms not only in his own country and in the kingdom over which he reigned, but also across the sea in Syria, Egypt, Africa, Jerusalem, Alexandria and Carthage.' (*Vita Caroli*, III, transl., Thorpe, *Two Lives of Charlemagne*, p. 80)

249. Whitelock (*E. H. D.*, i, 268, n.1) assumed that the author believed King Alfred had conferred grants of West Saxon land on these foreigners.

250. Count Gerald of Aurillac always employed a reader at his table, even when guests were present, and reading was suspended only to allow discussion of the text (Smyth, *Alfred the Great*, p. 206). Einhard also mentions Charlemagne's reading during meal times. The author, as a monk of the Benedictine Reform, emphasises the reading of prayers and of Holy Scripture at Alfred's court.

251. *comites* ('counts') translated 'ealdormen'.

252. The terms *ministeriales* and *familiares* for officers of the king's court are Frankish. Cf. Chapter 79. In spite of King Alfred's concern and friendship which was supposedly lavished on his *ministeriales* and *familiares*, not a single one of these magnates is ever mentioned by name in this *Life*, although the author as a self-proclaimed contemporary observer ought to have known them all as frequent visitors to the royal court.

253. 'By day and by night (*die noctuque*)' is a favourite phrase of this author, who uses it again, for instance in Chapter 77. An alternative version of the phrase – *cotidiana et nocturna* ('daily and nightly') occurs only a few lines further down in the text. *Life of Alfred*, ed. Stevenson, p. 60. These phrases are characteristically Byrhtferthian. See Smyth, *King Alfred the Great*, pp. 290–1.
254. The contents of Chapter 76A form part of Stevenson's Chapter 76.
255. Matthew vi. 33 from the Old Latin Bible (not the Vulgate text).
256. Ps. xxxv.8.
257. The metaphor of the clever bee derives from Aldhelm. See Keynes and Lapidge, *Alfred the Great*, n. 161. The ultimate source of the bee metaphor is Virgil's *Georgics*.
258. For Alfred's supposed lack of scholars in Wessex, cf. Chapters 24–5. We may compare also, Alfred's own lament regarding the state of English Latin scholarship in his preface to the *Pastoral Care* – a preface with which the author of the *Life* was familiar.
259. The *Life* of Alfred is the earliest authority for the attribution of Gregory's *Dialogues* to Bishop Wærfærth of Worcester. King Alfred, in his prose preface to the translation of the *Dialogues*, informs us that he commissioned his 'true friends' to produce that work. It is possible that Bishop Wærferth was the author not of the translated *Dialogues*, but of a verse preface originally written to accompany a copy of the translated text. See Smyth, *Alfred the Great*, pp. 544–8, and p. 95.
260. The phrase 'sometimes rendering sense for sense' (*aliquando sensum ex sensu ponens*) is based on Alfred's own account of his translation technique – *hwilum andgit of andgiete* as set out in the prefaces to his *Pastoral Care* and the *Consolation of Philosophy*. See Smyth, *Alfred the Great*, p. 548. The author of the *Life* was well read in the prefaces to Alfredian translations.
261. The *Life* cannot have been written before Plegmund's appointment to the archbishopric of Canterbury in 890. But the author makes it clear that Plegmund and others had joined Alfred's international 'team' prior to November 877. Plegmund died in 923.
262. *capellanos*, 'chaplains', a Frankish term (*Life of Alfred*, ed. Stevenson, p. 305). The historicity of Athelstan and Wærwulf as royal tutors is very much in doubt and the problematic charters which contain their names in witness lists cannot be used to shore up claims made in the *Life* of Alfred. The idea that Wærwulf was the same person of that name who was described in 899 as a friend of Bishop Wærferth – in a charter concerning lands at Ablington in Gloucestershire – is impossible to prove or disprove. See Smyth, *Alfred the Great*, pp. 253–4.
263. Earlier (Chapter 23) we have been told that the infant Alfred miraculously (*divina inspiratione*) learnt to read aloud the contents of an entire book, and we were told in Chapter 22 that he overcame his illiteracy in his twelfth year. We were also told in Chapter 76 that as king, Alfred zealously 'read Saxon books aloud' as well as learning Saxon poems by heart.
264. The author's inclusion of the names of Grimbald and John (see next note) was most probably inspired by the list of scholars whom King Alfred acknowledged in his preface to the *Pastoral Care*. In that preface, the king listed as his helpers, Archbishop Plegmund, Bishop Asser, and the Mass-priests, Grimbald and John. All that we know with certainty of Grimbald – apart from his role in the translation of the *Pastoral Care* – is that he died, still bearing the title of Mass-priest, in 901. Winchester propaganda of the late tenth century credited Grimbald with a hand in the foundation of the New Minster in Winchester and claimed that he was

offered and refused the archbishopric of Canterbury. See Smyth, *Alfred the Great*, pp. 255–60.

265. The priest John is associated with Grimbald as being one of those *magistri* or 'tutors' who were summoned to King Alfred's court from Gaul. It is nowhere stated but presumably understood that this John was the same person as John the priest and monk who was an 'Old Saxon by race' and who was supposedly appointed by King Alfred as abbot of Athelney. See Chapter 94.

266. The author inserted this narrative of his first encounter with King Alfred between the annals of 885 (mis-dated by the author to 884. Chapters 66–72) and 886 (Chapter 82) in his Latin translation of the Anglo-Saxon Chronicle. We are given to believe, therefore, that this first visit to Alfred took place in 885; the second visit in the latter half of 886; and that Alfred began to read and to translate in November 887.

267. For the significance of this Welsh directional idiom, see pp. 117–19.

268. Dean in Sussex refers to either East and West Dean near Eastbourne or East and West Dean in West Sussex. Whatever the true location, this so-called *villa regia* was probably meant to coincide with the Dean which King Alfred left in his *Will* to his younger son, Æthelweard. Keynes and Lapidge, *Alfred the Great*, p. 319, n. 41 and Stevenson, ed., *Life of Alfred*, p. 312.

269. *famina*, 'utterances', 'words' – and so 'exchanges' in a conversation.

270. The rare use of direct speech here attributed to King Alfred is based on the dialogue between Charlemagne and Alcuin as recorded in the *Life* of Alcuin. The *Life* of Alcuin also provided the model for the length of time Asser agreed to spend at King Alfred's court and also for the gifts which Alfred bestowed on Asser. See pp. 112–13.

271. Keynes and Lapidge unaccountably inserted here in their translation the phrase 'a short while after', for which there is no evidence in the original Latin. Keynes and Lapidge, *Alfred the Great*, p. 94.

272. Whitelock (*E.H.D.*, i, 269) translated *in Wintonia civitate* as 'in the city of Caerwent'. Keynes and Lapidge (*Alfred the Great*, p. 94) extended the sense to read 'the monastery of Caerwent'. Winchester, Hampshire, can be the only place which is meant here. *Wintonia* of Chapter 79 is clearly the same *civitas* as the *Wintonia* of Chapter 18 which according to this same author was attacked by Pagans in 860. That raid of 860 was unquestionably on Winchester and no amount of textual massage can move the supposed place of 'Asser's' convalescence from Winchester to Wales. See Smyth, *Alfred the Great*, pp. 354–5.

273. *indiculos* 'letters'.

274. *rudimenta*. Stevenson (*Life of Alfred*, p. 65) considered *rudimenta* to be a corrupt reading. But the author uses the same word with its original meaning of 'rudiments [of learning]' in Chapter 89. Cf. G.H. Wheeler, 'Textual Emendations to Asser's Life of Alfred', *Eng. Hist. Rev.*, xlvii (1932), 87–8.

275. *parochia*, 'the monastic jurisdiction' including other monasteries over which St. David's had control. The author of the *Life* uses the same term to describe the diocesan jurisdiction of Exeter in Chapter 81.

276. The author would seem to suggest that Hyfaidd's attacks on St. David's and on 'Archbishop' Nobis were an ongoing problem which drove 'Asser' to seek King Alfred's patronage in *c*. 885. But Nobis had died back in 873, so his persecution at the hands of Hyfaidd took place at least twelve years, if not more, before 'Asser's' defection to Wessex. See pp. 123–7.

277. *regiones* ('regions') is used to describe the early medieval kingdoms of Wales.

278. The notion that King Alfred controlled all – or indeed any – of South Wales in 885 and for 'a long time before' then was politically and militarily impossible.

279. For conflicting accounts of the true number of Rhodri's sons and for the manipulation of the Cottonian text by adherents of the 'genuine' Asser lobby, see pp. 127–9.

280. Eadred, *recte Æthelred*, ealdorman of the Mercians. The same error is repeated in Chapter 75 above. Eadred is described as a *comes* or 'count'.

281. *dominium et defensionem* ('lordship and protection') may be terms inspired by Carolingian feudal practice.

282. This supposed record of the submission of Welsh rulers to King Alfred as well as the cementing of their alliance through either baptism or confirmation was based on genuine records of similar events in the tenth century when Alfred's son Edward and his grandson Athelstan, did indeed expand their territories to the north and west. See pp. 126–7. Byrhtferth of Ramsey was well aware of those later tenth-century submissions of Welsh and Norse magnates to the West Saxons, from his own compilation of the Worcester Latin Chronicle.

283. Here the author does give the correct name *Æthered* (Æthelred) for the ealdorman or king of the Mercians who was the son-in-law of King Alfred. Æthelred of Mercia is also correctly referred to in Chapter 83 below.

284. *amor, tutela* and *defensio* may relate to Frankish feudal concepts of a later age. Keynes and Lapidge, *Alfred the Great*, n. 189, p. 264; F.L. Ganshof, *Feudalism* (London: 3rd edn., 1964), pp. 83–4; K.J. Hollyman, *Le développement du vocabulaire féodal en France pendant le Haut Moyen Age* (Geneva, 1957), pp. 52–3.

285. *Leonaford* cannot be identified, and in the form in which it is given, it would be a 'highly improbable [placename] in England', *Life of Alfred*, ed. Stevenson, pp. 318–20. I am grateful to Mr. Eric Christiansen, New College Oxford, for suggesting the possibility of Lyford in Berkshire – some four miles north of Wantage and six miles west of Abingdon. Lyford appears as *æt Linforda* in a grant by King Edmund to his thegn, Ælfheah, in 944 (Birch 798; Sawyer 494). *Linford (lindfordinga)* is also mentioned in the bounds of a charter granting lands by the same king, at Garford near Abingdon in 940 (Birch 761; Sawyer 471). There was clearly a large estate in royal ownership there from as early as the mid-tenth century.

286. *curto* ('court') is a Frankish word. The term is used in Chapters 22, 75, 81 and 100. Cf. *Life of Alfred*, ed. Stevenson, p. 219.

287. The claim that Asser was granted first Congresbury and Banwell and later the *parochia* of Exeter is modelled on Charlemagne's gifts to Alcuin, first of Ferrières and Troyes and later of Tours. See pp. 112–13.

288. The *pallium* or cloak referred to by the author might well have had liturgical significance.

289. The author's claim that King Alfred granted him the diocese (*parochia*) of Exeter has been the subject of much controversy. See pp. 112–13.

290. The phrase is modelled on the Preface to Einhard's *Life* of Charlemagne. Cf. a similar borrowing from Einhard in Chapter 16.

291. This was Alfred's thirty-eighth year according to the author's earlier reckoning.

292. The phrase *saepe memoratus exercitus* relating to an army which has not been mentioned since Chapter 66 may suggest that the Chronicle passages were translated into Latin in one, and perhaps a separate operation, and were later glossed and added to by the compiler of the *Life*.

293. The A-Text of the Chronicle (and Æthelweard) do not mention Paris by name here. But MS *A* mentions the 'bridge at Paris' in a continuation of this annal under 887.

Too much has been made of the author's supposed 'original contribution' to our knowledge of these events. Cf. Smyth, *Alfred the Great*, p. 488, as against Stevenson (*Life of Alfred*, p. 324, n.1) who believed that the author 'had been at Paris'.

294. The Chronicle does not describe Alfred in this passage or elsewhere as 'king of the Anglo-Saxons'.

295. Whitelock took this phrase to mean that Alfred had taken London after a bloody campaign against the Danes. The text does not warrant such an assumption. Other evidence suggests that London may not have come fully within West Saxon control until as late as 911. The Chronicle's claim that King Alfred entrusted London 'to the control of Ealdorman Æthelred' back in 886 may be West Saxon propaganda with a view to highlighting Alfred's presumed superiority over Æthelred of Mercia. London was a Mercian town, and it may have been well-nigh impossible for Alfred to have won acceptability as direct ruler there during his reign in Wessex proper.

296. *comiti*, literally 'count' of the Mercians. *comes* is a Frankish term. The use of *commendavit* ('he commended') to describe King Alfred's supposed handing over of London to Ealdorman Æthelred may be suggestive of Frankish feudal terminology.

297. This follows the reading of the Cotton manuscript as restored in the translation of Keynes and Lapidge (*Alfred the Great*, n. 199, p. 266).

298. The original Chronicle text referred to 'Danes', the author prefers *pagans*. Keynes and Lapidge (*Alfred the Great*, p. 98), mistranslate *pagani* as 'Vikings'.

299. This was Alfred's thirty-ninth year according to the author's earlier reckoning.

300. Keynes and Lapidge (*Alfred the Great*, p. 98), here and a few lines further on in the narrative, translate *regnum* ('kingdom') as 'empire'.

301. *conscissum est*, rare use of *conscindo*, 'to rend to pieces'. The word is used in the context of schism and the rending of garments, in ecclesiastical writing and in biblical exegesis of Late Antiquity and the Early Middle Ages.

302. This chapter is not only entirely dependent on the Anglo-Saxon Chronicle, but like the Chronicle, it is heavily retrospective in tone. All the events recorded here are given under the year 887, but the summary of Carolingian dynastic strife covers a three-year period from 887 to 889. Arnulf was proclaimed king in East Francia (Germany) in 887. His brother, Charles the Fat was deposed on 11 November 887, and Charles died on 13 January 888. The dismemberment of Carolingian lands did not take place until 888, and the civil war in Italy between Berengnar of Friuli and Guy, duke of Spoleto, continued until the spring of 889. There is nothing original in this account, and the Alfredian chronicler whose text the author followed, borrowed the material in the 890s from a set of Frankish annals of the Fulda type. See Smyth, *Alfred the Great*, pp. 486–90.

303. The Anglo-Saxon Chronicle does not identify Ealdorman Æthelhelm with Wiltshire at this point, but Æthelhelm is so identified at the record of his death under the annal for 897. This is the last annal (887) from the Anglo-Saxon Chronicle to be translated by the author.

304. The author abandons his translation of the Chronicle text here at 887. Because the first recension of the Chronicle – the *A-Text Precursor* – is thought to have continued down to include part at least of the annal for 892, it is assumed that the author (whenever he may have written) did have access to a Chronicle text continued thus far. He refers to West Saxon forts which were unfinished at a time when the Danes attacked (Chapter 91), and that is strongly suggestive of a similar reference to a 'half-made' fort in the Chronicle under 892. The 887 annal,

however, represents the last entry in the Chronicle translation undertaken by the author.

305. *regia cambra* ('the royal chamber') is a Frankish term.

306. This is clearly the same book which the author describes in Chapter 24 as being kept by Alfred from when he was a boy. The notion of the personal book of the king, kept always in his possession, is borrowed from Einhard's account of Charlemagne.

307. The author's statement that Alfred had read from a manuscript of his own making back in his youth flatly contradicts so much of what he says elsewhere of the king's supposed illiteracy. Keynes and Lapidge (*Alfred the Great*, p. 99) translate *legerat* ('he read') as 'he learned'.

308. After the words: *quod ego audiens et ingeniosam*, Wise identified a change of hand from this point on in the manuscript, and continuing down to the end of Chapter 98. This second hand was designated the *manus recentior* by Wise. See note 358 at the end of Chapter 98.

309. Source of quotation unknown.

310. *inhianter* 'open-mouthedly'. This word is repeated in Chapter 106B below.

311. The reference to *divinae scripturae* ('Divine Scriptures') shows that Alfred's miraculous acquisition of the art of reading and translation was associated in the monastic author's mind with the study of biblical exegesis.

312. Luke xxiii. 42.

313. Following the emendation by Keynes and Lapidge (*Alfred the Great*, p. 269, n. 215).

314. St. Martin's Day, 11 November 887.

315. The notion of the king's handbook containing a miscellany of notes was inspired partly by the account of the emperor's writing tablets in the *Life* of Charlemagne and partly perhaps by Byrhtferth of Ramsey's own handbook which he compiled as a teaching aid in the late tenth century.

316. Whitelock (*E.H.D.*, i, 272) significantly omitted this chapter from her translation. It did little to bolster her 'Genuine Asser' thesis. The author develops his notion of royal discipleship from the last chapter. His note of apology was probably inspired by the offensive allegory of an early medieval king – himself the dispenser of cruel justice – fixed to a gibbet.

317. Perhaps a Frankish quotation. See Keynes and Lapidge, n. 217, p. 269.

318. On the author's own calculation, if Alfred were born in 849, then his 45th year would have been in 893. The mysterious illness was alleged to have appeared in the king's 20th year, which on the same calculation would have been 868 – the year of Alfred's marriage, when as the author informs us (in Chapter 74) the king was indeed said to have contracted a mysterious illness during his wedding feast. Two important pieces of information are conveyed in this sentence therefore: the first that the author claims to be writing in AD 893, and the second that Alfred's illness was connected in some way in the author's mind with the marriage of the king back in 868.

319. Wheeler suggested that the word *sollicitudine* may have dropped out of the original text at this point. Wheeler, 'Textual Emendations', *Eng. Hist. Rev.*, xlvii (1932), 86.

320. Whitelock (*E.H.D.*, i, 272) unaccountably omits the word *Jerusalem* in her translation.

321. The text read *ab el* or *a bel. Life of Alfred*, ed. Stevenson, p. 77, and cf. Stevenson's extensive footnote, ibid., pp. 328–9.

322. Stevenson in one of his more naive comments wrote: 'The mention of gold and silver buildings is somewhat surprising, but there is no reason to suspect the accuracy of the reading' (*Life of Alfred*, ed. Stevenson, p. 329).

323. The Frankish *cambris* ('chambers') is again used. Cf. Chapter 88.

324. Keynes and Lapidge suggested that this passage refers to Alfred's demolition of existing buildings and his reconstruction of them on the same royal estates, citing Rahtz's account of successive building programmes at Cheddar. Keynes and Lapidge, n. 22, p. 270, and n. 25, p. 317. But in the case of Cheddar, a major rebuilding programme in stone took place significantly in the 930s (the reign of Athelstan) not in the 880s. The author is suggesting that King Alfred moved buildings and building materials from one location to another and the author may have acquired that idea not from any contemporary knowledge he had of King Alfred, but from what he read in Einhard's *Life* of Charlemagne. There he would have read that when Charlemagne was building his cathedral at Aachen:

> 'He was unable to find marble columns for his construction anywhere else, so he had them brought from Rome and Ravenna.' (Thorpe, transl., *Two Lives of Charlemagne*, p. 79)

325. Following the suggested emendation of Wheeler – 'Textual Emendations', *Eng. Hist. Rev.*, xlvii (1932), 87.

326. This criticism of King Alfred's 'people' who were unwilling to support the common good of his realm reads like Byrhtferth of Ramsey's criticism of the magnates of Æthelred the Unready in Byrhtferth's account of that reign in the Worcester Latin Chronicle.

327. This example of the pilot metaphor recurs in Chapters 21 and 73.

328. *Comites*, 'counts', translated here as 'ealdormen'.

329. *Ministros* ('ministers'), translated here as 'thegns'.

330. *Praepositos* might also refer to 'reeves' and is so translated by Keynes and Lapidge (*Alfred the Great*, p. 102), following Whitelock (*E.H.D.*, i, 273).

331. The author is here describing the *witan* or 'wise men' – bishops, ealdormen, thegns and heads of religious houses – who advised the king in their capacity as royal councillors.

332. A curious present tense in the midst of imperfects.

333. *castellis* ('fortifications' from the Frankish *castella*). This discussion on unfinished fortresses which were attacked from land and sea was almost certainly inspired by the account in the Anglo-Saxon Chronicle of the Danish capture of an unfinished (*samworht*) Alfredian fortress near the Lympne estuary in Kent in 892. The author's strong views on the need to defend the kingdom are remarkable at this point in his narrative and reflect the preoccupations of a writer who had to endure the uncertainties of the reign of Æthelred the Unready.

334. *imperialium diffinitionum* ('imperial decrees'). The spelling with *iff* is illiterate but not unparalleled. The phrase surely reflects a Frankish thought world and one which was alien to the embattled West Saxon kingship of the late ninth century.

335. *eulogii*. Keynes and Lapidge (*Alfred the Great*, n. 226, p. 271) take *eulogii* to be a genitive of *eulogium* ('fine utterance', 'excellent authority'). They then assume the loss of a noun from the original text and insert *per exemplum*. . . . before *eulogii* to read: 'to follow up the example of the excellent authority' on the assumption that the author was referring back to his appeal to the authority of Scripture shortly before.

336. This reads like yet another strongly critical comment by the author on the state of Anglo-Saxon society and its defences in the reign of Æthelred the Unready.

337. The Cotton text reads *cauticis* which has been taken by Stevenson (*Life of Alfred*, p. 80) and by subsequent translators to read *caudicis*. Another possibility is *nauticis*. See *Life of Alfred*, ed. Stevenson, p. 332.

338. There is no contemporary evidence from charters or elsewhere to indicate that the monastery at Athelney was founded by King Alfred. The place was too isolated during Alfred's precarious reign – and it was occupied by that king for too brief a period – to have suggested itself as a prudent location for a new and model monastery. Its foundation most likely took place during the more stable political situation which prevailed in the reign of Alfred's son, Edward the Elder. It would then have been a tenth-century thanksgiving foundation for the preservation of Alfred's dynasty during Alfred's time of refuge there in 878. See Smyth, *Alfred the Great*, pp. 264–6.

339. This passage reveals the mind of an author who is clearly concerned with issues relating to Monastic Reform, and betrays concerns of a writer from the late tenth century.

340. This chapter reflects the Ramsey author's late tenth-century zeal to return to a Benedictine type *regula* or *rule*. He was also influenced by the *Life* of the Frankish count, Gerald of Aurillac, who is said in his *Life* to have lamented about the difficulties of finding suitable monks for his monastic foundation at Aurillac. This in turn may have prompted the author to assert that Alfred eventually decided to colonise his monastery at Athelney with Gaulish monks. See Smyth, *Alfred the Great*, p. 262.

341. This was presumably the same John – also described as a priest and monk – who the author tells us back in Chapter 78 was summoned from 'Gaul' to act as a tutor to King Alfred in *c*. 885–7. His description of John here in Chapter 94 as an 'Old Saxon' would suggest that he hailed from continental Saxony (as opposed to England). But the author's understanding of where the 'Old Saxons' were located on the continent was – as is seen in Chapter 69 – lamentably confused. It is perhaps fruitless to attempt to make sense of details such as this in the author's work. In Chapter 76, for instance, he lists Franks (*Franci*) as being distinct from Gauls (*Galli*).

342. It is entirely inconsistent of the author to tell us in Chapter 93 that King Alfred regarded English infants as unsuitable material for his monastery 'because of the tenderness of their feeble' age, and now inform us that the king recruited Gaulish infants to swell the ranks of that same foundation at Athelney.

343. Much spurious or anachronistic detail in the *Life* of Alfred may well have been inspired by the author's genuine observations at Ramsey in the late tenth century. For instance, Byrhtferth and his circle must have known some pagan and many half-pagan sons of Danish magnates who attended the remarkable monastic school at Ramsey. So while the author's protestation that he himself was a witness to this fact ought to put us on our guard, nevertheless, he may have been writing from a personal experience of sorts. I have suggested elsewhere that there is a relationship between this observation regarding the supposed pagan youth in Alfred's monastery at Athelney, and Byrhtferth of Ramsey's account of the education of the young St. Oda who was alleged to have been the son of Danish parents. See Smyth, *Alfred the Great*, pp. 315–16.

344. References to *monachium habitum* ('monastic habit') are redolent of the language of late tenth-century monastic reformers.

345. The author's reference to 'tares and cockles' (*zizania et lolium*) mirrors a similar reference to the same weeds made by Byrhtferth of Ramsey in his *Life* of St.

Oswald. Significantly, both references draw together an allusion from Matthew's Gospel and Virgil's *Georgics* and that rare combination points as a powerful argument in favour of Byrhtferth of Ramsey's personal involvement in the authorship of the *Life* of King Alfred. See Smyth, *Alfred the Great*, p. 284.

346. This passage could be taken as a medieval hagiographer's charter, and underlines the fact that our author's primary objective was not to write a factual *life* of King Alfred, but to edify his readers and to moralise.

347. Matthew xxvii. 64.

348. This anecdote relating to the attack on Abbot John was part of the stock in trade of late tenth- and early eleventh-century hagiographers who were at pains to show how reforming abbots were threatened with murder and violence in the face of their heroic efforts to reform lax monastic communities. Whitelock found these chapters too embarrassing to include in her translation of King Alfred's *Life* for *English Historical Documents* (i, 274). See Smyth, *Alfred the Great*, pp. 262–3.

349. Keynes and Lapidge's 'rose briskly to meet them' (*Alfred the Great*, p. 105) scarcely does justice to *insurgens acriter* written in the context of describing a murderous affray.

350. *gronnae* ('fen'). See note 151 to Chapter 53.

351. Abbot John is described by the Frankish title, *senior* ('lord'). Cf. the description of King Æthelwulf in Chapter 13.

352. This unedifying tale of the torturing to death of abbot John's assailants and also of those who had plotted against him, is in marked contrast to the forgiveness extended by Bishop Æthelwold of Winchester to his would-be murderers. The tale is constructed through a mixture of folklore and hagiography. See Smyth, *Alfred the Great*, p. 263.

353. This is a typical continuity phrase (*his ita relatis, ad incepta redeamus*) frequently employed by the author and also by Byrhtferth of Ramsey throughout many of Byrhtferth's known works. See Smyth, *Alfred the Great*, pp. 291–3.

354. This statement assumes that the foundation of the nunnery post-dated the founding of the fortress or *burh* at Shaftesbury. William of Malmesbury's supposed evidence for the founding of the town of Shaftesbury by King Alfred in the eighth year of his reign in 880, is a piece of medieval antiquarianism based on a late version of the Anglo-Saxon Chronicle. See Smyth, *Alfred the Great*, p. 260.

355. Earlier, in Chapter 75, the author referred to Æthelgifu as being 'subjected to and and consecrated under the monastic rule of life'. The mention of *monasticae vitae regulis* is again suggestive of the ideals of late tenth-century monastic reformers. King Alfred was probably referring to Æthelgifu in his *Will* when he alludes to his 'middle' or second daughter, but there is no indication in that contemporary document connecting her either with Shaftesbury or with the monastic life. Even more significantly, the king did not leave any bequests to monasteries at either Athelney or Shaftesbury, although he did leave bequests to several other religious houses. It may be that Æthelgifu's genuine connection with Shaftesbury began after the death of her father and sometime in the early tenth century. Equally, it may be that the author wilfully confused the ninth-century Æthelgifu with the later Queen Ælfgifu, wife of King Edmund, who was buried at Shaftesbury in 944 and whose relics, according to the Chronicler Æthelweard, were working miracles at Shaftesbury at the very time when the author was writing the *Life* of King Alfred. Such confusion and half-truths were typical of this writer's approach to royal biography. See Smyth, *Alfred the Great*, pp. 264–6.

356. So, although King Alfred allegedly found it impossible to staff his monastery with

English monks, there was apparently no shortage of women to answer his call to Shaftesbury.

357. The earliest charters for both Athelney and Shaftesbury contain anachronisms and glaring chronological errors which have not deterred enthusiasts from attempting to rehabilitate them. See Smyth, *Alfred the Great*, p. 266 and p. 649, n. 150.

358. Wise noted that the second or later hand of the Cotton manuscript – his *manus recentior* which had taken over from early in Chapter 88, now ended at the end of Chapter 98. Wise did not state whether the final hand which took over in the manuscript at Chapter 98 was the same as the earlier hand which had worked down to Chapter 88 or whether this was a 'third' or altogether different hand from the other two. Stevenson argued with some conviction that the so-called later hand which begins in Chapter 88 was no later than the eleventh century. (Stevenson, *Alfred the Great*, pp. xliii–xlvi). Stevenson further surmised that 'there is evidence that the chapters in the later hand formed part of the original work in the similarity of style, and in the fact that the older hand or hands resumed, as we may conclude from Wise's silence, after the later hand ceased' (ibid., p. xlvi). See note 308 above.

359. This Chapter is modelled on purely hagiographical considerations.

360. The precise passage from Scripture may not be identifiable (Keynes and Lapidge, *Alfred the Great*, p. 273, n. 239), but surely Matthew xxv. 28–9 is relevant here: 'whenever a man is rich, gifts will be made to him and his riches will abound.'

361. The author is probably thinking here of the record in the Anglo-Saxon Chronicle of King Æthelwulf's grant by charter of a tenth of all his (personal) estates for his spiritual needs back in 855. King Alfred's biographer misinterpreted the Chronicle record in relation to Æthelwulf's donation (see Chapters 11 and 16 above) and is here attributing even more extravagant spiritual provisions to Æthelwulf's son, Alfred.

362. Genesis iv.7, Old Latin version.

363. Proverbs xxi.1.

364. *ministros,* 'ministers'.

365. The reference here to the *census,* and yet again at the beginning of Chapter 102 (where mention is also made of the royal *fiscus* or fisc), shows that the author had the king's royal or 'public' revenues in mind, rather than his private wealth. We are asked to believe that Alfred alienated half of the public purse for charitable purposes – income raised from tribute and the control of coinage; fines raised from the administration of justice; and profits from the collection of food rents, taxes and tolls. It is seriously open to question whether any late ninth-century kingdom such as Wessex, which had endured so much sustained external military pressure and extortion could have set aside such great sums for charity.

366. The complex division and subdivision of Alfred's taxation revenues represent unreal schematisations which reflect the mathematical and numerical preoccupations of Byrhtferth, the Ramsey schoolmaster. Thus Alfred's revenues were initially divided into two, with the first half then divided into thirds and the second half divided into quarters. See Smyth, *Alfred the Great*, p. 596.

367. The author's decision to divide Alfred's revenues between the king's *bellatores* ('fighters'), his *operatores* ('workmen' – see the next Chapter 101) and the promotion of good works, may have been suggested by King Alfred's own triple division of society into fighting men, working men and those who pray. See Smyth, *Alfred the Great*, p. 596.

368. *satellites* 'followers' is a Frankish term frequently employed by the author for the king's retainers.

369. The author's account of the three relays of service (*ministerium*) at King Alfred's court (*curtus regius*) is an embroidered version of a misunderstood passage in the Anglo-Saxon Chronicle. The Chronicle under the annal for 893 tells us that King Alfred 'had divided his army into two, so that always half its men were at home [and] half on service, apart from the men who guarded the fortifications.' The Chronicle describes what was essentially two divisions between those men in active service (including those defending the burhs) and those resting at home. The author developed this into three categories, describing a rota in three divisions, with each division having its rota further sub-divided into thirds (one third served at court, two-thirds at home). This division into thirds and ninths may be nothing more than the invention of the numerically minded Byrhtferth.

370. Cf. Alfred's *Will*. Keynes and Lapidge, *Alfred the Great*, p. 273, n. 244.

371. *operatoribus* ('workmen'). Cf. note 367 above. The author misunderstood Alfred's own reference in his translation of Boethius's *Consolation of Philosophy*, to his *weorcmen* – the serfs and labourers of his kingdom – and turned them into 'countless numbers' of craftsmen who erected imaginary buildings. See Smyth, *Alfred the Great*, p. 596.

372. *aedificio*, 'building technique'.

373. 2 Corinthians ix.7. It is impossible to accept that King Alfred alienated one sixth of all his annual public revenues for the maintenance of foreigners – even of those who had not requested support!

374. The first half of the king's revenue was divided into three and now the second half was supposedly divided into quarters. The unreal nature of the first and second half of the divisions becomes apparent when we note that Alfred supposedly allocated a sixth of his revenue in the first division (Chapter 101) to 'foreigners of every nation' while he also allocated (Chapter 102) one eighth of his revenues to 'the poor of every nation'. This means in effect that King Alfred supposedly and farcically alienated 0.30 (almost a third) of his annual revenue to strangers! We are also told in Chapter 102 that the king allocated yet more funds for foreign monasteries.

375. For this reference to annual revenue and the treasury (*census*), see note 365 above.

376. See Keynes and Lapidge, *Alfred the Great*, p. 274, n. 247.

377. The idea that Alfred allocated one eighth of his annual revenue to the monasteries of Athelney and Shaftesbury is not supported by contemporary evidence from the king's own *Will* where he makes no mention of those houses, and yet where he makes bequests to other monasteries including Winchester.

378. The idea that King Alfred gave so generously to the school which he himself supposedly founded, was probably prompted by Byrhtferth's own preoccupation with the monastic school at Ramsey at the turn of the millennium.

379. In addition to giving away almost one-third of his revenue to foreigners and to strangers, Alfred also gave away further annual revenue for the maintenance of monasteries overseas. This passage relating to Alfred's generosity to Welshmen, Cornishmen, Gauls, Bretons, Northumbrians and Irishmen, is based on Einhard's record of Charlemagne's interest in foreign peoples:

> 'He gave alms not only in his own country and in the kingdom over which he reigned, but also across the sea in Syria, Egypt, Africa, Jerusalem, Alexandria, and Carthage. Whenever he heard that Christians were living in want, he took pity on their poverty and gave them money regularly.'

And again:

> 'He loved foreigners and took great pains to make them welcome. So many visited him as a result that they were rightly held to be burden not only to the palace, but to the entire realm.' (*Two Lives of Charlemagne*, transl., Thorpe, pp. 76, 80).

It is important to note that the author includes Cornwall (*Cornubia*) among those regions, which as he wrote (supposedly) in the 890s were then regarded as being outside of English West Saxon and Mercian territories proper. Yet back in Chapter 74 we are told that Alfred went hunting in the heart of Cornish territory in his youth. It would have been highly improbable that the young Alfred ever hunted in Cornwall.

380. The passage is not from Scripture as the author claimed, but from St. Augustine's *Enchiridion de Fide*. Cf. Galbraith, p. 101; and Keynes and Lapidge, *Alfred the Great*, p. 274. n. 249.

381. The text reads: *externis divinis* which is a nonsense. I have followed Keynes and Lapidge here, as well as earlier editors in amending to *externis divitiis*. Keynes and Lapidge, p. 274, n. 250.

382. The supposed invention by Alfred of the lantern candle clock was inspired by the hagiographical account of the king's obsession with time management, and by an equally obsessive desire on the part of Alfred to measure half of all his time which he wished to give to God (see Chapter 103). The degree of credibility which we attach to this chapter, therefore, depends on how much weight we give to the hagiographical account in this *Life* of the deeds of *Saint* Alfred.

383. The candles, on Stevenson's reckoning, would have weighed only 5/8th of an ounce each and he was clearly uncomfortable with this finding because 'they would be very thin in proportion to their length'. Consequently their rate of burning would have been far too rapid to comply with the experiment described in this chapter. *Life of Alfred*, ed. Stevenson, p. 338. We know that Byrhtferth of Ramsey had an abiding interest in clocks, time-measurement, and the monastic hours. It was Byrhtferth's personal concerns and not King Alfred's which are reflected in this chapter. See Smyth, *Alfred the Great*, pp. 321–4.

384. The idea of King Alfred having candles burning continuously before holy relics which he took with him everywhere even while travelling with a tent, was suggested to the author by the *Life* of Count Gerald of Aurillac. See Smyth, *Alfred the Great*, pp. 323–4.

385. Alfred may well have been a conscientious judge (see Smyth, *Alfred the Great*, pp. 394–400) but his concern for justice as portrayed by the author may also have mirrored the *Life* of Count Gerald of Aurillac.

386. The verb is missing from this final sentence in this chapter. Wheeler ('Textual emendations', *Eng. Hist. Rev.,* xlvii [1932], 87) added the words *utilitati studebat* 'sought after advantage'. The author's attack on the corruption and self-interest of the magnates bears all the hall-marks of Byrhtferth's comments on the aristocracy of late tenth-century England.

387. Keynes and Lapidge (*Alfred the Great*, p. 275, n. 255) describe *studebat* as 'meaningless' and substituted Wheeler's *sedebat* 'he used to sit [in judgements]'. Wheeler, loc. cit.

388. *comitum et praepositorum* could be translated 'ealdormen and reeves'.

389. This picture of divisive debates and judgements in assemblies of the *witan* may well reflect conditions in late tenth-century England – conditions which

prompted the author to write this *Life* of King Alfred in the first instance, and to exaggerate Alfred's reign as a golden age.

390. I follow the emendations suggested by Keynes and Lapidge (*Alfred the Great*, p. 275, n. 257).

391. This is a typical exaggeration on the part of the author and should not be taken literally. But cf. P. Wormald, *The Making of English Law* (Oxford and Malden), i, 118, n. 5.

392. *fideles* 'followers'.

393. The author may here be echoing phrases in King Alfred's *Will*.

394. The author's reference to the 'office and status of Wise Men' (*sapientium ministerium et gradus*) is a direct reference to the *witan* or 'wise men' in the Anglo-Saxon royal council.

395. *comites, praepositi ac ministri* could translate as 'ealdormen, reeves and thegns'.

396. *litteralibus studiis* ('reading and writing').

397. The idea that the illiterate warlords of Wessex embraced learning with alacrity, or the idea that Alfred would have been in a position to force them to take up night-school, is a fantasy dreamt up by the schoolmaster of Ramsey 100 years after Alfred's death.

398. The ending here *pace* Keynes and Lapidge (*Alfred the Great*, n. 260, p. 275) is neither abrupt nor indicative of an unfinished work. The final sentence with its *hanc explicavimus* ('we have explained this') constitutes a standard rounding-off formula of a type used by the author to end other discrete sections of the *Life*.

## 1 A Tour around the Manuscripts

1. *Asser's Life of King Alfred*, ed. W.H. Stevenson (Oxford reprint 1959 of 1904 edn.), chapter 91, p. 76.
2. Nelson, 'Waiting for Alfred', *Early Medieval Europe*, vii (1998), 123.
3. T. Wright, 'Some Historical Doubts Relating to the Biographer Asser', *Archaeologia*, xxix (1842), 192–201.
4. Ibid., pp. 196, 199–200. Cf. *Life of Alfred*, ed. Stevenson, pp. xlix–l.
5. Ibid., pp. xcix, ciii.
6. *E.H.D.*, ed. Whitelock, i, 192.
7. The *Life of Alfred* provides a translation of the Alfredian Chronicle from AD 851 – supposedly the third year of Alfred's life – up until AD 887 (*Life of Alfred*, ed. Stevenson, chapter 3, p. 4 – chapter 86, p. 73).
8. Ibid., pp. xiii–xxxii.
9. Ibid., pp. 221–5; 294–6.
10. Ibid., p. xcvi.
11. Ibid., pp. c–ci; cviii.
12. Ibid., p. xcvii and cf. pp. xcvii–xcix.
13. V.H. Galbraith, 'Who Wrote Asser's Life of Alfred?', in Galbraith, *Introduction to the Study of History* (London, 1964), p. 122.
14. F.W. Maitland, 'The Laws of the Anglo-Saxons', *Quarterly Review*, cc (October 1904), 147–8.
15. Galbraith, p. 90.
16. Ibid., pp. 93–4, 110, 113–14, 120.
17. Ibid., pp. 91–2, 104–10.
18. Ibid., p. 113.

19. Ibid., pp. 99–103.
20. Ibid., pp. 99–100.
21. Ibid., p. 111.
22. J.L. Nelson, 'Myths of the Dark Ages', in L.M. Smith, ed., *The Making of Britain: the Dark Ages*, p. 155.
23. H.H. Howorth, 'Asser's Life of Alfred', *The Athenaeum* (1876), no. 2526, pp. 425–6; no. 2535, pp. 727–9; no. 2549, pp. 307–9; idem, 'Ethelweard and Asser', *The Athenæum* (1877), no. 2597, pp. 145–6. *Life of Alfred*, ed. Stevenson, pp. cx–cxv.
24. Because of the uncorrected dating in the Anglo-Saxon Chronicle, 901 rather than 899 was considered to have been the year of Alfred's death (*Two of the Saxon Chronicles Parallel*, eds. C. Plummer, and J. Earle (2 vols. Oxford 1965 reprint of 1896 edn.), i, 91).
25. Nelson, p. 149.
26. F.M. Stenton, *Anglo-Saxon England*, 2nd edn (Oxford reprint 1967), p. 261.
27. See Nelson, Plate 83, p. 156.
28. Stenton, p. 269, n. 1.
29. Ibid., p. 268.
30. D. Whitelock, *The Genuine Asser* (Stenton Lecture 1967; Reading, 1968), p. 3.
31. D. Whitelock, 'Recent Work on Asser's Life of Alfred', in *Life of Alfred*, ed. Stevenson, p. cxlvii.
32. *Willelmi Malmesbiriensis monachi de Gestis pontificum Anglorum libri quinque*, ed. N.E.S.A. Hamilton (London, Rolls Series, 1870) p. 177. *Willelmi Malmesbiriensis monachi de Gestis regum Anglorum*, ed. W. Stubbs (Rolls Series, 1887), i, 131.
33. See pp. 126–7 below.
34. Whitelock, *Genuine Asser*, p. 20.
35. Ibid., p. 8.
36. Ibid., p. 20.
37. S. Keynes and M. Lapidge (transl.), *Alfred the Great: Asser's Life of King Alfred and Other Contemporary Sources* (Penguin, Harmondsworth, 1983), p. 50.
38. Ibid.
39. Ibid., p. 51.
40. C.[R.] Hart, 'Byrhtferth's Northumbrian Chronicle', *Eng. Hist. Rev.*, xcvii (1982), 558–9.
41. K. Gazzard, 'Abbo of Fleury' (Unpublished Oxford D.Phil thesis, 2000).
42. *Life of Alfred*, ed. Stevenson, pp. li–liii.
43. Ibid., p. lii.
44. Ibid., pp. liii–liv.
45. Ibid., pp. xxi–xxviii.
46. Ibid., pp. xxviii–xxxi.
47. Ibid., pp. xxxii–iii.
48. Keynes and Lapidge, op. cit., pp. 224–5.
49. Stevenson, pp. xxxii–iii.
50. Ibid., pp. xv–xvi.
51. K. Sisam, *Studies in the History of Old English Literature* (Oxford, reprint 1962), p. 148, n. 3.
52. Stevenson, p. xliv.
53. P.H. Sawyer, *Anglo-Saxon Charters: an Annotated List and Bibliography* (Roy. Hist. Soc., London, 1968), no. 898. (Henceforward referred to as Sawyer, no. 898, etc.) Sisam, op. cit., p. 148, n. 3.
54. C.R. Hart, *Learning in Late Anglo-Saxon England: the School of Ramsey*, Chapter 22

(forthcoming). Hart, 'Byrhtferth's Northumbrian Chronicle', p. 576.

55. See pp. 67–76 below.
56. Stevenson, pp. xxxviii and n.1.
57. When James Ussher, archbishop of Armagh, wrote of the Cottonian manuscript sometime before 1639, he dated it to Asser's time (i.e. *c.* AD 900) or shortly afterwards. Ibid., p. xli. Stevenson wrongly described Ussher as archbishop of Dublin. Ibid., *Index,* p. 383.
58. Ibid., p. xlii and n. 1.
59. Ibid., p. xliii.
60. Ibid., p. xliii; Whitelock, 'Recent Work on Asser's Life of Alfred', pp. cxxvii–iii; Sisam, p. 148, n. 3.
61. Stevenson, p. xxxviii, n. 1.
62. Ibid., p. xliii.
63. C.[R.] Hart, 'Byrhtferth's Northumbrian Chronicle', *Eng. Hist. Rev.,* xcvii (1982), 558–82; M. Lapidge, 'Byrhtferth of Ramsey and the *Historia Regum',* A.S.E., x (1982), 97–122.
64. S.J. Crawford, 'Byrhtferth of Ramsey and the Anonymous Life of St. Oswald', in F.C. Burkitt, ed., *Speculum Religionis: Being Essays ... Presented to Claude G. Montefiori* (Oxford, 1929), pp. 99–111.
65. M. Lapidge, 'Byrhtferth and the *Vita S. Ecgwini',* Medieval Studies, xli (1979), 331–53.
66. P. Baker and M. Lapidge, eds., *Byrhtferth's Enchiridion* (Early English Texts Soc., Oxford, 1995).
67. Stevenson, p. lix.
68. P. Hunter Blair, 'Some Observations on the "Historia Regum" attributed to Symeon of Durham', in *Celt and Saxon: Studies in the Early British Border,* ed. K. Jackson *et al.* (Cambridge, 1964), pp. 100–2.
69. For a summary of the complex argument relating to Whitelock's views on the text of the abridged version of Alfred's *Life* in the Northumbrian Chronicle, see Smyth, *King Alfred the Great,* p. 628, n. 67.
70. Lapidge, 'Byrhtferth of Ramsey and the *Historia Regum',* A.S.E., x (1982), 121.
71. Keynes and Lapidge, *Alfred the Great,* p. 57.
72. Stevenson, pp. xlviii–xlix; lviii–lix.
73. Ibid., p. lix.
74. Lapidge entitled those same first five sections of the *Historia Regum* as Byrhtferth's *Historical Miscellany,* M. Lapidge, 'Byrhtferth and the Early Sections of the *Historia Regum',* p. 119. Lapidge's study applied only to the Durham recension or Hart's BNC D. Of the five sections which survive in BNC D, only sections 2–5 were originally included in BNC Y, and of those, Section 3 (material derived from Bede) is now missing. The account of the martyrdom of the Kentish Æthelberht and Æthelred (Section 1) does not appear to have been ever included in BNC Y.
75. W. Stubbs, ed. *Chronica Magistri Rogeri de Houedene,* 4 vols. (Rolls Ser., London, 1868–71), i, xxxvi–xxxviii.
76. I am grateful to C.R. Hart for information on Byrhtferth's Northumbrian Chronicle, York version.
77. Hart, 'Byrhtferth's Northumbrian Chronicle', pp. 563–4.
78. Ibid.
79. *Symeonis Monachi Opera Omnia,* ed., T. Arnold, 2 vols. (London, Rolls Ser. 1890–96), ii, n.*a,* p. 85.

80.  Hart, pp. 575–6.
81.  Hart, *Learning in Late Anglo-Saxon England* (forthcoming).
82.  Hart, *Learning in Late Anglo-Saxon England* (forthcoming). Idem, 'Byrhtferth's Northumbrian Chronicle', p. 578, where Hart set out his earlier views on dating.
83.  For the earlier part of the Worcester Chronicle, see *The Chronicle of John of Worcester: Volume II: the annals from 450 to 1066*, eds., R.R. Darlington and P. McGurk, transl. J. Bray and P. McGurk (Oxford, 1995).
84.  B. Thorpe, ed., *Florentii Wigorniensis monachi, Chronicon ex Chronicis* (English Historical Society, London, 1848–9), 2 vols. The attribution to Florence of Worcester goes back to William Howard's edition of the Worcester *Chronicon ex Chronicis* in 1592.
85.  *Chronicle of John of Worcester*, eds., Darlington and McGurk, pp. xvii–xx, lxvii–lxxxi.
86.  C.R. Hart, 'The Early Section of the Worcester Chronicle', *Journal of Medieval History*, ix (1983), 251–315.
87.  *Chronicle of John of Worcester*, eds. McGurk and Darlington, ii, lxxix–lxxxi.
88.  M. Lapidge, 'Byrhtferth and Oswald', in *St. Oswald of Worcester*, eds. N. Brook and C. Cubitt (Leicester, 1996), p. 76.
89.  Ibid., p. 78.
90.  This was nothing less than a tacit endorsement by Lapidge of Hart's findings that Byrhtferth was the compiler of the B-Text of the Anglo-Saxon Chronicle. Ibid., p. 78 and n. 53.
91.  Lapidge, 'Byrhtferth and the *Historia Regum*', p. 99.
92.  *Chronicle of John of Worcester*, eds. McGurk and Darlington, ii, lxxx.
93.  Ibid., pp. xlvi–xlvii; lv–lvii.
94.  C.[R.] Hart, 'The East Anglian Chronicle', *Journal of Medieval History*, vii (1981), 268; Keynes and Lapidge, p. 52.
95.  Hart, *Learning in Late Anglo-Saxon England*, Chapter 14 (forthcoming).
96.  Trinity College Cambridge MS R.7.28.2.
97.  *The Annals of St. Neots* in *The Anglo-Saxon Chronicle: a Collaborative Edition*, XVII, eds. D.N. Dumville and M. Lapidge (Cambridge, 1984), p. xv. The date of the original compilation of the Annals of St. Neots is disputed.
98.  Hart, 'East Anglian Chronicle', *Journal of Medieval History*, vii (1981), 249.
99.  Dumville and Lapidge, p. xxiii.
100.  Hart, pp. 250–1.
101.  Hart, 'East Anglian Chronicle', p. 280; idem, *Learning in Late Anglo-Saxon England*, Chapter 13 (forthcoming).
102.  Hart, 'East Anglian Chronicle', pp. 250, 280. The surviving text of the East Anglian Chronicle is found in a composite volume in Cambridge, Trinity College, MS R.7.28 (770) and was written between *c.* 1120 and *c.* 1140 (Dumville and Lapidge, pp. xv–xvi).
103.  Hart, p. 261; cf. Dumville and Lapidge, p. xxxix.
104.  Hart, pp. 261–4.
105.  Whitelock, *Genuine Asser*, pp. 18–19; Keynes and Lapidge, *Alfred the Great* (chapter 70), p. 88, and p. 253, n. 135.
106.  Whitelock was essentially agreeing with Stevenson here, for although Stevenson accepted that the manuscript of the *Life* of Alfred which was used in the compilation of the East Anglian Chronicle (*Annals of St. Neots*), agreed very closely with the Cottonian manuscript, he also held that in places, it displayed more correct readings. (*Life of Alfred*, ed. Stevenson, pp. xlix, lvii–lviii). Hart challenged

Stevenson's analysis, point by point. In the opinion of Stevenson and Whitelock, the copy of the *Life* of Alfred used by the compiler of the East Anglian Chronicle, was by implication a different manuscript from that of Cotton Otho A.xii. It is not clear what precise relationship was thought by Whitelock to have existed between the manuscript of Alfred's *Life* which lay behind the East Anglian Chronicle and that consulted by the compilers of the *Historia Regum* (*HR 1*) and – in one instance at least – *HR 2*, save the fact that they all preserved more accurate readings than those in the lost Cotton manuscript which formed the basis of Parker's edition. Whitelock's conclusions on the nature of the manuscript of the *Life* of Alfred, which was consulted by the compiler of the East Anglian Chronicle, were based on a much more limited study than that carried out by Hart.

107. Hart, p. 264.
108. *Annals of St. Neots*, eds., Dumville and Lapidge, p. xxiii.
109. Hart, pp. 274–7.
110. Dumville and Lapidge, pp. lxiv–v.
111. Ibid. p. xlv, n. 49.
112. Ibid., p. xlvii.
113. Ibid., p. xlvii.
114. Ibid., pp. xliii–vii.
115. Hart, pp. 251–3; 260.
116. Dumville and Lapidge, pp. xlix–lvi.
117. Ibid., p. xlvi.
118. Ibid., p. xlv.
119. Dumville and Lapidge (*sub annis*, 365, 369, 375, 527, 579, 585, 588 and 633), pp. 4–10.
120. Hart, p. 252.
121. *Encomium Emmae Reginae*, ed. A. Campbell. Camden Soc. 3rd Series lxxii (London, 1949), pp. xix–xxi; xxxv–vii.
122. Ibid., pp. 24–5.
123. *Life of Alfred*, ed. Stevenson, p. 5.
124. *Encomium Emmae*, ed. Campbell, pp. 24–5.
125. Stevenson, p. 28.
126. *Encomium Emmae*, ed. Campbell, pp. xxxvii, 24–5; 96. *Annals of St. Neots*, eds. Dumville and Lapidge, p. 78.
127. Campbell, p. xxxvii. Although the passage on the Raven Banner was included in Parker's edition of Alfred's *Life*, Wise later stated that the Raven Banner episode was an interpolation from the *Annals of St. Neots* into the Cottonian text. We must, therefore, either go against Wise's judgement and conclude that episodes such as the Raven Banner were original to the Cotton manuscript of Alfred's *Life*, or that the author of the *Encomium* found all three of his borrowed passages in another source. *Life of Alfred*, ed. Stevenson, p. 44.
128. Dumville and Lapidge (*sub anno* 851), p. 43.
129. Ibid. (*sub anno* 871), p. 66.
130. Ibid. (*sub anno* 878), p. 78; Hart, who noted that the East Anglian Chronicle regularly leaves out glosses on placenames from the *Life* of Alfred (Hart, 'East Anglian Chronicle', p. 262), did not include the omission of the gloss on Sheppey in his list. In view of the tendency on the part of the compiler of the *Annals of St. Neots* to omit such glosses, the inclusion of the gloss on *Æscesdun* is significant, and shows that such omissions were not universal practice on the part of the compiler of the *Annals of St. Neots*.

131. *Chronicle of John of Worcester*, eds., Darlington and McGurk, ii, 264, 288.
132. A.P. Smyth, *Scandinavian Kings in the British Isles, 850–80* (Oxford, 1977), pp. 248–9, 269–70. C.E. Wright, *The Cultivation of Saga in Anglo-Saxon England* (Edinburgh, 1939), pp. 126–37.
133. Whitelock, *Genuine Asser*, p. 8; Keynes and Lapidge, *Alfred the Great*, p. 57.
134. For a brief discussion on this topic, see S. Keynes in A. Campbell, ed., *Encomium Emmae Reginae* (Cambridge, 1988 reprint), n. 3, p. xl.
135. A detailed account of Emma's career and of her place in eleventh-century northern European society will be found in P. Stafford's *Queen Emma and Queen Edith* (Oxford, 1997).
136. *Memorials of St. Edmund's Abbey*, ed. T. Arnold (London, Rolls Series, 1890–6), i, 341.
137. C.[R.] Hart, *The Danelaw* (London and Rio Grande), p. 198 and notes. F.E. Harmer, ed., *Anglo-Saxon Writs* (Manchester, 1952), pp. 145–7, 435–7. Cf. Sawyer no. 1069.
138. Sawyer no. 980.
139. Hart, *Danelaw*, pp. 57–9, 62–6, 471–2.
140. *Encomium Emmae*, ed. Campbell, p. xlviii.
141. Sawyer no. 997. Harmer, ed., *Anglo-Saxon Writs* pp. 246, 257.
142. Lapidge, 'Byrhtferth and Oswald', p. 78, n. 52.
143. C.[R.] Hart, 'The Ramsey Computus', *Eng. Hist. Rev.*, lxxxv (1970), 29–44; idem, *Learning in Late Anglo-Saxon England*, Chapter 8 (forthcoming).
144. Hart, 'Ramsey Computus', p. 42. Hart had made subsequent emendments to his own edition of the Ramsey Annals to appear in his *Learning in Late Anglo-Saxon England*.
145. For the significance of the calculation of King Alfred's age at various points in his *life*, see pp. 176–81 below.
146. *Life of Alfred*, ed. Stevenson, pp. 41–2.
147. *Annals of St. Neots*, eds. Dumville and Lapidge, pp. 76–7.
148. Smyth, *Alfred the Great*, pp. 332–4.
149. We are told in the *Life* of Alfred (Chapter 74) that the young Alfred visited a church in Cornwall 'in which St. Gueriir lies in peace and now St. Neot lies there as well'.
150. Smyth, pp. 325–48.
151. The *Life* of St. Ecgwine was written for the monks of Evesham, which like Ramsey was a dependency of Worcester. Cf. M. Lapidge, 'The Medieval Hagiography of St. Ecgwine', *Vale of Evesham Historical Society Research Papers*, vi (1977), 78–9.
152. The immediate source of the Worcester Latin Chronicle's abridgement of the *Life* of Alfred may have been derived from the abridged version in the East Anglian Chronicle with further additions from the fuller Cottonian text. Information supplied by C.R. Hart.
153. Whitelock, *Genuine Asser*, pp. 19–20.
154. M. McKisack, *Medieval History in the Tudor Age* (Oxford, 1971), pp. 27–8.
155. *Annals of St. Neots*, eds Dumville and Lapidge, pp. xli–ii.
156. Ibid., p. xlii.
157. Corpus Christi College, Cambridge MS no. 100.
158. *Life of Alfred*, ed., Stevenson, pp. li–iii; Keynes and Lapidge, *Alfred the Great*, p. 225. The statement by Keynes and Lapidge that the Corpus 100 transcript 'reproduces the text of Asser as it stood in the Cotton manuscript before Parker's annotations were added and before the passages from other sources had been inserted' (ibid., p. 225) was a departure from the earlier caution of Stevenson (p. lii), who recognised

that it had been tampered with by Parker and copied by an indifferent scholar. If the judgement of Keynes and Lapidge on this transcript were indeed true, then the loss of its exemplar, Cotton Otho A. xii, would be of little consequence.

159. Stevenson, pp. lvi and lviii; cf. Dumville in *Annals of St. Neots*, eds Dumville and Lapidge, p. xlii.
160. Stevenson, p. xii.
161. Ibid., p. xxi.
162. J. Strype, *The Life and Acts of Matthew Parker, the first archbishop of Canterbury in the reign of Queen Elizabeth*, 3 vols. (Oxford, 1821), ii, 441.
163. Ibid., ii, 245.
164. Ibid., ii, 500.
165. Stevenson, p. xxi, n. 2.
166. Ibid., p. xxi, n. 2.
167. Ibid., p. xxix.
168. Strype, ii, 441–4.
169. Ibid., ii, 27–8, 53, 372.
170. Ibid., ii, 293–7.
171. Ibid., ii, 245–6, 251–2.
172. McKisack, p. 47.
173. Ibid.
174. Strype, ii, 501.
175. Stevenson, p. lii.
176. Ibid., p. xix.
177. Ibid., pp. lxvii–viii, n. 4.
178. Strype, ii, 456, 518.
179. McKisack, p. 35.
180. *Correspondence of Matthew Parker, D.D. Archbishop of Canterbury*, ed. J. Bruce and T.T. Perowne (Parker Soc., Cambridge, 1853), p. 388.
181. McKisack, p. 41.
182. Ibid., pp. 35–6.
183. Ibid., pp. 30–1.
184. V. Sanders, 'The Household of Archbishop Parker and the Influencing of Public Opinion', *Journal of Ecclesiastical History*, xxxiv (1983), 535–42.
185. McKisack, p. 28.
186. Sanders, p. 538.
187. McKisack, p. 35.
188. Ibid.
189. *Life of Alfred*, ed., Stevenson, p. xxxiv.
190. Ibid., p. xvi and n. 2.
191. Ibid., chapter 88, pp. 73–4.
192. Sanders, p. 536.
193. Strype, ii, 501.
194. *Matthaei Parisiensis Historia Anglorum*, ed. F. Madden, 3 vols. (London, Rolls Ser., 1866), i. xxxvii. Cf. Stevenson, p. xix.
195. Ibid., pp. xxxix, xli, n. 1.
196. Stevenson, p. xi.
197. Keynes and Lapidge, *Alfred the Great*, pp. 221, n. 110; 222, n. 118; 242, n. 72.
198. Stevenson, p. cxxxi.
199. D.P. Kirby, 'Asser and his Life of King Alfred', *Studia Celtica*, vi (1971), 13.
200. *Encomium Emmae*, ed. Campbell, p. xxi.

## 2 The Author of the *Life*

1. Smyth, *Alfred the Great*, pp. 175–9.
2. *Historia Regum*, ed. Arnold, ii, 66–8.
3. Smyth, pp. 544–8.
4. Ibid., pp. 3–9. Keynes ('On the Authenticity of Asser's Life of King Alfred', *Jrnl. Ecclesiastical Hist.*, xlvii (1996), 535), although dismissing my argument in regard to the disputed borderland between Wessex and Mercia, failed to answer my case. Howlett – more embarrassingly – did not understand the discussion (*Eng. Hist. Rev.*, cxii (1997), 943.
5. Smyth, op. cit., pp. 9–11.
6. *Life of Alfred*, ed. Stevenson, p. 164. Whitelock, by a circular argument, authenticated the presence of one *Sigewulf pincerna* (Sigewulf the Butler) in the doubtful charter by King Alfred relating to North Newnton, Wiltshire, by stating: 'There is nothing odd in the promotion of a cup-bearer to the position of ealdorman, for the cup-bearer held an office of dignity. Asser says that Alfred's maternal grandfather, Oslac, was King Æthelwulf's *pincerna*.' D. Whitelock, 'Some Charters in the Name of King Alfred', in M.H. King and W.M. Stevens, *Saints Scholars and Heroes: Studies in Medieval Culture in Honour of Charles W. Jones* (Minnesota, 1979), i, 81–2.
7. *Chronicle of John of Worcester*, eds. Darlington and McGurk, ii, 428–9.
8. See pp. 69–71 above.
9. Byrhtferth refers, for instance, to Cenred of Mercia as a *rex famossissimus* in his *Life* of St. Ecgwine. Smyth, *Alfred the Great*, p. 303.
10. Ibid., pp. 309–10.
11. Ibid., pp. 315–16.
12. Ibid., pp. 204–15.
13. Ibid., p. 199.
14. Ibid., pp. 205–10.
15. Nelson, 'Waiting for Alfred', *Early Medieval Europe*, vii (1998), p. 122.
16. The phrase is taken from King Alfred's Old English Prose Preface to the translation of Pope Gregory's *Pastoral Care*.
17. Nelson, loc. cit.
18. Ibid., and cf. M. Lapidge, 'A King of Monkish Fable', *Times Higher* (8 March 1996), p. 20. I do not accept Lapidge's insistence on the necessity to demonstrate verbal links between the *Lives* of Gerald and of Alfred in order to demonstrate a direct connection between the two works.
19. Smyth, *Alfred the Great*, pp. 597–600.
20. Although the place in Cornwall is described as the church of St. Gueriir, since the relics of St. Neot were preserved there, it would be pedantic not to assume that St. Neots in Cornwall was the place which was meant.
21. Smyth, pp. 210–12.
22. Ibid., pp. 181–5.
23. Keynes, 'On the Authenticity of Asser's *Life* of King Alfred', *Journal of Eccles. History* xlvii (1996), 536.
24. The influence of Einhard on the *Life* of Alfred can be found in Chapters 16, 73, and 81. Cf. M. Schütt, 'The Literary Form of Asser's *Vita Alfredi*', *Eng. Hist. Rev.*, lxxii (1957), 209–20.
25. Campbell, 'Alfred's Lives', *Times Literary Supplement* (26 July 1996), p. 30. It should be pointed out that Einhard is describing a division of property in Charlemagne's *Will*, while Alfred's biographer is describing a division of that king's revenues

during life. I am in agreement with Professor Campbell that the parallels are striking. There is no evidence from King Alfred's own *Will* (where bequests are set out
in some detail) to suggest that the divisions described by the pseudo-Asser had
any historical basis.

26. Nelson, p. 122 and n. 25.
27. See p. 212 and n. 6; p. 213 and n. 21.
28. See Smyth, *Alfred the Great*, pp. 189–91.
29. *Chronicle of John of Worcester*, eds. Darlington and McGurk (*sub anno* 992), ii,
    440–1.
30. Lapidge, 'Byrhtferth and Oswald', p. 78.
31. Smyth, pp. 187–8.
32. See pp. 93, 103, 147.
33. See Smyth, pp. 191–5, 310–11, 261–3.
34. *Life of Alfred*, ed. Stevenson, pp. xlix–l, lxxx–lxxxi.
35. Keynes and Lapidge, *Alfred the Great*, n. 47, p. 239.
36. Stevenson, pp. lxxiv–lxxv.
37. Keynes and Lapidge, n. 201, p. 266. Cf. ibid., n. 197, p. 266.
38. Smyth, p. 316.
39. Keynes, p. 543.
40. See Smyth, p. 299.
41. See pp. 168–71 below.
42. See pp. 164–6 below.
43. Stevenson, p. 325.
44. C.R. Hart, *Learning in Late Anglo-Saxon England*, Chapter 32 (forthcoming). Hart
    identified references to royal estates in the Worcester Latin Chronicle under
    annals for AD 571 (Limbury *et al.*); 893 (Milton); 901 (Twinham); 914 (Hook
    Norton); 924 (Farndon and Kingston); 946 (Pucklechurch); 977 (Calne); 994
    (Andover).
45. Ibid.; *Chronicle of John of Worcester*, eds. Darlington and McGurk, ii, 62–3.
46. *Historia Regum*, ed. Arnold, ii, 9.
47. *King Alfred's West Saxon Version of Gregory's Pastoral Care*, ed. H. Sweet (Early
    English Texts Soc., Original Ser. xlv (part 1), l (part 2); Oxford, 1958 reprint of
    1871 edn.), i. 6–7.
48. Sawyer no. 346; W. de G. Birch, ed., *Cartularium Saxonicum: A Collection of Charters
    Relating to Anglo-Saxon History*, 4 vols. (London, 1964 reprint of 1885–99 edn.), no.
    561. Afterwards referred to as Birch no. 561, etc.
49. Sawyer no. 348; Birch no. 567. See Smyth, pp. 374–5; D. Whitelock, 'Some
    Charters in the Name of King Alfred', in King and Stevens, eds., *Studies in Honour
    of Charles W. Jones*, i, 78–83.
50. The charters of Edward the Elder's reign which were witnessed by Bishop Asser of
    Sherborne are listed in *Asser's Life of Alfred*, ed. Stevenson, n. 3, pp. lxv–lxvi.
51. Keynes and Lapidge, p. 177, and nn. 93 and 95, p. 323.
52. Smyth, pp. 225–6.
53. Ibid., pp. 357–62.
54. Ibid., pp. 354–5.
55. Galbraith, 'Who Wrote Asser's Life of Alfred?', pp. 99–100.
56. Keynes and Lapidge, n. 193, p. 264.
57. Smyth, p. 504.
58. The intervening chapters in the *Life* of Alfred (Chapters 82–85) cover only those
    annals in the Anglo-Saxon Chronicle for the years 886–7, but although the author

of the *Life* abandoned his Chronicle at 887, his Chronicle exemplar most likely contained the record down to 893, as his knowledge of imperfect and abortive fortress-building (as recorded in the Chronicle under 893) suggests (Stevenson, chapter 91, pp. 78–9).

59. Stevenson, chapter 79, p. 64.
60. Ibid., chapter 81, p. 68.
61. Ibid., chapter 79, p. 65.
62. A.P. Smyth, 'The Origins of English Identity', in A.P. Smyth, ed., *Medieval Europeans: Studies in Ethnic Identity and National Perspectives in Medieval Europe* (London, 1998), pp. 31–2.
63. Ibid., p. 31, and n. 24, p. 50. *Bede's Ecclesiastical History of the English People*, eds. and transl. B. Colgrave and R.A.B. Mynors (Oxford, 1969), pp. 140–1.
64. King Alfred's political astuteness – not to say his ruthlessness and cunning – are evident in the twists and turns set out in his complicated *Will*. See Smyth, *Alfred the Great*, pp. 401–20.
65. *Chronicle of John of Worcester*, eds. Darlington and McGurk, ii, 354–5.
66. See pp. 198–9.
67. Keynes and Lapidge, p. 49.
68. W. Davies, *The Llandaff Charters* (Aberystwyth, 1979), no. 223, p. 121.
69. Ibid., n. 236, pp. 123–4.
70. *Asser's Life of Alfred*, ed. Stevenson, p. 314.
71. Davies, *Llandaff Charters*, p. 74.
72. Ibid., pp. 76–7, and nn. 45 and 56, p. 88, where Professor Davies relies on the *Life* of King Alfred to date the reigns of Hywel ap Rhys (king of Glywysing) and that of Elise ap Tewdwr, king of Brycheiniog.
73. W. Davies, *Wales in the Early Middle Ages* (Leicester, 1982), p. 200.
74. K. Hughes, *Celtic Britain in the Early Middle Ages: Studies in Scottish and Welsh Sources* (Woodbridge, 1980), p. 68.
75. These annals borrowed from Irish records are: the death of Áed mac Néill (878), the death of Cerball, King of Osraige (887), and perhaps the death of the scholar, Suibne (889), if this had not been borrowed direct from the Anglo-Saxon Chronicle.
76. The English entries relate to the deaths of King Alfred (900) and of Asser (908).
77. *Life of Alfred*, ed. Stevenson, chapters 9, 30, 49, 49, 55 and 57.
78. Ibid., chapters 42, 52, 54, 74.
79. Ibid., chapter 35, p. 27.
80. Ibid., chapter 52, p. 40.
81. Ibid., chapter 79, p. 64.
82. Ibid.
83. Ibid., chapter 80, p. 66.
84. Lapidge, 'Byrhtferth and the *Historia Regum*', p. 105.
85. Smyth, *Alfred the Great*, pp. 325, 340–1.
86. Thanet, Nottingham, Dorset, Exeter, Selwood and Cirencester. The author supplies four other British placenames, whose meanings are not explained.
87. Chippenham was in Alfred's possession. He had spent Twelfth Night there in 878, but in his *Will* he left Chippenham to his youngest daughter, which may suggest that his estate there did not pertain to the kingship of Wessex *per se*. *Select English Historical Documents of the Ninth and Tenth Centuries*, ed. F.E. Harmer (Cambridge, 1914), pp. 17–18, 51.
88. Reading was held by female members of the dynasty as late as the 970s or 980s,

when Æthelflæd, second wife of King Edmund, bequeathed it to Edward the
Martyr or to Æthelred the Unready. We are only certain of Reading's position as
a royal estate during the reign of Edward the Confessor. Keynes and Lapidge,
p. 241, n. 63.

89. Stevenson, chapter 84, p. 71.
90. Ibid., chapter 5, pp. 5–6.
91. Ibid., chapter 42, p. 33.
92. Ibid., chapter 57, p. 47.
93. Ibid., chapter 35, p. 27.
94. Ibid., chapter 26, p. 22.
95. *Historia Regum*, ed. Arnold, ii, 74, 77.
96. Lapidge, 'Byrhtferth and the *Historia Regum*', p. 105.
97. Keynes and Lapidge, *Alfred the Great*, p. 51.
98. Stevenson, p. xci.
99. Keynes and Lapidge, p. 54.
100. Stevenson, p. 326.
101. Ibid., chapter 89, p. 75.
102. Ibid., p. 326.
103. Sawyer, nos. 964 and 967. *Chronicon Monasterii de Abingdon*, ed., J. Stevenson, 2
     vols. (London, Rolls Ser., 1858), i, 438, 441.
104. *Life of Alfred*, ed. Stevenson, p. 255.
105. Ibid., p. 256.
106. Ibid., Chapter 18, p. 18; *ASC MS. A* (*sub anno* 860), ed. Bately, p. 46.
107. Stevenson, p. 179.
108. *ASC MS.A.*, ed. Bately, p. 44.
109. Stevenson, chapter 5, p. 6.
110. *Vita I S. Neoti*, eds. Dumville and Lapidge, p. 129.
111. *Armes Prydein: the Prophecy of Britain from the Book of Taliesin*, eds. I. Williams and
     R. Bromwich (Dublin, 1972), pp. 4–5, 12–13.
112. *Nennius: British History and the Welsh Annals*, ed. and transl. J. Morris (Chichester,
     1980), p. 67. Cf. Keynes and Lapidge, *Alfred the Great*, p. 229, n. 6; p. 232,
     n. 20.
113. Stevenson, chapter 30, p. 24, and pp. 230–1.
114. Smyth, *Alfred the Great*, p. 346.
115. *Life of Alfred*, ed. Stevenson, chapter 42, p. 33.
116. Ibid., chapter 54, p. 43.
117. Ibid., chapter 79, p. 64. Stevenson (ibid., p. 380) followed by Keynes and Lapidge
     (*Alfred the Great*, p. 367) omit all reference to the Severn in the index to their
     respective editions and translations of the *Life* of Alfred.
118. *Nennius*, ed. Morris, pp. 60, 74, 81, 82.
119. *Annales Cambriae*, ed. J.W. Ab Ithel (London: Rolls Ser., 1860), (*sub anno* 632),
     p. 7.
120. *Nennius*, ed., Morris, p. 81. Cf. *Annales Cambriae*, ed. Ab Ithel (*sub anno* 1257), p.
     92, where the form for the Severn is *Hafren*.
121. Stevenson, chapter 82, p. 69; chapter 84, p. 71. Cf. *Claudii Ptolemæi Geographia*,
     ed. C. Müller (Paris, 1883), i, 86.
122. Hart suggested that the author of the earliest *Life* of Neot had been brought as
     a novice by Ealdorman Æthelwine of East Anglia (the lay founder of Ramsey)
     from one of that ealdorman's West Country estates. This would explain the
     author's knowledge of Cornish topography and perhaps also his rudimentary

grasp of Celtic nomenclature. Hart, *Danelaw*, p. 610.

123. *Vita Oswaldi*, in J. Raine, ed., *The Historians of the Church of York and its Archbishops*, 3 vols. (London: Rolls Ser., 1965 reprint of 1879 and 1894 edn.), i, 431–3.

124. *The Historia Brittonum: iii, The 'Vatican' Recension*, ed. D.N. Dumville (Cambridge, 1985), pp. 18–19.

125. Stevenson, chapter 80, p. 66.

126. *A.S.C.* (*sub anno* 914) *E.H.D.*, ed. Whitelock, i, 194–5.

127. *A.S.C.: MS.A.* (*sub anno* 853), ed. Bately, pp. 44–5. *E.H.D.*, ed. Whitelock, i, 174.

128. A.P. Smyth, *Scandinavian York and Dublin: the History and Archaeology of Two Related Viking Kingdoms,* 2 vols. (Dublin, reprint 1987), i, 109–10; ii, 8–9, 62–72.

129. Æthelred of Mercia (d. 911) is twice referred to by the author of the *Life* as *Eadred.* This cannot be explained away as a later manuscript error, where the forms *Æthered* and *Eadred* sometimes become confused – understandable in an eleventh-century context. Why, for instance, is Alfred's older brother invariably referred to correctly as *Æthelred/Æthered*, while his namesake of the Mercians is wrongly named *Eadred*, here in Chapter 80 and earlier in Chapter 75? Darlington and McGurk (*Chronicle of John of Worcester*, ii, 296, n. 2) believed that John of Worcester may have corrected the erroneous *Eadred* to read *Æthelred* in the Worcester Chronicle version of the *Life.*

130. *sum dæl þæs Norðwealcynnes. A.S.C.: MS.A.* (*sub anno* 893), ed. Bately, p. 57.

131. W. Davies, *Wales in the Early Middle Ages* (Leicester, 1982), p. 114.

132. Smyth, *Scandinavian York and Dublin*, ii, 65–72.

133. Stevenson, p. 316.

134. D. N. Dumville, 'The "Six" Sons of Rhodri Mawr: a Problem in *Asser's Life of King Alfred*', *Cambridge Medieval Celtic Studies*, iv (1982), 9, n. 39.

135. Ibid., pp. 9–10.

136. Ibid., p. 6.

137. Ibid., p. 14.

138. Ibid., pp. 13–14.

139. Ibid., p. 15.

140. Ibid., p. 13.

141. Ibid., p. 14.

142. Ibid., p. 13.

143. It requires first, that the *sex* of Parker's text previously read *vi* ('by the force') and was later misconstrued as the Roman numeral *vi* ('six'). It also requires that Parker added yet another *vi* to his transcript between the words *Rotri* and *compulsus.*

144. *Annales Cambriae*, ed., Ab Ithel, p. 15.

145. Ibid.

146. Cf. H. Loyn, *The Vikings in Wales* (Dorothea Coke Memorial Lecture, University College London, 1976), pp. 4–5.

147. M. Schütt, 'The Literary Form of Asser's *Vita Alfredi*', *Eng. Hist. Rev.*, lxxii (1957), 210; Whitelock, 'Genuine Asser', p. 5.

148. Keynes and Lapidge, p. 250, n. 115.

149. Ibid., p. 56.

150. *Life of Alfred*, ed. Stevenson, Chapter 7, p. 7.

151. Ibid., chapter 38, p. 29.

152. *Armes Prydein*, ed. Williams, p. xxix and n. 2, ibid.

153. Keynes and Lapidge, n. 70, p. 242.

154. J. Campbell, E. John and P. Wormald, *The Anglo-Saxons* (Oxford, 1982), pp. 43, 55.

155. *Chronicon Galfridi le Baker de Swynebroke*, ed., E.M. Thompson (Oxford, 1889), p. 152.
156. Ibid., p. 153.

## 3 The Author's Latin Style

1. [*Life* of Count Gerald of Aurillac], *Vita Sancti Geraldi Auriliacensis Comitis*, in *Patrologiae Cursus Completus series Latina*, cxxxiii (Paris, 1853), ed., J.P. Migne, pp. 644–5; transl., G. Sitwell, *St. Odo of Cluny: Being the Life of St. Odo of Cluny by John of Salerno and the Life of St. Gerald of Aurillac by St. Odo* (London and New York, 1958), p. 97.
2. *Life* of Gerald, ed. Migne, p. 645; Sitwell, transl., p. 98.
3. *Life* of Gerald, ed. Migne, pp. 645–6; Sitwell, transl., pp. 98–9.
4. *Life of Alfred*, ed., Stevenson, Chapter 42, p. 32.
5. Ibid., chapter 76, pp. 59–60.
6. *Life* of Gerald, ed. Migne, pp. 649–50, 653–4; Sitwell, transl., pp. 104–5, 111–12.
7. *Life* of Gerald, ed. Migne, p. 670; Sitwell, transl., p. 134.
8. Lapidge, 'A King of Monkish Fable', *Times Higher Education Supplement*, 8 March 1996, p. 20.
9. J.A. Robinson, *The Times of St. Dunstan* (Oxford, 1969, reprint of 1923 edn.), pp. 134–6; Sitwell, p. xii.
10. *Historia regum*, ed. Arnold, ii, 85.
11. *Vita Oswaldi*, in *Historians of the Church of York*, ed. Raine, i, 420–1, 435.
12. Hart, *Danelaw*, p. 596; J.A. Robinson, *St. Oswald and the Church of Worcester* (British Academy Supplementary Papers 5: London, 1919), pp. 15–16.
13. Hart, more than any other scholar, has demonstrated the pre-eminence of Ramsey in late tenth-century England. Hart, *Learning in Late Anglo-Saxon England: The School of Ramsey* (forthcoming).
14. Hart, pp. 30–1, 472; A. Williams, A.P. Smyth and D. Kirby, *A Biographical Dictionary of Dark Age Britain* (London, 1991), p. 1.
15. *Byrhtferth's Manual A.D. 1011*, ed., S.J. Crawford (Early English Text Soc., Oxford, 1966, reprint of 1929 edn.). Baker and Lapidge, *Byrhtferth's Enchiridion* (Early English Text Soc., Oxford, 1995).
16. S.J. Crawford, 'Byrhtferth of Ramsey and the Anonymous Life of St. Oswald', in *Speculum Religionis*, ed. Burkitt, pp. 99–111; J. Armitage Robinson, 'Byrhtferth and the Life of St. Oswald', *Journal of Theological Studies*, xxxi (1930), 35–42; M. Lapidge, 'The Hermeneutic Style in Tenth-Century Anglo-Latin Literature', *ASE* iv (1975), p. 91.
17. Lapidge, 'Hermeneutic Style', pp. 91–3; idem, 'The Medieval Hagiography of St. Ecgwine', *Vale of Evesham Historical Soc.* vi (1977), 77–93; idem, 'Byrhtferth and the *Vita S. Ecgwini*', *Medieval Studies*, xli (1979), 331–53.
18. See pp. 67–9.
19. *Life* of Odo, ed. Migne, p. 84; Sitwell, Transl., pp. 26–7.
20. *Vita Oswaldi*, ed. Raine, i, 446.
21. *Life* of Odo, ed. Migne, pp. 80–2; Sitwell, transl., pp. 79–81.
22. Lapidge argued that there is no extant English manuscript of Odo's *Life* of Count Gerald, with the clear implication this suggested the work was unknown in late Anglo-Saxon England. This is a *non sequitur*, when in its Frankish homeland – again according to Lapidge – only four copies of the work survived. We have no

means of knowing what the full extent of library holdings at pre-Reformation Ramsey consisted of, nor of the fate of all the contents of that library in the sixteenth century.

23. Lapidge, 'Hermeneutic Style', pp. 67, 72.
24. Ibid., pp. 73, 78.
25. *Life of Alfred*, ed., Stevenson, p. xcii. Stevenson's list of Frankish borrowings into the text of the *Life* of Alfred (p. xciv) is supplemented elsewhere in his edition on pp. xciii, 255–6 and 312.
26. Ibid., pp. 313, 315–16.
27. Ibid., pp. 255–6.
28. Ibid., pp. 312–13.
29. Ibid., p. 313.
30. Lapidge, 'Hermeneutic Style', pp. 78–81.
31. *Memorials of St. Dunstan*, ed., Stubbs, pp. 3–52. Lapidge, pp. 81–3.
32. *Vita Oswaldi*, ed. Raine, i, 410.
33. Lapidge, pp. 99–100.
34. Campbell, 'Alfred's Lives', *Times Literary Supplement*, 26 July 1996, p. 30.
35. Stevenson, pp. xcii, 256; Crawford, 'Byrhtferth and the Anonymous *Life* of Oswald', pp. 102–3; Lapidge, pp. 71–3.
36. Stevenson, p. xciii; Keynes and Lapidge, *Alfred the Great*, pp. 54–5.
37. *Life of Alfred*, ed. Stevenson, p. 225.
38. Keynes and Lapidge, p. 54.
39. Stevenson, p. lxxxix.
40. Crawford, 'Byrhtferth and the Anonymous *Life* of Oswald', p. 102.
41. It is significant that those scholars who support the idea of the authenticity of the historical Asser's authorship of the *Life* of Alfred, concentrate on denying the possibility of an attribution to Byrhtferth of Ramsey. But these critics rarely engage with the much wider problem of the tenth-century flavour of the *Life* as a whole. It was precisely the same tactic which critics of Galbraith used in the 1960s when discrediting his attribution of the *Life* to Bishop Leofric of Exeter.
42. *Æthelweard*, ed. Campbell, p. xlv.
43. Ibid.
44. Campbell was aware of the danger of over-simplification when it came to classifying Anglo-Latin periods and styles, but his overall view of this subject still stands (ibid.).
45. Keynes and Lapidge, *Alfred the Great*, p. 53.
46. Lapidge later dismissed the possibility of a Ramsey or Byrhtferthian connection with the *Life* of Alfred on the grounds that Byrhtferth is never once found to cite the Old Latin version of the bible (Lapidge, 'A King of Monkish Fable', *Times Higher Education Supplement*, 8 March 1996, p. 20). The argument is from negative evidence, and besides, the author of the *Life* of Alfred cannot be shown to cite the Old Version exclusively. In five other biblical quotations, it is unclear whether the Old Latin or later Vulgate version is being quoted. Copies of Jerome's Vulgate were often contaminated with reminiscences of the Old Latin bible, and one cannot argue from isolated quotations. Stevenson, who was more cautious than his successors in this field, summed up the evidence well, when he wrote that 'these quotations are an argument in favour of the authenticity [of "Asser"], though perhaps not a conclusive one' (*Life of Alfred*, p. xcv). Stevenson's hesitation stemmed from his knowledge that familiarity with the Old Latin Bible was not peculiar to the Welsh or Celtic churches. It was also known in Francia – which

reintroduces the possibility of yet further Frankish influence via Ramsey on the *Life* of Alfred.

47. Stevenson, chapter 89, p. 75; *E.H.D.*, i, 272.
48. *Byrhtferth's Manual,* ed. Crawford, p. 133.
49. Lapidge, 'Byrhtferth and the *Historia Regum*', p. 99, n. 12.
50. M.L.W. Laistner, 'Notes on Greek from the Lectures of a Ninth Century Monastery Teacher', *Bulletin of the John Ryland's Library,* vii (1923), 421–56, especially pp. 422–6.
51. Lapidge, 'Hermeneutic Style', pp. 70–3.
52. *Einhardi Vita Karoli,* ed., Rau, *Quellen,* v, 196.
53. *Historia Regum,* ed. Arnold, ii, 75 and 84.
54. Ibid., p. 67.
55. Ibid., p. 89.
56. Stevenson, p. lvii.
57. Ibid., chapter 95, p. 82.
58. Keynes and Lapidge, p. 272, n. 234.
59. *Vita Oswaldi,* ed. Raine, i, 418.
60. Lapidge, 'Byrhtferth and the *Historia Regum*', p. 101.
61. [*Life* of Ecgwine], *Vita Quorundum Anglo-Saxonum,* ed. Giles (London, 1854), p. 352.
62. Stevenson, chapter 67, p. 50; chapter 100, p. 86.
63. Ibid., chapter 101.
64. Ibid., chapter 76.
65. Ibid., chapter 1. The word *rector* also appears in the *Life* of Ecgwine (ed. Giles, p. 379). Lapidge dismissed my list of agentive nouns, choosing to comment only on *rector,* claiming that 'none of these words is unusual or distinctive' (Lapidge, *Times Higher Educational Supplement,* 8 March 1996, p. 20). The point of my argument is that collectively such nouns are significant – as Lapidge himself argued elsewhere – and that *rector* when applied by the author to King Alfred's status as *omnium Brittanniae insulae ... rectori* reveals, in my opinion, a mid- to late tenth-century form of address. Keynes also chose to misinterpret my views on the significance of the term *rector* as applied to Alfred and to later tenth-century rulers (Keynes, 'On the Authenticity of Asser's Life of Alfred', *Journal of Ecclesiastical History,* xlvii (1996), p. 540. Cf. Smyth, *Alfred the Great,* pp. 479–80.)
66. Stevenson, chapter 80.
67. Ibid., chapter 79.
68. Ibid., chapter 91.
69. *Vita Oswaldi,* ed. Raine, i, 462.
70. Lapidge, 'Byrhtferth and the *Vita S. Ecgwini*', p. 352.
71. Stevenson, chapter 91, p. 77; *Byrhtferth's Manual,* ed. Crawford, p. 198.
72. Stevenson, chapters 15, 96.
73. Ibid., chapter 5.
74. Ibid., chapter 97.
75. Ibid., chapter 88.
76. Ibid., chapter 16.
77. Ibid., chapters 89, 90.
78. Lapidge, 'Byrhtferth and the *Historia Regum*', pp. 102–3; idem, 'Byrhtferth and the *Vita S. Ecgwini*', p. 336.
79. Keynes and Lapidge, *Alfred the Great,* p. 54.
80. Lapidge, 'Byrhtferth and the *Vita S. Ecgwini*', p. 336.

81. Ibid., 'Byrhtferth and the *Historia Regum*', p. 106.
82. Smyth, *Alfred the Great*, pp. 285–6. And see Hart, *Learning in Late Anglo-Saxon England* (forthcoming).
83. *Vita Prima Sancti Neoti (Life of St Neot)*, eds. Dumville and Lapidge, p. xcviii.
84. Stevenson, chapters 75 and 76.
85. Ibid., chapter 19.
86. *Life* of Ecgwine, ed. Giles, p. 383.
87. Stevenson, chapter 91.
88. Ibid., chapters 71, 76–8, 89.
89. Lapidge, 'Byrhtferth and the *Historia Regum*', p. 102.
90. Stevenson, chapter 15, p. 13; *Historia Regum*, ed. Arnold, ii, 67.
91. Ibid., ii, 86.
92. Ibid., ii, 44.
93. *Einhardi Vita Karoli*, in *Quellen*, ed. Rau, v, 164.
94. *excellentissimae* occurs in Chapter 92 of the *Life* of Alfred (Stevenson, p. 79).
95. *Vita Oswaldi*, ed. Raine, i, 427.
96. *Historia Regum*, ed. Arnold, ii, 11.
97. Stevenson, p. 1.
98. See pp. 193–6.
99. *Historia Regum*, ed. Arnold, ii, 84.
100. *Life* of St. Ecgwine, ed. Giles, p. 378.
101. Stevenson, chapter 91, p. 78.
102. Ibid., chapter 92.
103. Ibid., chapter 91.
104. Ibid., chapter 76, cf. ch. 100.
105. Ibid., chapter 92, cf. ch. 104.
106. *Vita Oswaldi*, ed. Raine, i, 412.
107. Stevenson, chapter 97.
108. *Life* of St. Ecgwine, ed. Giles, p. 394.
109. Stevenson, chapter 76.
110. *Byrhtferth's Manual*, ed. Crawford, p. 244.
111. *Annals of St. Neots*, eds. Dumville and Lapidge, pp. 39, 99.
112. *Chronicle of John of Worcester*, eds. Darlington and McGurk, ii, 426–7.
113. *Immo* appears in the *Life* of Alfred with particular frequency in chapters 12, 13 and 23. It also occurs in the *Life* of Oswald (ed. Raine, i, 412), and the *Life* of Ecgwine (ed. Giles, p. 376). For the *Life* of St. Neot, see Smyth, *Alfred the Great*, p. 338.
114. Lapidge, 'Byrhtferth and the *Historia Regum*', p. 102.
115. Lapidge, 'A King of Monkish Fable', *Times Higher Education Supplement*, 8 March 1996, p. 20.
116. *Historia Regum*, ed. Arnold, ii, 90.
117. Stevenson, chapter 12, p. 10.
118. Ibid., chapter 91.
119. Ibid., chapter 22.
120. *Historia Regum*, ed. Arnold, ii, 42.
121. Stevenson, chapters, 22, 74, 88 for *incessabiliter*. chapters 25, 91 for *incessabilius*.
122. Ibid., chapter 101.
123. *Vita Oswaldi*, ed. Raine, i, 413; *Life* of Ecgwine, ed. Giles, p. 352.
124. *Vita Oswaldi*, ed. Raine, i, 473.
125. *Chronicle of John of Worcester*, eds. Darlington and McGurk, *sub annis* 473, 714, 1010, 1011.

126. Stevenson, chapters 15, 42, 74, 81, 91 and 101.
127. *Vita Sancti Wilfridi*, in *Historians of the Church of York*, ed. Raine, i, 105.
128. Stevenson, chapter 92.
129. I never claimed such individual words as *breviter* or *pariter* were crucial to the attribution of authorship of the *Life* of Alfred, but following Lapidge's own methodology, I listed them as being significant in forming a class as a whole. The fact that any one individual word may be dismissed as 'common coin' does not invalidate my argument relating to rarer forms such as *incommutabiliter* or *intransmeabilis*.
130. For random examples of the authors' love of word-play, we have in the *Life* of Alfred (Chapter 15): *Sicut enim irrationabiliter in propria vixisse refertur, ita multo irrationabilius in aliena gente vivere deprehenditur*, which we may compare with: *atque lacrymulis lacrymis effusionem* in the *Life* of St. Oswald (ed. Raine, i, 406) or with *Eanbaldus ... in archiepiscopatum genti Northanhymbrorum solempniter confirmatus est... qua die celebratur solempnitas* in the Northumbrian Chronicle (*Historia Regum*, ed. Arnold, ii, 58). We may compare the use by the author of King Alfred's *Life* of *irrationabiliter ... irrationabilius* with Byrhtferth's *lacrymulis lacrymis* and *solempniter ... solempnitas* while bearing in mind that *sollemniter* was also an adverb used by the author of Alfred's *Life* (Chapter 74). We note the succession of polysyllabic adverbs in the following passage from the *Life* of Alfred (Chapter 99): *non inaniter incepta, utiliter inventa, utilius servata est. Nam iamdudum in lege scriptum audierat, Dominum decimam sibi multipliciter redditurum promisisse atque fideliter servasse, decimamque sibi multipliciter redditurum fuisse.* Here we have *inaniter, utiliter ... utilius, fideliter*, and the characteristic repetition of *multipliciter*, an adverb also found in Byrhtferth's *Life* of St. Oswald (ed. Raine, i, 456). The following passage from the *Life* of St. Oswald (ibid., p. 464) is part of an account of how Oswald observed a solemn church festival at Ramsey with his monks: *His sollemniter finitis, reversi sunt cuncti ad refectionem quam eis beatus dux praeparaverat dapsiliter ad edendum. Cuncta quae quondam Salomon suis regali potentia fretus dederat, omnia iste non solum carnaliter sed etiam spiritaliter peregerat. Dicatam Christo ecclesiam, quam nobiliter aeditui ornaverunt cortinis et palleis, et multiphariis accensis luminaribus, quis annuntiet?* Byrhtferth, too, piled up his polysyllabic adverbs within a single sentence – and bearing in mind that a significant amount of the repertoire of unusual polysyllabic adverbs in the *Life* of Alfred turn up again in Byrhtferth's works, we note the presence in this one sentence of *sollemniter, dapsiliter, carnaliter, spiritaliter* and *nobiliter*. *Sollemniter/solempniter* occurs in the *Life* of Alfred (Chapter 74) and in the *Life* of Ecgwine (ed. Giles, p. 390) and the Northumbrian Chronicle (*Historia Regum*, ed. Arnold, ii, 58). With *carnaliter* from the *Life* of Oswald, we may compare *corporaliter* in the *Life* of Alfred (Chapter 74).
131. Lapidge, 'Byrhtferth and the *Historia Regum*', p. 107.
132. *Life* of St. Ecgwine, ed., Giles, p. 376.
133. *Vita Oswaldi*, ed. Raine, i, 439.
134. Stevenson, chapter 91, pp. 76–7; *E.H.D.*, ed. Whitelock, i, 272.
135. See Smyth, *Alfred the Great*, p. 701.
136. Stevenson, chapter 22, p. 20.
137. *Historia Regum*, ed. Arnold, ii, 42 (*sub anno* 764).
138. Stevenson, chapter 22, p. 20; *E.H.D.*, i, 266.
139. Crawford, 'Byrhtferth and the Anonymous Life of Oswald', p. 108.
140. Stevenson, p. xci.
141. Ibid., p. 54.

142. *Karolus rex Francorum misit synodalem librum ad Britanniam, sibi a Constantinopoli directum, in quo libro, heu pro dolor! multa inconvenientia et verae fidei contraria reperientes, maxime quod poene omnium orientalium doctorum non minus quam trecentorum vel eo amplius episcoporum unanima assertione confirmatum, imagines adorare debere, quod omnino ecclesia Dei execratur.* Historia Regum, ed. Arnold, ii, 53.

143. Stevenson, chapters 22, 24, 25, 74 (x 2), 76, 79, 81, 100, 104 (x 2), 106.

144. Lapidge, 'A King of Monkish Fable', *Times Higher Education Supplement*, 8 March 1996, p. 20.

145. Stevenson, chapter 74.

146. Lapidge, 'Byrhtferth and the *Historia Regum*', p. 101.

147. *Historia Regum,* ed. Arnold ii, 13.

148. Stevenson, chapter 92.

149. Ibid., chapter 74.

150. Ibid., chapter 103, cf. chapter 99.

151. Ibid., chapter 103.

152. *Historia Regum*, ed. Arnold, ii, 55.

153. *Life* of St. Ecgwine, ed. Giles, p. 390.

154. Lapidge, pp. 105–8.

155. Stevenson, chapter 21.

156. Ibid., chapter 73.

157. *Vita Oswaldi*, ed. Raine, i, 429.

158. Ibid., p. 442.

159. Stevenson, chapter 97.

160. *Historia Regum* (*sub anno* 793), ed. Arnold ii, 55.

161. *Byrhtferth's Manual*, ed. Crawford, p. 216.

162. Ibid., p. 40.

163. *Vita Oswaldi*, ed., Raine, i, 403.

164. Stevenson, chapter 74.

165. Ibid., chapter 92.

166. *Vita Oswaldi*, ed., Raine, i, 454.

167. Stevenson, chapter 16.

168. *Byrhtferth's Manual*, ed., Crawford, pp. 232–3.

169. Ibid., pp. 182–3.

170. Ibid., pp. 180–1.

171. Ibid., p. 202 (and cf. *Vita Oswaldi*, ed. Raine, i, 462).

172. *Byrhtferth's Manual*, ed. Crawford, p. 18.

173. Stevenson, chapter 13.

174. *Byrhtferth's Manual*, ed. Crawford, pp. 232–3.

175. Lapidge, 'Byrhtferth and the *Historia Regum*', p. 105.

176. [*Life* of Alfred], *E.H.D.*, ed. Whitelock, i, 271; Stevenson, chapter 81, p. 68.

177. Ibid., chapter 88.

178. *Life* of St. Ecgwine, ed. Giles, p. 378.

179. Stevenson, p. 326.

180. Crawford, 'Byrhtferth and the Anonymous Life of Oswald', in *Speculum Religionis*, ed. Burkitt, pp. 108–9.

181. The 'place' (*locus*) in the phrase both *hoc in loco* for Byrhtferth and the author of the *Life* of Alfred is not a vague physical or geographical location, but a point in the writer's narrative.

182. Stevenson, chapter 81, p. 68; *E.H.D.*, i, 271.

183. Howlett, in a misrepresentation of my argument (review of Smyth, *King Alfred the*

*Great*, in *Eng. Hist. Rev.*, cxii (1997), p. 943), noted that 'any schoolboy might be expected to recognise *hoc in loco* used at all times and in all places in which the Latin language was written.' It is true that any schoolgirl might expect to find *in hoc loco*, but not *hoc in loco* used so often throughout the *Life* of Alfred and in precisely the same context of continuity phrases as it is found in Byrhtferth's *Manual*. Mr. Howlett did not have the courtesy to note my point that Crawford saw this phrase as a defining characteristic of the Latinity of the *Life* of St. Oswald which enabled him to attribute that work to Byrhtferth of Ramsey as early as 1929.

184. Byrhtferth of Ramsey in his other works frequently refers to Rome as 'the Romulean city' or as 'the threshold of the Apostles' (Lapidge, p. 104; idem, 'Byrhtferth and the *Vita S. Ecgwini*', p. 343). The author (in Stevenson's Parker-Cotton edition) mentions Rome some eleven times in his *Life* of Alfred, but nowhere in these terms. All the references to Rome in King Alfred's *Life* relate directly or indirectly to incidents in the Anglo-Saxon Chronicle, and because the author followed his Latin text of the Chronicle so closely, he had little scope to embroider his narrative at that point. Both Crawford and Robinson observed that in his other works, Byrhtferth's Latin was at his most 'sober' and lacking in 'efflo-rescent rhetoric' when he was following an established author such as Bede. Byrhtferth in his summary of the *Life* of Alfred in the Northumbrian Chronicle also writes of Rome simply as *Roma* when he is following passages from the Chronicle. There is, however, one notable exception, when Byrhtferth is summarising the account in the *Life* of Alfred of how King Æthelwulf took his son, Alfred, to Rome and how Æthelwulf arranged in his *will* for alms to be sent there. In this passage, Byrhtferth does refer to Rome as *Romuleas sedes* and *ad limina principis apostolorum* and *ad limina sancti Petri* (*Historia Regum*, ed. Arnold, ii, 72). It may well be, therefore, that the author of Alfred's *Life*, when following the Chronicle closely, referred to Rome simply as *Roma*, but that in the case of the account of Æthelwulf's bequests to Roman churches (which is not in the Chronicle) more 'precocious phrases' for Rome were used by him. Byrhtferth's summary of Alfred's *Life* in his Northumbrian Chronicle may, after all, offer equally good if not superior textual readings to those found in Parker's printed edition.

185. Stevenson, chapters 21 and 73.
186. Whitelock, 'Prose of Alfred's Reign', p. 80.
187. Howorth, *Athenaeum*, 4 August 1877, p. 146. The ship's metaphor occurs in *Æthelweard*, ed. Campbell, p. 38.
188. Stevenson, p. cxvii.
189. Keynes and Lapidge, p. 74; Stevenson, chapter 21, p. 19.
190. Keynes and Lapidge, p. 88; Stevenson, chapter 73, p. 54.
191 *Æthelweard*, ed. Campbell, pp. 38–9.
192. Stevenson, p. cxvii.
193. Howorth, *Athenaeum*.
194. *Byrhtferth's Manual*, ed. Crawford, pp. 14–17.
195. Ibid., pp. 14–15.
196. Ibid., pp. 142–5.
197. Ibid., p. 244.
198. *Vita Oswaldi*, ed. Raine, i, 423.
199. Stevenson, chapter 76; *E.H.D.*, ed. Whitelock, i, 268.
200. Stevenson, chapter 88, p. 74; *E.H.D.*, i, 272.

201. Stevenson, pp. 302–3; Keynes and Lapidge, pp. 258–9, n. 161.
202. *Memorials of St. Dunstan*, ed., Stubbs, p. 10.
203. Ibid., p. 387.
204. Stevenson, chapter 88, p. 74.
205. Ibid., chapter 53, p. 41.
206. Ibid., pp. 255–6.
207. Sawyer, 792, Birch 1297; C.R. Hart, *The Early Charters of Eastern England* (Leicester, 1966), pp. 165–86. The reference in the charter to *gronnis* is found in Hart, ibid., p. 166.
208. Leland, *De Rebus Britannicis Collectanea*, ed. T. Hearne (Oxford, 1774), iv, 23; Crawford, 'Byrhtferth and the Anonymous Life of St Oswald', p. 100.
209. Stevenson, chapter 88, p. 74.
210. Ibid., chapter 89, p. 75.
211. *Vita Oswaldi*, ed. Raine, i, 423.
212. *Regularis Concordia: The Monastic Agreement*, ed. T. Symons (London, 1953), p. 3.

## 4   The Author's Use of the Anglo-Saxon Chronicle

1. The author of the *Life* tells us in Chapter 91 that at the time he was writing, King Alfred's forty-fifth year was then in course. Since he gives us Alfred's year of birth as 849 (Chapter 1), then the king's forty-fifth year (on the author's reckoning) was 893.
2. Hart has shown that the Alfredian annals in the *Life* of Alfred are based on the A-Text Precursor with occasional additions from the B-Text.
3. Smyth, *King Alfred the Great*, pp. 174, 301, 310.
4. The author's translation of the Chronicle's text of events in East Kent which he dates to 864 belongs, in fact, to the 865 annal in the Anglo-Saxon Chronicle. The suggestion by Keynes and Lapidge (*Alfred the Great*, n. 43, p. 238) that since the Anglo-Saxon year began at this period in the autumn, so the author of Alfred's *Life* may have been correct in dating the raid on East Kent to 864 is unconvincing. There is no evidence to suggest that the author had any independent knowledge of the dating of events during the period 851–87. On the contrary, the evidence points consistently and overwhelmingly in the opposite direction. The author's misdating of Chronicle entries for 865 and 885 has to be set against complete dependence on the sequence of entries and chronology provided by a Manuscript A-type version of the Anglo-Saxon Chronicle.
5. The author of the *Life* of Alfred unusually supplied a date for the wedding of the king which he assigned to 868 (Chapter 29). He did this on the assumption that Alfred's marriage to a Mercian woman coincided with his brother's alliance with Burgred and with the expedition to Nottingham.
6. Smyth, *King Alfred the Great*, pp. 102–9.
7. Ibid., pp. 105–6.
8. P.H. Sawyer, *The Age of the Vikings* (London, 2nd edn, 1971), p. 19.
9. The years 888 and 889 appear to be devoid of Frankish material in the Anglo-Saxon Chronicle, but the Chronicle does contain (misplaced) information on Francia for those years (Smyth, op. cit., p. 101).
10. The dating of the Welsh dynastic insertion in the *Life* of Alfred is very ambiguous. The author refers to his own expulsion by King Hyfaidd from St. David's 'during this period' when his kinsman, Archbishop Nobis, had also been expelled. Nobis

died back in 873–4. His summary of Welsh history deals with a series of supposed submissions to King Alfred which might have taken place any time between 873 and 893.

11. Smyth, *King Alfred the Great*, p. 102.
12. For a discussion of the significance of the Frankish material in the Alfredian Chronicle, see Smyth, pp. 99–116.
13. Life of Alfred, ed. Stevenson, pp. 287–90.
14. Keynes and Lapidge, *Alfred the Great*, pp. 265, n. 197; 266, n. 201.
15. It should be said that Professor Janet Bately and Dr. Roy Hart were exceptional in this respect, and studied that version of the Chronicle in the *Life* of Alfred as a text in its own right.
16. Ibid., n. 130, p. 252; nn.133, 134, p. 253.
17. *E.H.D.*, ed. Whitelock, i, n. 10, p. 181.
18. *Chronicle of Æthelweard*, ed. Campbell, (*sub anno* 885), pp. 44–5.
19. Smyth, p. 475.
20. Ibid., p. 375.
21. Ibid., pp. 378–9.
22. Keynes and Lapidge, pp. 143–4.
23. Smyth, pp. 490–526.
24. Keynes and Lapidge, pp. 41–2, 56.
25. *Life of Alfred*, ed. Stevenson, pp. lxxxv–lxxxviii.
26. The terminal position of the Sandwich episode in the 851 annal of the Chronicle is shared by Versions B, C, D, E, F and the *Life* of Alfred.
27. Stevenson, p. lxxxviii.
28. I have argued for the compilation of the Chronicle archetype in the period 896–9. See Smyth, *Alfred the Great*, pp. 455–526.
29. C.[R.] Hart, 'The B Text of the Anglo-Saxon Chronicle', *Journal of Medieval History* viii (1982), 241–99.
30. Lapidge, 'Byrhtferth and Oswald', p. 78.
31. I still maintain that the Ramsey author of King Alfred's *Life* may have been inspired to bring it to an abrupt end in 892–3 because he had access to that first booklet of the A-Text or A-Text precursor which ended in 892–3 (Smyth, *King Alfred the Great*, pp. 504–6). Keynes has pointed out that if the Ramsey author 'had access to a copy of only the "first proto-booklet" which extended to *c*. 892', then he could not be expected to have been familiar with material in the second proto-booklet dealing with annals later than 893 (Keynes, 'On the Authenticity of Asser's Life of King Alfred', *Journal of Ecclesiastical History*, xlvii (1996), 547). Such reductive arguing takes no account of the fact that we already know how Byrhtferth as the leading authority on the Chronicle possessed several versions of that text – many of which were of his own compiling. He was quite capable of inventing a *Life* of Alfred based on a discrete section of the A-Text of the Alfredian Chronicle which came into his possession regardless of what other versions he already possessed.
32. *A.S.C. MS A.*, ed., Bately, p. 2.
33. 851, 853, 855, 860, 865, 866, 867, 868, 869, 870, 871, 872, 873, 874, 875, 876, 878, 879, 880, 881, 882, 883, 885, 886, 887.
34. The Northumbrian Chronicle which followed the Cottonian error in the labelling of Alfred's age from Chapter 32 (for AD 870) to Chapter 47 (for AD 875) did not follow the Cottonian additional error in Chapter 49 for AD 876. So the Cottonian version gives AD 876 as Alfred's twenty-sixth year, while the Northumbrian

Chronicle gives this as Alfred's twenty-seventh year. The Cottonian version gives AD 878 as Alfred's twenty-seventh year, while the Northumbrian Chronicle gives it as the king's twenty-eighth year. This shows that the version of the Northumbrian Chronicle was also following an exemplar which omitted the annal for AD 877. For had that exemplar included the annal for AD 877, then AD 878 would have been Alfred's twenty-ninth year according to the Northumbrian Chronicle.

35. *Life of Alfred,* ed. Stevenson, p. li.
36. Keynes and Lapidge, *Alfred the Great,* p. 230, n. 11.
37. Ibid., pp. 269–70, n. 218.
38. See p. 79.
39. C.[R.] Hart,'The Ramsey Computus', *Eng. Hist. Rev.,* lxxxv (1970), 29–44.
40. Hart, *Learning in Late Anglo-Saxon England* (forthcoming).
41. Lapidge, 'Byrhtferth and Oswald', p. 78.
42. Smyth, *King Alfred the Great,* pp. 173–4; cf. Keynes and Lapidge, *Alfred the Great,* n. 4, p. 228.
43. It would appear that mention of London was also absent from the summary of the *Life* of Alfred preserved in Byrhtferth's Durham recension of the Northumbrian Chronicle. *Historia Regum,* ed. Arnold, ii, 70.
44. *Bede's Ecclesiastical History of the English People,* eds. Colgrave and Mynors, (II, iii), pp. 142–3.
45. See Smyth, *King Alfred the Great,* pp. 12–17.
46. Ibid., pp. 303–6.
47. C. Hart, 'The Earldom of Essex', in K. Neale, ed., *An Essex Tribute for Frederick Emmison* (London, 1987), pp. 65–6. Smyth, pp. 303–4.
48. See pp. 101–2, 146, 150, 154.
49. Keynes,'On the Authenticity of Asser's Life of King Alfred', *Journal of Ecclesiastical History,* xlvii (1996), 545.
50. Keynes and Lapidge, *Alfred the Great,* p. 240, n. 55. Keynes significantly failed to address two further observations which I made on the gloss *honorabiliter* as applied to Bishop Ealhstan at the notice of his burial in Chapter 28. The first is that both Byrhtferth of Ramsey and the author of King Alfred's *Life* used the same two variants of a formula for the burial record of holy men or churchmen in their writings. This applies to Byrhtferth's *Life* of St. Oswald as well as to those sections of his Northumbrian Chronicle in the *Historia Regum* which are independent of Alfred's *Life.* Secondly, Keynes failed to comment on the remarkable coincidence that not only are the deaths of Bishop Ealhstan of Sherborne and Ealdorman Eanwulf of Somerset both entered under the same year (867) in the Chronicle of Æthelweard, but the records of their deaths are closely linked together in the text of that chronicle. See Smyth, *King Alfred the Great,* pp. 194–5, 311–12.
51. *Chronicle of John of Worcester,* eds. Darlington and McGurk, ii, 292, n.1.
52. Smyth, *Scandinavian Kings in the British Isles,* pp. 245–6.
53. Cf. *Life of Alfred,* ed. Stevenson, pp. 252–3; Keynes and Lapidge, *Alfred the Great,* n. 94, pp. 246–7.
54. The Worcester Chronicle contains a translated version of the Anglo-Saxon Chronicle's annal for 877, but the special pleading to the effect that part of the Danish army stayed on at Exeter and a part only moved off to Mercia reveals an attempt by a later compiler to reconcile the mangled version of the Anglo-Saxon Chronicle which he found in the Alfredian annals taken from King Alfred's *Life.*
55. *Life of Alfred,* ed. Stevenson, p. 253.

56. *A.S.C., MS A.*, ed. Bately (*sub anno* 877), p. 50.
57. *The Anglo-Saxon Chronicle: a Collaborative Edition*, iv. Manuscript B, ed. S. Taylor (Cambridge, 1983), (*sub anno* 876), p. 36.
58. Keynes and Lapidge, n. 94, p. 247.
59. Ibid., p. 247, n. 94.
60. *E.H.D.*, ed. Whitelock, n. 3, p. 179.
61. *Life of Alfred*, ed. Stevenson, pp. 261–2.
62. *7 Hamtunscir se del se hiere behinon se was. A.S.C. MS A.*, ed. Bately, p. 51.
63. *Et multos eiusdem gentis ultra mare compulit ... navigare, Life of Alfred*, ed. Stevenson, p. 40.
64. *omnes accolae Hamtunensis pagae, qui non ultra mare pro metu paganorum navigaverant.* Ibid., p. 45.
65. Whitelock naively argued that because Asser regarded Alfred as *veredictus* ('The Truthteller'), then Alfred must have accurately reported these events of 878 to his contemporary biographer. D. Whitelock, 'The Importance of the Battle of Edington', in Whitelock, ed., *From Bede to Alfred* (Studies in Early Anglo-Saxon Literature and History, 13, London, 1980), pp. 10–11.
66. Keynes and Lapidge, *Alfred the Great*, p. 85, pp. 249–50, n. 114.
67. Life of Alfred, ed. Stevenson, p. 329; Smyth, *Alfred the Great*, p. 595.
68. Keynes and Lapidge, p. 85.
69. Stevenson, p. 27.
70. Smyth, pp. 490–526.
71. Smyth, pp. 314–15. A.P. Smyth, 'The Solar Eclipse of Wednesday 29 October A.D. 878: Ninth-Century Historical Records and the Findings of Modern Astronomy', in J. Roberts and J.L. Nelson (eds.), *Alfred the Wise: Studies in Honour of Janet Bately on the Occasion of her Sixty Fifth Birthday* (Cambridge, 1997), pp. 187–210.
72. *Life of Alfred*, ed. Stevenson, p. 280.
73. Whitelock, *Genuine Asser*, p. 9.
74. Keynes, 'On the Authenticity of Asser's Life of King Alfred', *Journal of Ecclesiastical History*, xlvii (1996), 543–4.
75. Smyth, 'Solar Eclipse of A.D. 878', pp. 187–210.
76. *Historia regum*, ed. Arnold, ii, 87.
77. *A.S.C. MS. A.* ed. Bately, (*sub anno* 885), p. 52.
78. *Historia regum*, ed. Arnold, ii, 87.
79. *Life of Alfred*, ed. Stevenson, p. 291.
80. Anglo-Saxon Chronicle (*sub anno* 885), transl. Whitelock, *E.H.D.*, i, 182.
81. Smyth, 'Solar Eclipse of 878', pp. 206–8.
82. *Life of Alfred,* ed. Stevenson, p. 292. Keynes and Lapidge, *Alfred the Great,* p. 253, n. 133.
83. *Chronicle of John of Worcester*, eds. Darlington and McGurk, p. 320.
84. Hart, 'East Anglian Chronicle', p. 263.
85. Keynes, 'On the Authenticity of the Life of King Alfred the Great', *Journal of Ecclesiastical History*, xlvii (1996), 540.
86. Smyth, *King Alfred the Great*, pp. 386–7.
87. Smyth, 'The Emergence of English Identity', in Smyth, ed., *Medieval Europeans*, pp. 39–48.
88. Smyth, *King Alfred the Great*, p. 385.
89. *Westseaxna cyninges*, A.S.C. MS. A., ed. Bately (*sub anno* 885), p. 53.
90. Ibid. (*sub annis* 885 and 886), p. 53.
91. Sawyer no. 351; Birch no. 740, ii, 456–7.

92. Smyth, p. 391 and n. 114.
93. Keynes ('On the Authenticity', *Journal of Ecclesiastical History*, xvii (1996), 540) misrepresents my argument regarding the use of *rector* by the author of the *Life*.
94. Smyth, pp. 33–50; 67–98.
95. Ibid., pp. 174, 301.
96. *Life of Alfred*, ed. Stevenson, p. 186.
97. Ibid., p. 190.
98. Darlington and McGurk, eds., *Chronicle of John of Worcester*, ii, 440–1.
99. Simon Keynes's fascinating paper on 'Anglo-Saxon Entries in the "Liber Vitae" of Brescia' (*Alfred the Wise*, eds. Roberts, Nelson and Godden, pp. 106–19) prudently stops short of attempting to prove that the infant Alfred went to Rome either on one or two occasions. The evidence from the *liber vitae* in question is ambiguous and problematic in the extreme. There are also alternative explanations which are not discussed in the paper.
100. Smyth, op. cit., pp. 309–11.
101. Ibid., p. 312.
102. Keynes and Lapidge, *Alfred the Great*, p. 240, n. 52.
103. See pp. 100, 244, n. 379.
104. Smyth, pp. 210–12; 330–1.
105. *Chronicle of Æthelweard*, ed. Campbell, p. 49.
106. Sawyer no. 350. Birch no. 576, ii, 219–20. This charter relates to a grant of land at Farleigh, in Kent, by King Alfred to his *dux* or ealdorman, Sighelm.
107. *Two Lives of Saint Cuthbert: a Life by an Anonymous Monk of Lindisfarne and Bede's Prose Life*, ed. B. Colgrave (New York, 1969), (*Bede's Life of Cuthbert*) pp. 154–5.

## 5  Why Was the *Life* of King Alfred Written at Ramsey in *c.* AD 1000?

1. A.P. Smyth, *Scandinavian York and Dublin: the History and Archaeology of Two Related Viking Kingdoms,* 2 vols. (Dublin, reprint 1987).
2. McGurk and Darlington, eds., *Chronicle of John of Worcester*, pp. 476–7.
3. Smyth, *King Alfred the Great*, pp. 260–9.
4. Ibid., pp. 403–4.
5. Ibid., p. 313.
6. The 'English king' who took the relics of St. Neot from Cornwall is not named in the *Life* of St. Neot. See Smyth, p. 334.
7. Lapidge first dated the earliest *Life* of St. Neot to 'not long after the transfer, probably in the late tenth century, of the relics of St. Neot from their original location in Cornwall to a priory at Eynesbury' (Keynes and Lapidge, *Alfred the Great*, p. 197, and pp. 254–5).
8. *Vita Prima Sancti Neoti*, eds., Dumville and Lapidge, pp. xciv–xcv.
9. *E.H.D.*, i, ed., Whitelock, p. 839.
10. Lapidge, 'Byrhtferth and Oswald', p. 79.

# Index